Elementary Classroom Management

Elementary Classroom Management

Lessons From Research and Practice

Third Edition

Carol S. Weinstein

Andrew J. Mignano, Jr.

Boston   Burr Ridge, IL   Dubuque, IA   Madison, WI   New York
San Francisco   St. Louis   Bangkok   Bogotá   Caracas   Kuala Lumpur
Lisbon   London   Madrid   Mexico City   Milan   Montreal   New Delhi
Santiago   Seoul   Singapore   Sydney   Taipei   Toronto

McGraw-Hill Higher Education

A Division of The McGraw-Hill Companies

ELEMENTARY CLASSROOM MANAGEMENT
LESSONS FROM RESEARCH AND PRACTICE
Published by McGraw-Hill, a business unit of The McGraw-Hill Companies, Inc., 1221 Avenue of the Americas, New York, NY, 10020. Copyright © 2003, 1997, 1993 by The McGraw-Hill Companies, Inc. All rights reserved. No part of this publication may be reproduced or distributed in any form or by any means, or stored in a database or retrieval system, without the prior written consent of The McGraw-Hill Companies, Inc., including, but not limited to, in any network or other electronic storage or transmission, or broadcast for distance learning.
Some ancillaries, including electronic and print components, may not be available to customers outside the United States.

This book is printed on acid-free paper.

4 5 6 7 8 9 0 FGR/FGR 0 9 8 7 6 5 4

ISBN 0-07-232243-8

Editorial director: *Jane Karpacz*
Developmental editor: *Cara Harvey*
Editorial coordinator: *Christina Lembo*
Project manager: *Diane M. Folliard*
Production supervisor: *Susanne Riedell*
Coordinator of freelance design: *Mary E. Kazak*
Photo research coordinator: *Judy Kausal*
Photographer: *Suzanne Karp Krebs*
Cover design: *Asylum Studios*
Typeface: *10/12 Times*
Compositor: *Carlisle Communications, Ltd.*
Printer: *Quebecor World Fairfield Inc.*

Library of Congress Cataloging-in-Publication Data
Weinstein, Carol Simon.
    Elementary classroom management: lessons from research and practice/Carol S. Weinstein, Andrew J. Mignano, Jr.–3rd ed.
        p.cm.
    Includes bibliographical references and index.
    ISBN 0-07-232243-8 (alk. paper)
    1. Classroom management–United States–Case studies. 2. Education, Elementary–United States—Case studies. 3. Home and school–United States. 4. Handicapped children–Education–United States. I. Mignano, Andrew J. II. Title.
LB3013. W45 2003
372.110'24–dc21

2002024640

www.mhhe.com

About the Authors

Carol Simon Weinstein is professor of education in the Department of Learning and Teaching at Rutgers Graduate School of Education. She received her bachelor's degree in psychology from Clark University in Worcester, Massachusetts, and her master's and doctoral degrees from Harvard Graduate School of Education.

It was at Harvard that Dr. Weinstein first became interested in the impact of classroom design on students' behavior and attitudes. She pursued this topic for many years, writing about the ways that classroom environments can be designed to facilitate teachers' goals and to foster children's learning and development. Dr. Weinstein's interest in organizing classroom space eventually expanded to include classroom organization and management in general. She is the author of *Secondary Classroom Management* (McGraw-Hill, 2003), as well as numerous chapters and articles on classroom management and teacher education students' beliefs about caring and control. In 1998, she took part in writing and producing the CD-ROM, *Effective Classroom Management: An Interactive Multimedia Professional Development Tool for Educators.* Dr. Weinstein currently works with teachers on conflict resolution and peacemaking and is a trainer for *Second Step,* a violence prevention program.

In 2000, Dr. Weinstein was recognized for her efforts with the "Contributing Researcher Award" from the American Federation of Teachers for "Bridging the Gap between Theory and Practice in Effective Classroom Management."

Andrew J. Mignano, Jr., is principal of the Laura Donovan School in Freehold Township, New Jersey. He received his bachelor's degree in elementary and special education from Rutgers College in 1974 and his master's degree in educational psychology from Kean College in 1981. During his 15 years as a teacher he taught all levels from kindergarten to grade five, including one year teaching a special education class. His 13 years as principal have been characterized by his skills as an educational leader and professional developer. During his tenure he has been instrumental in the implementation of innovative programs in the areas of early literacy, early childhood education, writing workshop, strategic reading, inclusion and parent involvement. Mr. Mignano has worked closely with the Rutgers Office of Teacher Education. He has welcomed Rutgers' student teachers to his school and has also served as an adjunct professor for the seminar that accompanies student teaching.

Dedication

To Neil, Rachel, and Laura, for their unfailing support. C.S.W.

For my mother, Gwendolyn, whose unselfish love and strength enabled my father to live and die his way. A.J.M.

Brief Contents

Contents

Preface

In the years since the first and second editions of *Elementary Classroom Management,* the challenges of classroom management have grown dramatically. Classes are more heterogeneous than ever, with students from a wide range of cultural and linguistic backgrounds. Youngsters with disabilities are educated in classes with their nondisabled peers. Increasing numbers of youngsters come to school with emotional and psychological problems. The horror of Columbine and other incidents of school violence have heightened anxiety. At the same time, there has been more attention to the need to make schools safer, more caring places; more attention to problems of bullying and peer harassment; and greater effort to reach out to alienated, isolated youth.

Given these challenges, teacher education students and beginning teachers need clear, practical, research-based suggestions for organizing and managing classrooms. *Elementary Classroom Management* responds to that need. Our goal has been to write a book that uses research on teaching in a reasonable, responsible way, yet is accessible, even enjoyable to read. Chapters address the ongoing management tasks that teachers face, such as organizing physical space, creating community, teaching and enforcing norms for behavior, motivating students, and responding to misbehavior. Each of these topics is like a piece of a jigsaw puzzle; no one piece is sufficient by itself, but when they are all put into place the result is a classroom environment that is respectful, orderly, and productive.

A Case Study Approach

The full title of this book is *Elementary Classroom Management: Lessons from Research and Practice.* As the subtitle indicates, the book combines what research has to say about effective classroom management with knowledge culled from practice. This is done by weaving together discussions of research-based management principles with both the thinking and the actual management practices of four real elementary teachers. Barbara Broggi, Garnetta Chain, Ken Kowalski, and Viviana Love teach different grades in very different school districts, but they are all experienced teachers who are able to create productive, respectful classrooms. Readers will come to know these four teachers—to hear their thinking on various aspects of classroom management and to see the ways they interact with students. Their stories provide real-life illustrations of the concepts and principles derived from research.

One point about the structure of the book needs to be made explicit. This edition integrates material about Barbara, Ken, and Garnetta that was collected during 1991–1992, 1994–1995, and 2001. (Viviana retired to Puerto Rico just before we began writing the new edition.) In other words, we have created a composite picture of each teacher by portraying incidents that occurred in different years with different students at different grade levels as though they had all occurred in the same academic year with the same class. We have sacrificed absolute verity, but we have gained simplicity and coherence.

The Third Edition: New Coverage

Like the earlier editions, this edition of *Elementary Classroom Management* is more comprehensive than many management texts, with chapters on working with families, using time effectively, and helping students with special needs. The book also addresses the managerial challenges involved in a variety of instructional formats, such as independent work, recitations, discussions, and groupwork, topics more commonly found in general methods books. This material has been updated to reflect recent scholarship and current concerns. In addition, this edition contains three new chapters:

- *Creating Safer, More Caring Classrooms* (Chapter 5) addresses the need to build caring, supportive relationships with and among students, a theme that is echoed throughout the book. This new emphasis is intended to convey the message that classroom management is not simply about rules, rewards, and consequences, but also about building connections with students and creating safer, more caring classrooms.
- *Enhancing Students' Motivation* (Chapter 8) is an expanded version of the discussion of motivation that appeared in earlier editions as part of a chapter on gaining students' cooperation. The chapter begins by reflecting on what is realistic and appropriate with respect to motivating elementary students. It then examines the factors that give rise to motivation and considers a variety of motivational strategies drawn from research, theory, and the practice of the four teachers.
- *Preventing and Responding to Violence* (Chapter 14) is a sad necessity in this post-Columbine era, even at the elementary level. The chapter discusses the ways that individual teachers can build a climate of tolerance, teach conflict resolution, recognize the early warning signs of potential violence, de-escalate potentially explosive situations, and deal effectively with aggression and fighting.

Writing Style and Features

Although the subject matter is serious, we have written *Elementary Classroom Management* in a somewhat informal, conversational style. Readers of the previous editions have told us that the book is unlike any textbook they have read; we take that as a compliment. In addition, chapters contain photographs and cartoons; checklists of key points; models of letters, forms, assessments, and contracts; summaries of major ideas; activities to extend understanding; and suggestions for further reading. All of these features are intended to engage the reader, promote comprehension, and facilitate application of the material.

This edition of *Elementary Classroom Management* parallels the second edition of *Secondary Classroom Management* (Weinstein, 2003), so that instructors teaching courses with both elementary and secondary teacher education students can use the two books as a package. The major difference, of course, is that the "Lessons from Research and Practice" described in the secondary book are largely based on studies conducted in junior- and senior-high classrooms and on the practices of four secondary teachers. We hope that we will hear from faculty using both books, so we can learn if they do, in fact, work well together. (Contact Weinstein at csw@rci.rutgers.edu.)

Acknowledgements

We wish to express our gratitude to all the people who helped to make this edition a reality. A fervent thank you goes to Viviana, Garnetta, Barbara, and Ken for allowing us to observe in their classrooms and ask them endless questions. They have been gracious and welcoming, and they have generously shared the lessons they have learned in their combined 125 years of teaching. Thank you, also, to the superintendents and assistant superintendents who gave us permission to carry out this project in their districts: Ronald Larkin and Penelope Lattimer of New Brunswick; Marylu Simon of Highland Park; and Willa Spicer of South Brunswick. We are also grateful to Leslie Lillian and Tonia Moore, who took the time to speak with us about programs for students with special problems. Many thanks to the Rutgers student teachers who shared their frustrations and uncertainties, as well as their new understandings. We hope their comments and journal entries will resonate with readers who are also beginning the process of learning to teach. Special thanks go to Jeanne Barnes, Karen Boose, Mary Callahan, Jen Clemente, Mary Custy, Terri Ann Fleischman, Mary Porcelli, Janina Rzeszutik, Paulette Sato, Cynthia Szumowski, and Christine Zehnder. It should be noted that in several cases, details have been changed to avoid embarrassment to anyone, and at times, composite journal entries have been created.

We want to express our appreciation to Suzanne Karp Krebs, photographer and friend. Her ability to take such graceful photographs amid the hyperkinetic activity of elementary students is truly impressive. We thank Claire Swedberg for conscientiously performing so many of the tedious tasks that are involved in producing a manuscript (especially the pursuit of copyright permissions) and Nancy Lefkowitz for carefully checking references (while recovering from knee surgery). We are also grateful to the individuals who provided thoughtful, comprehensive, helpful reviews: Sonya Carr, Southeastern Louisiana University, Connie J. Erpelding, University of Northern Iowa, Calista Koval, St. Leo University, Lawrence Lyman, Emporia State University, Jane McCarthy, University of Nevada, Las Vegas, J. Cynthia McDermott, California State University, Dominguez Hills, Gina Post, University of Utah, Maura L. Roberts, Arizona State University, Ralph Shibley, University of Rio Grande, Rita Silverman, Pace University, Don Weinhouse, University of Southern Colorado, Karla B. Willis, Eastern Kentucky University. Thanks also to Lois Weiner from New Jersey City University, who reminded us about Molnar and Lindquist's work on changing problem behavior.

We also wish to acknowledge the expertise and encouragement of Cara Harvey, our editor at McGraw-Hill. She has been extremely patient during difficult times, and we appreciate her faith in us. To Diane Folliard, our thanks for being such a conscientious, efficient project manager. Finally, a special thank you to Neil, for putting up with all the whining (and everything else), to our children, Rachel and Laura, Alexa and Jon, for their unconditional love and support, and to Vince, for keeping Andy centered and making him laugh.

Carol Simon Weinstein
Andrew J. Mignano, Jr.

PART I

Introduction

Chapter One

The Elementary Classroom Environment: Crowded, Complex, and Potentially Chaotic

Guiding Assumptions

Plan of the Book

Summary

For many prospective and beginning teachers, entering an elementary classroom is like returning home after a long absence. So much is familiar: Bulletin boards still display "Good Work" studded with As, stars, and smiling faces; bells and buzzers still interrupt lessons to announce fire drills; the dusty odor of chalk still permeates the air. The familiarity of these sights, sounds, and smells makes us feel comfortable and at ease; in fact, it may lead us to think that the transition from student to teacher will be relatively easy. Yet, ironically, this very familiarity can be a trap; it can make it difficult to appreciate what a curious and demanding place the elementary classroom really is. Looking at the classroom as if we have never seen one before can help us recognize some of its strange characteristics and contradictions.

Viewed from a fresh perspective, the elementary classroom turns out to be an extremely crowded place. It is more like a subway or a bus than a place designed for learning. In fact, it is difficult to think of another setting, except prison, where such large groups of individuals are packed so closely together for so many hours. Nonetheless, amid this crowdedness, students are often not allowed to interact. As Philip Jackson (1968) has noted,

students must try to behave as if they were in solitude, when in point of fact they are not. . . . in the early grades it is not uncommon to find students facing each other around a table while at the same time being required not

*to communicate with each other. These young people, if they are to
become successful students, must learn how to be alone in a crowd. (p. 16)*

There are other contradictions in this curious place. Children are expected to work together in harmony, yet they may be strangers—even rivals—and may come from very different cultural backgrounds. Students are urged to cooperate, to share, and to help one another, but they are also told to keep their eyes on their own papers, and they often compete
for grades and special privileges. They are lectured about being independent and responsible, yet they are also expected to show complete, unquestioning obedience to the teacher's
dictates. (This peculiar situation is captured in the cartoon that appears in Figure 1-1.)

In addition to these contradictions, Walter Doyle (1986) has pointed out six features
of the classroom setting that make it even more complex. First, classrooms are characterized by *multidimensionality.* Unlike a post office or a restaurant, places devoted to a
single activity, the classroom is the setting for a broad range of events. Within its boundaries, students read, write, and discuss. They form friendships, argue, celebrate birthdays, and play games. Teachers not only instruct, they also collect milk money, take attendance, and settle disputes. They counsel students with problems and meet with
parents to discuss students' progress. Somehow, the classroom environment must be able
to accommodate all these activities.

*"I expect you all to be independent, innovative, critical thinkers who will
do exactly as I say."*

FIGURE 1-1. Students are urged to be independent and responsible, yet they
are also expected to show complete obedience to the teacher. (Reprinted by
permission of Warren.)

Second, many of these activities take place at the same time. This *simultaneity* makes the elementary classroom a bit like a three-ring circus. It is not uncommon to see a cluster of students discussing a story with the teacher, individuals writing at their desks or on computers, pairs of students playing a mathematics game, and a small group working on a social studies mural. Still other students may be passing notes about yesterday's soccer game. It is this simultaneity—this three-ring circus quality—that makes having "eyes in the back of your head" so valuable to teachers.

A third characteristic of classrooms is the rapid pace at which things happen. Classroom events occur with an *immediacy* that makes it impossible to think through every action ahead of time. A squabble erupts over the ownership of an action figure; a student complains that a neighbor is copying; a normally silent child makes a serious, but irrelevant comment during a group discussion. Each of these incidents requires a quick response, an on-the-spot decision about how to proceed. Furthermore, classroom events like these cannot always be anticipated, despite the most careful planning. This *unpredictability* is a fourth characteristic of classrooms. It ensures that being a teacher is rarely boring, but unpredictability can also be exhausting.

A fifth characteristic of classrooms is the *lack of privacy*. Classrooms are remarkably public places. Within their four walls, each person's behavior can be observed by many others. Teachers talk of feeling as though they are always "on stage" or living in a "fishbowl" (Lortie, 1975). Their feelings are understandable. With 20 or 30 pairs of eyes watching, it is difficult to find a moment for a private chuckle or an unobserved groan. But the scrutiny goes two ways: Teachers constantly monitor students' behavior as well. And in response to this sometimes unwelcome surveillance, students develop an "active underlife" (Hatch, 1986) in which to pursue their own personal agendas. With skills that increase as they progress from grade to grade, students learn to pass notes, comb their hair, read magazines, and doodle, all—they hope—without the teacher's ever noticing. Yet, even if they avoid the teacher's eyes, there are always peers watching. It is difficult for students to have a private interaction with the teacher, to conceal a grade on a test, or to make a mistake without someone noticing.

Finally, over the course of the academic year, classes construct a joint *history*. This sixth characteristic means that classes, like families, remember past events—both positive and negative. They remember who got yelled at, who was chosen to be the paper monitor, and what the teacher said about homework assignments. They remember who was going to have only "one more chance" before getting detention, and if the teacher didn't follow through, they remember that too. The class memory means that what happens today affects what happens tomorrow. It also means that teachers must work to shape a history that will support, rather than frustrate, future activities.

Contradictory, multidimensional, simultaneous, immediate, unpredictable, public, and remembered—this portrait of the classroom highlights characteristics that we often overlook. We have begun the book with this portrait because we believe that *effective organization and management require an understanding of the unique features of the classroom.* Many of the management problems experienced by beginning teachers can be traced to their lack of understanding of the complex setting in which they work.

Calvin and Hobbes   by Bill Watterson

FIGURE 1-2. Teachers work with captive groups of students.
(Calvin and Hobbes © Watterson. Dist. by Universal Press Syndicate. Reprinted with permission. All rights reserved.)

Past experiences with children may also mislead beginning teachers. For example, you may have tutored an individual student who was having academic difficulties, or perhaps you have been a camp counselor or a swim-club instructor. Although these are valuable experiences, they are very different from teaching in classrooms. Teachers do not work one-on-one with students in a private room; they seldom lead recreational activities that children have themselves selected. Teachers do not even work with youngsters who have chosen to be present. (See Figure 1-2 for Calvin's perspective on compulsory attendance.) Instead, *teachers work with captive groups of students, on academic agendas that students have not always helped to set, in a crowded, public setting.* Within this setting, teachers must gain the cooperation of students and get them involved in educational activities. This is not a simple task. As Tracy Kidder (1989) has noted:

> *The problem is fundamental. Put twenty or more children of roughly the same age in a little room, confine them to desks, make them wait in lines, make them behave. It is as if a secret committee, now lost to history, had made a study of children and, having figured out what the greatest number were least disposed to do, declared that all of them should do it. (p. 115)*

Elementary Classroom Management is designed to help prospective and beginning teachers understand the special characteristics of the classroom setting and their implications for organization and management. We hope to provide concepts and principles that you can use to think about the managerial tasks you will encounter as a teacher. For example, once you recognize that students are a captive audience, you are better able to see why it's necessary to stimulate interest in lessons. Being aware of the public nature of classrooms helps you to understand the importance of dealing with behavior problems in an unobtrusive way. Comprehending the crowdedness of the classroom leads you to appreciate the need to minimize congestion and provide needed privacy through the careful arrangement of your classroom furnishings. A group of strangers can become a cohesive learning community if you know how to foster an atmosphere of caring and mutual support. Simultaneity of classroom events is manageable if you teach students what to do when you are busy elsewhere—and if you hold them accountable for doing it.

Guiding Assumptions

Sometimes, we become so preoccupied with basic management issues (like getting everyone to sit down), we forget that classroom management is not about achieving order for order's sake; it's about achieving order so that productive learning can occur. In other words, *the ultimate goal of classroom management is to promote learning*—and effective management can do just that. In fact, an analysis of 50 years of research (Wang, Haertel, & Walberg, 1993/94) concluded that *classroom management is the single greatest influence on student learning*—greater than students' cognitive processes (e.g., general intelligence, prior knowledge), home environment, motivation, and socioeconomic status. (See Figure 1-3.) With this in mind, let us consider six underlying assumptions that have guided the content and organization of this book.

The first assumption is that *successful classroom management fosters self-discipline and personal responsibility.* Let's be honest: Every teacher's worst fear is the prospect of losing control—of being helpless and ineffectual in the face of unruly, anarchic classes. Given this nightmare, it's tempting to create a coercive, top-down management system that relies heavily on the use of rewards and penalties to gain obedience. Yet, such an approach does little to teach students to make good choices about how to act (Covaleski, 1993). Furthermore, as Mary McCaslin and Tom Good (1998) point out, "the success of a compliance model depends upon constant monitoring (if the teacher turns her or his back, students misbehave . . .)" (p. 170). An emphasis on external control is also inconsistent with current thinking about curriculum and instruction (McCaslin & Good, 1992, 1998). It doesn't make sense to design learning activities that encourage independence, problem solving, and critical thinking, and then use managerial strategies that encourage dependence on points, popcorn parties, and punishment. This is not to discount the importance of teachers' authority; clearly, in order to be effective, you must be willing to set limits and guide students' behavior. Nonetheless, what you are aiming towards is an environment in which students behave appropriately, not out of fear of punishment or desire for reward, but out of a sense of personal responsibility.

The second assumption is that *most problems of disorder in classrooms can be avoided if teachers use good preventive management strategies.* Thus, we emphasize the prevention of misbehavior, rather than strategies for coping with misbehavior. This emphasis is consistent with classroom management research conducted in the 1970s and 80s—research that dramatically changed the way we think about students' behavior. In a now classic study, Jacob Kounin (1970) set out to explain the differences between orderly and disorderly classes by examining how teachers responded to misconduct. To his surprise, he found that the reactions of effective and ineffective managers were quite

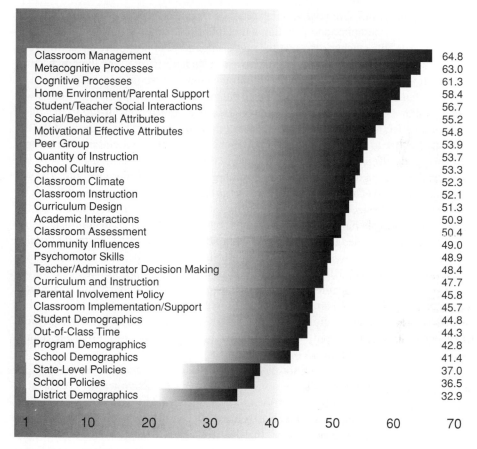

Classroom Management						64.8
Metacognitive Processes						63.0
Cognitive Processes						61.3
Home Environment/Parental Support						58.4
Student/Teacher Social Interactions						56.7
Social/Behavioral Attributes						55.2
Motivational Effective Attributes						54.8
Peer Group						53.9
Quantity of Instruction						53.7
School Culture						53.3
Classroom Climate						52.3
Classroom Instruction						52.1
Curriculum Design						51.3
Academic Interactions						50.9
Classroom Assessment						50.4
Community Influences						49.0
Psychomotor Skills						48.9
Teacher/Administrator Decision Making						48.4
Curriculum and Instruction						47.7
Parental Involvement Policy						45.8
Classroom Implementation/Support						45.7
Student Demographics						44.8
Out-of-Class Time						44.3
Program Demographics						42.8
School Demographics						41.4
State-Level Policies						37.0
School Policies						36.5
District Demographics						32.9

1	10	20	30	40	50	60	70

FIGURE 1-3. Relative influences on learning
(Source: Wang, Haertel, and Walberg, 1993/94. Reprinted with permission.)

similar. What accounted then for the differences in order? Kounin eventually determined that the orderly classes were more the result of a teacher's ability *to manage the activities of the group* than of particular ways of handling student misconduct. As a result of Kounin's study, we now distinguish between *discipline*—responding to inappropriate behavior—and *classroom management*—ways of creating a caring, respectful environment that supports learning (Evertson & Randolph, 1995).

A third assumption is that *the way teachers think about management strongly influences what they do.* Research has provided some fascinating examples of the relationship between teachers' beliefs about management and their behavior. Consider, Sarah, for example, a first-year teacher who was having difficulties managing her class (Ulerick and Tobin, 1989). Sarah's behavior in the classroom seemed to reflect her belief that effective teachers should use "charm and humor" to engage students in learning and gain their cooperation. In short, her thinking about management reflected a metaphor of "teacher as comedian." Eventually, Sarah reconceptualized the role of teacher, discarding the comedian metaphor and adopting a metaphor of teacher as "social director." As "social director," the teacher's job was to "invite students to appropriate, interesting, and meaningful learning activities" (p. 12), and to assist students in directing their own learning activities. This change in Sarah's thinking about classroom management led to changes in her behavior and dramatic improvements in the atmosphere of her classes.

In a similar study, Carter (1985) reviewed narrative descriptions of life in the classrooms of an effective and an ineffective classroom manager. Carter's analysis of the descriptions led her to conclude that the two teachers thought about classroom management in very different ways. She concluded that the effective manager saw her managerial role as "a driver navigating a complex and often treacherous route" (p. 89). From this perspective, her responsibility was to guide classroom events smoothly and efficiently; she emphasized the academic tasks that students needed to accomplish and did not allow minor misbehavior and interruptions to get her off course. In contrast, the ineffective manager seemed to see her role as "defender of a territory." Constantly vigilant for threats to order, she was careful to catch all misbehavior whenever it occurred and used reprimands and appeals to authority in order to control inappropriate behavior.

Taken together, these studies suggest that teachers who view classroom management as a process of guiding and structuring classroom events tend to be more effective than teachers who stress their disciplinary role or who see classroom management as a product of personal charm (Brophy, 1988). This perspective on classroom management is also consistent with an emphasis on prevention.

Fourth, *the need for order must not supersede the need for meaningful instruction.* Current educational reform efforts share a vision of students as active learners engaged in meaningful, complex tasks, problem-solving and critical thinking, collaboration and cooperative groupwork. This means that classrooms will be noisier and more active than in the past—more "a bee-hive of activity" than "a well-oiled machine" (Evertson & Randolph, 1995). Certainly, learning and teaching cannot take place in an environment that is chaotic and disorderly. On the other hand, excessive concerns about quiet and uniformity can hinder this kind of learning and teaching (Doyle, 1986). For example, a teacher may wish to divide the class into small groups for a hands-on science experiment, believing that her students will learn better by *doing* rather than by simply *watching.* Yet her anxiety about the noise level and her fear that students may not cooperate could make her abandon the small group project and substitute a teacher demonstration and an individual workbook assignment. In one respect this teacher is correct: A collaborative science experiment will not only be more intellectually and socially challenging, it will also be more challenging from a managerial perspective. Nonetheless, it is crucial that teachers not sacrifice opportunities to learn in order to achieve a quiet classroom. As Doyle (1985) comments, "A well-run lesson that teaches nothing is just as useless as a chaotic lesson in which no academic work is possible" (p. 33). The solution is to anticipate the specific managerial "hazards" that can arise in different situations (Carter, 1985) and try to prevent them from occurring.

Our fifth assumption is that the *tasks of classroom management vary across different classroom situations.* Ecological psychologists remind us that the classroom is not a "homogenized glob" (Kounin & Sherman, 1979, p. 150). Rather, it is composed of distinct "subsettings"—guided reading groups, whole class discussions, transition times, cooperative learning activities—and what constitutes order may be different in each of these subsettings. For example, "calling out" may be a problem during a teacher-directed question and answer session (often referred to as "recitation"), but it may be perfectly acceptable in a more student-centered discussion. Similarly, students may be prohibited from helping one another during a weekly quiz, but they may be encouraged to work together on cooperative science teams. Students have the right to know what is expected of them in these different classroom situations. This means that teachers must think about the behavior that is appropriate in each classroom subsetting and make a point of teaching students how they need to behave. To assist in this task, *Elementary Classroom Management* discusses the specific management "hazards" associated with independent work, groupwork, recitations, and discussions (Carter, 1985) and suggests ways of preventing these hazards from occurring.

Our final assumption is that *becoming an effective classroom manager requires knowledge, reflection, hard work, and time.* Despite numerous books that provide "101 guaranteed ways of creating classroom order," classroom management cannot be reduced to a set of recipes or a list of "how to's." As we have seen, the classroom environment is crowded, multidimensional, fast-paced, unpredictable, and public. In this complex setting, pat answers just won't work. Similarly, well-managed classrooms are not achieved by following "gut instinct" or doing "what feels right." Classroom management is a *learned craft.* That means that you must become familiar with the knowledge base that undergirds effective management. You must also be ready and willing to anticipate problems, analyze situations, generate solutions, make thoughtful decisions—and learn from your mistakes.

Plan of the Book

Elementary Classroom Management focuses first on ways of creating a classroom environment that supports learning and self-regulation, such as designing an appropriate physical setting, developing standards for behavior, building an atmosphere of caring and respect, and using time wisely. It then moves to the managerial tasks directly related to instruction—for example, motivating students to learn, organizing groupwork, and managing student-centered discussions. Finally, the book examines the inevitable challenges associated with classroom management, such as responding to inappropriate behavior, helping students with special needs, and preventing and coping with violence.

Throughout the book, concepts and principles derived from research are woven together with the wisdom and experiences of real elementary teachers. In particular, we focus on four individuals who teach in central New Jersey. You learn about the classes they teach and about the physical constraints of their rooms; you hear them reflect on their rules and routines and watch as they teach them to students. You listen as they talk about motivating students and fostering cooperation, and as they discuss appropriate ways to deal with misbehavior. In sum, *this book focuses on real decisions made by real teachers as they manage the complex environment of the elementary classroom.* By sharing these stories, we do not mean to suggest that their ways of managing classrooms are the only effective ways. Rather, our goal is to illustrate how four reflective, caring, and very different individuals approach the tasks involved in classroom management.

Now, let's meet the teachers.

Summary

This chapter examined some of the contradictions and special characteristics of classrooms. It argued that effective management requires an understanding of the unique features of the classroom environment and stressed the fact that teachers work with captive groups of students on academic agendas that students have not always helped to set. It then discussed six assumptions that guided the content and organization of the book.

Contradictions of the classroom environment:

- Classrooms are crowded, yet students are often not allowed to interact.
- Children are expected to work together harmoniously, yet they may not know or like each other.
- Students are urged to cooperate, yet they often work in individual or competitive situations.
- Students are encouraged to be independent, yet they are also expected to conform to the teacher's dictates.

Characteristics of the classroom environment:

- Multidimensionality.
- Simultaneity.
- Immediacy.
- Unpredictability.
- Lack of privacy.
- History.

Guiding assumptions of the book:

- The ultimate goal of classroom management is to promote learning.
- Successful classroom management promotes self-regulation.
- Most problems of disorder can be avoided if teachers use good preventive management strategies.
- The way teachers think about management influences the way they behave.
- The need for order must not supersede the need for meaningful instruction.
- Behavioral expectations vary across different subsettings of the classroom.
- Becoming an effective classroom manager requires knowledge, reflection, hard work, and time.

In an effort to illustrate various ways of managing classrooms effectively, the book focuses on real decisions made by real teachers as they manage the complex environment of the elementary classroom.

References

Brophy, J. (1988). Educating teachers about managing classrooms and students. *Teaching and Teacher Education, 4*(1), 1–18.

Carter, K. (March–April 1985). Teacher comprehension of classroom processes: An emerging direction in classroom management research. Paper presented at the annual meeting of the American Educational Research Association, Chicago.

Covaleskie, J. F. (1993). Discipline and morality: Beyond rules & consequences. In J. W. Noll (Ed.), *Taking Sides: Clashing views on controversial educational issues.* Guilford, CT: The Dushkin Publishing Group, pp. 319–326. Reprinted from *The Educational Forum,* Winter 1992, 56(2).

Doyle, W. (1985). Recent research on classroom management: Implications for teacher preparation. *Journal of Teacher Education, 36*(3), 31–35.

Doyle, W. (1986). Classroom organization and management. In M. C. Wittrock (Ed.), *Handbook of research on teaching.* New York: Macmillan, pp. 392–431.

Evertson, C. M., & Randolph, C. H. (1995). Classroom management in the learning-centered classroom. In A. C. Ornstein (Ed.), *Teaching: Theory and practice.* Boston: Allyn & Bacon.

Hatch, J. A. (March 1986). Alone in a crowd: Analysis of covert interactions in a kindergarten. Presented at the annual meeting of the American Educational Research Association, San Francisco. ERIC Document Reproduction Service No. 272 278.

Jackson, P. (1968). *Life in classrooms.* New York: Holt, Rinehart & Winston.

Kidder, T. (1989). *Among schoolchildren.* Boston: Houghton Mifflin.

Kounin, J. S. (1970). *Discipline and group management in classrooms.* New York: Holt, Rinehart & Winston.

Kounin, J. S., & Sherman, L. (1979). School environments as behavior settings. *Theory into Practice, 14,* 145–151.

Lortie, D. (1975). *Schoolteacher.* Chicago: University of Chicago Press.

McCaslin, M., & Good, T. L. (1992). Compliant cognition: The misalliance of management and instructional goals in current school reform. *Educational Researcher, 21*(3), 4–17.

McCaslin, M., & Good, T. L. (1998). Moving beyond management as sheer compliance: Helping students to develop goal coordination strategies. *Educational Horizons,* Summer, 169–176.

Ulerick, S. L., & Tobin, K. (March 1989). The influence of a teacher's beliefs on classroom management. Paper presented at the annual meeting of the American Educational Research Association, San Francisco.

Wang, M. C.; Haertel, G. D.; & Walberg, H. J. (1993/1994). What helps students learn? *Educational Leadership, 51*(4), 74–79.

Meeting the Teachers (and Their Students)

All four of our teachers work in central New Jersey, a densely populated area characterized by ethnic, racial, and socioeconomic diversity. *Viviana Love* is a first-grade bilingual teacher at Roosevelt School in New Brunswick, a midsized urban district. Also in New Brunswick is *Garnetta Chain,* who teaches third grade at McKinley School. Across the Raritan River from New Brunswick is Highland Park, where *Barbara Broggi* is a fourth-grade teacher at Bartle School. Finally, *Ken Kowalski* teaches fifth grade at Brunswick Acres School in nearby South Brunswick. This chapter introduces all four teachers and briefly describes the districts within which they work. Then the chapter considers what their students have to say about the characteristics of successful classroom managers. We begin with New Brunswick.

Of the 6,500 students who attend this district's 10 schools, 54 percent are Latino and 41 percent are African American. Many of the children come from poor or low-income families, evidenced by the fact that 80 percent of the students qualify for the federal free or reduced-price lunch program. The socioeconomic conditions breed other conditions typical of urban areas—drug abuse, transiency, homelessness, teenage pregnancy, physical abuse.

About 20 years ago, after receiving some of the lowest scores in New Jersey on a statewide standardized test, New Brunswick instituted a highly structured curriculum. Objectives were developed for every subject at every grade level, along with timelines for teaching each objective. Teachers must submit plan books and grade books to building principals, who closely monitor when each objective is taught and evaluated and how students are progressing.

Critics argued that the new curriculum restricted creativity and burdened teachers with unnecessary paperwork, but academic achievement has steadily increased in the last decade. This improvement is evident in the scores on the High School Proficiency Test (HSPT) that New Jersey requires for graduation. In 1998, 87.2 percent of 11th-graders passed the reading portion of the test; 86.2 percent passed the math portion; 88.3 percent passed the writing portion; and 74.5 percent passed all three portions. These results compare favorably with other urban school districts in the state, and teachers and administrators are convinced that New Brunswick has been moving in the right direction. Financial support from local corporations (in particular, Johnson & Johnson, whose world headquarters is located in the city) and collaborative projects with Rutgers, the state university, have also aided the district's quest for improvement.

Viviana Love

Roosevelt School is in the heart of downtown New Brunswick, surrounded by single- and multifamily dwellings. It is an old, but well-cared for building with a capacity for 700 students. On the first floor, in a spacious, carpeted room next to the office, we find Viviana Love, a first-grade bilingual teacher.

Viviana was born in a small town in Puerto Rico. Although her parents had only a third-grade education, they instilled in Viviana a desire to learn and a strong ambition to succeed. Her mother taught her to read and write, and with these skills Viviana began her teaching career at the age of seven. She tutored neighborhood children, and much to her delight, she sometimes received a quarter for her services! From the very beginning, Viviana knew teaching felt right.

Viviana Love

An image of her first-grade teacher, Mrs. Hernandez, is as strong today as it was 50 years ago:

> *She wore a lot of bracelets and when she went to the board . . . oh, those bracelets! I loved the chiming of the bracelets. I used to just look at them and say to myself that the first thing I'll do when I am a teacher is buy a lot of shiny bracelets—and I did. The bracelets, for me, were a glamorous symbol of high social status. I couldn't wait to write on the board with my shining bracelets.*

Viviana began her professional teaching career in Puerto Rico, before she even completed college. She taught for seven years in a small two-room schoolhouse while pursuing her bachelor's degree; she then moved to the island of St. Croix where she taught Spanish for half a year. In 1970, she arrived in New Jersey. She has taught in New Brunswick ever since—a total of 37 years of teaching.

With no children of her own, Viviana "adopts" her students: "They are my children," she says. "I will do anything for them, just like mothers do for their own children. I want them to be the best." Sometimes she feels like taking them home with her, so she can give them the love and stability some of them lack. Above all, she seeks to stimulate her students' desire to learn.

Viviana's commitment to her students is evident in her first-grade bilingual classroom. With an energy level that is rare, she motivates, prods, instructs, models, praises, and captivates her students. Most instruction is delivered to the whole class, as required by the district. The pace is brisk, and Viviana clearly has a flair for the dramatic; she uses music, props, gestures, facial expressions, and shifts in voice tone to communicate the material.

Viviana's 25 students have all emigrated from the Dominican Republic, Mexico, Puerto Rico, and Honduras. Eighteen attended kindergarten here; seven are "port-of-entry" (POE) children who have just arrived in this country. Early in the school year, Viviana instructs primarily in Spanish. She moves to English as soon as possible, however, using Spanish whenever she perceives problems in comprehension. Viviana is vehement about not wanting her children segregated or labeled as disadvantaged because they are not fluent in English. She uses every available minute for instruction, even turning interruptions or unexpected events into "teachable moments." When a visitor comes to her classroom, for example, she asks her students to use English to describe the person's clothing, hair color, and height. Her efforts pay off: Although her children begin the year speaking little or no English, they leave in June generally having achieved the normal first-grade objectives for New Brunswick.

Knowing that her children come from poor families, Viviana provides all the materials they need to complete class assignments. "My children cannot say they couldn't complete a project because they didn't have a magazine or scissors. I give them what they need so that there is no excuse for failure." Some people say that Viviana is strict and demands too much of first-grade students, but her students don't seem daunted by her high expectations. They look enthusiastic and speak proudly about their accomplishments.

Viviana also sets high standards for herself. A firm believer in continuing professional development, she has a master's degree in urban education and additional credit hours in bilingual education. She frequently serves as a cooperating teacher for student teachers and regularly attends workshops and courses. She is part of the Rutgers–New Brunswick Math Project, a program that emphasizes the importance of mathematical problem solving and the use of manipulative materials. She recently volunteered to participate in another Rutgers–New Brunswick collaboration on literacy. When we comment on her continuing efforts to improve her teaching, she shrugs: "Teachers have to keep current. . . . Education changes because students change. Our teaching must reflect the changes of the world around us." Viviana's success in the classroom and her commitment to her profession have been acknowledged by the district and the state: She is the proud recipient of the Governor's Teacher Recognition Award.

Viviana is also valued and appreciated by the parents of the children she teaches. On the first day of school, she talks openly with the parents who have accompanied their children to school: "At home, *you're* the parents . . . but at school, *I'm* the mother. We're all family, one big family, all Hispanic, and we all help each other." She communicates frequently with parents, not simply to discuss children's progress in school, but also to counsel parents on discipline, guide them in their search for employment, and suggest ways they can help their children learn.

Despite having lived here for 31 years, Viviana maintains strong ties with her parents who are still in Puerto Rico. She is grateful for the love of learning and the drive to succeed that they stimulated in her. She hopes to share these same gifts with her students and their families.

Garnetta Chain

We move now to the outskirts of New Brunswick, where McKinley School sits amid low-income housing projects and worn-looking factories. In a brand new addition to the building, we meet third-grade teacher Garnetta Chain. Garnetta's classroom belies the stereotype of the urban school. The blue-gray carpeting that covers two-thirds of the classroom creates a feeling of warmth and homeyness, while the linoleum on the other third provides a suitable flooring for messy activities. From the back wall, next to the sink, juts a peninsula of shelving and cabinets. Two aquariums with long-haired guinea pigs sit on the formica countertop, and math manipulatives of all sizes and colors fill the shelves. Brightly colored posters suggest the topics the class will be studying—the solar system, "exploring emotions," the cursive alphabet. In one corner is a library center; on the opposite wall is a collection of board games.

Garnetta, a mother of three children, has been teaching for 25 years, two of which were spent as director of a day care center in New York. Although she began college intending to become a biochemist, she soon realized she'd much rather work with children than with test tubes and changed her major to education. Her family supported this decision, especially her grandmother, a teacher herself for 30 years. Garnetta eventually

Garnetta Chain

received a master's degree in elementary education; she has taught third grade for the last 13 years. This year her class is small, only 15 students; three are Latino and 12 are African American. It's quite a change from last year, when she had a class of 39 children and had to teach in the library, since no classroom was large enough!

Garnetta speaks candidly of the difficulties her students face. Too many of them have been victims of physical and sexual abuse. Drugs, teenage pregnancy, and violence plague the community in which they live. It is no wonder that Garnetta feels that her main goals as a teacher are to impart moral values, give plenty of love and attention, and teach her students to feel good about themselves and to enjoy learning.

She also aims to offer a secure and safe environment. Class rules are clearly posted in her room. Garnetta feels that her children live with so much uncertainty in their lives that they need to know there is one place they can count on consistency. She tells us: "They need to know that a no or yes answer will remain that way, whether it's Monday or Friday. They have to have limits; there need to be consequences for their behaviors so that they'll develop responsibility for their actions."

Along with limits, Garnetta provides praise and affection. We watch her calm an angry child with a soft word and prevent a disruption with a hand on a shoulder, and it's easy to see why her students come to respect and trust her. It's not unusual for students to return to her classrooms years after they've moved on, just to chat or to discuss a problem.

Garnetta's caring, like Viviana's, goes well beyond the classroom walls. This fact was strongly impressed upon us one day in April as we sat watching her teach. Suddenly, a little boy appeared outside her window, his face pressed against the glass. The child had been in Garnetta's class, but a social service agency had removed him from his foster home and placed him with his father in a neighboring town. Although Garnetta had strongly opposed the move, she had not been able to convince the authorities that he was better off where he was.

On that April day, Garnetta invited him in. He found his old chair and a sweatshirt he had left behind. The children accepted him, and you could tell by the smile on his face that he felt at home. Once again, Garnetta tried to intervene. She had heard the boy wasn't attending his new school regularly and was seen out late at night unsupervised. She immediately got on the telephone with the boy's caseworker. Suggesting he return to McKinley, Garnetta even volunteered to pick him up at his new address and drive him each day. It didn't work. Garnetta gave him all the love she could that day and then gently told him he had to return to his new school.

When we asked Garnetta how she maintains her optimism and enthusiasm for teaching, she replied:

I always hope that there's somebody out there that I will reach and that I'll make a difference. I know society has a strong hold on my students and I may fail, but if someone makes something of themselves, and I've had a role in making a difference, then it's all worthwhile. I have to believe this.

If making a difference depends on energy and enthusiasm, then Garnetta will surely succeed. She's a veritable whirlwind. She not only participates in the Rutgers–New Brunswick Math Project, she's also one of three McKinley teachers involved in New Jersey's "Statewide Systemic Initiative," designed to upgrade mathematics and science education. Her classroom also participates in "Project 2000," in which Merrill-Lynch executives serve as teaching assistants and role models one day per week, and "Family Science," a program that invites families to come to school and participate in science activities with their children. In addition, Garnetta regularly supervises student teachers and coordinates several extracurricular programs—the yearly bazaar, the African-American History Week program, and holiday dessert night. One of her favorite projects is "career week," when students learn about vocational opportunities. (On "aerospace day," she even had a helicopter pilot land his helicopter in the school yard!) Garnetta also spends a lot of time on the phone, trying to generate parent support. It's not easy; most families are caught up in their own lives and have difficulty maintaining contact with the school. But she keeps after them.

In class, Garnetta never sits down. She is everywhere, all at once, making sure that her students are actively involved. When they learn about liquid measurement, she gives them water and containers for pouring and measuring. Sometimes she has them work in pairs, interviewing each other and then describing their partners in oral reports to the class. When they begin the fearsome topic of long division, they work with Unifix cubes, and it's suddenly not so scary. When they read about bread baking in their reading books, they make bread in class. Although Garnetta is required to present new concepts and skills to the whole class, she frequently uses small groups for reinforcement and enrichment. She strongly believes in the value of students teaching each other and stresses the importance of their learning to work together.

Garnetta is hopeful that all her extra efforts will pay off and that a potential drop-out will become a high school graduate. She tries to serve as a model for her students, and she wants them to see the pride she has in herself and her career. She tells us, "I want them to see that teaching is as great as being a doctor or lawyer."

Barbara Broggi

The tree-lined borough of Highland Park lies on the other side of the Raritan River from New Brunswick. The population of this small community is extremely diverse. The district's three schools serve children who live in homes valued at $500,000 as well as those from low-income apartment complexes. The student population of 1,650 is 53 percent European American, 17 percent African American, 14 percent Latino, and 16 percent Asian American. About 26 percent of the children qualify for the federal free or reduced-price lunch program. HSPT results from Fall 1998 indicate that 96.3 percent of 11th-graders passed the reading portion of the test; 100 percent passed the math portion; 100 percent passed the writing portion; and 96.3 percent passed all three portions. These results reinforce Highland Park's reputation as a district that works hard to promote excellence, no mean accomplishment in the face of budget problems and changing demographics.

Barbara Broggi, also a mother of three children, is a product of the Highland Park school system. She currently teaches fourth grade at Bartle School, the district's intermediate school. Bartle houses 450 students in grades three through six. This year, Barbara has 25 students. Like Highland Park itself, her class is diverse in terms of racial/ethnic composition: 16 of her students are European American, four are African American, three are Latino, and two are Asian American. The class is also heterogeneous in terms of academic ability and achievement: Six students qualify for enrichment; three students have been classified as having learning disabilities; and three children receive extra "basic skills instruction." In addition, one boy has autism, and another is classified as emotionally disturbed; both of them have "child-specific aides" who stay with them all day. Their inclusion in Barbara's classroom exemplifies the district's policy of educating students with disabilities in neighborhood schools instead of sending them to special schools out of the district.

Barbara never thought of becoming anything but a teacher. Her mother taught high school in Highland Park, and Barbara grew up with an insider's view of the profession. She was present when students dropped by to talk with her mother or to ask for extra help, and it was this close personal connection with people that first attracted Barbara to teaching. Even now, after 23 years in the classroom, it's the relationship with students that means the most to her:

Everyday contact with my students is what makes teaching so special for me. I want to get to know them as people—not just names on a seating chart. I want them to know me, to see that I'm a person with strengths and needs just like them. If I cry when I'm reading them a sad passage from a novel, they see that I have feelings and that I'm not afraid to express them. And they learn that it's okay to express their feelings as well. I tell my students, "We're in this together. We're going to learn, work, and play together. And our common goal is to get the most out of every single day."

Barbara Broggi

For the last several years, Barbara has participated in a program called "Creating an Original Opera," sponsored by the Metropolitan Opera Guild. Teachers in this program learn how to act as facilitators who help children produce their own opera. Not only do the students decide on the theme and thesis of the story, they also write the actual dialogue, the music, and the lyrics. In addition, they do every other task involved in staging an opera except the directing: sets, lighting, props, costumes, make-up, public relations, advertising, and, of course, performing. According to Barbara, participation in the opera project has had an impact on the way she teaches all areas of the curriculum:

> *Philosophically, I've always believed that classrooms should be student centered. But this project has given my teaching definition and direction. It has taught me so much about how to turn over ownership of learning to kids, and how much kids can do when they're given the chance. When you see children functioning really well as carpenters and set designers, it makes you more aware of their talents. For some kids, it's the first time that someone's found out what they're good at. You begin to honor those talents and to think: How can we use these talents in the classroom?*

Barbara's classroom reflects her belief in the importance of creative expression and active participation. Students' work covers the walls and hangs from the ceiling. Science experiments are always in progress, and illustrations of novels enliven a bulletin board. Three computers remain on all day so students can write and edit and do research.

Barbara is given quite a bit of latitude in the materials and teaching strategies she uses. Nine years ago, for example, she stopped using basal readers and is now an avid supporter of literature-based reading instruction. She selects novels that touch her, · *Bridge to Terabithia* (Paterson, 1977), *The War with Grandpa* (Smith, 1984), *Sarah,*

Plain and Tall (MacLachlan, 1985), novels that will be meaningful to her students: "During literature discussions, I can tap into a whole range of student feelings on a wide variety of subjects. And as we share ideas, we grow closer together." Barbara also uses children's literature as a springboard for teaching vocabulary, grammar, writing, and spelling.

Barbara enjoys living in the town where she teaches. She likes being able to run into parents at the local food store, at a soccer game, or in the sports collectibles card shop that she and her husband own. Parents appreciate this accessibility, and the informality of their encounters helps Barbara to establish a partnership with them. She is on a first-name basis with the parents of her students—an indication of their open, easy relationship.

Barbara volunteers for many district committees and plays a very active role on them. She says it's out of nosiness, but it's clear that she is seriously committed to educational improvement. Always seeking better and more interesting ways to teach, she frequently participates in professional development activities. She regularly supervises student teachers and conducts workshops on learning styles and cooperative learning for her colleagues and teachers from other districts.

Each afternoon when the dismissal bell has sounded, students of all ages cluster around the door to Barbara's classroom. They come to share some news, to complain about a perceived injustice, or simply to see what's going on in her room. It was the promise of close personal relationships with children that lured Barbara into teaching. Now, as we watch Barbara surrounded by her present and former students, it's clear that the promise has been realized.

Ken Kowalski

Not far from New Brunswick is the community of South Brunswick. The school district has a reputation for innovation. Four of its 11 schools have been designated "Blue Ribbon Schools" by national review panels assembled by the United States Department of Education, and three have received New Jersey "Star School" status. In recent years, the district has worked closely with the Educational Testing Service to pilot procedures for the National Board for Professional Teaching Standards. South Brunswick has also devoted considerable effort to developing alternative ways to measure student understanding, such as portfolio and performance assessments.

This well-regarded school district currently has about 7,500 students and is gaining more than 400 a year. The student population is becoming increasingly diverse; it is now 64 percent European American, 20 percent Asian American, 10 percent African American, and 6 percent Latino. More than 50 different first languages are spoken—in particular, Spanish, Gujarati, Hindi, Cantonese, and Arabic—and like Highland Park, the socioeconomic range is striking. Although many people think of South Brunswick as a middle- to upper-middle class community, a sizable number of its children live in low-cost mobile home parks. About 12 percent are eligible for the federal free or reduced-price lunch program. The HSPT results from Fall 1998 show that 95.5 percent of 11th-graders passed the reading portion of the test; 96.6 percent passed the math; 98.6 percent passed the writing; and 93.2 percent passed all three portions.

At first glance, Brunswick Acres School looks as if it's situated in the middle of a park. It's surrounded by woods and grassy fields; a wooden foot bridge spans a creek flowing nearby. Built in 1975, the school serves 502 students from kindergarten through fifth grade. A new addition was recently completed, and a gym is currently being transformed into classrooms to accommodate the growing population in this area.

Brunswick Acres is an "open space" building. The main instructional area is a huge space that can accommodate at least 10 "classrooms." There are few permanent interior walls; instead classroom boundaries are delineated by folding walls, file cabinets, bulletin boards, shelves, and cubbies. As we walk through the "hallways," on our way to Ken Kowalski's teaching area, we can see what's happening in various classes. We watch students traveling from one area to another, constructing models, discussing a story, and working in the media center.

Ken, who has a 16-year-old daughter, is a fifth-grade teacher. He came to teaching in a roundabout way. After graduating from college with a degree in sociology, he became a writer. He began working in an after-school program in New Brunswick to supplement his income. As he came to know the children in his charge, he realized that they needed more than arts and crafts, but he wasn't sure how to help them:

I had gone to a parochial school as a kid, and there were 50 to 60 students in a class. The nuns were just overwhelmed by that many students; they had little time for individuals. I couldn't draw on my own personal experiences to help "my kids," and I didn't know intuitively what to do. If teaching is an art, then I came into it with no colors on my palette.

Ken Kowalski

Ken decided to enroll in a teacher certification program so he could "do something" for his at-risk students. He soon had children playing word games and dropping by his house to talk or listen to stories. His career in teaching had begun.

Sometimes, Ken regrets that his route to teaching was indirect: "Too many people 'end up' teaching—and it seems so much less noble than knowing from the very start that you want to be a teacher." Despite the serendipitous way he entered teaching, Ken has a strong commitment to the profession and a deep attachment to his colleagues. He received two master's degrees, one in reading and one in computer education, and regularly participates in in-service courses. Over the years, he has achieved a reputation as a master teacher. Like Viviana, Garnetta, and Barbara, Ken frequently serves as a cooperating teacher and is active on district committees. He constantly questions what he does in the classroom, searching for the best ways to help his students grow.

This year, Ken has 23 students in his class; there are 3 Asian Americans, 1 African American, and 19 European Americans. A number of Ken's students were in his fourth-grade class the year before, so the relationship between them is easy and familiar from the very beginning. Since he knows his students, Ken can "pick up" from the previous year and develop plans that he knows will be intellectually challenging. His students will continue to do "process writing"—they will write first drafts, discuss them with peers, revise, edit, and finally "publish" their work. They will also gather information about ocean ecosystems, using a software program called *A Field Trip to the Sea* (Sunburst, 1999). During social studies, they will do two simulation games, one on coming of age in Native American cultures and the other on the colonization of America.

In addition, Ken is very concerned about his students' social and emotional development. This past summer, he attended an institute on the "responsive classroom," an approach to teaching that emphasizes the importance of integrating academic, social, and emotional learning. As Ken puts it:

Geometry is an exciting, necessary lesson, but to say that geometry is more important than sitting with kids and dealing with issues like teasing and humiliation is a mistake. If the kids sit there feeling miserable, then school is a sham—a place to come and feel terrible while you're trying to learn. Instead, school should be a place where you come to deal with the most important problems—which are how do you deal with people—and then you're ready to learn some geometry. Geometry can be fun when kids don't have to worry about other things.

Ken works hard to create an atmosphere of understanding, responsibility, and mutual respect. During class, he appears relaxed and patient. When students speak to him, he listens intently. His students know that they can confide in him; they often use their daily journals as an opportunity to tell him about concerns. Ken knows that writing offers a privacy that's difficult to achieve in the classroom, and he always writes back.

Most instruction occurs in small groups, with lots of cooperative learning and opportunities for student decision making. Whether students are in clusters working out a math problem, conferencing about their writing, or discussing a recently read novel, Ken pushes them to think critically, to reason, and to solve problems. His emphasis on critical thinking even extends to outdoor activities. He is a firm believer in daily physical exercise and takes his class outside almost every day. But here too, Ken stresses the importance of *strategy*. And as always, he's in the middle of it all—running and dodging, coaching and exhorting.

Ken may have begun teaching with no colors on his palette, but he has certainly become a master of even the most subtle hues.

What Do the Students Say?

While working on this chapter, we became curious about the perceptions of students in the classrooms of our four teachers. In particular, we were interested in their reasons for cooperating with their teachers. In each class, we met with students in small groups, either in a corner of the room or out in the hallway. We asked them to explain "why the kids in this class behave." They answered with disarming honesty, and within each class, students demonstrated extraordinary consistency.

Viviana's first-graders seemed to have difficulty even understanding the concept of misbehavior. For them, behaving well was the only possible course of action. "We gotta behave," they told us, "because she's grown up and she's a teacher." Over and over, they insisted that "kids hafta listen to the teacher," that "we have to behave because she tells us to be good." When we described situations in which students *didn't* behave well, they looked at us blankly, as if they could not conceive of that possibility. One boy even told us, "My mother has educated me to behave well, so I never misbehave. *I'm not allowed to misbehave.*" A few children talked about wanting Mrs. Love to be happy: "Mrs. Love is good, and she's happy when we're good. She feels good when we listen." And one boy said he behaved well so that he would learn: "If you don't listen to the teacher you might not learn, and when you grow up someone might ask you a question and you won't know the answer, and you won't be able to have a good job, and then you won't make money."

In contrast, Garnetta's third-graders had no difficulty understanding our question. They talked enthusiastically about the stickers they receive for good behavior. They proudly showed us their sticker folders, making certain we saw their favorites. They also told us about the candy they sometimes get when they've been "especially good," and about the pizza parties that they've earned. In addition, they emphasized that "Ms. Chain is real nice." We heard several variations on this theme: "Ms. Chain doesn't yell." "Ms. Chain cares about us." "Ms. Chain treats us real good. If we ask her to go somewhere, like the bathroom, she let's us go. Other teachers say wait until the other kids go." "Ms. Chain bought the guinea pigs for us—only the eighth-grade kids got guinea pigs." Students also described some of the projects they do, claiming that "in this room, we get interesting stuff to do." One boy talked excitedly about their research on the solar system, while another claimed: "This teacher is better than any other teacher I had because she teaches us a lot of things and gives us lots of science and math." One girl reported that "in this class, we get to bake bread (the story in our reading book was about making bread, so she let us do that). And she's going to let us make cupcakes, and she let us go with her to get fish for the bazaar." Finally, students described some of the "consequences" that they received if they broke the rules.

In Barbara's class, the students also stressed how "nice" their teacher was, how "she doesn't yell," and how "she makes things fun, even things we don't like." They talked about their science experiments, the arts and crafts activities they had done, the books they read, and the journals they kept. They were appreciative of the fact that they were allowed to work with other students and that they were given choices: "When we come in each day, we can write in our journals or read our books." "When we do science, we can do a poster, or a model, or a report." "When we watch movies, we can sit anywhere we want—even on top of our desks!" "When we read, we can go over to the library corner and lay on the rug." Finally, they talked about the way Barbara gives them free time, and how she plays board games with them ("not like *mothers,* who never play games with kids"). And one child seemed to sum it all up when he said: "She gives us what *we* want, so we give her what *she* wants."

We heard the same themes in Ken's class. These fifth-grade students talked about how "he makes work fun" and how "nice" he is—how he jokes, how he cares about kids, and how he really listens. One girl liked the way "we can tell him about our problems. We have journals and if we have a problem, we can write it down and tell him and he'll write back (like if you don't want to sit next to somebody or if you want to be in another reading group)." Students also mentioned the occasional use of rewards ("we get to play an extra game outside if we do a lot of good stuff") and penalties ("we have to stay in for recess and discuss what we did wrong"). The main theme, however, was the fact that "in Mr. K's class kids get to make decisions." Repeatedly, students talked about the options they were given (e.g., "we get to decide what order to do the work in"). They proudly pointed out the Students' Bill of Rights and the Student-of-the Week program. One boy earnestly described the difference between Mr. K and "other teachers": "In here, kids make up the class rules. Some teachers don't care what kids think about what the rules should be. They come in the first day, hand out a paper with rules on it and say, 'These are the rules.' But in here, we can say what we think the rules should be."

Examining the similarities and the differences among these responses is intriguing. To some extent, the differences across classes seem to reflect developmental changes that occur in children's understanding of authority and obedience. William Damon (1977), for example, has pointed out that very young children view authority figures as having an inherent right to be obeyed. Thus, most of Viviana's children insist, "we gotta behave because she's grown up and she's a teacher." Later, Damon observes, authority comes to be understood as a reciprocal relationship: One person obeys another in return for the other's assistance and favors. We hear this type of reasoning when Garnetta's students tell us "she gives us stickers and candy" and when Barbara's students cite the way "she plays games with us." At a still later age, children begin to see authority as an earned commodity; those who have acquired specific abilities and experiences are entitled to obedience. According to Damon, the authority figure's respect for the welfare and rights of the subordinate is seen as particularly important. Although this theme emerged in discussions with both Garnetta's and Barbara's students, it was most striking in our talks with Ken's fifth-graders, who repeatedly emphasized that "in Mr. K's class, kids get to have a say in what we do."

Beyond these developmental differences, we can see that students' responses largely reflect three themes—*respect, motivation,* and *limits.* The students we spoke to described the ways their teachers demonstrate concern and caring; the times they are allowed to exercise choice and self-regulation; the assignments they get that are interesting to do. In addition, students talked about their teachers' "limits" and described the penalties that are invoked "if kids act up."

Students' descriptions closely matched the behavior that we saw during our observations. We were repeatedly struck by the caring and sensitivity teachers showed to students, by their efforts to stimulate students' interest and engagement in lessons, and by the authoritative, "no-nonsense" attitudes. We will address these themes in the three sections of the book that follow.

Concluding Comments

Viviana, Garnetta, Barbara, and Ken teach in very different settings. Grade levels range from Viviana's first grade to Ken's fifth grade. The racial composition of the four classes differs dramatically: Barbara's class is extremely heterogeneous, Viviana's children are all Latino, Ken's class is predominantly European American, and Garnetta's class is predominantly African American. Viviana and Garnetta work in a district where 80 percent of the children are eligible for free lunch, compared with the 26 percent figure in Barbara's district and the 12 percent figure in Ken's district. And while Viviana and Garnetta must follow a carefully prescribed curriculum, Ken and Barbara are given a great deal of freedom. In order to be effective, our four teachers must be sensitive and responsive to these differences in age, race, culture, socioeconomic conditions, and district policy.

Despite these differences, Viviana, Garnetta, Barbara, and Ken are alike in many ways. Obvious similarities emerge when they talk about the tasks of classroom management. In Chapter 1, we discussed our assumption that the way teachers think about management strongly influences how they behave. We cited research suggesting that teachers who view classroom management as a process of guiding and structuring classroom events tend to be more effective than teachers who stress their disciplinary role. Interestingly, when Viviana, Garnetta, Barbara, and Ken speak about classroom management, they rarely use the words *discipline* or *punishment, confrontation* or *penalty.* Instead, they stress the need to develop a "caring community," in which all children are contributing, valued members (Battistich, Watson, Solomon, Lewis, & Schaps, 1999); they speak about involving students and helping them to achieve; they talk about the importance of being organized and well prepared.

These views are captured in the metaphors they hold for classroom management. Viviana's metaphor is "mothering"—just as mothers teach their children how to behave in various situations, so must teachers. Barbara speaks of "gardening," and Ken talks about "coaching." For Garnetta, management is "choreography": "You're setting the stage for the dance, helping everyone to do the right steps, to make one big beautiful dance together. . . ." These metaphors reveal the difficulty the teachers have separating classroom management from instruction. To them, it's "all of a piece."

It's important to remember that Viviana, Garnetta, Barbara, and Ken are real human beings working in the complex, uncertain environment of the elementary classroom. Although they are intelligent, skillful teachers who are extremely effective at preventing misbehavior, their classrooms are not free of problems. (In fact, Chapter 12 focuses specifically on the ways they deal with misbehavior.) Like all of us, they make mistakes; they become frustrated and impatient; they sometimes fail to live up to their image of the "ideal" teacher. By their own testimony, they are all still learning how to run more effective classrooms.

It is also important to remember that these four teachers do not follow recipes or prescriptions for classroom management, so their ways of interacting with children often look very different. Nonetheless, *underlying the differences in behavior, we often detected the same guiding principles.* In the chapters that follow, we will try to convey the ways these four excellent teachers tailor the principles to fit their own particular contexts.

Finally it is necessary to point out that these teachers do not work in schools where conditions are so bad that classes have to be held in stairwells or storage closets, where windows remain broken for years, and where 40 students in a class have to share a handful of books. Nor do they teach in schools that have installed metal detectors or where students regularly carry weapons. In recent years, New Brunswick, Highland Park, and South Brunswick have all experienced an increase in serious problems—but violence is certainly not an everyday occurrence. Whether the strategies discussed here are generalizable to severely troubled schools is not clear. Nevertheless, we hope that *Elementary Classroom Management* will prove to be a useful starting point for teachers everywhere.

Summary

This chapter introduced the four teachers whose thinking and experiences will be described throughout the rest of the book. They work in three school districts in central New Jersey.

- **New Brunswick**: an urban district of 6,500 students (54 percent Latino and 41 percent African American); 80 percent of the students qualify for the federal free or reduced-price lunch program.
    Viviana Love: First-grade bilingual teacher at Roosevelt School.
    Garnetta Chain: Third-grade teacher at McKinley School.

- **Highland Park**: a small district of 1,650 students (53 percent European American, 17 percent African American, 14 percent Latino, and 16 percent Asian American); about 26 percent of the students qualify for the federal free or reduced-price lunch program.

Barbara Broggi: Fourth-grade teacher at Bartle School (grades 3–6).

- **South Brunswick**: a district of about 7,500 students and growing fast; student population is 64 percent European American, 20 percent Asian American, 10 percent African American, and 6 percent Latino; about 12 percent of the students are eligible for the federal free or reduced-price lunch program.
  Ken Kowalski: Fifth-grade teacher at Brunswick Acres School.

Although these four teachers teach different grade levels in very different settings, they are alike in many ways. In particular, they speak about classroom management in very similar terms: They emphasize the prevention of behavior problems, mutual respect, involving students in learning activities, and the importance of being organized and well prepared.

The four teachers' views of effective classroom management mirror their students' conceptions. When asked why they behave well in certain classes and not in others, students consistently voiced three themes: relating to students with caring and respect; teaching in a way that is motivating and interesting; and setting limits and enforcing them. We will return to these three themes in subsequent chapters.

References

Battistich, V., Watson, M., Solomon, D., Lewis, C., & Schaps, E. (1999). Beyond the three R's: A broader agenda for school reform. *The Elementary School Journal, 99*(5), 415–432.

Damon, W. (1977). *The social world of the child.* San Francisco: Jossey Bass.

MacLachlan, P. (1985). *Sarah, Plain and Tall.* New York: Harper & Row Junior Books.

Paterson, K. (1977). *Bridge to Terabithia.* New York: Harper & Row.

Smith, R. K. (1984). *The War with Grandpa.* New York: Dell.

PART II

Establishing an Environment for Learning

Chapter Three

Designing the Physical Environment

Six Functions of the Classroom Setting

The Teacher as Environmental Designer

Designing a Fourth-Grade Classroom

Summary

Discussions of organization and management often neglect the physical characteristics of the classroom. Unless it becomes too hot, too cold, too crowded, or too noisy, we tend to think of the classroom setting as merely a backdrop for interaction. Yet, this setting can *influence the way teachers and students feel, think, and behave.* Careful planning of the physical environment is an integral part of good classroom management. Moreover, *creating a comfortable, functional classroom is one way of showing your students that you care about them.*

Environmental psychologists point out that the effects of the classroom environment can be both *direct* and *indirect* (Proshansky & Wolfe, 1974). For example, if students seated in straight rows are unable to carry on a class discussion because they can't hear one another, the environment is *directly hindering their participation.* Students might also be affected *indirectly* if they infer from the seating arrangement that the teacher does not really want them to interact. In this case, the arrangement of the desks is sending a message to the students about how they are supposed to behave. Their reading of this message would be accurate if the teacher had deliberately arranged the seats to inhibit discussion. More likely, however, the teacher genuinely desires class participation, but has simply not thought about the link between classroom environment and student behavior.

This chapter is intended to help you develop *"environmental competence"* (Steele, 1973)—awareness of the physical environment and its impact and the ability to use that environment to meet your goals. Teachers who are environmentally competent can plan spatial arrangements that support their instructional plans. They are sensitive to the messages communicated by the physical setting. They know how to evaluate the effectiveness of a classroom environment. They are alert to instances when physical factors might be contributing to behavioral problems, and they can modify the classroom environment when the need arises.

As you read this chapter, remember that classroom management is not simply a matter of dealing with misbehavior. As we stressed in the first two chapters, successful managers *promote students' involvement in educational activities, foster self-regulation, prevent disruption, and relate to students with care and respect.* Our discussion of the classroom environment reflects this perspective: We are concerned not only with reducing distraction or minimizing congestion through good environmental design, but also with ways the environment can foster children's security, increase their comfort, and stimulate their interest in learning tasks.

Throughout this chapter, we will illustrate our major points with examples from the classrooms of the teachers you have just met. At the end of the chapter, we will revisit Barbara's classroom and listen to her reflect on the ways her classroom environment helps her to achieve her goals.

Six Functions of the Classroom Setting

Chapter 1 emphasized the wide variety of activities that occurs in classrooms. Although we normally think of the classroom as a place for instruction, it is also a place for Halloween parties and making friends, for collecting book club money and passing notes. It is a setting for social interaction, for trying out new roles, and for developing trust, confidence, and a sense of personal identity. Fred Steele (1973) has suggested that physical settings serve *six basic functions*: security and shelter, social contact, symbolic identification, task instrumentality, pleasure, and growth. These six functions provide a useful framework for thinking about the physical environment of the elementary classroom.

They make it clear that designing the physical setting is far more than decorating a few bulletin boards.

Security and Shelter

This is the most fundamental function of all built environments. Like homes, office buildings, and stores, classrooms should provide protection from bad weather, noise, extreme heat or cold, and noxious odors. Sadly, even this most basic function is sometimes not fulfilled, and teachers and students must battle highway noise, broken windows, and leaky roofs. In situations like this, it is difficult for any of the other functions to be met. Physical security is a *precondition* that must be satisfied, at least to some extent, before the environment can serve students' and teachers' other, higher-level needs.

Physical security is a particularly important issue in classes like science and art, where students may come into contact with potentially dangerous supplies and equipment. It is essential that teachers of these subjects know about their state's safety guidelines regarding proper handling, storage, and labeling. The art teacher in Viviana's school, for example, is careful to store supplies according to state specifications. She also keeps informed about regulations regarding the kinds of materials she can order; pointed scissors and rubber cement are definitely out!

Physical security is also a matter of special concern if you have students in wheelchairs, with leg braces, on crutches, or with unsteady gaits (from muscular dystrophy, for example). Navigating through crowded classrooms can be a formidable and dangerous task. Be sensitive to the need for wide aisles and space to store walkers and crutches when not in use. The physical or occupational therapists working in your school can provide consultation and advice.

Often, schools provide *physical* security, but fail to offer *psychological* security—the feeling that this is a safe, comfortable place to be. Psychological security is becoming increasingly crucial as more and more children live in impoverished, unstable, and sometimes unsafe home environments. For them, in particular, schools must serve as a haven. Psychological security is also particularly important in open space settings, like Ken's, where background noise and large interior spaces can be unsettling.

One way of enhancing psychological security is to make sure your classroom contains some "softness." With their linoleum floors, concrete block walls, and formica desks, classrooms tend to be "hard" places. But children (and adults) tend to feel more secure and comfortable in environments that contain items that are soft or responsive to their touch. In Garnetta's classroom, we find plants, fish tanks, and bean bag chairs in which to relax; Viviana's room contains a leather couch, two arm chairs, and pillows to sit on while reading. Other soft elements that teachers can use are stuffed, feathered, or furry animals—but make sure that none of your students are allergic to them. Warm colors, bright accents, and varying textures (e.g., burlap, wood, and felt) can also help to create an atmosphere of security and comfort.

Another way of increasing psychological security is to arrange classroom space so that students have as much freedom from interference as possible. In the crowded envi-

Barbara uses pillows and stuffed animals to create a "soft" reading area.

ronment of the classroom, it is easy to become distracted. You need to make sure that students' desks are not too near areas of heavy traffic (e.g., the pencil sharpener, the sink, a learning center), and that noisy activities are separated from quiet ones (e.g., block play from the literacy center).

It's also helpful to create cozy corners with pillows and a rug where students can retreat when things get too hectic. Low partitions will allow children to feel separated and private, but still enable you to see what's going on. In addition, you might set up a few study carrels or "private offices" where children who want more enclosure can work alone, or provide folding cardboard dividers (three pieces of heavy cardboard bound together) that they can place on their desks. All of us need to "get away from it all" at times, but research suggests that opportunities for privacy are particularly important for children who are distractible and for those who have difficulty relating to their peers (Weinstein, 1982). Barbara recognizes this need for privacy:

I always arrange the desks in clusters because I use a lot of small-group activities, but I've had kids who ask to sit all alone, and I allow them that opportunity. What I've found is that they usually want to be back in the group after a while. I've never put a child by him or herself, because then that child can't be part of the activities I plan—for example, with your table group, write a couplet that describes what happened in this chapter; or write a math riddle that another table will solve. I want the kid to be part of the cluster, but have the right to buy out when he or she can't handle it. If I see a kid having trouble at a table, I might say, "Look if you would like to go work by yourself, go ahead, but you can't ruin this for everyone." Or the kid might ask me to go work alone. He or she can move their desk to a corner or find a little enclosed place on the floor.

Freedom from distraction is especially crucial for children with attention-deficit/ hyperactivity disorder (ADHD), a neurobiological disability that interferes with an individual's ability to sustain attention. Children with ADHD have difficulty focusing attention, concentrating, listening, following instructions, and organizing tasks; they may also exhibit behaviors associated with hyperactivity—difficulty staying seated, fidgeting, impulsivity, lack of self-control. You can help children with ADHD by seating them away from noisy areas, near well-focused students, and as close to you as possible so that it's easy to make eye contact. For these children, study carrels, folding dividers, and retreat spaces are especially important. Although many teachers seat distractible students in the center-front (given a traditional row arrangement), Perlmutter (1994) suggests that the *second* seat from the front in the end rows may be more effective in limiting distractible stimuli.

Social Contact

Interaction among Students

As you plan the arrangement of students' desks, you need to think very carefully about how much interaction among students you want. Clusters of desks promote social contact since children are close together and can have direct eye contact with those across from them. In clusters, children can work together on activities, share materials, have small-group discussions, and help each other with assignments. The proximity is particularly helpful for facilitating interaction among children from different linguistic and cultural backgrounds and among children with disabilities and their nondisabled peers (Lambert, 1994).

On the other hand, rows of desks make it easier for children to concentrate on individual assignments (Bennett & Blundell, 1983; Bonus & Riordan, 1998; Wheldall and Lam, 1987; Wheldall, Morris, Vaughan, & Ng, 1981). This appears particularly true for students who have behavior and learning problems. For example, when a primary class was moved from groups to rows, Hastings and Schwieso (1995) found a marked increase in students' average time-on-task (from 48 percent to 78.5 percent). But the improvement was even more dramatic for three particularly distractible, disruptive boys whose average time-on-task went from 16 percent to 91 percent—an increase of 75 percentage points!

It is clear that clusters of desks are most appropriate if you plan to emphasize group-work and cooperative learning. *But it is unwise and inconsistent—even inhumane— to seat children in clusters and then give them individual tasks and tell them not to talk.* If you do that, students receive two contradictory messages: The seating arrangement is communicating that it's all right to interact, while your verbal message is just the opposite!

You might also consider putting desks in horizontal rows. (See Figure 3-1.) This arrangement orients students toward the teacher, but still provides them with close neighbors on each side. Another option, advocated by Frederic Jones (2000), is shown in Figure 3-2. Here, an "interior loop" allows you to "work the crowd with the fewest steps" (p. 34).

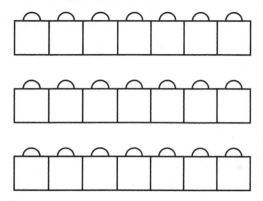

FIGURE 3-1. A horizontal arrangement

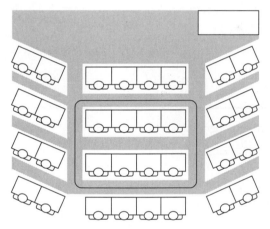

FIGURE 3-2. Fredric Jones's interior loop arrangement

Figures 3-3 to 3-5 illustrate the ways Viviana, Garnetta, and Ken have arranged their classrooms. As you can see, Viviana uses a horseshoe arrangement. This layout is consistent with the teacher-directed nature of her instructional program, but it also allows students to work easily with the individuals sitting on either side. Viviana explains this choice of layout:

> *I like the desks in a horseshoe because this way everyone can see what's going on in the front of the room. They can see the work on the board or demonstrations at the small round table. But it's also a good arrangement*

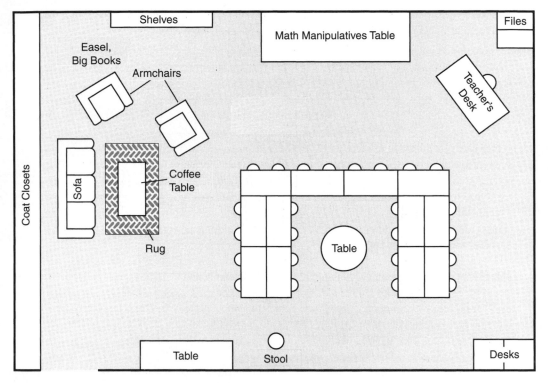

FIGURE 3-3. Viviana's room arrangement

for working with a partner. The horseshoe also lets me see everybody and to get close to them.

Garnetta also used to arrange desks in a horseshoe, but this year she has created three clusters of five desks each. The change was instigated by McKinley's adoption of a new reading series that supports integrated language arts instruction and encourages peer interaction. By arranging the desks in clusters, Garnetta has organized the physical environment to support the new approach.

While Garnetta is teaching in a brand-new classroom that is far more spacious than the classrooms she has had in previous years, Ken's classroom space this year is much smaller than the spaces he used to have. Given the cramped size, Ken has decided to put individual desks into clusters. Fortunately, this arrangement is compatible with his teaching strategies and goals, since he emphasizes cooperative small-group activities:

By pushing the desks together, I not only save space, I also create clusters that are appropriate for small group work and provide a nice big surface for art work and projects. I've oriented the desks so that practically no one has

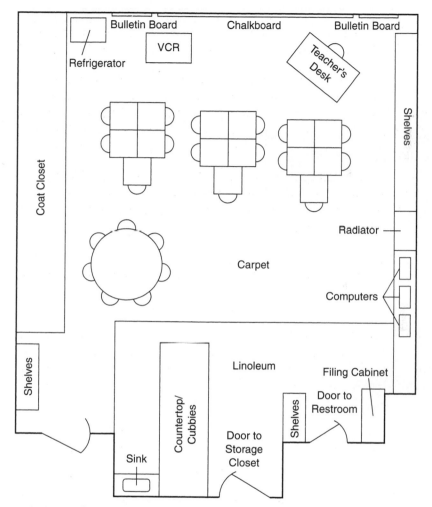

FIGURE 3-4. Garnetta's room arrangement

to turn completely around to face the front of the room. It's real easy for them to communicate with one another, yet they can still see presentations that are done with the overhead. By clustering the desks, I'm also able to create a big space where we can sit on the rug for "morning meetings."

Interaction between the Teacher and the Students

The way students are arranged can also affect interaction between the teacher and the students. A number of studies have found that in classrooms where desks are arranged in rows, the teacher interacts mostly with students seated in the front and center of the classroom.

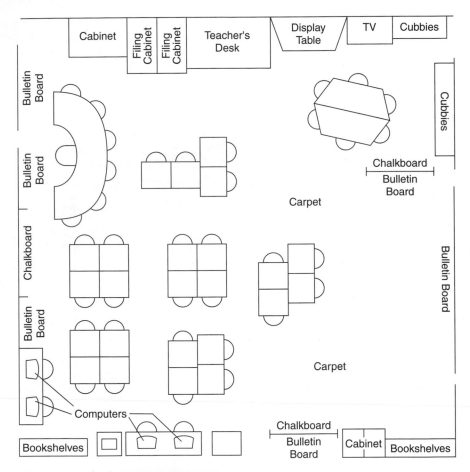

FIGURE 3-5. Ken's room arrangement

Students in this "action zone" (Adams & Biddle, 1970; Kashti, Arieli, & Harel, 1984) participate more in class discussions and initiate more questions and comments.

Educational researchers (e.g., Levine, O'Neal, Garwood, & McDonald, 1980) have tried to tease out the reasons for this phenomenon. Do students who are more interested and more eager to participate select seats in the front, or does a front seating position somehow produce these attitudes and behaviors? This issue has not yet been fully resolved, but the weight of the evidence indicates that a front-center seat does encourage participation, while a seat in the back makes it more difficult to participate and easier to "tune out."

Although research on the action zone has only examined row arrangements, it is easy to imagine that the same phenomenon would occur whenever teachers direct most of their comments and questions to the students who are closest to them. Keep this in mind and take steps to ensure that the action zone encompasses your whole class. Some suggestions are to (1) move around the room whenever possible; (2) establish eye contact with students seated farther away from you; (3) direct comments to students seated in the rear and on the sides; and (4) periodically change students' seats so that all students have an opportunity to be up front.

Symbolic Identification

Steele's third function refers to the information provided by a setting about the people who spend time there. The key questions are: What does this classroom tell us about the students—their interests, activities, backgrounds, accomplishments, and preferences? And what does the classroom tell us about the teacher's goals, values, and beliefs about education?

Too often classrooms resemble motel rooms. They are pleasant but impersonal, revealing nothing about the people who use the space. Yet it is not difficult to "personalize" a classroom setting, and by doing so you communicate to children that they are important and special. Barbara describes an introductory activity she does at the beginning of school:

One of the first things I do with kids is a writing activity and an art activity. They write a piece about why they're unique (for example, maybe somebody's a ballerina or likes computers). Then we turn that into a banner made out of felt. Each person has a banner, even me. We put our names on the banners with puff paint and hang them all around the edge of the classroom. Then we take the essays and hang them on the writing bulletin board. The banners stay up all year long.

There are innumerable ways to personalize classroom space: You can post children's photographs, art work, and projects, the stories they dictate or write, and charts listing heights, weights, or birthdays. You can decorate your room with silhouettes of the children or with life-size bodies traced on large paper. You can set aside a bulletin board for the "student of the week." You can display children's best work. One idea we especially like is to allow each child to select his or her own best piece of work each week. In this way, you encourage children to be self-evaluative, and you avoid the danger of continually posting the work of only a few children.

You can also personalize space by displaying materials that reflect the cultural backgrounds of the children in your class. For example, you might post a map of the world highlighting students' countries of origin. At the beginning of the year, you could create a welcome sign written in the different languages spoken by your students or their families. You might exhibit photographs of children from around the world, list accomplishments of notable people from your children's native countries, or hang posters showing art from different cultures. In Viviana's room, colorful fabric parrots from Puerto Rico hang from the ceiling; bulletin board displays are labeled in both English and Spanish; and paper flags of the Dominican Republic, Nicaragua, Mexico, Ecuador,

Puerto Rico, Cuba, Peru, Honduras, and Columbia decorate one wall. Displays like these communicate respect for your students' diverse cultural backgrounds.

In addition, consider ways you can use the environment to communicate something about your *own* cultural background, experiences, and idiosyncrasies. You might want to hang your favorite art prints, display pictures of your family, or exhibit your collections of "precious objects." We've seen hippopotamuses of all sizes, paperweights, kaleidoscopes—even hubcaps. In Barbara's classroom, giraffes sit on her desk and perch on the top of cabinets. Not only do they encourage students to take risks and to "stick their necks out," they allow students to see that Mrs. Broggi is a real person.

Task Instrumentality

This function concerns the many ways the environment helps us to carry out the tasks we need to accomplish. Think about the tasks and activities that will be carried out in your classroom. Will students work alone at their desks on independent assignments? Will they work cooperatively on activities and projects? Will you instruct the whole class from the chalkboard? Will you work with small reading groups? Will students do research using the Internet? Will they rotate among learning centers? Will they engage in dramatic play, block play, arts and crafts, science experiments?

For each of these tasks, you need to consider the physical design requirements. For example, if you plan to meet with small reading groups, you have to think carefully about where to locate the small-group area. Do you want it near a chalkboard or a bulletin board? In any case, its location should not be distracting to students working independently. You also want to be able to monitor the rest of the students while you are working with the small group.

This year, Ken is lucky enough to have four computers in his room, and Barbara and Garnetta each have three. This is substantially better than having only one computer per classroom (or none), a situation that exists in many schools, but it still means that the computer is a scarce but precious resource. This increases the need to think carefully about location. If students are going to work at the computer in pairs or in small groups, place it in an area where clusters of students can gather round without creating traffic congestion and distraction. Also keep in mind that the computer is often "a social event" (Genishi, 1988); the upright position of the screen invites comment and inquiry from students walking past or sitting nearby. How you feel about this spontaneous interaction should be a factor in your decision about the computer's location.

Whatever tasks will occur in your classroom, there are a few general guidelines you need to keep in mind. These are listed in Figure 3-6.

Pleasure

The important question here is whether students and teachers find the classroom attractive and pleasing. To the already overworked teacher preoccupied with covering the curriculum, raising test scores, and maintaining order, aesthetic concerns may seem irrelevant and insignificant (at least until parent conferences draw near). Yet given the amount of time that you and your students spend in your classroom, it is worth thinking about

Make sure that frequently used classroom materials are accessible to students. Materials like crayons, pencils, paper, dictionaries, rulers, and staplers should be easy to reach. This will minimize the time spent preparing for activities and cleaning up. Decide which materials will be kept in students' desks and which will be kept on shelves.

Organize shelves and storage areas so that it is clear where materials and equipment belong. It is useful to label shelves so that everyone knows where things go. (For very young children, you can use picture labels.) This will make it easier to obtain materials and to return them. You should also have some sort of a system for the distribution and collection of students' work (e.g., in–out boxes or individual student mailboxes).

Plan pathways through the room to avoid congestion and distraction. Paths to the water fountain, pencil sharpener, trash can, and coat closet should be clearly visible and unobstructed. These high traffic areas should be as far from students' desks as possible. Make sure that your pathways don't go through work areas. For example, you don't want children to have to walk through a literacy corner in order to get something from the coat closet. Children shouldn't have to walk behind the small-group reading area in order to get a needed dictionary. Are pathways wide enough for students with walkers or wheelchairs?

Plan enough space for the children to line up at the door (Clayton & Forton, 2001).

Allowing about nine inches between each child, you can estimate the space you will need for students to line up without bumping into furniture or each other.

Design a seating arrangement that allows students to have a clear view of instructional presentations. If possible, students should be able to see instructional presentations without turning their desks or chairs around.

Provide students with a place to keep their belongings (lunch boxes, backpacks, skateboards, etc.). This is especially important if your classroom doesn't have desks with storage space.

Decide where to put your desk (or get rid of it!). The location depends on where you will be spending your time. If you will be constantly moving about the room, your desk can be out of the way, in a corner perhaps. If you will use your desk as a conference area or as a work station, then it needs to be more centrally located. But be careful: With a central location, you may be tempted to remain at your desk for long periods of time, and this cuts down your ability to monitor students' work and behavior. All four of our teachers have their desks off in a corner or in the back of the room.

Separate incompatible activities. If you plan to set aside spaces for particular activities, think carefully about their relative locations. Make sure to separate activities that don't go well together: noisy-quiet, messy-neat, and wet-dry (e.g., the computers should be far away from the sink!).

FIGURE 3-6. Guidelines for ensuring task instrumentality

ways to create a pleasing environment. In Garnetta's room, plants line the window sill; Barbara uses large pieces of boldly patterned wrapping paper to cover bulletin boards; and Viviana's colorful parrots create a festive air.

The classic study on environmental attractiveness was conducted by Maslow and Mintz (1956). These experimenters compared interviews that took place in an "ugly" room with those that took place in a "beautiful" room. Neither the interviewer nor the subject knew that the real purpose of the study was to assess the impact of the environment on their behavior. Maslow and Mintz found that interviewers assigned to the ugly room complained of headaches, fatigue, and discomfort. Furthermore, the interviews *finished more quickly* in the ugly rooms. Apparently, people in the ugly room tried to finish their task as quickly as possible in order to escape from the unpleasant setting.

Identifying specific characteristics that everyone considers pleasing has been difficult. Nonetheless, there are some principles to keep in mind when thinking about ways to create an attractive classroom. In general, people seem to respond positively to the presence of *variation*. In other words, they seem to enjoy being in environments that contain both warm colors and cool colors; open, spacious areas and small, cozy corners; hard surfaces and soft surfaces; textures that are smooth and those that are rough (Olds, 1987). However, it is important that this variation be moderate and orderly. A lack of stimulus variation can lead to monotony, but too much variation can produce feelings of anxiety and chaos, especially if it lacks patterning or predictability.

Growth

Steele's last function is particularly relevant to classrooms, since they are settings specifically intended to promote children's development. This function is also the most difficult to pin down, however. While it's easy to see that environments should be functional and attractive, it's less obvious that they can be designed to foster growth. Furthermore, growth can refer to any number of areas—learning to tie one's shoes, increasing your self-confidence, learning to cooperate. For simplicity, we will restrict our discussion to ways in which the environment can promote children's *cognitive development.*

Psychologists have found that the opportunity to explore rich, stimulating environments is related to cognitive growth. Your classroom should be more than a place where children listen to instruction, complete workbook pages, and demonstrate mastery of skills. It should be a setting that *invites children to explore, observe, investigate, test, and discover.* This means that in addition to the standard readers, dictionaries, and workbooks, your classroom should contain a wide variety of materials such as puzzles, brainteasers, math manipulatives, science equipment, and art supplies.

When stocking your classroom, it is useful to think about materials that are "open"— water, paint, clay—and those that are "closed"—puzzles, workbooks, tracing patterns (Jones and Prescott, 1978). Location on an open–closed continuum describes the extent to which a material or object dictates *one right answer.* For example, children have many options when creating with clay, but there is only one right way to complete a wooden puzzle. Materials like blocks, Lego, and Tinker Toys lie somewhere in the middle of the continuum: Although these materials impose some restrictions on what can be done with

Viviana reads a story to her class in the "living room."

them, they still invite experimentation and improvisation. Analyzing materials in terms of openness can help you to structure a setting that promotes creativity and divergent thinking.

The environment can also foster children's growth by stimulating their interest in books. Morrow (2001) encourages teachers to provide children with the opportunity to have pleasurable experiences with literature: to read daily to children, to discuss the stories, to schedule recreational reading periods, and to integrate literature with other areas of the curriculum. An appealing, well-organized literacy center can support these literature activities. Viviana, for example, has created a "mini-living room" in her classroom, complete with a leather-upholstered sofa and arm chairs (salvaged from a school storage closet). A coffee table overflows with newspapers, books, and magazines, and a small rug and pillows allow children to sit comfortably on the floor. Viviana tells us why she has provided this center:

For many of my children, the only thing they do in the living room is watch television. I want them to realize that you can sit in the living room and read a good book. Every day I sit on the sofa and have them sit around me on chairs and pillows. I read a story or an article from the day's newspaper (which I bring in). Then I let someone take the newspaper home. The kids love our "living room," and I feel so good when I see them curled up on the sofa with a book.

Here are a few simple guidelines to keep in mind if you decide to include a literacy center in your classroom (Morrow & Weinstein, 1982, 1986).

Locate your literacy center in a quiet area of the room, with low partitions that provide protection from distraction and intrusion, but that still permit you to see what's going on.

Display at least some of the books so that the covers are clearly visible. In this way, children can see the illustrations on the front. The spine of a book rarely contains more than the title, and this is often hard to read unless you crane your neck sideways.

Include some element of softness in the literacy center (e.g., pillows, beanbag chairs, rockers, plants) to provide a comfortable, cozy feeling.

Stock the center with a wide variety of magazines, newspapers, and books (novels, reference books, poetry, catalogues, cook books, biographies, travel books, appliance manuals, picture books, etc.) at a wide variety of reading levels. If possible, include audiotapes of books that children can listen to and read along with.

Include literature props, such as felt-board stories, roll movies, and puppets, as well as materials that children can use to make their own books (e.g., paper, staplers, cardboard, markers, pencils). If particular books are associated with specific activities that could be carried out in the classroom, include the materials that children will need. For example, a book about magnets might be displayed next to a tray with magnets, paper clips, nails, and tacks (Loughlin & Martin, 1987). You could also include paper on which children can record the results of their investigations.

Place a bulletin board in the literacy center, where you can post children's book reviews, the jackets of featured books, and sign-up charts for students who want to read aloud to classmates or to children in younger grades.

Plan set times for students to use the literacy center. Too many teachers design and equip literacy centers and then don't provide opportunities for children to use them. Some teachers allow children to go to the center only if they are finished with their "real work." This means that children who work slowly may never get to use the center. It also conveys the message that the activities done in the literacy center are not considered as important or valuable as those done at desks under the teacher's direct supervision.

Figure 3-7 contains a checklist that you can use to evaluate and improve the literacy environment of your classroom (Morrow, Strickland, & Woo, 1998).

The Teacher as Environmental Designer

Steele's six functions give you a way of thinking about the environment, but they don't provide you with an architectural blueprint. If you think about the various roles that settings play, you will realize that the functions not only overlap, they may actually conflict. Seating that is good for social contact may be bad for testing. Room arrangements that provide children with privacy may be poor for monitoring and maintaining order. As you think about your room and your own priorities, you will have to determine which functions will take precedence over others.

THE LITERACY CENTER

_____ Children participate in designing the center (develop rules, select a name for center, and develop materials).
_____ Area placed in a quiet section of the room.
_____ Visually and physically accessible, yet partitioned from the rest of the room.
_____ Rug, throw pillows, rocking chair, bean bag chair, and stuffed animals.
_____ Private spot in the corner such as a box to crawl into and read.
_____ The center uses about 10 percent of the classroom space and fits five to six children.

THE LIBRARY CORNER

_____ Bookshelves for storing books with spines facing outward.
_____ Organizational system for shelving books.
_____ Open-faced bookshelves for featured books.
_____ Five to eight books per child.
_____ Books representing three to four grade levels of the following types: (a) picture books, (b) picture story-books, (c) traditional literature, (d) poetry, (e) realistic literature, (f) informational books, (g) biogra-phies, (h) chapter books, (i) easy to read books, (j) riddle and joke books, (k) participation books, (l) series books, (m) textless books, (n) televi-sion-related books, (o) brochures, (p) magazines, and (q) newspapers.
_____ Twenty new books circulated every two weeks.
_____ Check-out/check-in system for children to take out books daily.
_____ Head sets and taped stories.

_____ Felt board and story characters with the related books.
_____ Materials for constructing felt stories.
_____ Other story manipulatives (roll movie or puppets with related books).
_____ System for recording books read (e.g., 3 × 5 cards hooked onto a bulletin board).

THE WRITING CENTER
(THE AUTHOR'S SPOT)

_____ Tables and chairs.
_____ Writing posters and a bulletin board for children to display their writing by themselves.
_____ Writing utensils (pens, pencils, crayons, felt-tipped markers, colored pencils).
_____ Writing materials (many varieties of paper in all sizes, booklets, and pads).
_____ Typewriter or computer.
_____ Materials for writing stories and making them into books.
_____ A message board for children to post messages for the teacher and students.
_____ A place to store "Very Own Words."
_____ Folders for children to place samples of their writing.

CONTENT-AREA LEARNING CENTERS

_____ Environmental print, such as signs related to themes, directions, and rules.
_____ A calendar.
_____ A current events board.
_____ Appropriate books, magazines, and newspapers in all centers.
_____ Writing utensils in all centers.
_____ Varied types of paper in all centers.
_____ A place for children to display their literacy work.

FIGURE 3-7. A checklist for evaluating and improving the literacy environment
Source: Morrow, Strickland, & Woo, 1998.

In this section of the chapter, we describe a process that you can follow as you design your classroom.

Think about the Activities the Room Will Accommodate

The first step in designing a classroom is to decide on the activities your room is to ac-commodate. For example, if you are teaching a kindergarten or primary classroom, you may wish to create areas for sharing time, reading aloud, small-group reading instruction, whole group math instruction, blocks, housekeeping, computers, and arts and crafts. An intermediate grade teacher might want to accommodate whole-group literature discussions, small-group work, media presentations, "hands-on" projects, and testing. List these activities in a column and next to each activity, note if it poses any special physical requirements. For example, art and science areas should be near a sink, and the literacy center should be in a quiet area of the room. Computers need to be near electrical outlets and away from chalkboards to avoid chalk dust. For access to the Internet, the location of the computer will also be dictated by hard wiring.

Draw a Floor Plan

Before actually moving any furniture, draw a number of different floor plans and select the one that seems most workable. (Figure 3-8 depicts symbols that may be useful.) As you decide where to place furniture and equipment, consider the special requirements noted on your list of activities, as well as the room's "givens"—the location of the outlets, the chalkboard, the windows, the built-in shelves, computer wiring, permanently installed TV monitors, and phones. Also keep in mind our discussion of psychological security, social contact, and task instrumentality.

It may be helpful to begin by deciding where you will conduct whole-group instruction (if at all) and the way students will be seated during this time. Think about where the teacher's desk should be; if frequently used materials are stored on shelves or in cabinets that are accessible to you and your students; and if pathways are clear. Remember, there is no one right way to design your classroom. The important thing is to make sure that your spatial arrangement supports the teaching strategies that you will use and the kinds of behaviors you want from your students (Bonus & Riordan, 1998; Wengel, 1992).

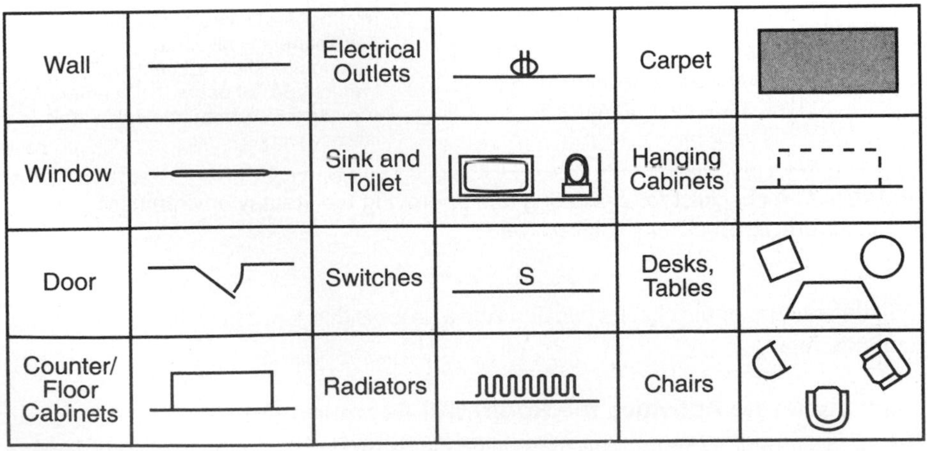

FIGURE 3-8. Drawing a floor plan: Some useful symbols

Involve Students in Environmental Planning

Although a great deal can be done before the start of school, it is a good idea to leave some things *undone,* so your students can be involved in the design process. You might solicit children's ideas for room design and then select those that seem most feasible. You might also rotate responsibility for some aspect of the environment among small groups of students (e.g., each group could have an opportunity to design a bulletin board display). Inviting children to participate in environmental planning not only helps to create more responsive physical arrangements, it also allows them to voice their opinions and to share in meaningful decision making. (See our discussion of sharing responsibility in Chapter 5.)

Try the New Arrangement, Evaluate, and Redesign

Use Steele's six functions of the environment as a framework for evaluating your classroom design. For example, does the classroom provide opportunities for retreat and privacy? Does the desk arrangement facilitate or hinder social contact among students? Do displays communicate information about the students and their work? Are frequently used materials accessible to students? Does the room provide pleasure? Does it contain materials that invite children to explore and to extend their interests and abilities?

As you evaluate the effectiveness of the classroom setting, stay alert for behavioral problems that might be caused by the physical arrangement. For example, if a small cluster of students suddenly becomes inattentive when their desks are moved next to the hamster cage, it is likely that an environmental change is in order, rather than detention. If students rarely demonstrate interest in reading during free choice time, it may be due to the way the books are displayed. If the classroom floor is constantly littered despite your appeals for neatness, the underlying problem may be an inadequate number of trash cans.

Improving your room does not have to be tedious and time consuming. In fact, small modifications can bring about gratifying changes in behavior. This was demonstrated by Krantz & Risley (1972), who found that when kindergartners crowded around a teacher who was reading a story, they were inattentive and disruptive. Just spreading the children out in a semicircle markedly improved their attentiveness. In fact, this simple environmental modification was as successful as a complicated system of rewards and privileges that the experimenters had devised! If you prefer to have students in a cluster rather than a semicircle, you can put stickers on the carpet to designate individual student spaces. This allows you to maintain a feeling of intimacy (e.g., for a shared reading experience), but still give students their own space.

Designing a Fourth-Grade Classroom

This chapter has tried to provide you with a way of thinking about classroom environments and an outline of the design process. Now we'll take a closer look at Barbara's fourth-grade classroom (see Figure 3-9). As you can see, she has arranged the desks in

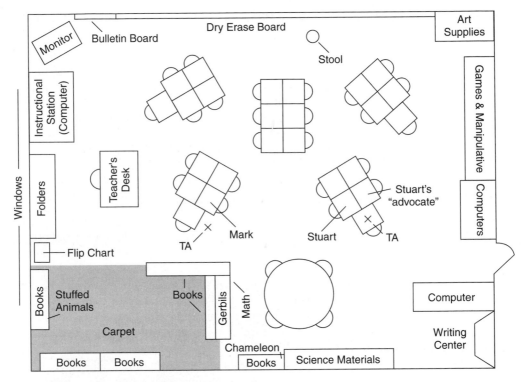

FIGURE 3-9. Barbara's room arrangement

clusters because she does a lot of cooperative learning activities. Her own desk is off to the side of the classroom, out of the way and near the literacy center. The class computers are placed on either side of the doorway.

As Barbara planned her room at the beginning of the school year, she shared her thoughts with us. The following transcript illustrates the way that one teacher thinks through the process of designing the classroom environment:

> *The first thing I think about is what has to stay where it is (like the bulletin boards), where the outlets are located, and other kinds of constraints. For example, in order to attach to the network, the computers need to be near the drops [where the network connections are located], which are near the door to the classroom. In our buildings, the instructional station and monitor are always located on an outside wall. Based on where the whiteboard is and where the instructional station is, I decide where the main whole-group instructional area will be.*
>
> *After that I go on to the things that I personally value. I'm involved in a cooperative learning science project, and my students have to sit in groups.*

I don't want to change the seating every day just for science, so I designed the room with that need in mind.

This year I also had to think carefully about where Stuart [the child with autism] and Mark [the child with an emotional disorder] would be seated and make room for their TAs [teaching associates or full-time, child-specific aides], Mr. C and Mr. T. They each have a chair next to the student they're assisting, but they also share a student desk [next to Stuart] for storage of any materials they might need. Based on the IEPs [individualized education plans] for both students, Stuart and Mark need to be able to leave the classroom and take a walk in the hallway whenever they get overstimulated or out of control. This means they have to be near an edge so the coming and going isn't disruptive. Stuart's IEP also says that he needs to be seated in the same cluster with one of two students that are his "advocates"—they've both gone to school with him since he entered the mainstream classroom, and they understand his social needs, body language, and vocalizations. Stuart uses a laptop, and if it's not fully charged it needs to be near an outlet, so that was another thing I needed to keep in mind.

I also think about where to put storage for things that kids will need. For example, I've set out all the art supplies on a bookcase in the front of the room, so that kids can have easy access to markers, paper, glue, etc. I want the kids to be independent and feel that they have control over their needs. A kid shouldn't have to come to me and ask if he can get into the closet for a marker. I've found that you can't have everything the kids need in the same place, because then you have too many kids in the same place at the same time. It becomes chaotic. So I spread supplies around—paper is over here, art supplies over there. I also have three pencil sharpeners (one by the door and one on top of a bookshelf, and a battery-operated one on my desk).

I've put the literacy center on the outside wall because I like it near the windows. There's a bookcase there filled with stuffed animals that kids have given me that go along with pieces of literature that we've read—lots of penguins for Mr. Popper's Penguins! There's also a collection of books that I've built up over my years in fourth grade. On the other side of that bookcase are some math manipulatives. Although people also play board games on the rug, I've stored them on the other side of the room so kids don't have to climb over other kids in order to get a game. On top of the bookcase near the round table are the gerbils. I have a child with ADHD in my math class, and one of the suggestions in his IEP is to have a classroom pet, which is a calming influence. I know it sounds weird, but when he gets too distracted, he can sit at the round table, watch the gerbils and do his math.

The round table gets to be the best place in the whole room because you can use it for science projects, manipulatives, conferencing for writing. Next to the table I've stored the resource books—encyclopedias and dictionaries, thesaurus, etc. And on the top of that bookcase is the aquarium with our chameleons. (They're great pets—they don't bite, nobody's allergic to them, they're neat to watch, and you can use them to teach about habitat. They're the best pets I've ever had—but I won't touch them.)

I couldn't live without my flip chart; it can go anywhere in the classroom—and does. Suppose I'm teaching about plants and talking about root structure. I can draw it on the flip chart and leave it. Then the next day, I can start on the stem and draw that part. Kids are pulled out of science for basic skills class, and if you miss the notes, it's tough. This way the notes and illustrations can remain there for the week, and the kids won't miss it.

We'll start off the year with this arrangement, but of course, we'll have to see how it works and we'll probably change things around. I try to give the kids a say in how things are arranged. We have a deal: Sometimes I make the final decision, and sometimes they do. Whichever, we agree to live with the arrangement for a designated period of time. Then if we don't like it, we can change it. Last year my class decided they wanted the round table in the center of the room with the desks in a horseshoe around it. I hated this, but I lived with it for a month. Then I told them exactly why I didn't like it: I had no privacy, and all the noise faced the front of the room. So together we changed the arrangement.

I think a lot about the way the room looks. I hate dull, boring classrooms. Rooms need to be filled with children's work and to reflect your own personal touch. I decorate with wrapping paper. On one bulletin board I put bright yellow paper with flowers of purple and red. Then I put black paper on the bulletin boards on either side and made flowers to match the center paper. One of those areas will be for displays related to the opera we create; one other will be for children's own personal writing; and the third will be for activities that we do with literature. When you put up bulletin boards, they need to be neat and attractive because that shows the children that you took time and effort, and they need to do the same thing. I don't think we should expect more from kids than we're willing to give. We're models of what we expect from them.

I tend not to be the neatest person in the world, and unfortunately my kids model that behavior too. So there comes a time when we have to say, "OK, let's clean up. Dump your desk and let's make a clean start." It's wonderful if you can be neat, but I'm not. In an elementary classroom, you go from activity to activity, and if you use a lot of materials, you tend to end up with a mess. But I don't want to forgo an activity because it makes a mess.

One very annoying constraint I have is a lack of running water in the room. I usually leave two buckets of clean water under the round table just in case I need it. Kids can wash hands in one bucket, and get water (e.g., for water colors) out of the other bucket. I also keep paper towels there. The custodians are not wild about it, but it's nice not to have to run down the hall every time someone spills juice. I usually change the water at lunch time because I need water in the afternoon for science.

I've tried to create a room that's flexible and that can adapt to our changing needs at different times of the year; a room that's inviting and attractive and personal; a room that encourages kids to work together but that also provides them with an opportunity to be alone; a room that helps them to be independent. Now we'll just have to wait and see what happens.

Summary

In this chapter we discussed how the physical environment of the classroom influences the way teachers and students feel, think, and behave. We stressed the need for teachers to be aware of the direct and indirect effects of the physical environment. This awareness is the first step to developing "environmental competence." We suggested ways to design a classroom that will support your instructional goals, using Steele's six functions of the environment as a framework for discussion.

Security and shelter:
- Add elements of softness.
- Arrange space for freedom from interference.
- Create a "retreat" area.

Social contact:
- Consider how much interaction among students you want.
- Think about whether you are making contact with *all* of your students.

Symbolic identification:
- Personalize your classroom space so that it communicates information about you and your students.

Task instrumentality:

- Make sure frequently used materials are accessible to students.
- Make it clear where things belong.
- Plan pathways to avoid congestion and distraction.
- Plan adequate space for students to line up by the exit door.
- Arrange seats for a clear view of presentations.
- Offer students a personal space in which to keep belongings.
- Locate your desk in an appropriate place (off to the side helps to ensure that you will circulate), or get rid of it.
- Separate incompatible activities.

Pleasure:

- Use a variety of colors and textures to create an aesthetically pleasing environment.

Growth:

- Stock your room with a variety of activities, both "open" and "closed."
- Create a literacy center.

Careful planning of the physical environment is an integral part of good classroom management. When you begin to design your room, think about the activities it will accommodate and invite your students to participate in the planning process. Try your arrangement, evaluate it, and redesign as necessary.

Activities

The following activities are intended to help you think about classroom physical environments. The activities are appropriate for in-service teachers with their own classrooms, as well as preservice teachers engaged in pre-student teaching field experiences or student teaching.

1. Visit an elementary classroom, draw a classroom map, and evaluate the physical layout in terms of Steele's six functions of the environment. The following questions, adapted from Bruther (1991), may be helpful.

Security and shelter:

1. Does the classroom feel like a safe, comfortable place to be?
2. Does it contain furnishings and materials that are soft and responsive to touch?
3. Do children have freedom from intrusion and interference?
4. Is there any opportunity for retreat or privacy?

Social contact:

5. Does desk arrangement facilitate or hinder social contact among students? Is this compatible with the explicit objectives?

Symbolic identification:

6. Are there displays of students' work throughout the room?

7. Is there evidence of the students themselves displayed throughout the room (e.g., name tags, photographs, silhouettes, brown paper bodies, multicultural materials, "star of the week" bulletin board, etc.)?

Task instrumentality:

8. Are frequently used classroom materials accessible to students?
9. Are shelves and cabinets well organized so that it is clear where materials and equipment are stored?
10. Are pathways clearly visible?
11. Do pathways allow easy access in and out of all areas?
12. Does the seating arrangement allow students to see instructional presentations without difficulty?

Pleasure:

13. Does the room make people feel good?
14. Does the room contain some type of softness (e.g., carpeting, pillows, beanbag chairs, cushions, rocking chair)?
15. Are there any amenities present (e.g., plants, aquarium, etc.)?
16. Is the classroom colorful and brightly decorated?

Growth:

17. Does the classroom contain a wide selection of supplemental reading materials?
18. Are the books displayed in a way that encourages students to engage in voluntary reading?
19. Does the classroom contain a variety of materials and equipment (e.g., science materials, art materials, puzzles, computers, etc.)?

2. Have students compose a "wish poem" (Sanoff, 1979) by responding to the phrase "I wish my classroom . . ." This is an excerpt from one written by the kindergartners of a student teacher who tried this activity (with the original spellings and translations):

I wish my classroom had a firv truk (a fire truck).
I wish my classroom had a gold fish.
I wish my classroom wasn't hot and I wish my classroom was quiet.
I wus my classroom wus nis (was nice).
I wish my classroom it cmptr (had a computer).

3. Consider the following seating arrangements. For each one, think about the types of instructional strategies for which it is appropriate or inappropriate. The first one has been done as an example.

Arrangement	Instructional Strategies for Which This Arrangement Is Appropriate	Instructional Strategies for Which This Arrangement Is Inappropriate
Rows	Teacher or student presentations; audio-visual presentations; testing	Student-centered discussions; small-group work
Horizontal rows		
Horseshoe		
Small clusters		
Circle		

4. Scrutinize this floor plan (Figure 3-10) of a first-grade room where the teacher is experiencing difficulty with classroom management. According to the teacher, there are four primary problems: (1) children at the small group table are frequently distracted; (2) clean-ups and transitions between activities take too long; (3) there is conflict between children in the library corner and those playing with puzzles and games; (4) when the teacher is working with a small group, the children who are not in the group have difficulty staying on task.

Think about the ways in which the environment might be contributing to the problems. How would you rearrange the room?

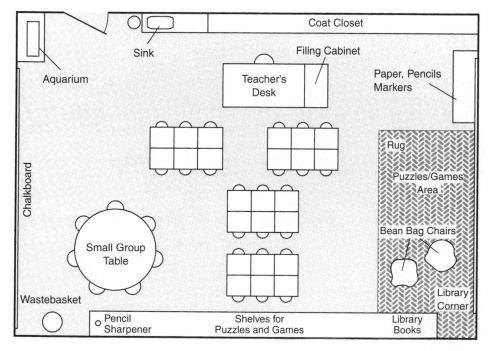

FIGURE 3-10 Floor plan of first grade room

For Further Reading

Clayton, M. K., with Forton, M. B. (2001). *Classroom spaces that work.* Greenfield, MA: Northeast Foundation for Children.
Jones, F. H. (2000). *Tools for teaching.* Santa Cruz, CA: Fredric H. Jones & Associates.
Loughlin, C. E. (1994). Classroom physical environment. *The International Encyclopedia of Education (2nd ed.), X,* 161–164.
Weinstein, C. S., & David, T. G. (Eds.) (1987). *Spaces for children: The built environment and child development.* New York: Plenum Press.

Organizational Resources

The Americans with Disabilities Act (ADA) Technical Assistance Program. Offers resources for making physical accommodations for children with special needs (www.adata.org).

References

Adams, R. S., & Biddle, B. J. (1970). *Realities of teaching: Explorations with video tape.* New York: Holt, Rinehart, & Winston.

Bennett, N., & Blundell, D. (1983). Quantity and quality of work in rows and classroom groups. *Educational Psychology, 3,* 93–105.

Bonus, M., & Riordan, L. (1998). *Increasing student on-task behavior through the use of specific seating arrangements.* Chicago: Saint Xavier University & IRI/Skylight Field-Based Masters Program. ERIC Document Reproduction Service No. ED 422 129.

Bruther, M. (1991). Factors influencing teachers' decisions about their classroom physical environments. Unpublished doctoral dissertation, Rutgers Graduate School of Education.

Clayton, M. K., with Forton, M. B. (2001). *Classroom spaces that work.* Greenfield, MA: Northeast Foundation for Children.

Genishi, C. (1988). Kindergartners and computers: A case study of six children. *Elementary School Journal, 89,* 185–201.

Hastings, N., & Schwieso, J. (1995). Tasks and tables: The effects of seating arrangements on task engagement in primary classrooms. *Educational Research, 37*(3), 279–291.

Jones, E., & Prescott, E. (1978). *Dimensions of teaching learning environments. II: Focus on day care.* Pasadena, CA: Pacific Oaks College.

Jones, F. H. (2000). *Tools for Teaching.* Santa Cruz, CA: Fredric H. Jones & Associates.

Kashti, Y., Arieli, M., & Harel, Y. (1984). Classroom seating as a definition of situation: Observations in an elementary school in one development town. *Urban Education, 19*(2), 161–181.

Krantz, P. J., & Risley, T. R. (September, 1972). The organization of group care environments: Behavioral ecology in the classroom. Paper presented at the Annual Convention of the American Psychological Association, Honolulu. ERIC #ED 078 915.

Lambert, N. M. (1994). Seating arrangements in classrooms. *The International Encyclopedia of Education* (2nd ed.), *9,* 5355–5359.

Levine, D. W., O'Neal, E C., Garwood, S. G., & McDonald, P. J. (1980). Classroom ecology: The effects of seating position on grades and participation. *Personality and Social Psychology Bulletin, 6*(3), 409–412.

Loughlin, C. E., & Martin, M. D. (1987). *Supporting literacy: Developing effective learning environments.* New York: Teachers College Press.

Maslow, A. H., & Mintz, N. L. (1956). The effects of esthetic surroundings: I. *Journal of Psychology, 41,* 247–254.

Morrow, L. M. (2001). *Literacy development in the early years: Helping children read and write* (4th ed.). Needham Heights, MA: Allyn and Bacon.

Morrow, L. M., Strickland, D. S., & Woo, D. G. (1998). *Literacy instruction in half- and whole-day kindergarten: Research to practice.* Newark, DE: International Reading Association.

Morrow, L. M., & Weinstein, C. S. (1982). Increasing children's literature use through program and physical design changes. *Elementary School Journal, 83*(2), 131–137.

Morrow, L. M., & Weinstein, C. S. (1986). Encouraging voluntary reading: The impact of a literature program on children's use of library centers. *Reading Research Quarterly, 21*(3), 330–346.

Olds, A. R. (1987). Designing settings for infants and toddlers. In C. S. Weinstein & T. G. David (Eds.), *Spaces for children: The built environment and child development.* New York: Plenum Press, 117–138.

Perlmutter, B. F. (1994, August 12). Teaching distractible students: Modifications in seating arrangements and classroom strategies. Paper presented at the Annual Convention of the American Psychological Association, Los Angeles, CA.

Proshansky, E., & Wolfe, M. (1974). The physical setting and open education. *School Review, 82,* 557–574.

Sanoff, H. (1979). *Design games.* Los Altos, CA: William Kaufmann.

Steele, F. I. (1973). *Physical settings and organization development.* Reading, MA: Addison-Wesley.

Weinstein, C. S. (1982). Privacy-seeking behavior in an elementary classroom. *Journal of Environmental Psychology, 2,* 23–35.

Wengel, M. (1992). *Seating arrangements: Changing with the times.* Research/Technical Report. Eric Document Reproduction Service No. ED 348 153.

Wheldall, K., Morris, M., Vaughn, P., & Ng, Y. (1981). Rows versus tables: An example of the use of behavioral ecology in two classes of eleven year-old children. *Educational Psychology, 1*(2), 171–184.

Wheldall, K., & Lam, Y. Y. (1987). Rows versus tables. II. The effects of two classroom seating arrangements on classroom disruption rate, on-task behaviour, and teacher behaviour in three special school classes. *Educational Psychology, 7*(4), 303–312.

Chapter Four

Establishing Norms for Behavior

Research on Effective Classroom Management

Defining Your Expectations for Behavior

The First Few Days of School: Teaching Students How to Behave

Concluding Comments

Summary

The first day of a new academic year can be scary, even for students who have been in school several years. There are so many unknowns: What will the teacher be like? Who will be in my class? Will I be able to find my room? And, of course, there are all those "what if" questions: What if I have to go to the bathroom? What if my pencil point breaks? What if the teacher asks me a question and I don't know the answer?

Beginning teachers have their *own* set of "what ifs": What if the kids don't listen to me? What if a student asks me a question and I don't know the answer? Nonetheless, as adults, we may underestimate the intensity of students' September anxieties. To understand what students are feeling, try to recall a time when your unfamiliarity with cultural norms and customs made you uncomfortable and insecure. Perhaps you visited a shop in a foreign country and weren't certain whether it was appropriate to bargain with a vendor. Maybe you attended a service in a church of a different faith and wondered whether to kneel with the rest of the congregation. Or perhaps you had dinner in an unusually elegant restaurant and felt unsure about proper table etiquette.

In each of these situations, *not knowing what was expected* caused insecurity, discomfort, and self-consciousness. All of us feel more competent when we understand the norms for appropriate behavior, and elementary students are no exception. Indeed, a study on motivation in the classroom provides research support for this commonsense notion. Skinner and Belmont (1993) hypothesized that clearly structured classroom environments (i.e., those that provided information about how to achieve desired outcomes) would satisfy children's need for competence. Consistent with this hypothesis, they found that third-, fourth-, and fifth-graders were more likely to work harder and to be more persistent when they perceived their teachers as providing clear expectations. The message is apparent: *Well-defined norms for behavior can help to dispel the "what ifs" and enhance feelings of safety and security.*

Clear expectations for behavior have another major benefit. As we have emphasized in earlier chapters, classes are crowded, complex settings in which individuals engage in a wide variety of activities. *Well-defined norms decrease the complexity of the classroom.* They minimize confusion and prevent the loss of instructional time. They enable you and your students to carry out "housekeeping" tasks (e.g., taking attendance, distributing materials, collecting homework) smoothly and efficiently, so that time for learning and teaching is maximized.

In this chapter we describe research that demonstrates the importance of classroom norms. We then discuss some principles to guide you in establishing norms for your own classrooms. We'll also learn how Viviana, Garnetta, Barbara, and Ken introduce norms to their students and what they think about this central task of classroom management.

Research on Effective Classroom Management

Prior to 1970, teacher preparation programs could offer only limited advice about classroom management to beginning teachers. Teacher educators shared useful "tricks of the trade" (e.g., flick the lights for quiet), stressed the importance of firmness and consistency, and warned prospective teachers not to smile until Christmas. But research identifying the behaviors of effective managers was unavailable, and it was simply not clear why some classrooms function smoothly while others are chaotic.

That situation changed in 1970, with the publication of Jacob Kounin's study of orderly and disorderly classrooms. You may recall from Chapter 1 that Kounin set out to compare teachers' methods of responding to misbehavior. To his surprise, he found that the reactions of good classroom managers were not substantially different from the reactions of poor classroom managers. What *did* differ were the strategies that teachers used to *prevent* misbehavior. Effective classroom managers constantly monitored students' behavior. They displayed what Kounin called "withitness": They were aware of what was happening in all parts of the room, and they communicated this awareness to students. They also exhibited an ability to "overlap"—to do more than one thing at a time—certainly a desirable skill in a setting where so many events occur simultaneously! Furthermore, effective managers kept lessons moving at a brisk pace, so that there was little opportunity for students to become inattentive and disruptive.

Kounin's work led researchers to wonder how effective managers began the school year. In the late 1970s, a series of studies was launched at the Research and Development

Center for Teacher Education, located at the University of Texas at Austin. One project (Emmer, Evertson, &Anderson, 1980) involved observations of 27 self-contained, third-grade classrooms in an urban district. During the first three weeks of school, researchers observed extensively in each classroom and kept detailed records of what occurred. Observations were then stopped, but were resumed in November and continued until the end of the school year. On the basis of the November through May data, the researchers identified more and less effective managers. They then went back to the information collected at the beginning of the year and compared what the teachers had done during the first three weeks of school. Striking differences were apparent—even on the very first day of school!

Among the major differences documented by Emmer, Evertson, and Anderson was the way teachers handled rules and routines. *Effective managers had clear rules for general conduct* (e.g., "Be prepared for class"), *as well as procedures or routines for carrying out specific tasks* (e.g., going to the restroom). Furthermore, effective managers spent much of the first few days teaching these rules and procedures to students—as carefully as they taught academic content—and they continued to review during the first three weeks of school.

In contrast, the ineffective teachers did not have well-defined rules or procedures. One new teacher, for example, had no routines for going to the restrooms, using the pencil sharpener, or getting a drink of water. As a result, children wandered about, coming and going as they pleased. Although ineffective managers did have rules, the rules were often vague ("Be in the right place at the right time") and were not clearly explained. Ineffective managers frequently introduced rules casually, neglecting to teach them to students in a careful, deliberate way.

The research conducted by Emmer, Evertson, and their colleagues has helped to clarify what effective managers do to create order in their classrooms. This work underscores the importance of *(1) deciding how you want your students to behave and (2) making these expectations absolutely clear to students.* Let's look at each of these steps separately.

Defining Your Expectations for Behavior

Before the first child enters your classroom, you need to think about how you expect your students to behave. Not only do you need to decide on *norms for students' general conduct,* you also need to identify the *behavioral routines or procedures* that you and your students will follow in specific situations. For example, when students arrive in the morning, are they to hang up their coats, go immediately to their desks, and take out a book? Or may they chat quietly with neighbors, sharpen pencils, and play games? When students need paper for an assignment, will they get it themselves, will you have a "paper monitor," or will you distribute it yourself? When students have to use the restroom, are they to ask permission or simply get a pass and leave? When students are working at their seats, may they help one another or must they work individually?

Because these seem like such trivial, mundane issues, it is easy to underestimate their contribution to classroom order. But lessons can fall apart while you try to decide how to distribute paper, and students feel anxious if they're unsure whether answering a classmate's question during seatwork is helping or cheating. As we will see, behavioral norms may vary from class to class, but no class can function smoothly without them.

Planning Norms for General Conduct

Emmer, Evertson, and their colleagues found that effective managers typically have three to six general rules of conduct. These rules describe the behaviors that are necessary if your classroom is to be a good place in which to live and work—for example, "respect other people's property," "keep your hands to yourself," and "follow directions." In Garnetta's classroom, she and the children decided upon the following rules:

Be respectful.

Raise your hand to talk.

Don't fight; settle disagreements peacefully.

Listen when someone is talking.

Stay in your seat.

Think before you do something.

As you reflect on rules for your own classroom, there are four principles to keep in mind. These are summarized in Table 4-1 (and violated in the cartoon in Figure 4-1). First, *rules should be reasonable and necessary.* Think about the age and characteristics of the children you are teaching, and ask yourself: What rules are appropriate for them? For example, it is unreasonable to require kindergartners to "sit quietly at your desks at all times." Given young children's irresistible need to move, establishing such a rule will only result in squirming, fidgeting, and frustration.

TABLE 4-1. Four Principles for Planning Classroom Rules

Principle	Questions to Think About
1. Rules should be reasonable and necessary.	What rules are appropriate for this grade level? Is there a good reason for this rule?
2. Rules need to be clear and understandable.	Is the rule too abstract for students to comprehend? To what extent do I want my students to participate in the decision-making process?
3. Rules should be consistent with instructional goals and with what we know about how people learn.	Will this rule facilitate or hinder my students' learning?
4. Classroom rules need to be consistent with school rules.	What are the school rules? Are particular behaviors required in the halls, during assemblies, in the cafeteria, etc.?

Mrs. Mutner liked to go over a few of her rules on the first day of school.

FIGURE 4-1. (CLOSE TO HOME © 1993 John McPherson. Reprinted with permission of Universal Press Syndicate. All rights reserved.)

Also ask yourself whether each rule is necessary. Is there a compelling reason for it? Will it make the classroom a more pleasant place to be? Will it increase children's opportunity to learn? A second-grade teacher we know established a strict "no talking" rule during snack time (while children sat at four-person clusters of desks). It was difficult for students (and for us!) to understand why they should be forbidden to talk quietly while eating. Although the teacher was able to enforce the rule, her class perceived it as arbitrary and unfair.

Second, *rules need to be clear and understandable.* Because rules are often stated in very general terms ("be polite"), they may be too abstract for children to comprehend. When planning your rules, you need to think of specific examples to discuss with students. For example, Barbara's most basic rule for general conduct is "be courteous." She makes sure that "courtesy" is spelled out in terms of real behaviors: "When you play with someone who's being left out." "When you listen politely when someone's speaking." "When you don't tease." "When you don't call people names." "When you say please and thank you."

Many teachers believe that rules are more understandable and more meaningful when students are allowed to participate in the decision-making process. Participation, especially at higher grade levels, may increase students' willingness to "buy into" the rules, may make them more invested in seeing that rules are followed, and may help to prepare students for adult life (Solomon, Watson, Delucchi, Schaps, & Battistich, 1988). One advocate of involving students in rule setting is Daniel Meier, who writes about his first-grade teaching experiences in *Learning in Small Moments: Life in an Urban Classroom* (1997). (Figure 4-2 contains an excerpt from Meier's book that describes how Meier's co-teacher, John Sierra, introduced rules to their first-graders.) Notice that John first writes students' ideas on the board, retaining their language, and then groups the ideas

"Boys and girls," John said . . . with a quick clap of his hands. "Since this is your classroom, Mr. Meier and I want you to make your own rules so that we can all get along together this year. Who has a rule that would help us get along?"

Rule-setting is a common practice in classrooms in order to promote prosocial behavior, but John and I wanted the children to play an integral role in the process. The children took their cue and eagerly participated in the rule-making as John wrote their suggestions on a large piece of chart paper clipped to the blackboard.

With a softness he would retain all year, Matthew said, "You shouldn't hit anybody because they could get hurt."

"Yeah," Charles added with his already unique sense of humor, "and no kicking them or punching them or giving any karate chops."

"And I don't think," Michele said with maturity, "kids should tease other kids because they'll get their feelings hurt."

John synthesized all the suggestions, retaining the children's original intent and language.

Don't hit nobody.

No spitting.

Don't bother people when they're doing their work.

Share all the things you work with.

Don't hit.

Don't tease.

Be nice.

No stealing.

Don't kick.

No kung fu or karate.

Don't make people feel bad.

Ask someone to play if they don't have somebody to play with.

Don't get into no trouble.
(my favorite)

John stepped back from the list and studied it as if it were a painting.

"These are good rules. But there're too many of them. Also, some of the rules talk about the same thing. So we need to *group* them together and make just a few rules. Watch what I'm going to do. Is everybody watching?"

John paused to make sure.

"This rule about 'no kicking' is like this rule about 'no karate.' Why? Because they both have to do with hurting people physically. So I'm going to circle both rules with a blue marker. Okay, now, see this rule about 'being nice' and this other rule about 'not teasing'? These two are alike because they both involve people's feelings. I'll circle both rules with a red marker."

John circled and grouped the remaining rules.

"Now let's go back and look at all the blue rules. What's one rule we could write that would say something about all the blue rules?"

No one raised a hand.

"This is hard. Since all the blue rules have to do with getting hurt on the outside of our bodies, let's write, 'Don't hurt anybody.'"

John continued the process until he crystallized a final list.

1. Play fair.
2. Do not damage anything.
3. Take turns talking.
4. Keep your hands and feet to yourself.
5. Don't hurt other people's feelings.

John taped the final list to the wall, where it would remain for the rest of the year. (pp. 11–12)

FIGURE 4-2. Involving students in rule setting
Source: D. R. Meier, *Learning in Small Moments: Life in an Urban Classroom,* 1997.

that are similar in order to eliminate redundancy. (Note, also, that John does *not* always state rules in the positive, something that we generally recommend.)

Garnetta and Ken also involve students in setting classroom norms, although Ken has his sixth-graders draft a "Bill of Rights," rather than a set of rules. According to Ken, "The bill of rights changes the way kids think about classroom behavior. I hear kids say to other kids, 'This place is different; we have rights here.' If kids get teased, they're empowered to say, 'This shouldn't happen. I shouldn't be made fun of, people shouldn't tease me. It's not just a rule; it's my right.'" (We will return to the way Ken and Garnetta introduce rule setting later in the chapter.)

A third principle to keep in mind is that *rules should be consistent with instructional goals and with what we know about how people learn.* The first chapter discussed the assumptions underlying this book. One assumption was that the need for order should not supersede the need for meaningful instruction. As you develop rules for your classroom, think about whether they will *facilitate or hinder the learning process.* For example, a second-grade teacher we know had a "no erasures" rule for written work done in class. Her reason was clear: Children tended to create holes in their papers when they erased, and the results were messy and difficult to read. Unfortunately, not being allowed to erase created a good deal of anxiety; some students actually became more focused on not making mistakes than on what they were writing. Although the rule was well-intended, it interfered with children's learning.

In the pursuit of order, teachers sometimes prohibit talking during independent seatwork assignments. Or they may refrain from using cooperative learning activities for fear that students will be too rowdy. Obviously, such restrictions are necessary at times, but it is sad if they become the status quo. Educational psychologists who study the ways children learn stress the importance of children's interaction. Much of this thinking is based on the work of the Soviet psychologist, Lev Vygotsky, who believed that children's intellectual growth is fostered through collaboration with adults who serve as coaches and tutors and with more capable peers (Wertsch, 1985). Interestingly, research on the use of small groups indicates that these interactions benefit the *tutor* as well as the person being tutored. Noreen Webb (1985), for example, has found that children who provide explanations for their peers also show increased achievement. Given the important role that interaction plays in children's learning and cognitive development, it seems sensible not to eliminate interaction, but to spend considerable time teaching children how to behave in these situations. (We will address this topic more fully in Chapter 10.)

Finally, *classroom rules need to be consistent with school rules.* For example, some schools require students to possess a pass when they leave the classroom; if this is the case, you need to establish the same rule. Your school may hold an orientation meeting for new teachers where school rules and procedures are explained. If not, see if there is a school handbook and consult with office staff and other teachers. In particular, find out about behaviors that are expected during assemblies, in the cafeteria and library, and on the playground. You also need to know about any administrative procedures for which you are responsible (e.g., taking attendance, collecting lunch money, supervising fire drills, communicating with parents).

Planning Routines for Specific Situations

So many different activities occur in classrooms that trying to define behavior for specific situations can be daunting. Researchers at the Learning Research and Development Center at the University of Pittsburgh have observed the behavior of effective classroom managers and have categorized the routines they use (Leinhardt, Weidman, & Hammond, 1987). We have adapted their three-category system to provide you with a way of thinking about routines for your own classroom.

Class-Running Routines

These are *nonacademic routines* that enable you to keep the classroom running smoothly. This category of routines includes *administrative duties* (taking attendance, recording the number of students who are buying lunch each day, distributing school notices), *procedures for student movement* (entering the room at the beginning of the day; leaving the room at the end of the day; leaving the room to go to the bathroom, the nurse, the library, or lockers; lining up to go to "specials" such as art, music, and physical education; fire drills; moving around the room to sharpen pencils, use learning centers, or get materials), and *housekeeping routines* (cleaning chalkboards, watering plants, storing personal items such as book bags and coats, cleaning out desks, maintaining storage for materials used by everyone).

Without clear, specific class-running routines, these activities can consume a significant part of the school day. Research on the way time is used in second-grade classrooms has indicated that, on the average, noninstructional activities (transitions, waiting, housekeeping) consume almost 20 percent of the time spent in the classroom—more than the amount of time spent in mathematics instruction (Rosenshine, 1980). This figure is undoubtedly higher in classrooms that are not well managed.

By defining how children are to behave in these specific situations, you can save precious minutes for instruction. You also enable children to carry out many of these routines without your direct supervision, freeing you to concentrate on instruction. For example, Barbara allows her students to take a laminated cardboard pass and go to the bathroom without asking permission—as long as the class is not in the middle of a lesson. Having a single pass means that only one child can be out of the room at a time and, of course, Barbara makes sure that no one leaves the room an unreasonable number of times. With these safeguards in place, the routine runs smoothly and saves Barbara from innumerable interruptions.

Lesson-Running Routines

These routines *directly support instruction by specifying the behaviors that are necessary for teaching and learning to take place.* They allow lessons to proceed briskly and eliminate the need for students to ask questions like "Do I have to use pen?" "Should we number from 1 to 20?" and "What do I do if I'm finished?"

Lesson-running routines describe what items students are to have on hand when a lesson begins, how materials are to be distributed and collected, what kind of paper or writing instrument is to be used, and what should be done with the paper (folded into eight boxes; numbered from 1 to 10 along the left margin; headed with name, date, and subject).

In addition, lesson-running routines specify the behaviors that students are to engage in at the beginning of the lesson (e.g., have books open to the relevant page, silently sit and wait for instructions from the teacher) and what they are to do if they finish early or if they are unable to finish the assignment by the end of the time period.

Homework procedures can also be considered lesson-running routines, since the pace and content of a lesson often depends on whether students have done their homework assignments. You need to establish routines for determining quickly which students have their homework and which do not, as well as routines for checking and collecting assignments.

Interaction Routines

These routines refer to the *rules for talk*—talk between teachers and students and talk among students themselves. Interaction routines specify *when talk is permitted and how it is to occur.* For example, during a whole-class discussion, students need to know what to do if they want to respond to a question or contribute a comment. All four of our teachers, like many others, usually require students to raise their hands and wait to be called on, rather than simply calling out. In this way, the teachers can distribute opportunities to participate throughout the class and can ensure that the conversation is not dominated by a few overly eager individuals. The teachers can also check on how well the class understands the lesson by calling on students who do not raise their hands.

It's often hard to keep track of which students have had an opportunity to speak. In order to avoid this problem, Ken sometimes uses "the cup system"—a coffee mug containing popsicle sticks with students' names. He shakes the cup, pulls out a name, and then places the popsicle stick on the side.

During some lessons, you may want students to respond chorally rather than individually (e.g., counting by fives). A simple signal can be used to indicate that the rules for talk have changed. Viviana, for example, uses hand gestures. When she wants students to raise their hands, she shoots her arm into the air as she asks the question. When she wants a choral response, she reaches out both hands, palms up, in a clear invitation to respond.

Barbara also suspends the normal rules for talk at times. For example, during a "great books discussion," she encourages her students to respond directly to one another. It's amazing how difficult they find this to be, at least at first; students repeatedly seek her permission to talk, despite her frequent reminders that they can comment without first being called on.

Interaction routines also include *procedures that students and teachers use to gain each other's attention.* For example, if students are busy working and you need to give additional instructions, how will you signal that you want their attention? Will you say, "Excuse me," as Garnetta does, or will you clap your hands, flick the lights, or ring a bell? Conversely, if you are busy working with a small group or an individual, and students need your assistance, how will they communicate that to you? Will they be allowed to call your name or leave their seats and approach you? Will they turn over a "help" sign at their desks, or perhaps raise a red flag?

Finally, you need to think about the rules that will govern *talk among students.* When 20 to 30 students sit so close to one another, it's only natural for them to talk. You must decide when it's all right for students to talk about the television show they saw last night (e.g., during recess and free time) and when their talk must be about academic work (e.g., during cooperative learning activities or peer conferencing). You also need to think about times when students may talk quietly (e.g., during independent work or writing workshop), and when you need to have absolute silence (e.g., when you are giving instruction or during a test).

Table 4-2 summarizes the three types of routines we have just discussed.

TABLE 4-2. Summary of Classroom Routines

CLASS-RUNNING ROUTINES: Nonacademic routines that enable the classroom to run smoothly

Administrative routines
>   Taking attendance
>   Recording lunch orders
>   Distributing school notices

Routines for student movement
>   Entering the room at the beginning of the day
>   Leaving the room at the end of the day
>   Going to the restroom
>   Going to the nurse
>   Going to the library
>   Going to "specials"
>   Fire drills
>   Sharpening pencils
>   Using learning centers
>   Getting materials

Housekeeping routines
>   Cleaning chalkboards
>   Watering plants
>   Storing personal items (books, bags, coats)
>   Cleaning desks
>   Maintaining common storage areas

LESSON-RUNNING ROUTINES: Routines that directly support instruction by specifying the behaviors that are necessary for teaching and learning to take place

>   What to bring to the lesson
>   Collecting homework
>   Recording who has done homework
>   Returning homework
>   Moving in and out of centers
>   Responsibilities during writing workshop
>   Distributing materials

(continued)

TABLE 4-2. Summary of Classroom Routines *(continued)*

Preparing paper for assignment (heading, margins, type of writing instrument)
Collecting in-class assignments
What to do when assignments have been completed

INTERACTION ROUTINES: Routines that specify when talk is permitted and how it is to occur

Talk between teacher and students

During whole-class lessons
When the teacher is working with a small group
When the teacher needs the group's attention
When students need the teacher's attention

Talk among students

During independent work
During center time
During peer conferencing
During cooperative learning activities
During small-group work
During free time
During transitions
During loudspeaker announcements
When a visitor comes to speak with the teacher

The First Few Days of School: Teaching Students How to Behave

Learning how to behave in school is not always easy. Too often, students have to guess the rules for appropriate behavior from teachers' indirect statements like "I see someone whose hands are not folded" [translation: students' hands should be folded now] (Shuy, 1988) or "I don't see any hands" [translation: students should raise their hands if they wish to speak] (Gumperz, 1981). Students must also be sensitive to cues provided by nonverbal behavior, like voice tone and pitch, posture, tempo and rhythm of speech, and facial expression. Sometimes students "misbehave" simply because they have misinterpreted these subtle cues! And take note: Misinterpretation is especially likely when teachers and students come from different cultural backgrounds.

In order to minimize confusion, you need to teach students rules and routines as deliberately and thoroughly as you would teach academic content. As we indicated earlier in this chapter, Emmer, Evertson, and Anderson (1980) found that effective managers spent a large portion of the first few days of school teaching rules and procedures and then reviewed and reinforced them during the first three weeks. Subsequent research has confirmed this finding. In fact, Leinhardt, Weidman, and Hammond (1987) found that during days one through four, teachers and students spent *more time on management issues than on academic content.* This may seem like an unreasonable amount of time to invest in rules and routines, but your investment should pay off later when your class runs smoothly.

Teaching Norms for General Conduct

It's not enough to state norms for general conduct and expect students to understand or remember them. Instead, you need to *define terms* as clearly as possible, *discuss rationales,* and *provide examples.* Let's see what this looks like in action. On the morning of the first day of school, Barbara taught students her most basic norm: "Be courteous." During this discussion, she also explained the difference between "talking quietly" and "being silent." Notice how she solicits examples, explains why certain behaviors are necessary, comments on students' attentiveness, and checks to see that students understand how to whisper.

BARBARA: I guess it's time now to talk about fourth grade. This is a big step for you. People have a lot of expectations of fourth graders. Let's discuss some of those expectations. I expect you to *be courteous.* What does that mean? What are some examples of being courteous?

STUDENT: Not being rude.

BARBARA: That's right, but give me an example of not being rude.

STUDENT: Not slamming the door on somebody.

BARBARA: Good. What's another example?

STUDENT: Listen to people when they're talking.

BARBARA: Yes. I can see that you people don't have any problem with that, because you're listening now as we're talking. Another example of being courteous? [Students can't think of any.] Let's say we're having a lesson and someone walks in to talk to me. What could you do to be courteous?

STUDENT: Sit quietly.

STUDENT: Whisper quietly.

BARBARA: Good. It's important for you to know that it's all right with me if you whisper quietly. But I need to know that you know what whispering quietly means. So go ahead and do that. [Students whisper.] All right, I can live with that. That was fine. Okay, so you can *sit silently,* or you can *whisper quietly.* What else?

STUDENT: You can read a book.

BARBARA: Yes, that's a good idea. Do you think you could get up and walk around? [Students murmur no and shake their heads.] Right, because as soon as the person leaves we'll resume the lesson, and we'll lose time if you're all around the room. Is there anything else you could do when I'm speaking with someone?

STUDENT: Continue working on our work.

BARBARA: Absolutely. Let's talk some more about what courtesy means. Let's suppose I'm teaching a lesson and your pencil point breaks. What will you do?

> STUDENT: Take out another pencil.
> BARBARA: Wonderful solution. What else?
> STUDENT: Ask if we can sharpen our pencil.
> BARBARA: Okay. When someone's talking, it's impolite to just get up and sharpen a pencil. As long as we're talking about sharpening pencils, let me give you another example of courtesy: If the pencil sharpener drops and makes a mess, I don't go crazy, but I do expect you to clean it up. That's being courteous. You know, we're going to be living here together all day long, and we're going to be friends. We're going to be like a family. So we have to treat each other courteously and learn to care about one another.

Later in the morning, Barbara came back to her theme about "quiet" and "silence."

> BARBARA: Most of the time I want the class to be quiet when we're working. To me, being quiet is different from being absolutely silent. Can someone tell me the difference?
> STUDENT: When you're quiet you can whisper, but when you're silent, you can't even whisper.
> BARBARA: Absolutely. Now, there are certain times when you'll be working that I'll ask for silence, but most of the time I expect you to be quiet. That means that you can talk quietly. When might you need to talk as you're doing your work?
> STUDENT: When we're helping someone with a problem.
> STUDENT: When we ask someone for help.
> BARBARA: Right. Is this the time you arrange whose house you're visiting after school?"
> CLASS: No-o-o-o.
> BARBARA: Good. There are different times for different kinds of conversations, and conversations about visiting or what you did over the weekend should take place during lunch or recess or before school begins.

As this example illustrates, teaching students norms for general conduct doesn't have to be unpleasant or oppressive. Interestingly, Barbara doesn't even use the word *rule* as she discusses her expectations for students' behavior. Nor does she post rules on a bulletin board, although many effective managers do. When we asked her about this, she explained her reasoning:

> *Even if a rule is stated positively, the word* rule *itself has a negative connotation. From a child's perspective, rules are made up by adults to tell kids, "These are the things you can't do, and these are the things you have to do, and if you don't follow the rules you get punished." I also think that children think the rules are only for* them, *not for the teacher. I much prefer to talk about the way we all need to treat each other. When I talk about the need for courtesy, I try to make it clear that I need to be courteous too, not*

just the children. I also want to communicate that there is no question in my mind that we will all be courteous, so I don't talk about penalties or punishments, or what will happen if people aren't courteous.

Viviana also prefers not to use the word *rule* or to post rules. Nonetheless, she clearly communicates her expectations to her first-graders by giving explicit directions, reinforcing appropriate behavior, and correcting inappropriate behavior. During one interview, she shared her thinking with us:

Sure I have rules—listen when someone is talking, follow directions—but I don't tell the children "this is a rule." I teach the rules as the need arises. For example, with talking, if I'm talking and someone talks, then I say, "Wait a minute, I'm talking and you're not listening. How will you know what to do? You won't hear the directions." Everyone hears what I say, and they get the message, "I'm not supposed to talk when she talks." I also tell them how pleased I am when they're being quiet and how that way everyone can hear the directions. I don't post rules or talk about rules. I don't think that would be meaningful for my children. Instead I explain what to do when the opportunity comes up. Then it has an impact.

Teaching Routines for Specific Situations

Teaching students how to carry out behavioral routines is much like teaching them how to add or subtract. Emmer, Evertson, and Anderson (1980) found that effective classroom managers *explained and demonstrated procedures,* allowed students to *practice* them, *provided feedback* to students about their performance, and then *retaught* the procedures if necessary. Such thoroughness is particularly important at lower grade levels, when children have had little experience with the routines of school and when new instructional strategies are introduced (e.g., writing workshop, literature circles, centers).

As Viviana explained in her previous comments, she teaches her first-graders how to behave when the need arises. On the first day of school, for example, she taught them to turn their chairs around to face her when she gives instruction to the whole group. Even though the whole process lasted less than a minute, Viviana managed to demonstrate the behavior, had students practice, provided feedback, and explained the rationale for the routine.

> VIVIANA: All right children, I want you to turn your chairs around to face me. Let me show you how to do that. [She selects a child, stands her up and turns her chair around to demonstrate.] Did you all see that? José, can you do that? [The child turns his chair around properly.] Good for you. Now let me see everyone's chair like that. [She makes a big thing of looking up and down each row checking the chairs.] Very, very good. You did that very well. By turning your chairs around like this, you won't have to strain your necks trying

> to see what I'm doing [she twists her neck around to illustrate], and I'll be able to see everybody's beautiful face.

Throughout the day, Viviana reinforces this procedure repeatedly: "Turn your chairs around and face me. Very good, you remember how."

Different Approaches to Teaching Rules and Routines

Barbara, Garnetta, Viviana, and Ken all have clear expectations for students' behavior and make these expectations absolutely clear to students. Nonetheless, the four teachers introduce rules and routines in very different ways. These differences reflect their beliefs about what works best for their particular students in their particular contexts.

Ken and Garnetta provide an interesting contrast. In the following transcriptions, you can see how they introduce rules to their students on the first day of school.

Ken: The Bill of Rights

Instead of rules, Ken prefers to talk in terms of students' rights, as well as the laws that are required to protect those rights. Note how Ken allows all suggestions (as long as they were seriously contributed), but indicates that further refinement will be needed. Figure 4-3 presents the list of rights that emerged from continuing discussion.

> KEN: I want to spend some time thinking about what your rights in school are. I want to do a brainstorming session and write down things that you consider a right in school. I'm going to do a little editing, something I don't usually do, but I don't want to waste time on silly things, like throwing water balloons in the classroom. OK, what rights do you think you should have? (Ken moves to black-board and calls on children. As children state rights, Ken writes down what they say; sometimes he rewords a bit if student gives him permission.)
>
> STUDENT: The right to whisper when the teacher isn't talking.
>
> STUDENT: The right to be treated nicely, politely.
>
> STUDENT: The right to not have people take your things.
>
> STUDENT: The right to a two-minute break between every working period.
>
> STUDENT: The right to work and learn without being bothered.
>
> STUDENT: The right to a snack everyday.
>
> STUDENT: The right to sit next to whoever you want. (Ken writes: "The right to choose a table.")
>
> STUDENT: The right for the table to stay together unless it wants to break up.
>
> KEN: That's really an elaboration of the previous right, so I won't write it down, OK?
>
> STUDENT: The right to privacy—so no one else takes what you have. So no one touches your stuff without permission.
>
> STUDENT: The right to use chairs on the floor to lean.
>
> KEN: Can I write down, "The right to be comfortable?" (Boy agrees.)

MR. KOWALSKI'S CLASS'S BILL OF RIGHTS

The right to be treated nicely, politely, respectfully, fairly, kindly, welcomed, equally.

The right to whisper when the teacher isn't talking.

The right to a two-minute break between work periods.

The right to have choices about the day's schedule.

The right to work and learn without being bothered.

The right to talk to the class without anyone else talking.

The right to choose a table.

The right to privacy.

The right to be comfortable.

The right not to have people take your things.

The right to play with anyone during recess.

The right to a snack every day.

The right to stand up for others.

The right to apologies.

The right to learn.

The right to make mistakes.

The right not to be copied.

The right to ask for help.

The right to ask questions.

The right to have fun while learning.

The right to have silence.

The right to work independently.

The right to study.

The right to have feelings.

The right to help other people at the right time.

The right to chew gum without blowing bubbles or making a mess.

The right to go outside almost every day.

FIGURE 4-3. The final Bill of Rights

> STUDENT: The right to chew gum, without blowing bubbles. (Everyone begins to murmur, "yeah. . .")
>
> KEN: We'll put it up, but we'll have to think about it. I like the way you qualified it about the bubbles.
>
> STUDENT: The right to make choices about the day's schedule.
>
> STUDENT: The right to free work time.

Suggestions appear to be at an end. A few kids mutter things like "There must be more things to put up that we haven't thought about." Ken stands silently and waits. Kids are unable to come up with much more.

> KEN: I don't think this is complete yet. But I'm going to copy this down and post it. We're going to have to work on this, and define things more carefully, especially the chewing gum.

In the next few days, Ken and his students continue to revise and refine the Students' Bill of Rights. When they are all satisfied with the final list, Ken turns the discussion to the "laws" needed to protect those rights. As Ken tells it, "That's when the kids start saying, "You have to do what the teacher says." They expect *me* to protect their rights, and I *do* accept that responsibility. But I also tell them that we have to work *together* on this." After Ken and his students decide on laws that will safeguard their rights, Ken types the list, trying hard to preserve students' actual language. (See Figure 4-4.)

Later, Ken shared his thoughts with us about the whole process:

You know, I think every teacher should do this every year. The bill of rights teaches you so much about the kids in your class; the list always reflects their concerns and their views of what classrooms are all about. You can see where they're from, what's happened to them in the past, what their expectations are. Making a bill of rights forces them to open up . . . to think about what they'd really like the classroom to be. It almost becomes a wish list—we wish we had these things. And then, of course, it forces me to ask myself, why not? Why can't they have these things? After all, if they're willing to take on the responsibilities, well, then, why shouldn't they enjoy the rights?

Some of the things on the list seem a lot more "special" than they really are. Take the two-minute break between classes, for example. In reality,

---

LAWS TO PROTECT OUR RIGHTS

1. Follow directions the first time.
2. Speak nicely, be courteous, and respect other people, their feelings and their things. Follow the Bill of Rights.
3. Laugh at the right time for the right time.
4. Respect others' Right to Learn. Do not distract others. Don't be nosy. Don't yell. Remember to get quiet at countdown.
5. Talk at the right times with the right tone of voice and volume.
6. Transitions and movements are calm, quiet, careful and elegant.
7. Follow all classroom and school procedures, like: bathroom; pencil; lunch and recess; morning; dismissal; and . . .

FIGURE 4-4. Laws to Protect Our Rights

every time you switch classes, it takes about that long anyway. So you define it as the break. You're acknowledging that it takes that long and saying that it's all right to talk during that time. Instead of fighting them for two minutes, you're saying, "I know it's going to take that long and it's OK" I'm not sure why it's so important to them, when they know they'll have time between classes. In any case, allowing students to have that two-minute break in the bill of rights legitimizes something that's going to happen anyway.

Another thing—you read the literature on gifted and talented education, and it talks about how we want kids to be fluent idea-producers, to be able to make choices, to engage in problem solving, to critique ideas. Well, here's a real life problem—what rights should you have in this classroom and what laws do we need to protect them? It's so much more real than anything you find in a G&T [gifted and talented] catalog. The kids have to live with the list they come up with; it stares them in the face every day. And it makes the classroom more real.

Garnetta: Stranded on an Isolated Island

In the following scenario, we see how Garnetta helps to make the need for rules vivid for her third-grade students. Notice how her students readily suggest classroom rules, consequences, and rewards. In fact, Garnetta needs to do little prompting during the discussion. Her students' responses reflect their experiences at McKinley, where teachers have been taught *Assertive Discipline,* a program developed by Lee and Marlene Canter (Canter & Canter, 1992). Assertive Discipline emphasizes the right of teachers to determine and insist upon appropriate behavior from students; it distinguishes teachers who interact with students in an assertive manner from those who are nonassertive ("wishy-washy") or hostile. In classrooms using Assertive Discipline, it is common to see a set of posted rules, rewards, and penalties.

> GARNETTA: We're going to go on an imaginary trip, on a boat. [She describes what the boat is like.] But a storm comes up and the boat capsizes, and we all go overboard. Luckily, we find a lifeboat. We all get on the little lifeboat, and we get to an island. Things are real nice for a few days, but after a while they get kind of disorganized. [She elaborates on how kids begin to take other kids' clothes, other kids' food, how people do whatever they want to do.] So we have a problem. We're missing something we need to make life on the island better for us all. What are we missing?
>
> STUDENT: Rules.
>
> GARNETTA: Right. We need to make some rules. What would be some good rules for our island?
>
> STUDENT: Don't mug somebody.
>
> STUDENT: Don't snatch somebody's food.

STUDENT: Don't take anybody's clothes.

STUDENT: Don't beat nobody up.

GARNETTA: These are really fine rules for our island . . . But what if somebody didn't follow them, what if someone did something wrong?

STUDENT: Make them do 15 pushups.

GARNETTA: What do we call that?

STUDENT: Consequences.

GARNETTA: Right. What are consequences?

STUDENT: If you break the rules, you gotta pay the price.

GARNETTA: Let's say that everyone did everything just right. What could we do then?

STUDENT: We could get rewards. [Students begin to murmur: Yeah, we could get some treats, some candy, some popcorn parties.]

GARNETTA: Yes, we could have some wonderful treats. Life on the island would be a lot better then. But, you know, we have to leave the island and come home, because school is starting. We build a new boat and we come back to New Brunswick, and we come to school. Now let's think about what we need in our class. How can we make it good in *here*?

STUDENT: We gotta have rules and consequences and rewards here too.

GARNETTA: Okay, you want to suggest a rule?

STUDENT: Stay in your seat. [Garnetta writes what students say on the board.]

STUDENT: Raise your hand to be recognized.

GARNETTA: Excellent rule.

STUDENT: Think before you do something.

GARNETTA: Oh, I like that one. Yes I do.

STUDENT: Don't play around. No horseplay.

STUDENT: No fighting.

GARNETTA: Definitely. That's certainly a rule we want to have.

STUDENT: Don't run in the classroom.

STUDENT: Don't chew gum.

STUDENT: Don't talk when the teacher's talking.

GARNETTA: Well, what if *you're* talking or giving a report?

STUDENT: Listen to *whoever's* talking.

GARNETTA: Oh, I like that, because when you listen quietly to someone who's talking, you're showing what?

STUDENT: Respect. Show respect for other people.

GARNETTA: Okay, I'm going to add those rules: "Be respectful" and "Don't talk while others are talking or giving reports." Okay, now let's think of consequences. If you break the rules, what could we do?

STUDENT: If you be bad, the teacher can call your parents and talk to them and talk to the principal.

STUDENT: If we have a party that week, the person can't go, they gotta go to the office.

STUDENT: Stay after school.

GARNETTA: Yes, definitely.

STUDENT: Write your spelling words 300 times each.

STUDENT: No, a thousand times.

GARNETTA: I'm going to just write "do a written assignment" instead. You all come up with these really big punishment assignments, but if I ever did anything like that, you'd just hate it. You know, all of these are pretty severe. What about consequences for something more minor.

STUDENT: No treats.

STUDENT: No special games.

GARNETTA: Okay, that's more balanced. Now let's look at rewards. What kind of rewards can you suggest?

STUDENT: Give the kids something, like a piece of cake or stickers.

GARNETTA: I'm going to write "stickers or other treats." That can include lots of things.

STUDENT: You get to go outside.

GARNETTA: Okay, you could get to go outside to play.

STUDENT: Have a party.

GARNETTA: Oh, yes, we like parties, don't we?

STUDENT: See a movie.

STUDENT: A peanut hunt—we did that last year. [She explains.]

GARNETTA: Gee, that's out of sight. I'll have to find out more about how to do that. Any more suggestions? [Class is quiet.] Okay, well this is a good list, but I'm going to add one more thing to the rewards list: "Send a good note home to parents." I especially like that. That's going to be one of our most important ones. [She and the students discuss why that's a good thing to do.] Okay, on this list we have all the rewards we use in this school. Let's go over these lists real quick and review, and then I'll write them up on posters. We'll be talking some more about these in the days to come. [The class reads the lists out loud with her. A boy wants to add "Don't name call" to the list of rules. Garnetta agrees to add it.]

Later in the day, Garnetta talked with us about her approach to setting rules:

I talk with them a lot about why we need rules. I think they need a very clear structure to follow, especially since some of them come from homes where there's very little structure. The rules need to be clear and they need to understand what happens if you follow the rules and what happens if you don't follow them. You can see that they're very used to talking about rules, consequences, and rewards, because everyone in the school uses the same kind of system. They know what kind of behavior is expected here, and they know what happens if you misbehave. But I don't tie a particular reward or consequence to a particular rule. And what's on the board is not the order of severity. First would be "no treats," then "stay after school," then "do a written assignment" (that's often an essay about what happened or a letter of apology), then "send to office," and last "call parents."

Concluding Comments

Viviana, Garnetta, Barbara, and Ken all have well-defined expectations for student behavior, and they make these expectations absolutely clear. Nonetheless, the four teachers have somewhat different expectations, and they introduce rules and routines in different ways. These differences reflect their beliefs about what works best for their own particular students in their own particular contexts. Viviana prefers to teach her expectations for behavior in context; Garnetta uses a framework of rules, rewards, and consequences; Barbara's norms flow from the basic principle of courtesy; and Ken and his students formulate a bill of rights and a set of laws to protect those rights.

As a beginning teacher, you would be wise to adopt a deliberate, thorough approach to teaching and reviewing rules and routines. Once you've gained experience—and a reputation—you might try a less formal approach. Also keep in mind that rules and routines are not invented in a single year, polished and fully developed. Instead, they will evolve over time, products of your experience and creative efforts.

One final note: A while back, we heard a professor of education recount the story of her daughter's first week of kindergarten (Delpit, 1995). After each of the first four days of school, the mother asked her daughter what she had learned. The child's answers were succinct: On the first day she learned "to sit still"; on the second day she learned "to walk in a straight line"; on the third day she learned "to raise her hand"; and on the fourth day she learned "to be quiet." On the fifth day, the mother decided not to ask any more questions!

Obviously, the teacher in this story did a thorough job of teaching her students how to behave, and it's likely that she had few behavior problems in succeeding weeks. Nonetheless, we find this story somewhat sad and disturbing. Although we have emphasized the importance of establishing behavioral expectations early in the year, rules and routines should not be the *most salient* aspect of schooling for children. As you plan the first few weeks, make sure that you balance the teaching of rules and routines with a variety of learning activities that students will find meaningful, enjoyable, and memorable. We want our students to understand that they will learn more in our classes than simply how to behave.

Summary

This chapter discussed two important functions of classroom norms: (1) to provide a structure and predictability that help children to feel safe and secure; and (2) to reduce the complexity of classroom life, allowing you and your students to concentrate on teaching and learning. We outlined two broad categories of behavioral expectations—*rules for general conduct* and *routines for specific situations*—and emphasized the need to teach these explicitly.

When deciding on rules for general conduct, make sure they are

- Reasonable and necessary.
- Clear and understandable.
- Consistent with instructional goals and with what we know about how people learn.
- Consistent with school rules.

Plan routines for specific situations:

- Class-running routines.
    - Administrative duties.
    - Procedures for student movement.
    - Housekeeping responsibilities.
- Lesson-running routines.
    - Routines governing use and distribution of materials.
    - Routines for paper headings, homework procedures, what to do if you finish early.
- Interaction routines.
    - Routines specifying when talk is permitted and how it is to occur.
    - Routines for students and teachers to use to get each other's attention.

Teach rules explicitly:

- Define terms.
- Discuss rationales.
- Provide examples.

Teach routines carefully:

- Explain.

- Demonstrate.
- Practice.
- Give feedback.
- Reteach.

Remember, developing good rules and routines is only the first step. For rules and routines to be effective, you must actively teach them and then review them on a regular basis. Time spent on rules and routines in the first weeks of school will pay off in increased instructional time throughout the year. Make sure, however, to balance the teaching of rules and routines with learning activities that are meaningful and memorable.

Activities

1. Thinking about rules:

   a. Develop a set of rules for your classroom. About five rules should be sufficient. For each rule, think of ways to make the rules more meaningful (e.g., modeling expected behaviors, providing examples, discussing hypothetical scenarios).

   b. Obtain a copy of the school handbook, or talk to the principal or another teacher, to determine the school rules. Check your rules against the school rules to ensure that there is no conflict.

   c. Think about which rules are most important to you and why.

2. Thinking about routines:

   a. Table 4-2 is a list of areas for which you will need specific behavioral routines. Use this list to help you think through the ways you expect your students to behave.

   b. Not all of the routines you thought about in Activity 2-a can be taught that first day. You need to decide on priorities and teach routines when it is most appropriate (and most likely to be remembered). Decide which ones are necessary for the first day.

3. If you are teaching or student teaching, keep a reflective journal on developing and teaching rules and routines. Using the routines listed in Table 4-2, note which routines cause the most problems, the nature of the problems, and how you might respond to those problems. Also note which routines work particularly well.

4. You may decide, as Ken has, that developing a Bill of Rights is the strategy that best suits you and your students. During the brainstorming session, you may be

confronted with some unexpected suggestions from your students. This can be problematic: On the one hand, you don't want to squelch student initiative by vetoing too many of their ideas; on the other hand, you are the adult in charge and know what you and the school can tolerate.

A little practice on what to say to "unusual" ideas might help. Listed below are some student suggestions. What would be your response? Is there a way to incorporate or modify a suggestion to make it workable for you? Is there a way to say no in a manner that makes sense to the student? Give it a try!

a. We should be able to walk around the classroom without our shoes on.

b. We deserve stickers for bringing in our homework every day.

c. We should be able to bring toys to school.

d. We should have a joke-telling time every day before lunch.

e. We should be able to select one day a week when we don't have to do homework.

f. We should be able to write notes to each other.

g. We should be able to call you by your first name.

h. We should be able to lie down on the floor to do our work.

We posed the first situation to our group of teachers and asked their opinions, first privately and then as a group. These are their thoughts:

VIVIANA: I would tell them that it would be all right to take off their shoes as long as they wouldn't play with them and they could pay attention to what is going on in class. I, too, take off my shoes!

GARNETTA: I would say, fine, but what would happen if you stepped on a staple. You know how the carpet seems to collect staples. I would see what their solutions would be. I know there are days when my feet have had enough and I take off my shoes.

KEN: That's fine. It sounds sort of comfortable. But I'd ask them, "Are there any problems with this idea?" Someone might say, "Yeah, it will smell," or "We might trip over our shoes," or "You could step on a tack," or "You could stub your toe." I would then say, "Okay, how can we try to make sure these things don't happen?" And it would go on from there.

BARBARA: I originally wrote down OK as long as we were careful, but then I changed my mind. I would tell them that I wish we could take off our shoes, but if a fire drill happened no shoes could be a safety hazard. It wouldn't be safe to leave the building with no shoes on.

When the teachers came together, Barbara's thought about the fire drill shed some new light on the situation. Ken quickly agreed with Barbara and brought up the point that parents would be irate if they knew their children went outside without shoes in the winter. He also added that there was broken glass on the blacktop and the children could get cut. He envisioned law suits brought against him and the school.

Viviana and Garnetta, however, both still felt that taking shoes off was OK in their settings. Viviana felt that perhaps a fire drill occurring during this time was more like real life: "Do you keep your shoes on all the time at home, just in case a fire breaks out? No, you exit the house the way you are dressed or undressed, whichever the case may be. I want my children to experience life and feel like the classroom is their home."

Garnetta was also unwilling to sacrifice the comfort of those special times when children can unwind and cuddle up to a good book or work in a group on the carpet. "My school yard is well kept and free of any glass," she told us. "It would be OK in an emergency to take my children outside without their shoes."

This exercise clearly demonstrates that responses vary according to personal preference, district practices, expected parent response, and school environment. Once your students arrive at a list of rights, it's a good idea to share the list with some of your colleagues and get their input. They may come up with a "red flag" that you hadn't thought of. The children will understand the legitimate reasons for editing their original list as long as you provide an explanation.

For Further Reading

Evertson, C. M. (1994). Classroom rules and routines. *International Encyclopedia of Education* (2nd ed.). Oxford: Pergamon Press.

Meier, D. R. (1997). *Learning in small moments: Life in an urban classroom.* New York: Teachers College Press.

References

Canter, L., & Canter, M. (1992). *Assertive discipline: Positive behavior management for today's classroom.* Santa Monica, CA: Lee Canter & Associates.

Delpit, L. (May 1995). Informal comments at a conference celebrating the retirement of Courtney Cazden from Harvard Graduate School of Education, Cambridge, MA.

Emmer, E. T., Evertson, C. M., & Anderson, L. M. (1980). Effective classroom management at the beginning of the school year. *The Elementary School Journal, 80*(5), 219–231.

Gumperz, J. J. (1981). Conversational inference and classroom learning. In J. Green & C. Wallat (Eds.), *Ethnography and language in educational settings.* Norwood, NJ: Ablex.

Kounin, J. S. (1970). Discipline and group management in classrooms. New York: Holt, Rinehart and Winston.

Leinhardt, G., Weidman, C., & Hammond, K. M. (1987). Introduction and integration of classroom routines by expert teachers. *Curriculum Inquiry, 17*(2), 135–175.

Meier, D. R. (1997). *Learning in small moments: Life in an urban classroom.* New York: Teachers College Press.

Rosenshine, B. (1980). How time is spent in elementary classrooms. In C. Denham & A. Lieberman (Eds.), *Time to learn.* Washington, DC: U.S. Department of Education.

Shuy, R. (1988). Identifying dimensions of classroom language. In J. L. Green & J. O. Harker (Eds.), *Multiple perspective analyses of classroom discourse.* Norwood, NJ: Ablex.

Skinner, E. A., & Belmont, M. J. (1993). Motivation in the classroom: Reciprocal effects of teacher behavior and student engagement across the school year. *Journal of Educational Psychology, 85*(4), 571–581.

Solomon, D., Watson, M. S., Delucchi, K. L., Schaps, E., & Battistich, V. (1988). Enhancing children's prosocial behavior in the classroom. *American Educational Research Journal, 25*(4), 527–554.

Webb, N. M. (1985). Student interaction and learning in small groups: A research summary. In R. E. Slavin, S. Sharan, S. Kagan, R. Hertz-Lazarowitz, C. Webb, & R. Schmuck (Eds.), *Learning to cooperate, cooperating to learn.* New York: Plenum.

Wertsch, J. V. (1985). *Vygotsky & the Social Formation of Mind.* Cambridge, MA: Harvard University Press.

Chapter Five

Creating Safer, More Caring Classrooms

Ways of Showing Care and Respect

Building Caring Relationships among Students

Concluding Comments

Summary

Some years ago, we supervised a student teacher named Mollie, who had been placed in a fourth-grade classroom. One of us had taught Mollie in a course on campus and had some concerns about her organizational ability. Nevertheless, we weren't prepared for what occurred during the first visit to her classroom. Mollie was teaching a lesson on quotation marks. Although it wasn't exactly captivating, it wasn't awful. But her stu-

dents' behavior *was.* They chatted, rummaged through their desks, and completely ignored the lesson. Furthermore, throughout the period, a steady stream of students walked
up to Mollie, asked to go to the restroom, and left the room. We watched in disbelief as
a student left about every three minutes; at one point, five or six students were out at the
same time. Yet Mollie never asked students to wait until she had finished teaching or until the previous person had returned.

When the period was over, and we met with Mollie to discuss the lesson, we asked
her to talk about the students' behavior. We wondered how she interpreted the students'
lack of interest in her lesson and their obvious desire to leave the room. We also wanted
to know why she had never said "no" when a student asked to leave the room. We remember her answer clearly:

> *I want to show the children that I care about them. I don't want to rule this
> classroom like a dictator. If I say no when someone asks to go to the
> bathroom, that would be showing them that I don't respect them.*

Mollie never did create the atmosphere of mutual respect she desired; in fact, she
never completed student teaching. Her commitment "to care"—which she defined as
"never say no"—led to a situation so chaotic and so confused that no learning, teaching,
or caring was possible.

Over the years, we have thought a lot about Mollie, particularly her definition of caring. And we've heard echoes of Mollie's thinking in other prospective teachers with
whom we've worked. Like Mollie, these teacher education students believe that good
teachers have to be caring teachers. They also believe they have the capacity to care
deeply and to create strong bonds with students. They imagine themselves nurturing students' self-esteem, rejoicing in their successes, and watching over their well-being. They
envision classrooms characterized by warmth, affection, and mutual respect.

And then these prospective teachers begin student teaching. Over the weeks, the talk
about caring begins to fade away, replaced by talk of control. Talk of empathy and compassion becomes overshadowed by talk of discipline and detention. Students lament the
fact that they were "too nice" at the beginning and conclude that they should have been
"meaner." Some even seem to believe that caring and order are mutually exclusive.

The tension between wanting to care and needing to achieve order is not uncommon among novice teachers (McLaughlin, 1991; Weinstein, 1998). But caring and order are not irreconcilable goals. Indeed, the two go hand in hand. *When classrooms are
orderly, organized environments, caring relationships can flourish.* With clear rules
and routines, there is less likelihood of confusion, misunderstanding, and inconsistency—and more likelihood that teachers and students can engage in warm, relaxed
interactions.

At the same time, *one of the ways teachers create an orderly, productive environment is through acts of caring.* As the elementary students of our four teachers made
clear when we spoke with them about classroom management (see Chapter 2), *students
are more likely to cooperate with teachers who are caring and respectful.* Research confirms this contention: A comprehensive review of the literature on students' need for

belongingness in school (Osterman, 2000) indicates that when children feel supported, they are more inclined to accept the authority of others and to regulate their own behavior consistent with classroom norms.

But gaining cooperation is certainly not the only reason for developing respectful, supportive relationships with students. If we want children to be seriously engaged in learning, to share their thoughts and feelings, to take risks, and to develop a sense of social responsibility, then we need to organize classrooms so that students feel safe and cared for—emotionally, intellectually, and physically. If we want students to feel a sense of connectedness and trust, then we must work to create classroom communities where students know that they are needed, valued members of the group (Roeser, Eccles, & Sameroff, 2000; Sapon-Shevin, 1999). If we want students to accept and appreciate diversity—ethnic, racial, gender, class, ability/disability—we must model that behavior.

This chapter begins by considering what it really means to show caring and respect for students. We then turn to relationships among students themselves and discuss strategies for creating a "caring community of learners" (Battistich, Watson, Solomon, Lewis, & Schaps, 1999) in which students feel respected, trusted, and supported by one another. As you read, keep in mind the characteristics of classroom groups that were discussed in Chapter 1. Recall that, unlike most other social groups, students do not come together voluntarily. They are a captive audience, often required to work on tasks they have not selected and in which they may have little interest. Remember, too, that classroom groups are formed somewhat arbitrarily; students do not usually choose their peers *or* their teachers, yet they are expected to cooperate with both. Recalling these special characteristics makes it easier to see why teachers must work to create cohesion, cooperation, and a sense of community. (Figure 5-1 illustrates the difficulty Calvin's teacher has in gaining his cooperation.)

Calvin and Hobbes   by Bill Watterson

FIGURE 5-1. Calvin's teacher has difficulty gaining his cooperation. (Calvin and Hobbes © *Watterson. Dist. by Universal Press Syndicate. Reprinted with permission. All rights reserved.*)

Ways of Showing Care and Respect

Be Welcoming

One of the simplest ways to be welcoming is to smile. An old Chinese proverb tells us that "a man without a smiling face must not open a shop" (Charles, 2000, p. 39). Although the proverb was written long ago (note the use of gendered language!), the sentiment is still applicable—and as relevant to teachers as to shopkeepers.

In addition to smiling, you can welcome students by standing at the classroom door and greeting students at the beginning of the day. This not only ensures that students enter the room in an orderly fashion, it also gives you an opportunity to say hello, comment on a new book bag, and ask how things are going. If you have students who are not native English speakers, learn a few phrases in their native languages. It can mean a lot to students if you can welcome them to your class each day with a few words from their homeland: "*Ka hue?*" ("What's happening?" in Fijian); "*Apa khabar?*" ("How are you?" in Malaysian); "*¿Que tal?*" ("How goes it?" in Spanish) (Kottler, 1994). Ken tells about a girl in his class who had recently come from Mexico and was feeling unhappy and uneasy in her new setting:

> *One day she came in, and I said, "Buenas dias," and she got this huge grin on her face. When I saw her reaction, I tried to learn some common Spanish phrases. Whenever I'd use them—in my awful accent—she'd smile and correct me. It was really something; it changed the whole nature of our relationship.*

At the beginning of the school year, learn students' names (and any preferred nicknames) as quickly as possible. You also need to learn the correct pronunciation, especially for names that are unfamiliar. In the classes of our four teachers, for example, there are children whose names can be a challenge: Isatu ("eye-sa-too"); Nanatsu; Iaesi ("ee-si"); Wei Hou ("wee-how"); Hiji ("Hai-jai"); Yevgenyi; Zureyma; Daniel ("Donny-el"); Aminatu; Ayesha and Aisha (pronounced identically). In order to convey your respect for your students, it's important to spend time learning how they pronounce and spell their names.

Be Sensitive to Children's Concerns

In essence, this means thinking about classroom events and activities from a student's point of view. Sitting next to someone you dislike, for example, can make life in school very unpleasant. For this reason, Barbara allows students to have input whenever she changes the seating:

> *I ask students to write down a list of three students they'd like to sit next to. I tell them that I'll do my best to see that they sit next to one of their*

choices, but I explain that I'm counting on them to make wise choices—to choose someone who can act as a partner, someone they can sit next to without causing a commotion or interfering with others. . . . When I decide on the seating, I try to honor their requests, but I can also separate overly social kids or kids who just don't get along. In this way, I can prevent problems from occurring. The kids really like this system. They realize I'm trying to be considerate of their feelings, but I'm also protecting their opportunity to learn.

Another way of showing sensitivity to students' concerns is by remembering the very public nature of classrooms (described in Chapter 1) and keeping grades as private as possible. Most students don't want their peers to know if they've gotten a poor grade, and public announcements are less likely to increase motivation than to generate resentment. Even if you announce only the As, you can embarrass students. A fifth-grader we know was mortified when her teacher held her test up in front of the whole class and announced that "Laura was obviously the only one who studied!" And what does an announcement like that convey to the student who normally receives Ds, but studied really hard and earned a C?

Sensitivity also means discussing inappropriate behavior quietly and privately. Public reprimands are humiliating—and humiliation will surely poison your relationship with students. In the following vignette, Garnetta deals with an overly exuberant child in a sensitive manner:

Garnetta's class is learning to count money. Garnetta tells each table group to work together to draw as many combinations of $.35 as possible, using dimes, quarters, and pennies. The students are very excited. Leon seems about to burst. Standing up, he waves his arms and yells, "We got six [combinations]!" Then, "We got seven!" Garnetta walks over to him, bends down low, and speaks softly. Leon sits down and continues working with his group; he is still engaged and excited, but he no longer yells. It appears that other students have paid scant attention to the interaction.

Sensitive teachers also understand that students' energy levels ebb and flow, and dramatic mood changes from day to day are not uncommon. Halloween, Valentine's Day, food fights, and special events can all affect "student weather" (Gordon, 1997, p. 58)—as can disputes on the playground:

Barbara stands by the door waiting to greet her children after recess. It's clear as they enter the classroom that they're angry and upset. The story quickly comes out: A new kid from a higher grade caused an unbelievable amount of conflict and fighting out on the playground. So many kids were sent to the principal that he had to meet with them in the auditorium! Unfortunately, Barbara doesn't have a chance to discuss the situation with her class because they have to change rooms for science and social studies. She tells them that they'll talk the next day. Later, she describes what happened: "The delay worked out well, actually, because it allowed them to calm down a little before we talked. Because of the schedule, it worked out that the only time we could talk was during language arts period—and would you believe it—I was being observed by the principal. I began by reading them 'All I Really Need to Know I Learned in Kinder-garten.' I love that poem—especially the part about a snack and a nap every afternoon. We talked about what stood out for them as they heard it. Somebody picked up on the part about how wars happen because people butt in. I asked, 'Is that what happened yesterday?' Then it all began to pour out . . . I wasn't reprimanding or laying blame; I just tried to help them find alternative ways of dealing with the problems they were encountering. . . . Kids need a safe place to discuss heated, emotionally charged issues, and I try to create that kind of classroom."

Be Fair

It seems obvious that caring teachers must strive for fairness. But it's not always so simple. Indeed, teachers who are trying to treat students well often experience a tension between two moral orientations. Being fair generally involves "making judgments of students' conduct and academic performances without prejudice or partiality" (Katz, 1999, p. 61). In terms of classroom management, this translates into ensuring that rules apply to everyone, no matter what. On the other hand, being fair can also imply a recognition that people may need different, personalized treatment, and being caring certainly seems to demand that we acknowledge students' individuality. From this perspective, treating everyone the same is *unfair.* So what is a teacher to do?

This dilemma is especially salient for Barbara, since her class includes Stuart, a child with autism, and Mark, a child who has been classified as emotionally disturbed. Barbara is well aware of the fact that she needs to make special accommodations for both Stuart and Mark, but she wanted to make sure that their peers understood the reasons for the differential treatment. To provide an opportunity for the nondisabled children to discuss what it was like to be in class with Stuart and Mark, Barbara led "share circles" on a day when the two boys were not present. Discussion revealed that students were very understanding and tolerant of Stuart. When he walked around the room at will, or made noises during silent reading time, students attributed his behavior to his autism. In contrast, they considered Mark to be "sort of normal" and believed that he should be able to control his behavior. This made his occasional refusals to work or his aggressive outbursts confusing, and students expressed resentment about the special privileges Mark sometimes received (e.g., getting to use the computer while they were doing class work). Learning this, Barbara has worked hard to explain how "different students have different needs, so always treating everybody the same is not fair." She has also explained about "visible" and "invisible" disabilities and has emphasized the fact that invisible disabilities require students to be more sensitive and understanding. Her efforts appear to have paid off: Subsequent discussions with students indicated increased acceptance of Mark's outbursts and his special treatment.

Research confirms the fact that students generally appreciate the need for accommodations. Fulk and Smith (1995) explored the perceptions of 98 students in grades 1–6 regarding the acceptability of teachers' differentiating academic work and rules and rewards to meet the diverse needs of students with learning and behavior problems. Students were individually interviewed and asked two "yes" or "no" questions regarding management: "Pretend there is a student in your room who gets in trouble a lot for not following school rules. Would it be OK with you if this student got special rewards for behaving better that other students did not get?" "Would it be OK with you if the teacher gave this student extra chances or different rules while he or she learned to behave better?" Overall, most students favored special rewards (72 percent) and extra chances or different rules (67 percent); only first-graders, with a 53 percent "no" response, were split on the acceptability of differential treatment. Interestingly, students explained their responses not only in terms of the effect on students with problem behavior ("Because he needs more help with his behavior than other kids. He may someday get to be like us if he works hard and gets special things"), they also spoke about the effect of inappropriate behavior on the class as a whole ("His bad behavior affects others, so special rewards would be better for everyone"). Fulk and Smith conclude, "Teachers may be more concerned about equal treatment of students than students are" (p. 416). (We return to this topic in Chapter 12, when we discuss "the issue of consistency.")

Be a Real Person (Not Just a Teacher)

Beginning teachers often puzzle over the extent to which they should share information about their personal lives. We remember having teachers who refused to reveal their first names—as if that would somehow blur the boundary between teacher and student and diminish their authority. On the other hand, there are teachers who are extremely open. In an article on "Building Community from Chaos" (1994), Linda Christensen, a high school English teacher in Portland, Oregon, writes:

> *Students have told me that my willingness to share stories about my life— my father's alcoholism, my family's lack of education, my poor test scores, and many others, opened the way for them to tell their stories. . . . And through their sharing, they make openings to each other. Sometimes a small break. A crack. A passage from one world to the other. And these openings allow the class to become a community. (p. 55)*

As a new teacher, it's probably wise to find a happy medium between these two extremes and to discuss limited aspects of your out-of-school life, past and present (Jones & Jones, 1998). Students love to hear about your trips and vacations, cultural and athletic activities, hobbies, pets, and school experiences. As you gain experience and confidence, you can decide if you want to share more information about your personal life. But Garnetta suggests that you think about the *reason* for disclosing personal stories:

Why do you want to share information? Is it to get students' attention? to enhance a lesson? to model how to share during sharing time? to build a relationship with the children? There needs to be a purpose. Don't tell about your life just to tell.

Viviana thinks it's also important to consider the *audience* you are addressing: "Things that a teacher would share with fifth-graders might not be appropriate for me to share with my first-graders."

Another way of showing your humanity is to admit when you don't know something. Teachers sometimes feel that they have to be the "sage on the stage," but it can be beneficial for students to see that even "experts" don't know all the answers all the time. The best way to encourage students to take risks in the process of learning is to take risks yourself.

It's also important to apologize if you make a mistake. The following excerpt comes from a student teacher in middle school:

The class was working productively [on their creative writing assignments and posters for Grandparents' Day] when I heard one student, Gary, [who was] sitting on the floor by David's desk say to David, "Please stop kicking me." I heard David reply back, "I'm not kicking you." I watched the two of them for the next few minutes and observed their behavior. Gary continued drawing on the poster on the floor, while David sat at his desk writing. Then I saw it, as David swung his leg repetitively forward, kicking Gary several times in the back. . . . I rose to tell David that I needed to speak to him privately, took him into the farthest corner of the room, and said softly to him, "You need to stop doing that immediately." He said, "I really didn't know I was doing that!" Then I said, "I think you do and I'd like you to stop." Shortly after that, the class ended . . . and the students left. [Later] I had the chance to speak with another teacher about what happened. She had David in previous years, so I felt she could give me accurate feedback. "It's possible he's telling you the truth," she said. "He does have Tourettes Syndrome and occasionally he can have involuntary body movements."

I had been aware of David's Tourettes . . . having looked at his file. But I only noticed that he had trouble with occasional tics and sudden spoken outbursts. I went to find him in his next class. He came out of the class and I asked him again, "Did you mean to kick Gary the way you did?" He immediately said no, and meeting my glance, said, "I really did not mean to do that." At that point I realized I might have made a mistake so I explained to him that I had thought it had been intentional, and that I might have been wrong in thinking that way. Then I said that I would like for us to speak more often and keep open communication so that we can understand each other better. He agreed to do this, and then returned to class.

One final comment about being a "real person": We personally find it grating when teachers refer to themselves in the third person rather than in the first person (e.g., when Mrs. Smith says, "Mrs. Smith wants you to line up quietly" rather than "I would like you to line up quietly"). Real people don't speak that way.

Promote Autonomy by Sharing Responsibility

Providing opportunities for students to participate actively in classroom decision making, planning, and goal setting contributes to their feelings of being connected and supported (Osterman, 2000). We already touched on this topic in the last chapter, when we discussed the idea of allowing students to participate in rule setting. But shared decision making doesn't end on the first day of school; it is an ongoing process. For example, Ken sometimes allows students to select the novels they will read in small groups:

I brought in about a dozen sets of novels and had the kids examine them when they had some free time. They know there have to be three or four reading groups. They talked with one another about the books. I'd hear them say, "This looks good. Would you want to read this with me?" You know, it's funny. Teachers say, "You can't do this. Kids will just pick the books their friends read." I say, "That's right. And that's OK. In fact, that's exactly what adults do." When a friend says a book is good, that's when you want to read it. Kids are no different.

Anyway, after everyone had a chance to peruse the books, we took about 30 or 40 minutes one day to set up the groups. I told the kids, "Some people have picked this book, and this one. No one picked that one." Of course, we ended up with one group of only four and one group of nine, but generally, the kids were really cooperative. For example, one boy said, "I really wanted to read Treasure Island, *but no one else picked it, so I'll take* Dies Drear *instead." I also tried to steer the not-so-good readers to fairly straightforward books, but in some cases, I decided to let them try a more challenging book.*

After Ken's students read a chapter in their novels, they construct their own questions about the material and then answer them. Ken teaches his students to use Bloom's taxonomy of cognitive objectives (knowledge, comprehension, application, analysis, synthesis, and evaluation) and has them select the level at which they will construct their questions.

Ken also allows his class to have input into the daily schedule. He'll tell them, "It's 1:45 and we have three things to do. What order should we do them in?" Sometimes, students are allowed to select the two assignments they will do in class and the one they will bring home for homework.

Like Ken, Barbara tries to build choice into the curriculum. During one visit late in the school year, we watched Barbara introduce a new project—writing a newspaper based on *Tuck Everlasting,* the novel they had just finished reading. In the following vignette, Barbara not only allows individuals to select the topic on which to write, but also to decide whether they will work alone or in groups.

> BARBARA: Should we work in groups or not? [Students raise their hands in response to her question.] Edward?
>
> EDWARD: I personally don't want to work in groups. I have an idea about what I want to do and how I want to do it, and it would be better if I could work alone.
>
> BARBARA: Are there people who feel differently? How do you feel, James?
>
> JAMES: I'd like to work in pairs.
>
> BARBARA: Why?
>
> JAMES: Because it's easier. You get more work done quickly.
>
> EDWARD: I don't mind pairs either, just not a large group.
>
> ISATU: I go to enrichment, and it would help if I had a partner so I'd know what to do when I come back.
>
> BARBARA: That's a good point. Jill?
>
> JILL: Sometimes I prefer to work alone because I have serious thinking to do.
>
> BARBARA: OK, here's what we're going to do. You changed how I was thinking. I was thinking of having you work in threes, but you convinced me that pairs and singles would be good. . . . You get yourselves organized, and then come over to the round table and tell me what you want to write about and if you're single or pairs.

Although it is easier to share decision making with students in higher grades, Viviana and Garnetta also try to create opportunities for students to exercise independent judgment. For example, instead of assigning classroom jobs, Garnetta puts the list on the board and allows children to choose the two that they would like to do. She makes an effort to give students their first choice. When Viviana's first-graders work on spelling words, they have the option of using the spelling word in a sentence, drawing and labeling a picture showing the word, or incorporating the word in a sentence that describes a magazine picture.

Sharing decision making can be difficult for teachers. When you're feeling pressured to "cover the curriculum" and to maximize learning time, it's easier to make the decisions by yourself. Involving students can be "messy" and time-consuming, and allowing students to make decisions about their own behavior means that they'll sometimes make the wrong decisions. Nonetheless, a "short-term investment of time" can lead to "a long-term gain in decision-making ability and self-esteem" (Dowd, 1997).

Reduce the Use of Extrinsic Control

Another way of increasing students' experience of autonomy is to decrease the use of extrinsic rewards and punishments. None of us like to feel controlled or manipulated, and we generally experience external regulation as alienating (Ryan & Deci, 2000). Indeed, Kim, Solomon, and Roberts (1995) found a *negative* relationship between the use of external control and student engagement; this is critical, since student engagement is, in turn, significantly related to sense of community. What seems clear is that the more students feel externally regulated, the less they show interest and effort and the more they tend to disown responsibility for negative outcomes (Ryan & Connell, 1989). This hardly makes for a caring community.

Instead of imposing lots of rewards and penalties, our four teachers try to help students think about and understand the importance of making the classroom a good place to be. When problems occur, they typically take a "teaching" or problem-solving approach, rather than an approach based on punishment. When Viviana's children become distracted by the rubbery spider rings that are popular at Halloween time, Viviana doesn't direct students to put them away. Instead she says, "If you can pay attention and wear the ring, fine. If you think you'll have trouble, then take it off and put it in the desk."

Similarly, Ken calls class meetings to discuss persistent behavioral problems instead of simply handing out punishments:

Every day, the class would come back from playing outside and complain about kids being too aggressive—pushing, grabbing the ball, fighting. Finally, we had a class meeting. I said to them, "According to the Bill of Rights, everyone in this class has the right to go outside almost every day. [See Chapter 4.] But everyone also has the right to be treated nicely and to not be disturbed. So what are we going to do?"

It would have been a lot easier to just impose the consequences by myself, without deliberation. Meeting with students to discuss what to do is really time consuming. But I'm convinced that this is the way kids develop responsibility for their own behavior. And when I do bench someone, it's not because I'm mean or nasty; it's because that's what the class decided.

You really have to do this a lot in September and October. Later on everyone's too hysterical about standardized tests. But no one objects if you take a lot of time at the beginning of the school year; that's when you're supposed to be setting the tone. And in the long run, student decisions save time. There is less misbehavior when students help to decide.

Be Inclusive

In recent years, "inclusive education" has been used to refer to the practice of placing students with disabilities in general education classrooms, rather than segregating them in special classrooms or schools. But the term can also be used more broadly, to describe classes in which differences related not only to disability, but also to race, class, ethnicity, gender, cultural and linguistic background, religion, and sexual orientation are acknowledged, understood, and respected. As Mara Sapon-Shevin (1999) asserts:

The goal of having an inclusive classroom is not to homogenize those differences, pretending that they are not there or do not have an impact on students or their lives. The goal is to acknowledge those differences and create a classroom community that works with those differences (and sometimes around those differences) so that every student can feel a sense of connection and belonging. (pp. 63–64)

This, of course, is easier said than done. Before we can "create a classroom community that works with differences," we need to recognize that we are often afraid and suspicious of those differences. Sometimes, we deny even *seeing* differences. It is not uncommon, for example, for our European-American teacher education students to pride themselves on being color-blind, assuming that "to be color-blind is to be fair, impartial, and objective" (Nieto, 1996). Yet, to deny cultural or racial differences is to deny an essential aspect of people's identity—and recognizing those differences does not make us racist.

In addition to *acknowledging* differences, creating inclusive classrooms means learning about disabilities, or cultures, or races, or religions that we've never before encountered. For example, you can't acknowledge, understand, and respect behaviors that have cultural origins if you have no idea that the behaviors are rooted in culture. Teachers may be shocked when Southeast Asian students smile while being scolded if they are unaware that the smiles are meant not as disrespect, but as an admission of culpability and an effort to show that there is no grudge (Trueba, Cheng, & Ima, 1993). Similarly, teachers who are not cognizant of the fact that Pacific Islanders value interpersonal harmony and the well-being of the group may conclude that these students are lazy when they are reluctant to participate in competitive activities (Sileo & Prater, 1998). Teachers who are unaware that the culture of most American Indians tends to emphasize deliberate thought may become impatient when those students take longer to respond to questions (Nieto, 1996).

It's unrealistic to expect beginning teachers (or even experienced ones!) to be familiar with all of the cultures that might be represented in their extremely diverse classrooms. Certainly, developing this kind of "cultural literacy" takes time and effort. Some specific suggestions are listed in Table 5-1.

Search for Students' Strengths

In *Teaching to Change the World* (1999), Jeannie Oakes and Martin Lipton argue that when teachers and students have a caring relationship, they work together to find competence: "The student's search is his own discovery of what he knows and how he knows it. The teacher's search—an act of care and respect—is also discovering what the student knows and how he knows it" (p. 252).

Ken feels strongly about the importance of searching for students' strengths. During one meeting, he put it this way:

It's really important to build a schedule and design activities that will lead to success, not just reaffirm that the kid fails a lot. Teachers have got to work with children's strengths and interests, not just their weaknesses. A lot of the time, teachers say, "These are the areas where the child has problems, so I've got to spend all the time on remediating these." But skills are all interdependent; they can be taught in the context of activities that kids find

TABLE 5-1. Developing Cultural Literacy

1. **Explore students' family backgrounds.** Where did the student come from? Was it a rural or urban setting? Why did the family move? How long has the student been in this country? How many people are in the family? What are the lines of authority? What responsibilities does the student have at home? What are parents' beliefs with respect to involvement in the school and in their child's education? Do they consider teachers to be experts and therefore refrain from expressing differences of opinion? Is learning English considered a high priority?

2. **Explore students' educational background.** If students are new to this country, how much previous schooling have they had? What kinds of instructional strategies are they used to? In their former schools, was there an emphasis on large-group instruction, memorization, and recitation? In students' former schools, what were the expectations for appropriate behavior? Were students expected to be active or passive? independent or dependent? peer oriented or teacher oriented? cooperative or competitive?

3. **Be sensitive to cultural differences and how they may lead to miscommunication.** How do students think about time? Is punctuality expected or is time considered to be flexible? Do students nod their heads to be polite or to indicate understanding? Do students question or obey authority figures? Do students put their needs and desires before those of the group or vice versa? Are expressions of emotion and feelings emphasized or hidden?

4. **Use photographs to communicate without words.** Take pictures of the children engaged in various activities to take home to parents; display photographs around the room; invite students to bring in pictures of themselves and their families; use photographs for get-acquainted activities.

5. **Develop a portfolio for each child.** Make a list of everything the child can do without using language (build, sort, match, categorize, sequence, copy, draw, mimic, make faces, pantomime). Note interactions with other people. Determine which instructional activities the student enjoys the most and which he or she tries to avoid. Think about whether these preferences might reflect cultural values. Find out what activities the child pursues after school. Include photographs of the child and samples of work.

Source: Kottler, 1994; Sileo & Prater, 1998.

interesting and appealing, activities that they can succeed on. Children need to learn hope and success as much as they need to learn academic skills.

Nancy Keller (1994), a middle school science teacher in Vermont, provides an excellent example of building on children's strengths. Keller had been teaching science for three years as a part of a sixth- to eighth-grade team, when a new sixth-grade student arrived who had learning disabilities as well as behavioral and emotional problems. Andy was extremely loud and aggressive, and his verbal and physical threats frequently disrupted class. An emergency meeting of Andy's regular teachers, a special educator, and the special services administrator was held to review the records from Andy's previous school and to consider ways of helping him develop more positive social behaviors.

Keller describes the meeting and its aftermath as follows:

What stands out most for me about the initial IEP meeting was the positive manner and genuine concern that permeated the discussion . . . The problem was defined not in terms of Andy's negative behavior, but in terms of how we could use his strengths to address his needs.

I remember Andy being described as someone with a sense of humor, someone who regularly came to school, someone who liked being given special jobs or chores—someone who wanted to belong. Because Andy possessed these qualities, the problem was defined as finding ways we could build on them to help him become more successful in our classrooms. For example, because Andy liked being helpful, we gave him specific jobs to complete in each class . . . Andy's jobs also provided occasions when we could work on his social skills. . . . I purposely planned tasks he could complete in which he had to use his "quiet voice." These tasks—such as distributing science supplies on lab days—were of genuine assistance. . . [and involved] appropriately asking a classmate what supplies were needed and then handing them out. (pp. 83–84)

Keller goes on to describe the kinds of classroom and peer supports that were put into place for Andy (e.g., having a regular teacher and a special educator team teach; using cooperative groups, peer buddies, and peer tutoring) and the progress he made over the next three years. Andy's time in middle school was "not a progression of one amazing success after another, but rather a series of stops and starts . . . successes and setbacks" (p. 89). Nonetheless, his story is a cogent example of the impact teachers can have when they work together as a team, when they have the support they need, when they are willing to try a variety of instructional formats, and when they focus on what children *can* do, rather than on what they *cannot* do.

Develop Communication Skills

Another way of showing students that you care is by being a good listener. This means being attentive, demonstrating empathy, asking appropriate questions, and helping students solve their own problems. Let's briefly examine each of these.

Attending and Acknowledging

Giving a student your complete, undivided attention is the first and most basic task in being helpful (Kottler & Kottler, 1993). It is rare that individuals are fully attentive to one another. Have you ever tried to talk with someone who was simultaneously organizing papers, posting articles on the bulletin board, or straightening rows of desks? Divided attention like this communicates that the person doesn't really have time for you and is not fully paying attention.

Attending and acknowledging involve both verbal and nonverbal behaviors. Even without saying a word, you can convey that you are totally tuned in by orienting your body toward the student, establishing eye contact, nodding, leaning forward, smiling, or frowning. In addition, you can use verbal cues. Thomas Gordon (1974) recommends "empathic grunting"—the little "uh-huhs" and phrases (e.g., "Oh," "I see," "Mmmmm") that communicate, "I'm really listening." Sometimes, when a student needs additional encouragement to talk more, you can use an explicit invitation, what Gordon calls a "door opener"— "Tell me more," "Would you like to say more about that?" "Do you want to talk about it?" "Want to go on?"

One of the hardest ideas for teachers to accept is that a person can help another simply by listening. But Kottler and Kottler (1993) remind us that attending can be a powerful helping tool:

> *You would be truly amazed at how healing this simple act can be—giving another person your full attention. Children, in particular, are often so used to being devalued by adults that attending behaviors instantly tell them something is different about this interaction: "Here is a person who seems to care about me and what I have to say." (p. 40)*

Active Listening

Attending and acknowledging communicate that you are totally engaged, but they do not convey if you really *understand.* Active listening takes the interaction one step further by having you reflect back what you think you heard. This feedback allows you to check out whether you are right or wrong. If you're right, the student knows that you have truly understood. If you're off target, the student can correct you, and the communication can continue. Examples of active listening appear in Table 5-2.

If you're new to active listening, you may find it useful to use the phrase, "You feel . . ." when you reflect back what you heard. Sometimes, novices feel stupid, as if they're simply parroting back what the person just said. (In fact, when Carol was first learning to do active listening, a student became really annoyed and demanded to know why she kept repeating what he had said!) As you gain more skill, however, you are able to *paraphrase* what you hear, and the interaction becomes far more subtle.

Keep in mind that active listening is not easy. Student teachers with whom we work often want to reject it out of hand; they find it unnatural and awkward, and they would much prefer to give advice, not simply communicate that they understand. But knowing that someone really understands can be profoundly important, especially to children who often feel misunderstood. In addition, active listening provides an opportunity for students to express their feelings and to clarify their problems. It can also help to defuse strong feelings without taking the responsibility away from the student for solving the problem.

Questioning

When people tell us their problems, we often want to ask them questions in order to find out more information. Kottler and Kottler (1993) caution teachers to be careful about this practice:

> *The problem with questions, as natural as they may come to mind, is that they often put the child in a "one down" position in which you are the interrogator and expert problem solver. "Tell me what the situation is and I will fix it." For that reason, questions are used only when you can't get the student to reveal information in other ways. (p. 42)*

If you must ask questions, they should be open ended—requiring more than a one-word response. Like active listening, open-ended questions invite further exploration

TABLE 5-2. Examples of Active Listening

STUDENT:	Wait till my mom sees this test grade. She's gonna flip out.
TEACHER:	You think she'll be really mad at you?
STUDENT:	Yeah, she expects me to come home with all As.
TEACHER:	Sounds like you're feeling really pressured.
STUDENT:	Well, I am. You'd think that getting a B was like failing. My mom just doesn't understand how hard this is for me.
TEACHER:	So you think a B is an OK grade because this is really tough for you, but she thinks that you can do better.
STUDENT:	Yeah, she has this thing that if I come home with a B I'm just not working.
TEACHER:	That's rough. I can see how that would make you feel like she doesn't appreciate the efforts you're making.
STUDENT:	I can't believe I have to be home at 9.30! It's crazy! All my friends have a later curfew—
TEACHER:	So you think your parents are a lot stricter than the other kids' parents.
STUDENT:	Well, they are! I mean, I know it's 'cause they care about me, but it's really a pain to have to be home earlier than everyone else. I feel like a dork. And besides, I think I'm responsible enough to have a later curfew.
TEACHER:	So you're not just embarrassed, you're mad because they don't realize how responsible you are.
STUDENT:	All along she's been telling me how we'll be best friends forever, and then she goes and gets a best friend charm with Mira.
TEACHER:	When something like that happens, you feel really abandoned.
STUDENT:	I don't want to go to School-Base [for mental health counseling]. Only crazy kids go to School-Base!
TEACHER:	Going to School-Base is kind of embarrassing . . .
STUDENT:	Yeah. My friends are gonna give me a really hard time.
TEACHER:	You think they're going to say you're crazy.
STUDENT:	Yeah. I wanna go, but I don't want people to make fun of me.
TEACHER:	I can understand that. It's really rough when people make fun of you.
STUDENT:	I had the worst nightmare last night! I mean, I know it was just a dream, but I just can't get it out of my head. This bloody guy with a knife was chasing me down this alley, and I couldn't get away.
TEACHER:	Nightmares can be so scary.
STUDENT:	Yeah, and I know it's babyish, but I just can't shake the feeling.
TEACHER:	Sometimes a bad feeling from a nightmare stays with you a long time . . .

and communication, whereas close-ended questions cut off communication. Compare these questions:

What are you feeling right now? versus Are you feeling angry?

What do you want to do? versus Do you want to tell your father?

Kottler and Kottler point out one notable exception to the rule of avoiding questions whenever possible: that is, when it is important to get very specific information in a potentially dangerous situation, such as when a student is discussing suicide. Then it would be appropriate to ask specific questions: Have you actually tried this? Will you promise not to do anything until we can get you some help?

Problem Solving

Instead of trying to solve students' problems, you can guide them through a process that helps them to solve their *own* problems. In problem solving, students define their problem, specify their goals, develop alternative solutions that might be constructive, narrow the choices to those that seem most realistic, and put the plan into action (Kottler & Kottler, 1993).

In the following example, we see how Barbara used this approach to solve a problem her students were experiencing at the end of recess each day. Note how she makes certain that everyone agrees on what the problem is, that she doesn't allow students to evaluate suggestions during the brainstorming phase of the activity, that she herself speaks against suggestions she doesn't like, and that she doesn't have students vote on the solution, but instead works for consensus.

BARBARA: A few weeks ago, you were very upset about what was happening when you came in from the playground at the end of recess. We let it go for a while to see if the problem would go away by itself, but lately people have been telling me that things are still pretty bad out there. [Students begin to murmur in agreement and to comment on what is happening.] Can you tell me exactly what happens?

STUDENT: When the aide blows the whistle to come in, everyone gets in a big clump in the little alleyway by the door and then everybody pushes and shoves, and people start to fight, and then the aides get mad, and people get sent to the office . . .

BARBARA: Wait. [She draws a map of the playground and the school on the board.] Now let's see if I understand. Everyone clumps up right here? OK, so this is the problem. We're all agreed on what it is? [There are signs of agreement.] Now, let's brainstorm some solutions. Remember, when we brainstorm, we let everyone have their say without evaluating. We'll evaluate all the suggestions at the end.

STUDENT: We come in a double door, and the doors are always kept closed until after we're lined up, and everyone gets smushed in so then it's hard to open the doors. If they were left open all the time, we could get in easier. [Barbara writes on board: "#1. Leave doors open all the time."]

BARBARA: Another idea? [She continues to solicit ideas and to write down each suggestion in a numbered list on the board.]

STUDENT: Open the doors right before the whistle is blown.

STUDENT: Have classes go in different doors.

STUDENT: Line up by class in different places, and the quietest two classes go in first, one through each door.

STUDENT: Two classes line up by the fence, and two classes line up by the brick wall.

STUDENT: I agree with that idea . . .

BARBARA: Let's not evaluate now; we're still thinking of solutions.

STUDENT: Get more aides. Right now there are only two.

STUDENT: The classes play until the teachers come and get them.

STUDENT: Have a different whistle signal for each class, one whistle for one class, two for another, etc.

BARBARA: Are there any more ideas? [Suggestions seem to be at an end.] OK, our next job is to quietly read these suggestions and think about them. Take two or three minutes to discuss the suggestions with your table group. . . . [Students discuss the suggestions in their small groups.] OK, what we'll do now is discuss each one and decide what we think about each suggestion. [As students state positive or negative reactions, Barbara puts a plus or a minus sign by each suggestion that is mentioned.]

STUDENT: I like the idea of using more doors because that way kids would be separated and there wouldn't be so much pushing and shoving.

STUDENT: I like the one about more aides. If there were more aides then they could stop kids from pushing.

STUDENT: I don't think that's a good idea because it would cost money and the school doesn't have the money.

BARBARA: I'm going to write a dollar sign next to this one so you can think about the issue of money.

STUDENT: I like the idea of the teachers picking up the classes, but I don't think the teachers would like it.

BARBARA: Let me give you my perspective on that. . . . Even though I adore you, my lunch time is very precious to me and I would not appreciate giving up part of that time every day to come pick you up.

STUDENT: Our table likes the idea of having two classes by the wall and two by the fence.

STUDENT: Our table likes #2, open the doors just before the whistle.

STUDENT: I like the idea of lining up by class in different places. It works in the morning, so it would probably work in the afternoon.

STUDENT: I don't really like the idea of two classes lining up by the wall and two by the fence. Kids would still be too close, and they would still push. It might be better if they were farther apart, like maybe two classes could line up here and two could line up on the other side of the playground.

BARBARA: So you're really saying you like the idea of having classes line up in designated places. [Student agrees.]

STUDENT: Why don't we vote?

BARBARA: I don't want to vote because then there are winners and losers. But let's see if there are some we can eliminate. Let's sift out the ones that we think won't work. For example, I'm telling you that the one about having the teachers pick up the classes won't work because the teachers won't want to give up lunch. Let's look at the suggestions that have no marks next to them and the ones that have minus signs next to them. [She points to each one and asks, "Do you think this would work?" For each, the class says "no," and she erases.] Okay, there are three left. Does anyone have any objection to these three? [One girl has reservations about one and explains why.] Do you think you could live with it? [Girl indicates that she is willing to go along with the class.] Well, I think these three make a good package that we can present to [the principal]. Let's talk tomorrow about how we want to present these ideas.

A Note about Touching

In recent years, the fear of being accused of sexual harassment and physical abuse has made teachers wary of showing students any physical affection. Although our four teachers share this wariness, they do not want to forgo all physical contact. Ken still pats students on the back when he's praising them for particularly fine work. When children reach out to hug Barbara and Viviana, they still hug back. And Garnetta tells us:

> *There was a time when I actually stopped hugging or touching in any way because of the bad publicity, but I just couldn't continue doing that. I felt like I just didn't bond as well with that class. My children are young, and they need love. But you do have to be careful.*

It's important to remember that these teachers have been in their districts for many years and have solid reputations. As a new teacher, you are in a very different situation. Speak with your colleagues about the policy in effect in your school; some schools actually direct teachers to "teach but don't touch." Even if there is no explicit prohibition against touching children, you need to be cautious so that your actions are not misconstrued. For example, when children stay after school, keep the door open or make sure that other students or teachers are around. Give your hugs in front of others. Give "high fives" instead of hugs (Jones & Jones, 1998).

Building Caring Relationships among Students

A great deal has recently been written on ways of fostering supportive, trusting relationships among students. As Sapon-Shevin (1995) reminds us:

> *Communities don't just happen. No teacher, no matter how skilled or well intentioned, can enter a new classroom and announce, "We are a community." Communities are built over time, through shared experience,*

Ken's class begins each day with a "morning meeting."

and by providing multiple opportunities for students to know themselves, know one another, and interact in positive and supportive ways. (p. 111)

It is clear that our four teachers work hard to provide opportunities for students to know one another and to interact. Here are some of their suggestions, along with some from educational writers interested in students' social and emotional learning.

Hold Class Meetings

This year, as a result of having attended the "responsive classroom" institute, Ken decided to begin each day with a "morning meeting" (Kriete, 1999). He and his students sit in a circle on the floor and *greet each other* by name; they may pass a handshake around the circle, give a high-five, or toss a ball to the student they are greeting. *Sharing* comes next; during this phase of the morning meeting, a few students present news they wish to share, and others ask questions and comment. Ken's goal is to make sure that everyone gets to share once during the week, although he admits that this does not always happen. After sharing, the class engages in a *group activity*—a game, song, chant, or poem—designed to build community and create group identity. *Electricity* and *Zoom* are two of his class's favorite games. Finally, during *news and announcements,* Ken and his students discuss what they will be doing during the day. According to Ken, morning meeting has been a tremendous help in creating a sense of caring and belonging.

Nelsen, Lott, and Glenn, developers of *Positive Discipline in the Classroom* (2000), recommend a somewhat different type of class meeting. These educators believe that class meetings not only promote social skills, such as listening, taking turns, and hearing different points of view; they also encourage students and teachers to work together to solve classroom problems. Nelsen, Lott, and Glenn recommend that class meetings

1. Express compliments and appreciation.
2. Follow up on earlier solutions applied to problems.
3. Go through agenda items that students and teachers have written in a special notebook. Discuss ways of solving the problems that are brought up.
   a. Share feelings while others listen.
   b. Discuss without fixing.
   c. Ask for problem solving help.
4. Make future plans for class activities (e.g., field trips, parties, projects).

FIGURE 5-2. Class meeting format
Source: Nelsen, Lott, & Glenn, 2000.

follow a prescribed agenda (shown in Figure 5-2). The goal is to provide a safe time and place for everyone to develop an attitude of caring and concern for others and to learn the skills necessary for cooperation and problem solving.

Model and Recognize Prosocial Behavior

Teachers frequently exhort students to treat one another with respect. Yet exhortation is unlikely to be effective unless teachers themselves are respectful. As Mary Williams (1993) tells us, "Do as I say, not as I do" clearly does not work" (p. 22). Williams was interested in learning how respect was taught and learned by students in middle school classrooms (grades six through eight). She found that respect was best taught through modeling. According to students, teachers "have to follow the values themselves" (p. 22). Students resented teachers who told them to be kind and to respect others, yet exhibited favoritism, treated students "like babies," didn't listen, and gave "busywork."

Viviana is teaching a lesson on feelings. She shows the class pictures of people with different kinds of feelings: happiness, excitement, anger, love. They talk about what each picture is portraying. She shows a picture of a little boy by a fence with a ball and bat. "What do you think he's feeling?" "Sad," says one girl. "Lonely," volunteers another. Viviana asks, "Why do you think he's sad and lonely?" "Because the other children won't let him play ball with them." "What could you do to fix things?" "Invite him to play." After the pictures, she has the children portray different feelings. They get to the feeling of love, and they all joke about the fact that her name is Mrs. Love. One by one the children hug her to express "their love for Mrs. Love." Afterwards she tells us: "I try to teach them how to deal with their feelings. I tell them that sometimes I get angry at my husband and I count to 10 so that I don't say something I may regret later. I tell them, if you get angry, count to 10 or do something until you cool off. You can hop, jump, ride a bike. Then you can talk with the person about what made you angry and you're less likely to say words you'll regret later on."

A few weeks later, we watch Viviana teach a phonics lesson. A child at the chalkboard is having difficulty and writes a word incorrectly. Viviana reminds the class, "Remember, we don't laugh." She goes to help the boy and makes a mistake herself. "Oh my goodness, I made a mistake. Are you going to laugh at me? If you do, how will I feel?" The children tell her she'll feel sad. "Yes, I'll feel sad, like this boy over here. [She points to a picture of a boy with a very sad face.] "Instead of laughing, what do you need to do?" she asks the class. "Help you." "That's right, you need to help me."

In addition to modeling, it's important to promote and recognize the prosocial behavior of your students. For example, Allan Beane, author of *The Bully Free Classroom* (1999), suggests that teachers encourage kindness by having a "kindness box" into which students drop brief notes about acts of kindness they do or witness. Periodically, the teacher pulls out a note and reads it aloud. Other strategies include assigning students "kindness pals," for whom they do random acts of kindness; having a "kindness reporter," who watches for acts of kindness, briefly describes them in a notebook, and reports at the end of the week; and collaboratively writing "Our Big Book of Kindness."

Provide Opportunities for Students to Get to Know One Another

In order to build community, our four teachers create opportunities for students to learn about one another and to discover the ways in which they are similar and different. For example, on the first day of school, Ken has his students create personalized CD covers with a title, an illustration, and 12 song titles that tell something important about themselves. By the end of the period, he has learned a good deal about the self-perceptions of his students, and they have learned about each other.

Similarly, Garnetta begins the school year by having students pair up and interview each other with a set of questions that she and the class have formulated. After the children have interviewed their partners, they introduce each other to the class. Then they write up their interviews, affix them to photographs that Garnetta takes of each child, and post them on a bulletin board.

Viviana reads her class *The Important Book* (1949) by Margaret Wise Brown. Each child then makes a banner proclaiming what is important about himself or herself—and what is *most* important (e.g., "The important thing about Juanita is that she is smart, she can speak Spanish, she likes to skate, she loves pizza, etc. But *the most important thing* is that she is smart.").

"Find Someone Who" is an introductory activity that Barbara likes to use. Students must find one person in the class who fits each of the descriptions (e.g., someone who "has the same favorite television show as you do," "someone who went to DisneyWorld this summer"). When Barbara writes the descriptions, she tries to incorporate multiple intelligences: "someone who likes to draw cartoons," "someone who likes to hike," "someone who read more than six books this summer."

"Find Someone Who" can be especially useful if you include items relating to race, cultural and linguistic background, and disability and solicit information in addition to a signature. Consider these examples (Sapon-Shevin, 1995):

Find someone who grew up with an older relative. What's one thing that person learned from the older relative?

Find someone whose parents come from another country. What's one tradition or custom that person has learned from his or her parents?

Find someone who has a family member with a disability. What's something that person has learned by interacting with the person with a disability?

Here are some additional getting acquainted activities that you can use at the beginning of the year:

GUESS WHO? Have students write a brief autobiographical statement (family background, hobbies, extracurricular activities, etc.), which they do not sign. Collect the statements, read each description, and ask students to write the name of the individual they believe wrote the description. (You can participate too.) After all the descriptions have been read, reread them and ask the authors to identify themselves. Ask students to indicate how many classmates they correctly identified (Jones & Jones, 1998).

TWO TRUTHS AND A LIE (OR TWO FACTS AND A FICTION) Have students write down and then share three statements about themselves, two of which are true and one of which is a lie. For example, Carol might write, "I once played the princess in *Once Upon a Mattress,* and one night during a performance I fell from the top of 15 mattresses and herniated a disk in my back," "I won third prize in the All-Alaska Logging Championship for the rolling pin toss," and "I trekked through Nepal on my honeymoon." Students guess which one is the lie, and then she tells the truth. (she didn't trek through Nepal; she backpacked through Colorado and Wyoming.) The activity can be done as a whole class or in small groups. In either case, since the activity allows students to select what to disclose about themselves, there is little chance of embarrassment. It also provides opportunities for students to discover common interests and experiences and to test assumptions and stereotypes. (Sapon-Shevin, 1999).

LITTLE-KNOWN FACTS ABOUT ME This is a variation of the previous activity. Students write a statement about themselves that they think others won't know. The papers are folded, collected, put in a box, and shaken. Students take turns drawing a paper and reading the statement aloud. Everyone guesses who wrote the little-known fact (Sapon-Shevin, 1999).

LIFELINES Each student draws a line on a piece of paper and then marks 6 to 10 points representing important events in their lives that they are willing to share (e.g., the birth of a sibling, the death of a close family member, the time they starred in the school play, when they moved to this school). Students then get into pairs and share their life stories. Members of each pair could also introduce each other to the rest of the class, referring to points on the lifeline (Sapon-Shevin, 1999).

Sometimes, the curriculum itself provides opportunities for students to look beyond their own world, reflect on the experiences of others, and develop empathy. For example, Ken's class reads *Wanted . . . Mud Blossom* (Byars, 1993), *Dear Mr. Henshaw* (Cleary, 1983), *Because of Winn-Dixie* (DiCamillo, 2000), and *Joey Pigza Swallowed the Key* (Gantos, 1998), all of which portray children in low-income, single-parent families. Ken continually pushes his students to think about the characters' emotions and decisions and to make connections between the characters' lives and their own life experiences.

Curb Peer Harassment

"Boys call me cow." "Boys call one girl popcorn because she has zits." "One time a kid missed the ball . . . , and they called him a f———fag." According to Shakeshaft and her colleagues (1997), verbal assaults like these permeate middle, junior, and senior high school. Shakeshaft's research team spent three years interviewing more than 1,000 Long Island, New York, students from eight different schools and from all socioeconomic levels. Everywhere they went, they found that "kids made fun of other kids" (p. 22). The primary targets were girls who were unattractive, unstylish, or physically mature and boys who didn't fit the "stereotypic male mold" (p. 23).

Such pervasive, hurtful peer harassment is certainly disturbing, but what is also disturbing is the fact that teachers rarely intervened, leading students to conclude that teachers just didn't care. For example, one girl reported that "in science class, the boys snap our bras. The [male] teacher doesn't . . . say anything. . . . The boys just laugh" (p. 24). When teachers did intervene, their responses were minimal. One student commented,

> *For name-calling, they'll [teachers] just say, "I don't want to hear that," and then that's it. They really don't do anything else. . . . I wish teachers would stop it right away; even if they hear only one thing. (p. 25)*

Another put it this way:

> *They [teachers] don't take as much control as they should. They say, "Don't do it next time." And when they [the harassers] do it the next time, they [the teachers] keep on saying the same thing. They don't take control. (p. 25)*

Peer harassment is not limited to the upper grades. It's not unusual to hear elementary students use "gay" and "lesbian" as derogatory labels for peers whose behaviors are outside the norm. Gordon (1994) reports that even first-graders use terms like "faggot" to ridicule others. In a "game" called "Smear the Queer," one child attacks another, knocks him to the ground, shouts "fag," and runs away.

In a study of 25 kindergarten through third-grade classrooms in racially, culturally, and economically diverse public schools, Froschl and Gropper (1999) found that teasing and bullying are common reactions to perceived differences among peers. Moreover, boys initiated more than three times as many incidents as girls; in one kindergartner's words, "Boys usually chase girls, because that's what boys do—boys chase." And once again, the research documented that teachers rarely intervened; indeed, teachers or other adults were uninvolved in or ignored *71 percent* of the observed incidents of teasing and bullying.

Curbing peer harassment requires a multifaceted approach. Shakeshaft and her colleagues recommend that teachers use reflective activities in order to raise awareness. For example, students can read fiction that relates to the topic of harassment and bullying; in math, they can conduct surveys and analyze the results; in art classes, students can depict their feelings about name calling and put-downs. In addition, students and faculty can work together to define the behaviors that are appropriate to inclusive, caring schools.

Other educators (Lundeberg, Emmet, Osland, & Lindquist,1997; Froschl & Gropper, 1999; Froschl, Sprung, & Mullin-Rindler, 1998) give additional recommendations for activities that are particularly appropriate for children in the primary grades. Kindergartners, for example, can explore the concept of human difference by creating a chart about how they are the same and different. First-graders can tell stories and draw pictures about when they had the courage to stand up for a friend who was being teased. Children can build a wall of blocks that represent the kinds of things that keep people from being friends and discuss ways to remove the barriers. They can have open meetings on name calling, teasing, and bullying and discuss appropriate and inappropriate responses. (Note that peer harassment is also discussed in Chapter 14, "Preventing and Responding to Violence.")

Be Alert for Student-to-Student Sexual Harassment

On May 24, 1999, in a case called *Aurelia Davis v. Monroe County Board of Education,* the Supreme Court ruled five to four that any school district receiving federal money can face a sex-discrimination suit if they are "deliberately indifferent" to information about "severe, pervasive, and objectively offensive" harassment among students (Walsh, 1999).

The Davis case started as a lawsuit brought by the mother of a Georgia schoolgirl who was *in fifth grade* when she began to experience what her family describes as five months of sexual harassment by the 11-year old boy who sat next to her. According to the plaintiff's brief to the Court, the boy "repeatedly attempted to touch [the girl's] breasts and vaginal area, . . . told her in vulgar terms that he want[ed], . . . to get in bed with her, . . . placed a doorstop in his pants and behaved in a sexually harassing manner" (Gorney, 1999). Meanwhile, the girl and her family made repeated requests for help from school officials, who are accused of ignoring their pleas. These allegations have not yet been proved in a court of law, but they illustrate the fact that worry about student-to-student sexual harassment is not confined to high schools.

Sexual harassment is generally defined as *unwanted and unwelcome sexual attention.* This includes a wide range of behaviors:

leering, pinching, grabbing, suggestive verbal comments, pressure for sexual activity, spreading sexual rumors, making sexual or sexist jokes,

pulling at another student's clothing, cornering or brushing up against a
student in a sexual way, insulting comments referring to students' sexual
orientation, date rape, sexual graffiti about a student, or engaging in other
actions of a sexual manner that might create a hostile learning environment.
(Hyman, 1997, p. 318)

It can sometimes be difficult for you—and your students—to distinguish between harmless teasing and sexual harassment. When you're faced with this situation, it's helpful to keep in mind the fact that whether harassment has occurred is truly in the "eye of the beholder." In other words, the determining factor is "how the person on the receiving end is affected by the behavior, not with what the other person means by the behavior" (Strauss with Espeland, 1992, p. 15). Kissing, touching, and flirting that the recipient likes or wants is *not* sexual harassment (although it is certainly inappropriate and may be an indicator that either child is the victim of sexual abuse; see Chapter 13).

In recent years, an increasing number of districts have written and distributed sexual harassment policies for both students and school personnel. These generally define sexual harassment, outline the procedures to follow when you learn about an incident of sexual harassment, and spell out the consequences. It's important that you obtain a copy of this policy and follow the specified procedures. Remember, the Supreme Court's ruling in the Davis case means that you must take complaints seriously and intervene. If you don't, you may be accused of "deliberate indifference" (Gorney, 1999).

Use Cooperative Learning Groups

Research suggests that there are few opportunities for interaction among students during the school day (Osterman, 2000). These findings are disturbing in light of innumerable studies attesting to the power of cooperative learning to promote the development of positive peer relations. More specifically, cooperative learning facilitates interaction and friendship among students who differ in terms of achievement, sex, cultural and linguistic background, and race; fosters the acceptance of students with disabilities; increases positive attitudes toward class; and promotes empathy (Good & Brophy, 2000).

David and Roger Johnson (1999), two prominent researchers in the field of cooperative learning, distinguish among three types of cooperative learning. In *formal cooperative learning,* teachers assign students to small heterogeneous groups that work together on carefully structured tasks; groups may stay together for anywhere from one class period up to several weeks. In *informal cooperative learning,* students work together in "temporary, ad-hoc groups" that might last from a few minutes to a whole period (Johnson & Johnson, 1999, p. 128). For example, during a whole-class presentation, Garnetta frequently tells her students to "turn to your neighbor and talk about how you'd tackle this problem." Finally, *cooperative base groups* are long-term, heterogeneous groups in which students support one another's academic progress and emotional well-being. Members of the base group can collect assignments for absent students and provide assistance when they return, tutor students who are having problems with the course material, check homework assignments, and provide study groups for tests. According to Jones and Jones (1998), it's helpful to have base groups meet several times a week for 5 to 15 minutes: "At the very least, the base group provides a setting in which at least three members of the class are concerned about each student's learning" (p. 133). (See Chapter 10, "Managing Groupwork," for a more detailed discussion of cooperative learning.)

Concluding Comments

Alfie Kohn (1996) suggests that it would be helpful if we all reflected on "what makes school awful sometimes" (p. 114). Then we might be more inclined to make sure that those kinds of situations don't happen for students in our classrooms. We recently followed his advice. With our students, we reminisced about the awful times we had experienced. Here are some of our students' memories:

In fourth grade, we were told we would have current events on Fridays—one article summarized and brought in to read aloud to the class. On the first Friday, I forgot, along with eight others, to do the assignment. The teacher made all those who forgot stand up while she harshly rebuked us in front of the class. Then she went around and we each had to say why we forgot it. Then she made us write a letter to our parents explaining why we would never forget current events again . . .

Looking back, first grade to about sixth grade was not too good for me. . . . I was always the forgotten kid. Teachers would rarely call on me because I was so quiet and because I never raised my hand for fear of saying the wrong thing, fear of being in the spotlight, fear of being embarrassed. That was also the case among my peers. My views or ideas were always ignored. . . .

In second grade, my teacher took off two gold stars which I had accumulated by my name. (To give some background: There was a huge poster on one bulletin board with everyone's name on it. Your goal was to collect stars of different colors for different achievements. Gold stars were the highest prize.) She did this in front of the class, and it humiliated me. What had I done to receive such harsh punishment? Well, I picked my nose . . .

In first grade, I had to go to speech therapy because I had a difficult time pronouncing my THs. So when it was time to go my teacher would say "Okay, all the kids who don't know how to talk right, line up at the door."

For too many children, school is a place where they feel humiliated, threatened, ridiculed, tormented, teased, powerless, and betrayed. Think about when school was awful for *you*. If you can keep those times in mind and try to ensure that they never happen to your students, you will be well on your way to creating a safer, more caring community.

Summary

This chapter began by discussing the tension that novice teachers often feel between wanting to care and needing to achieve order. We stressed the fact that caring and order are not irreconcilable goals and concluded that it is possible to create a classroom that is not only relaxed and comfortable, but also orderly and productive. The chapter then considered ways of showing students that you care about them and ways of building caring relationships among students.

Ways of showing care:

Be welcoming.
Be sensitive to students' concerns.
Be fair.
Be a real person (not just a teacher).
Promote autonomy by sharing responsibility.
Reduce the use of extrinsic control.
Be inclusive.
Search for students' strengths.
Develop communication skills:

Attending and acknowledging.
Active listening.
Open-ended questioning.
Problem solving.

Building caring relationships among students:

Hold class meetings.
Model and recognize prosocial behavior.
Provide opportunities for students to get to know one another.
Curb peer harassment.
Be alert for student-to-student sexual harassment.
Use cooperative learning groups.

For too many students, school is a place where they feel humiliated, threatened, ridiculed, tormented, teased, powerless, and betrayed. Teachers who can "remember when school was awful" are better able to create a safe, caring community for their students.

Activities

1. Interview a few elementary students about their definitions of caring teachers. Ask them to identify the ways in which teachers show caring to students.
2. Think about the teachers you had in elementary school. Select one teacher who showed caring to students and one teacher who did not. Write a paragraph on each teacher, providing details and examples to illustrate what each teacher actually did.
3. Do some planning for the first week of school. First, plan a way of showing students that you welcome their input. (Will you have students verbally share their suggestions and opinions about rules, lessons, assignments, or grouping? Write a letter to you? Answer specific questions?) Second, plan an introductory activity designed to help students become acquainted.
4. In the following bits of conversation, students have confided in teachers about problems they are experiencing, and the teachers have responded in ways *not* suggested in this chapter. Provide a new response for each case, using the communication skills discussed in this chapter: acknowledging, active listening, asking open-ended questions, and problem solving.

   > STUDENT: My parents won't allow me to go out on weekends like the other kids. They say they trust me, but then they don't show it!
   >
   > TEACHER: Well, I'm sure they have your best interests at heart. You know, you really shouldn't gripe. You're pretty young, and after all, a lot of kids don't have parents who care about them. I see a lot of kids whose parents let them do anything they want. Maybe you think you'd like that, but I'm sure you wouldn't. . . .
   >
   > STUDENT: I can't stand my stepmother. She's always criticizing me and making me come home right after school to watch my sister, and making me feel really stupid.
   >
   > TEACHER: Oh, come on now, Cinderella. I'm sure it's not that bad.
   >
   > STUDENT: My sister told me she thinks she's pregnant. She made me promise not to tell our folks, but I'm really scared. I think they should know. I'm scared she's going to try to get rid of it by herself. What do you think I should do?
   >
   > TEACHER: I think you should tell your parents.

5. Think about when school was awful for you. Share your experiences with others, either in writing or verbally, and look for commonalities. What themes emerge from these anecdotes?

For Further Reading

Beane, A. L. (1999). *The bully free classroom: Over 100 tips and strategies for teachers K–8.* Minneapolis, MN: Free Spirit.

Byrnes, D. (undated). *"Teacher, they called me a————!"* New York: Anti-Defamation League.

Charney, R. S. (1991). *Teaching children to care: Management in the responsive classroom.* Greenfield, MA: Northeast Foundation for Children.

Elias, M. J., Zins, J. E., Weissberg, R. P., Frey, K. S., Greenberg, M. T., Haynes, N. M., Kessler, R., Schwab-Stone, M. E., & Shriver, T. P. (1997). *Promoting social and emotional learning: Guidelines for educators.* Alexandria, VA: Association for Supervision and Curriculum Development.

Froschl, M., Sprung, B., & Mullin-Rindler, N. (1998). *Quit it! A teacher's guide on teasing and bullying for use with students in grades K–3.* New York: Educational Equity Concepts, Inc., Wellesley College Center for Research on Women, and NEA Professional Library.

Kohn, A. (1996). *Beyond discipline: From compliance to community.* Alexandria, VA: Association for Supervision and Curriculum Development.

Kriete, R. (1999). *The morning meeting book.* Greenfield, MA: Northeast Foundation for Children.

Nelsen, J. L., Lott, L., & Glenn, H. (2000). Positive discipline in the classroom (3rd ed.). Roseville, CA: Prima.

Oakes, J., & Lipton, M. (1999). *Teaching to change the world.* Boston: McGraw-Hill. (See, in particular, Chapter 7, Classroom Management: Caring and Democratic Communities, pp. 234–277).

Stein, N. (1999). *Classrooms and courtrooms: Facing sexual harassment in K–12 schools.* New York: Teachers College Press.

Organizational Resources

The Anti-Defamation League (ADL), 823 United Nations Plaza, NY, NY 10017 (www.adl.org; 1-800-343-5540). Dedicated to combating anti-Semitism, hate crime, and bigotry through programs, services, and materials. (The *ADL Material Resource Catalog* is a wealth of resources, including lesson plans, curriculum guides, and lists of children's books.)

The Southern Poverty Law Center, 400 Washington Avenue, Montgomery, AL 36104 (www.teachingtolerance.org). The Teaching Tolerance project provides teachers at all levels with ideas and free resources for building community, fighting bias, and celebrating diversity.

The Northeast Foundation for Children, 71 Montague City Road, Greenfield, MA 01301 (413-772-2066; www.responsiveclassroom.org). Offers professional development programs, workshops and resources on the "responsive classroom," designed to help educators integrate the teaching of social and academic skills.

References

Battistich, V., Watson, M., Solomon, D., Lewis, C., & Schaps, E. (1999). Beyond the three R's: A broader agenda for school reform. *The Elementary School Journal, 99*(5), 415–432.

Beane, A. L. (1999). *The bully free classroom: Over 100 tips and strategies for teachers K–8.* Minneapolis, MN: Free Spirit.

Brown, M. W. (1949). *The important book.* New York: Harper & Row.

Byars, B. C. (1993) *Wanted . . . Mud Blossom.* New York: Bantam Doubleday Dell Books for Young Readers.

Charles, C. M. (2000). *The synergetic classroom: Joyful teaching and gentle discipline.* New York: Longman.

Christensen, L. (1994). Building community from chaos. In B. Bigelow, L. Christensen, S. Karp, B. Miner, & B. Peterson (Eds.), *Rethinking our classrooms: Teaching for equity and justice.* Milwaukee, WI: Rethinking Schools Limited, 50–55.

Cleary, B. (1983). *Dear Mr. Henshaw.* New York: Morrow.

DiCamillo, K. (2000). *Because of Winn-Dixie.* Cambridge, MA: Candlewick Press.

Dowd, J. (1997). Refusing to play the blame game. *Educational Leadership, 54*(8), 67–69.

Froschl, M., & Gropper, N. (1999). Fostering friendships, curbing bullying. *Educational Leadership, 56*(8), 72–75.

Froschl, M., Sprung, B., & Mullin-Rindler, N. (1998). *Quit it! A teacher's guide on teasing and bullying for use with students in grades K–3.* New York: Educational Equity Concepts, Inc., Wellesley College Center for Research on Women, and NEA Professional Library.

Fulk, C. L., & Smith, P. J. (1995). Students' perceptions of teachers' instructional and management adaptations for students with learning or behavior problems. *The Elementary School Journal, 95*(5), 409–419.

Gantos, J. (1998). *Joey Pigza swallowed the key.* New York: Farrar, Strauss, and Giroux.

Good, T. L., & Brophy, J. E. (2000). *Looking in classrooms* (8th ed.). New York: Longman.

Gordon, L. (1994). What do we say when we hear "faggot"? In Bigelow, B., Christensen, L., Karp, S., Miner, B., & Peterson (Eds.). *Rethinking our classrooms: Teaching for equity and justice.* Milwaukee, WI: Rethinking Schools, Ltd.

Gordon, R. L. (1997). How novice teachers can succeed with adolescents. *Educational Leadership, 54*(7), 56–58.

Gordon, T. (1974). *T. E. T.—Teacher Effectiveness Training.* New York: Peter H. Wyden.

Gorney, C. (June 13, 1999). Teaching Johnny the appropriate way to flirt. *The New York Times Magazine, 43*–47, 67, 73, 80–83.

Hyman, I. A. (1997). *School discipline and school violence: The teacher variance approach.* Boston: Allyn and Bacon.

Johnson, D. W., & Johnson, R. T. (1999). The three Cs of school and classroom management. In H. J. Freiberg (Ed.), *Beyond Behaviorism: Changing the classroom management paradigm.* Boston: Allyn & Bacon, pp. 119–144.

Jones, V. F., & Jones, L. S. (1998). *Comprehensive classroom management: Creating communities of support and solving problems.* Boston: Allyn & Bacon.

Katz, M. S. (1999). Teaching about caring and fairness: May Sarton's *The Small Room.* In M. S. Katz, N. Noddings, & K. A. Strike (Eds.), *Justice and caring: The search for common ground in education.* New York: Teachers College Press, pp. 59–73.

Keller, N. (1994). Integrating Andy. In M. Dalheim (Ed.), *Toward Inclusive Classrooms.* Washington, D.C.: National Education Association, 83–84, 89.

Kim, D., Solomon, D., & Roberts, W. (April 1995). Classroom practices that enhance students' sense of community. Paper presented at the annual convention of the American Educational Research Association, San Francisco.

Kohn, A. (1996). *Beyond discipline: From compliance to community.* Alexandria, VA: Association for Supervision and Curriculum Development.

Kottler, E. (1994). *Children with limited English: Teaching strategies for the regular classroom.* Thousand Oaks, CA: Corwin Press.

Kottler, J. A., & Kottler, E. (1993). *Teacher as counselor: Developing the helping skills you need.* Newbury Park, CA: Corwin Press.

Kriete, R. (1999). *The morning meeting book.* Greenfield, MA: Northeast Foundation for Children.

Lee, V. E., Croninger, R. G., Linn, E., & Chen, X. (1996). The culture of sexual harassment in secondary schools. *American Educational Research Journal, 33*(2), 383–417.

Lundeberg, M. A., Emmett, J., Osland, P. A., & Lindquist, N. (1997). Down with put-downs! *Educational Leadership, 55*(2) 36–37.

McLaughlin, H. J. (1991). Reconciling care and control: Authority in classroom relationships. *Journal of Teacher Education, 42*(3), 182–195.

Nelsen, J. L., Lott, L., & Glenn, H. S. (2000). *Positive discipline in the classroom* (3rd ed.). Roseville, CA: Prima.

Nieto, S. (1996). *Affirming diversity: The sociopolitical context of multicultural education* (2nd ed.). White Plains, NY: Longman.

Oakes, J., & Lipton, M. (1999). *Teaching to change the world.* Boston: McGraw-Hill.

Osterman, K. F. (2000). Students' need for belonging in the school community. *Review of Educational Research, 70*(3), 323–367.

Roeser, R. W., Eccles, J. S., & Sameroff, A. J. (2000). School as a context of early adolescents' academic and social-emotional development: A summary of research findings. *The Elementary School Journal, 100*(5), 443–471.

Ryan, R. M., & Connell, J. P. (1989). Perceived locus of causality and internalization. *Journal of Personality and Social Psychology, 57,* 749–761.

Ryan, R. M., & Deci, E. L. (2000). Self-determination theory and the facilitation of intrinsic motivation, social development, and well-being. *American Psychologist, 55*(1), 68–78.

Sapon-Shevin, M. (1995). Building a safe community for learning. In W. Ayers (Ed.), *To become a teacher: Making a difference in children's lives.* New York: Teachers College Press.

Sapon-Shevin, M. (1999). *Because we can change the world: A practical guide to building cooperative, inclusive classroom communities.* Boston: Allyn & Bacon.

Shakeshaft, C., Mandel, L., Johnson, Y. M., Sawyer, J., Hergenroter, M. A., & Barber, E. (1997). Boys call me cow. *Educational Leadership, 55,* 22–25.

Sileo, T. W., & Prater, M. A. (1998). Creating classroom environments that address the linguistic and cultural backgrounds of students with disabilities: An Asian Pacific American perspective. *Remedial and Special Education, 19*(6), 323–337.

Solomon, D., Battistich, V., Kim, D., & Watson, M. (1997). Teacher practices associated with students' sense of the classroom as a community. *Social Psychology of Education, 1,* 235–267.

Strauss, S., with Espeland, P. (1992). *Sexual harassment and teens: A program for positive change.* Minneapolis, MN: Free Spirit.

Trueba, H. T., Cheng, L. R. L., & Ima, K. (1993). *Myth or reality: Adaptive strategies of Asian Americans in California.* Washington, DC: Falmer Press.

Walsh, M. (June 2, 1999). Harassment ruling poses challenges. *Education Week, 18*(38), 1, 22.

Weinstein, C. S. (1998). "I want to be nice, but I have to be mean": Exploring prospective teachers' conceptions of caring and order. *Teaching and Teacher Education, 14*(2), 153–163.

Williams, M. (1993). Actions speak louder than words: What students think. *Educational Leadership, 51*(3), 22–23.

Working with Families

"I had no idea his mother lost her job and his father hasn't been around for a month. No wonder he's been so belligerent!"

"Her grandmother has been so good about checking her assignment pad every night and making sure she's doing her homework. She really's working with me on this."

"His father comes in to read to the class whenever he has a day off. He provides such a fabulous role model!"

Comments like these can be heard in teachers' rooms all across the country. They reflect some of the benefits that accrue when teachers and families establish positive, productive relationships. First, *knowing about children's home situations provides insight into their classroom behavior.* It's easier to understand why John seems so listless if you're aware that his mother is undergoing chemotherapy, and Jana's anxiety about getting all As is understandable if you appreciate how much her parents pressure her to succeed.

Furthermore, these insights can help you decide what course of action to take when dealing with a child's problems. You don't want to suggest that a parent read to a child if the parent can't read, or send a note home if it will lead to a beating.

Second, *when families understand what you are trying to achieve, they can provide valuable support and assistance.* Most parents want their children to succeed in school and will do what they can to help. But they can't work in a vacuum. They need to know what you are trying to achieve and how you expect children to behave in your classroom. Familiarizing parents with your curriculum, routines, and policies minimizes confusion, misinterpretations, and conflict.

Third, *families can help to develop and implement behavior management plans.* Parental cooperation can be especially helpful because families have so many rewards at their disposal that are unavailable to teachers—a trip to the beach, a movie, pizza for dinner, or a new CD. Garnetta shares this example:

> I had this boy in my class who was extremely disruptive. He wouldn't work, kept "forgetting" his homework, distracted other children, wandered around the room. You name it; he did it. The three of us—the mother, the boy, and I—talked about what we could do, and we decided to try a system of home rewards. We agreed that I would send a note home each day, reporting on the boy's behavior. For every week with at least three good notes, his mother let him rent a video game. In this way, the child's access to video games was directly dependent on his behavior. This system really made a difference!

Finally, *parent volunteers can make classroom management easier by assisting in the classroom.* Parents can staff learning centers, read to children, help during writing conferences, and carry out some of the clerical and housekeeping duties that eat up a teacher's time. In the crowded, fast-paced, unpredictable world of the elementary classroom, an extra pair of hands (and eyes) can be a lifesaver.

Despite the many benefits of close communication and collaboration, parents and teachers are often at odds with one another. What causes this adversarial relationship and what can teachers do to avoid it? In this chapter, we examine three barriers to close working relationships—teacher reluctance to involve parents, parent reluctance to become involved, and the changing nature of families. We then turn to our teachers and to the literature on parent involvement in order to suggest ways that families and schools can work together to *overcome* the barriers.

Barriers to Family–Teacher Cooperation

Teacher Reluctance to Involve Families in Schooling

A primary reason for teachers' reluctance to work with families is the *extra time and energy that are required.* Teaching is physically and emotionally exhausting, and reaching out to parents is sometimes viewed as one more burdensome task. Epstein and Becker (1982) remind us how much time it takes to make just one call home: "If a teacher telephones 30 parents and talks for 10 minutes to each, the teacher spends 5 hours voluntarily on the telephone with parents" (p. 103). Since this is obviously in addition to planning lessons and activities, grading papers, organizing cooperative learning groups, and creating bulletin board displays, it's understandable if teachers wonder whether the extra time required is worth the trouble.

In addition, *teachers' perceptions of families* undoubtedly contribute to the reluctance to seek greater parental involvement. Many teachers recognize that time is often a scarce commodity for parents, limited by responsibilities at work, household chores, and caring for other family members. The teachers question whether it is fair to ask already burdened parents to spend time working with children on academic activities or assisting in school (Epstein & Becker, 1982). As Ken told us one evening:

> *Some parents are really stressed out. One family I'm thinking about owns their business. They work unbelievable hours. Meanwhile, I'm telling them to read to their kid. C'mon, are they going to do the accounts, or are they going to read to their kid? They're going to do the accounts. It's understandable.*

Other teachers have been burned by encounters with angry, irresponsible, or apathetic parents. (See Figure 6-1 for a perspective on parental apathy.) They would tend to agree with Walde and Baker (1990) that "far too many parents—and not just disadvantaged ones—simply don't give a damn. For them, school is a free babysitting service" (p. 322).

PARENTAL APATHY? I DON'T KNOW - WE HAVEN'T THOUGHT MUCH ABOUT IT ONE WAY OR THE OTHER!

FIGURE 6-1. Parental apathy is sometimes viewed as a problem. (Reproduced by permission of Luci Meighan.)

Another reason for teachers' reluctance to involve parents is *the worry that parents may not understand their role in the classroom.* Some parent volunteers intervene when they shouldn't (e.g., imposing their own punishments for inappropriate behavior instead of consulting the teacher); they may instruct students in ways that contradict what the teacher has demonstrated; or they may violate confidentiality by sharing student records and relaying sensitive information. When situations like these occur, teachers may wonder if parent volunteers are more of a hindrance than a help.

Finally, teachers may be reluctant to involve parents because *they want to protect their "turf."* As public servants, teachers are often exposed to criticism. Parents may blame them for children's problems or question their professional competence. As Sara Lawrence Lightfoot (1978) writes:

> *The only sphere of influence in which the teacher feels that her authority is ultimate and uncompromising seems to be with what happens inside the classroom. Behind the classroom door, teachers experience some measure of autonomy and relief from parental scrutiny . . . (p. 26)*

Lightfoot concludes that teachers who are "more confident of their skills, expertise, and abilities" (p. 30) will be more likely to reach out to parents, and research supports her contention. In a study of factors that facilitate parent involvement, Hoover-Dempsey, Bassler, and Brissie (1987) found that *teacher efficacy* (teachers' beliefs that they can teach and that their students can learn) was the factor most strongly related to parent involvement.

Parent Reluctance to Become Involved in Schooling

Just as there are teachers who are reluctant to work closely with families, there are families who resist involvement. Griffith (1998), for example, found that *lower socioeconomic* status was associated with lower parent participation in schooling. Among the most obvious reasons for this association are the competing demands of work. Low-income households are more likely to have two parents who work full time, parents who have two or more jobs, parents who have to work evenings and nights, and parents who have jobs with inflexible or unpredictable hours.

In addition, there are more subtle reasons for reluctance to become involved. Some adults have *unhappy memories of their own experiences* as students. Listen to this father describe his reasons for not participating more fully in his son's schooling:

> *They expect me to go to school so they can tell me my kid is stupid or crazy. They've been telling me that for three years, so why should I go and hear it again? They don't do anything. They just tell me my kid is bad.*
>
> *See, I've been there. I know. And it scares me. They called me a boy in trouble but I was a troubled boy. Nobody helped me because they liked it when I didn't show up. If I was gone for the semester, fine with them. I dropped out nine times. They wanted me gone. (Finders and Lewis, 1994, p. 51)*

Other families simply *do not see involvement in schooling to be part of their role as parents* (Hoover-Dempsey & Sandler, 1997). They may believe that schooling should be left to the professionals or that they are showing their support for teachers by not interfering. They may even suspect that efforts to seek their involvement are attempts to shift responsibility and resent being asked to do the teacher's job.

It's important to note that beliefs like these may be culturally influenced. Asian-American families, for example, generally hold high expectations for their children's academic success; nonetheless, they tend to view educational matters as the province of the school (Fuller & Olsen, 1998). Similarly, Latinos typically perceive their role as ensuring their children's attendance; instilling respect for the teacher; encouraging good behavior in school; meeting their obligations to provide clothing, food, and shelter; and socializing children to their family responsibilities (Chrispeels & Rivero, 2000). Becoming involved in school is *not* a key component of this role.

Still other families *feel guilty* when their children have difficulties in school. They may become defensive and uncooperative when teachers try to discuss their child's problem or may be too embarrassed to disclose troubles they are having at home. Rather than deal with the child's problem, these families may try to deny what is occurring and to avoid communication with the teacher.

Finally, some families *are unnerved by the "threatening monolith" we call school* (Lightfoot, 1978, p. 36). This is particularly so when parents are poor, uneducated, or have limited proficiency in English. Some may find teachers and administrators unresponsive to their requests (Gutman & McLoyd, 2000); others may even fear teachers, viewing them as authority figures who must not be questioned (Lindeman, 2001). Immigrant parents may be confused by educational practices that are different from their own; they may not know the words (e.g., *standards, student-centered, cum file, grade equivalence*) that would allow them to have a meaningful exchange.

Chrispeels and Rivero (2000) interviewed 11 Latino families about family involvement in schooling. They report that 9 of the 11 felt they had little influence on what happened at school and left decisions in the hands of the teacher. Mrs. Andres was typical:

> *My daughter's report card from fourth grade arrived with all Bs. In third grade she came out with excellence and an A. We waited for the next report card and again she got all Bs. . . . She told me, "My teacher says that she will not give any As because that will make the children who get an F feel bad." My daughter said that in that case she would not try hard because she was not going to get an A. (p. 22)*

Although Mrs. Andres felt this was unfair, she did not ask the teacher for an explanation:

> *In a way I felt that the teacher could say, "Well, who tells you that your daughter deserves an A?" My fear of that comment kept me from going to ask. (p. 22)*

The Changing Nature of the Family

In 1955, 60 percent of American households consisted of a working father, a homemaker mother, and two or more school-age children (Hodgkinson, 1985). Teachers sent letters home addressed to "Dear Parents," reasonably confident that two parents would read them, and schools scheduled "Parent Conferences" with the expectation that parents were the primary caregivers of their children.

Times have changed. The typical family of the 1950s now represents less than 10 percent of our households (Cushner, McClelland, & Safford, 2000). Today, almost half of all marriages end in divorce (Swap, 1999), and 50 percent of our children will live in a single-parent family at some point during their childhood (Children's Defense Fund, 1999). In 1999, 32 percent, or nearly 23 million children, were not living with two parents (*Kids Count Data Book,* 1999). Most are growing up with a single parent, but for some, the significant adults in their lives are not their parents at all, but grandparents, aunts, uncles, brothers, sisters, or neighbors. The "stay-at-home" mother is vanishing; indeed, 50 percent of all preschoolers (Children's Defense Fund, 1999) and 70 percent of school-aged children (Swap, 1999) have mothers in the work force. With a surge in immigration from Central and Latin America, the Middle East, Southeast Asia and the Pacific, and Russia and Eastern Europe, many students come from homes where a language other than English is spoken, and their families are unfamiliar with schools in the United States.

The changing nature of the American family has made communication and collaboration more difficult than ever. Nonetheless, research has found that it is *teachers' attitudes and practices—not the educational level, marital status, or workplace of parents— that determine whether families become productively involved in their children's schooling* (Epstein, 2001; Griffith, 1998). In other words, it's the teacher that makes the difference. For this reason, you must not only understand the barriers to parent involvement, you must also be aware of the ways that families and schools can work together.

Overcoming the Barriers: Fostering Collaboration between Families and Schools

Joyce Epstein and her colleagues at Johns Hopkins University have studied comprehensive parent involvement programs and have identified different types of family–school collaboration (Epstein, 1995). Four of Epstein's categories provide a framework for our discussion.

Type 1: Helping Families to Fulfill Their Basic Obligations

This category refers to the family's responsibility to provide for children's health and safety, to prepare children for school, to supervise and guide children at each age level, and to build positive home conditions that support school learning and behavior. Schools can assist families in carrying out these basic obligations by providing workshops on child development and parenting skills; establishing parent-support groups; creating parent resource centers and toy-lending libraries; communicating with families through newsletters, videotapes, and home visits; and referring families to community and state agencies when necessary.

Asking teachers to assume responsibilities for the education of *families,* in addition to the education of *children,* may seem onerous and unfair. Not surprisingly, some teachers hesitate to become "social workers," a role for which they are untrained. Others feel resentful and angry at parents who do not provide adequate home environments; in particular, teachers may "write off" parents who are poor and minority, believing that these families cannot or will not assist in their children's education (Olson, 1990).

Although these attitudes are understandable, you need to remember that your students' home environments shape their chances for school success. As the number of distressed, dysfunctional families grows, assisting families to carry out their basic obligations becomes increasingly critical. Furthermore, research on parent involvement indicates that *most families want to become more effective partners with their children's schools* (Brandt, 1989); they simply do not know how to help.

What can you, as a teacher, realistically do to assist families in carrying out their basic obligations? Although you will probably not be directly involved in planning parent education workshops, writing newsletters on parenting, or creating videotapes, you can play an important *indirect* role. You can photocopy and share relevant articles from journals and magazines. You can let families know about available materials, motivate and encourage them to attend programs, bring transportation and child care problems to the attention of appropriate school personnel, and help families to arrange car pools (Greenwood & Hickman, 1991).

You can also educate families about relevant school-based resources (e.g., guidance counselors, psychologists, social workers, and school nurses), as well as community and state agencies. Viviana, for example, routinely sends home the addresses and phone numbers of the Salvation Army, Catholic Charities, family planning organizations, dental clinics, and food distribution centers. Sometimes, she personally intervenes to connect her families with appropriate agencies. Listen to her story of Santiago, a child who had come from Nicaragua:

Right away I noticed that Santiago had a lot of difficulty sitting still and paying attention. Sometimes he seemed like he was in another world. One day, shortly after school began, I talked with his grandmother when she came to school to pick him up. She told me that Santiago's father was still in Nicaragua and that Santiago lived with her, his mother, an older sister, and two little ones. She told me that Santiago had terrible problems sleeping, that he would wake up crying and fanning himself—as if he was trying to get flies away from him. She told me that Santiago had seen lots of people killed in Nicaragua, that he had seen bodies lying in the street, decomposing and covered with flies. I told the grandmother that we needed to get professional help for him and that I would see what I could do.

The next day, I found out that there was a Spanish-speaking person at a local mental health clinic, and I gave the grandmother the phone number. I told her to give the number to the mother, and I urged her to call. The clinic gave them an appointment right away and told the mother to bring all members of the family. It was such a good thing that they did! They found out that Santiago's older sister was contemplating suicide! As for Santiago, after working with him a number of times, they decided he needed medication to calm him down.

The change in Santiago was unbelievable. He was able to sit still, to pay attention, to do his work. He did fine after that. The mother came to see me and said, "Mrs. Love, you saved my family. My daughter was going to kill herself, and I didn't even know it." But she was worried about Santiago's medication; I assured her that they knew how much to give Santiago. We talked about her family and her jobs—she was working three jobs! Later, I found out the mother was laid off from two of the three jobs, and she didn't know what to do. I helped her go to welfare.

In addition to playing this indirect assistance role, there are times when it may be appropriate to work *directly* with families. You might be able to help them communicate more effectively with their children. If kindergartners are worried about separation, for example, you could share information with parents or caretakers about active or empathetic listening (see Chapter 5); if sixth-graders are arguing about curfews, you might be able to encourage parents to provide necessary limits. Barbara remembers a child with many behavior problems, both at home and in school:

The mother really wanted him in my class, and I agreed to take him—with the stipulation that she listen to my suggestions about how to handle him at home. She was at her wit's end with the boy, so she agreed. I had to teach her how to say no to her son and how to reward his good behavior. The mother, the child's therapist, and I worked together as a team, and eventually we saw a lot of improvement in his attitude toward school and his relationship with his mother. It was a lot of work, and it was discouraging at times. But we were able to reach a very difficult child, and we got to the point where he was controllable in class. This not only made him feel good, it also caused less of a distraction to the rest of the class. It was worth the trouble.

Occasionally, a child's desperate plight prompts our teachers to take an even more direct role in helping families. Viviana, for example, tells us that every year her children seem to come from more impoverished families:

In New Brunswick, rents are very high, so two and three families rent an apartment together. Three families might rent a three bedroom apartment, with a whole family sleeping in one bedroom. This means that some of the kids have to sleep on the floor. This year I have a girl in my class who used to fall asleep every day. I asked her, "Why are you so sleepy?" She told me that she has to sleep on the floor; there are eight in her family and they all sleep in one room with two beds. I had a folding bed that I had bought for when my nephew came to visit. I went to her house and asked the mother if she could accept it. I said, "Do you mind if I give you the folding bed?" She was very pleased, and the girl doesn't fall asleep anymore.

If you have students whose families have recently immigrated to this country, you might also help them to understand the expectations and norms of American schools. For example, immigrant parents sometimes view extracurricular activities as distractions from serious study and family responsibilities. Ruth Pianochka, a colleague who teaches courses in English as a Second Language, shares this story:

My parents, who immigrated from the Ukraine, did not permit me to work on the school paper . . . They did not give my brother permission to play soccer (although he signed the permission slip himself and played). . . . If someone had told my parents that extracurricular activities are really part of the holistic education of their children, I think they would have responded positively.

Type 2: Fulfilling the Basic Obligations of Schools—Communicating with Families

It's the first day of school in New Brunswick. In Viviana's classroom, 19 parents are standing around the sides and the back of the room. The children are seated boy-girl and according to height. Viviana speaks in Spanish to the parents. She introduces herself and explains how she seated the children. She explains that they're the parents at home, but she's the mother in school. She says that they are all family, one big family, all Hispanic, and that they should come in if they need help; they are not alone.

She discusses the importance of homework and attendance. She explains that she is very firm about both. She will give a zero if children do not bring in their homework. She tells the parents that she gives homework every day but not on weekends, so the children can relax. She says that parents should not let their children fool them about being sick and not able to come to school. She says the school has a nurse and can check their children and send them home if they're really sick.

Viviana moves to a round table in the front of the room where workbooks are displayed. She picks up each workbook and explains that there is much

Vivian welcomes parents on the first day of school.

work ("mucho trabajo") this year: spelling, social studies, English, math, science, health. Again, she emphasizes that the children must attend school in order to master the skills they need for first grade.

Viviana asks if the parents have any questions or comments. A woman in pink thanks her for her comments about being one big family. Then Viviana invites the parents to introduce themselves. They go around the room, saying who they are and pointing to their children. After the introductions are complete, the parents leave, kissing their children goodbye on the way out.

Epstein's second category of family–school involvement refers to the school's obligation *to communicate about school programs and children's progress.* Communications include the kind of face-to-face interaction that Viviana has on the first day of school and at open houses and parent–teacher conferences, as well as report cards, progress reports, memos, e-mail messages, newsletters, and phone calls. This is certainly the most commonly accepted way to work with parents, and there is no doubt that these communications are essential. The crucial question, however, is not only *whether* these communications occur, but *when they occur, whether they are being understood, and whether they lead to feelings of trust and respect or alienation and resentment.*

All of the teachers stress the importance of communicating with families early in the school year—*before* stressful situations occur. As Ken reminds us:

It takes effort for teachers to contact a parent, and so they often wait until some problem arises. Because of this, "communication" begins to have a negative connotation. We've got to communicate with parents even when

there is no problem—when we've got good things to tell—and the more
communication the better. If you develop a personal connection with
parents early, you have an easier time approaching them when you do
have a concern.

Given Ken's attitude, it is not surprising that he was part of an experiment this year
in which 64 South Brunswick teachers held parent conferences *before school began.*
The focus of the conferences was to hear "parents' hopes and dreams for the coming
year for their child" and to learn "one important thing they want their child to learn
this year." Ken hopes that "these early conferences will make it clear that parents and
teachers are *partners* in the education of the children." (Sometimes, partnership is
threatened by the use of educational jargon that parents may find difficult to understand; see Figure 6-2.)

It is clear that the four teachers with whom we are working are able to establish productive partnerships with families, and the next few sections of this chapter describe
some of the ways they do this. In addition, Table 6-1 lists some suggestions for communicating with parents who are particularly hard to reach.

Memos, E-mails, Newsletters, and Websites

So often, parents have no idea what is happening to their children for the six hours of
each school day. Hungry for information, they appreciate a note—electronic or paper—
about current projects, future activities, and children's progress. One or two weeks before school begins, Barbara sends home a letter addressed to her students and their families (see Figure 6-3). In it she talks about schedules, snacks, the curriculum, and
homework policies. But the letter conveys more than this basic information: it communicates her desire for an open, ongoing relationship and sets the stage for the year ahead.

In order to facilitate the process of writing positive notes and memos, it's helpful to
write each student's name on an envelope and place the envelopes in a convenient, obvious place. Once or twice a week, you can pull out an envelope and jot a brief, positive
note to the family of that student. When all the envelopes are gone, you'll know that

FIGURE 6-2. The use of educational jargon sometimes impedes communication.
(FRANK & ERNEST reprinted with permission of Newspaper Enterprise Association, Inc.)

TABLE 6-1. Reaching "Hard to Reach" Parents

Step #1: Try to figure out why parents are hard to reach. Ask yourself (or someone in the school who would know):

Do parents speak English?

Do parents come from cultures that do not identify parent involvement as a priority? Do they come from cultures that believe schooling should be left to the educators?

Do parents have work schedules that conflict with conferences?

Do parents live far from the school? Do they have transportation?

Do parents know where the school is?

Are the parents homeless (and therefore have no good address for receiving written communications from school)?

Step #2: Develop outreach strategies to address the underlying issue. For example,

Make sure that parents receive messages in their native language.

Figure out how to get messages to parents who are homeless.

Schedule conferences at flexible times to accommodate parents with conflicting work schedules.

See if neighbors or friends can be used as a liaison.

Determine if meetings can be held in a more convenient, more familiar, more neutral location.

Arrange for home visits (with appropriate security).

Source: Adapted from Swap, 1993.

you've communicated once with each family (Gruber, 1985). It's also a good idea to make a "communication card" for each student on which to jot down any extra contact you have with a family member by phone, e-mail, or in person.

Weekly newsletters also help to keep parents informed about what is happening in school. In the lower grades, you can have a class meeting right before dismissal to review and record the day's events. On Fridays, you can fill in the newsletter just before lunch (see the form in Figure 6-4) and then duplicate and send it home at the end of the day (Gruber, 1983). In the higher grades, students can fill out the form themselves at the end of each day or write a letter to parents on Fridays describing five events that occurred during the week. Some teachers also send out monthly newsletters, giving highlights of the past month and previewing the upcoming weeks. (See Figure 6-5.)

In recent years, Ken and Barbara have used electronic mail and the Internet to facilitate communication with parents. Barbara has created a website for her class that lists class assignments and due dates, links that might help in doing assignments, links to the Internet Public Library (IPL), the weekly schedule, news about current and upcoming events, requests for supplies or assistance, and photographs of class activities. (Note that children's pictures can appear on the website only if parents give permission.)

Although Ken has not established a class website, he takes five minutes at the end of each school day to send an e-mail message to all parents with Internet access (about 75 percent). In the message, he lists homework assignments, shares highlights of the day, and suggests topics to discuss over dinner. Ken makes a point of sending the e-mail to parents' work addresses: "I want parents to get it *before* they leave for home. My goal is

Welcome!!!!   Let's Have a Whale
of a Year

August 20

Dear   and Family,

I hope you all had a fun-filled summer. I certainly did. But now I'm ready for a new school year. As I think about our time together there are some bits of information for me to share with you.

Specials: 10:28–11:08   Mon.   PE
Tue.   PE
Wed.   Music
Thurs.   Art
Fri.   Health

Lunch: 11:57–12:37   We will share the cafeteria with the other fourth grade next door.

Snack: We will have a 15-minute break each morning for snacks and free time. I would encourage healthy snacks that we can eat while we play or talk.

Homework: You will be expected to do 20 minutes of reading outside of school each day. The books may be of your own choosing. You may also read with a parent, brother, or sister. Other homework assignments will be given as necessary to reinforce classroom skills, writing, or research. Everyone will develop a sense of responsibility for his/her own assignments, so an assignment pad will be helpful.

Mr. H. and Mr. T. will be working with us as Teacher Associates. They will be assisting students with special needs, but will be available for all of us to enjoy.

Our language arts curriculum will be literature-based. That means that most of our reading will be done through novels and related activities. The other major component of our class is a program called, "Creating an Original Opera." We will discuss this further as the year progresses, but I assure you it will be fun and challenging.

Well, if I tell you much more I won't have any surprises and any new information for Back to School Night on September 27th.

I am really looking forward to a great year. If you have any questions, please e-mail me at _____ or call me at home _____.

Love,

Mrs. Broggi

FIGURE 6-3. Letter from Barbara Broggi to her students and their families

OUR WEEKLY NEWSLETTER WEEK OF_____	
LITERACY	
MATHEMATICS	
SOCIAL STUDIES	
SCIENCE	
HEALTH	
ADDITIONAL NOTES	

FIGURE 6-4. A sample newsletter format

to get rid of the question, 'Do you have any homework?'" Ken also uses e-mail to communicate with parents when special situations arise:

> *I'm too social to make a short phone call. But I can send a short e-mail message letting them know their son had a great day, their daughter cried today, their child didn't have homework. It's easy and effective.*

We do have a few words of caution about using electronic mail to discuss sensitive issues or problems. E-mail doesn't allow you to convey your message in a calm, quiet tone of voice or to "soften" it with smiles, gestures, or body language; nor can you see or hear parents' reactions. For this reason, e-mail may be more likely to lead to misinterpretations than face-to-face interactions or even phone calls. On the other hand, written messages (whether e-mail or snail mail) enable you to choose your words carefully and deliberately, an advantage you may not have when you're interacting with parents in "real time."

CLASSROOM TIMES

Teacher: _____ Date: _____

NOVEMBER

Special Events

Hats Off To...

*Fifth Grade Track Meet WINNERS:

Long Jump:	Nick	1st place
	Bobby	6th place
Softball Throw:	Gloria	1st place
Shot Put:	Jason	1st place
Shot Put	Gloria	1st place
200m Dash	Jon	3rd place
50m Dash	Jon I	1st place
100m Dash	Bobby	1st place
	Nick	3rd place

*Very creative scarecrows...
70's Phoebe and Inmate Bobby were in a class of their own!

*Extremely scary, funny and creative gourd decorating!

Winners:
*Scariest: Joe for "Goblin"
*Funniest: Kristina for "Frankenstein's Wife"
*Most Creative: Bobby for "Crazy Mary"
*Best use of materials: Brianne for "Witch"

November Babies: Alex   11/8
               Jason   11/17

HALLOWEEN WAS "BOO-TIFUL IN ROOM 406!

*Mrs . Thomas along with some of our parents organized a yummy celebration for us.
*We had some super Halloween costumes! Everyone looked marvelous!
*Our Halloween M&M Estimation winners were:
    *Math - Joe   (estimate: 360 / actual: 340)
    *Homeroom - Alex   (estimate: 950 / actual: 990)
*Congratulations to...Kristina and Matt for being EXTREMELY lucky during Halloween Bingo AND...to Brianne, Matt, Christina S., & Ronnie for solving our Halloween Pun Fun Puzzlers.
*Our in-class trick-or-treating was enjoyed by all!
*We all enjoyed ending the day by parading around our school for the parents, staff and teachers!

HELP WANTED

I would like our class to participate in a "Thanksgiving dessert feast." On Wednesday, 11/25, I would like to have <u>the students prepare a dessert</u> with their group. We would do this in the morning and then enjoy the desserts after lunch. We would need at least 3-4 parents to assist with the cooking. We would also need some parents to send in some of the ingredients, bowls, or pans, and paper goods. I will send home more detailed information once I know whether I can get enough parents for that morning (Approx. 8:00 - 10:00) to make this even possible. Please let me know by <u>THIS MONDAY</u> if you can help out that morning! THANK YOU!!!

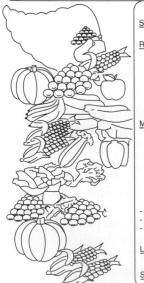

HIGHLIGHTS

<u>Spelling</u>: Due to the short weeks in November, we'll be taking 2 weeks to cover most lessons, and tests may not be on Fridays.

<u>Reading</u>: Voyage of the Dawn Treaders:
    *We'll be working on a mini-project about fantasy worlds.
    <u>Dive to the Coral Reefs</u>:
We'll be reading and discussing this nonfiction selection shortly.
    *Depending on the students' interest level, we may read and do a project on related topics.
    <u>Read Alouds:</u> Each day during snack time, I read "Stories with Holes" to the class. They have to figure them out through a questioning strategy. They're getting very good! Ask them about it!

<u>Math</u>:
    Chapter 2: "Addition and Subtraction of Whole Numbers and Decimals"
        *estimating sums and differences for whole numbers and decimals: rounding, front-end, and compatible numbers
        *adding and subtracting whole numbers and decimals
        *addition properties
        *equivalent decimals
        *Problem Solving:
           - writing number sentences to solve problems
           - solving multi-step problems
- Weekly quizzes
- Notebook notes and examples should be used when doing homework.
- We do a problem of the Day (Daily Math). Each requires logical/critical thinking. Ask your child about them!

<u>Language</u>:
     - Descriptive writing using adjectives, similes, and other figurative language
     - Nouns

<u>Science</u>: *Moon phases   *Eclipses   *The Planets

DON'T FORGET

11/3   - No school for students

11/11 - School picture day (dress up!)
        - Report cards go home

11/12 - No school
11/13 - No school

11/18 - Half day & Evening conference
11/19 - Half day & Evening conference
11/20 - Half day & Afternoon conferenc
        (Reminders forthcoming)

11/26 - No school
11/27 - No school

*Half days: 12:00 dismissal & no lunch
*Library is on day 2
*2nd Marking Period schedule check
        *days 2 & 3 - HEALTH
        *days 5 & 6 - GYM
*W.E.B. sheets due by Wednesday eac
        week for the previous week

FIGURE 6-5. Example of a monthly newsletter

We asked Barbara, Ken, Garnetta, and Viviana to share the guidelines they keep in mind when they draft memos, e-mails, and newsletters to families. Here are their responses:

> Memos, e-mails, and newsletters should be written in clear, concise language and should be edited for any misspellings or grammatical errors.

> Don't use educational jargon; it's a turn-off to parents. Remember that you won't be there to clarify what you meant.

> When writing a note to a family, make sure you know the last name of the parent or guardian to whom you are writing. Often, the parent and the child do not have the same last name.

> Tell children what is in the note. Not going behind their back is a sign of respect.

> If families don't read English, memos and notes should be written in their native language. (In Barbara's school, volunteer parents work as "parent advocates" to help teachers communicate with families who are Chinese, Filipino, Hispanic, Indian, Israeli, Japanese, Portuguese, and Russian.)

> Send lots of positive notes home, such as "happygrams," award certificates, and success stories. Parents love to hear when their children are doing well.

> End letters with an invitation to call or meet with you if there is any question about the contents.

> Don't write notes and letters in anger. If you're communicating about a problem, wait until you've calmed down, and think carefully about what you want to say.

This last guideline deserves some additional comment. Be prepared for the fact that parents will not always follow this advice and will write notes to you when they are angry or upset about something their child has told them about school. The note may sound angry or even abusive. Understand that the parent jotted the note in anger and try not to let the tone of the letter detract from dealing with the issue. If the incident is explained and the teacher uses active listening, most conflicts can be diffused and resolved.

Phone Calls

At the beginning of the school year, all four teachers find out when and how to contact the families of their students by telephone. (They're also careful about checking school records to see which parent should be contacted in cases of divorce.) Some businesses have strict policies about employees' receiving phone messages, and a call during work hours may result in a reprimand. In cases like this, it's better to call in the evening or to send a note home. Garnetta says that she sometimes has to call at 10:30 in the evening to reach working parents.

All of the teachers also let parents know when they can receive telephone calls during the school day. (Barbara and Ken even give parents their home phone numbers; they say that no parent has ever abused the information.) If parents call the school and leave a message, our teachers are prompt to return the call so that parents know they care.

Like memos and notes, phone calls should not be reserved for problems. Parents like to hear about their children's successes and improvement. If you've made contacts like these, it's easier to call when a problem *does* arise. Ken recalls a sensitive situation that occurred not too long ago:

The class was having a discussion about drug abuse. I was talking about peer pressure to use drugs. I noticed this boy wasn't paying attention and doing a lot of talking, so I said something like, "Kids will try to convince you to use drugs, just like they try to convince you to talk when we're having a class discussion." The boy stopped talking, looked at me, and said, "Are you saying I'm going to use drugs?" We talked about what I had meant, and things were OK, but I realized I needed to call home in order to head off trouble. I didn't want the boy to go home and say, "Mr. K. said I'm gonna use drugs." I called home right after school. I was really glad that I had already spoken to these parents a lot, so that we had a good relationship going. I began by telling the parent that I was generally concerned about the boy's behavior in class lately (which I was), and that I felt something was going on. We talked about that for a while, and then I said, "By the way, this happened in school today. . . ." It was really important for me to talk about this with the parents, so that the situation didn't get misinterpreted.

Home Visits

Visiting students' homes is not very common, but it can be a valuable way of learning about students' lives and reaching parents who are reluctant to come to school. During the visit, you can discuss how the child benefits when the home and school work together, invite parents to visit your classroom, and encourage them to call you if they have questions or concerns.

In some school districts, teachers are encouraged to visit the homes of all students before school begins in order to listen and to learn about each family. Other districts have created the position of home visitation coordinator or parent educator; this person is responsible for regularly visiting students' homes to discuss important events in the family's life, the child's progress in school, and ways parents can support and extend their child's learning (Olmsted, 1991).

Garnetta and Viviana stress the need to know about the community before you venture out. Both of them used to make regular home visits, but they are now far more cautious. Garnetta tells us:

A while back, I visited a child's home to talk about her progress in school and just to connect with the family. We had a nice visit. But two or three days later, I learned that her mom and dad and the older children were found guilty of possessing and selling drugs. I could have been in their home when the drug bust was made! Experiences like this have made me leery. I want to know the setting I'm walking into before I visit a parent's home these days.

Viviana has had similar experiences. As a result, she now asks another person (e.g., the school security guard) to go with her when she makes a home visit. She also asks for assistance from the district's Bilingual Community Liaison Coordinator, who is responsible for visiting children's homes.

Report Cards

Report cards have been the traditional way of communicating with families about a child's progress in school. Unfortunately, they are often not very informative. What exactly does it mean when children receive a C in reading? Are they on grade level or not? Are they having problems with vocabulary? With comprehension? With decoding? To clarify or elaborate on students' grades, it's a good idea to write narrative comments. Avoid bland, general statements such as "Maia did a lovely report." Power & Chandler (1998) suggest taking a few brief notes during the marking period about accomplishments or behaviors and then using sentence stems such as "Jessica's best work of the quarter was . . . ," "Jonathan has shown improvement in . . . ," "This term I was glad to see Connor . . . ," "Ask Sarah to talk about . . . ," "This term Melissa challenged herself by . . ." (p. 80).

Another common problem with report cards is timeliness. During discussions with our four teachers, they repeatedly emphasized that parents need to know how their children are doing *throughout the marking period.* In other words, the report card should never come as a shock.

Some schools formalize the process of keeping parents informed. Garnetta and Viviana, for example, are required by their district to write progress reports for all of their children every four weeks. These summarize strengths the children possess, as well as areas that need improvement.

In addition to sending home letters and progress reports, you may want to develop a comment sheet to accompany the report card so that parents can easily write back to you. A comment sheet like this can tell you a lot about the clarity of the report card and the concerns that parents may have. Most parents will appreciate this opportunity to communicate and feel that you value their participation.

Back-to-School Night

For many parents, open house or back-to-school night is the first opportunity to meet you and to see the classroom. It's also the first opportunity *you* have to show parents all the great things you've been doing and to tell them about the plans you have for the future. As Barbara says, "I put a lot of time, effort, and energy into my teaching, and I'm proud of it. I'm enthusiastic about what I do, and I want to share this with my parents. Plus, I like to show off!"

Keep in mind that first impressions *do* matter, so you need to think carefully about how you will orchestrate this event. Here are some guidelines that have emerged during our discussions with Viviana, Garnetta, Ken, and Barbara:

> In order to increase attendance, don't just rely on the notices sent to parents by the school. Send a special invitation to families, indicating how much you are looking

forward to meeting them. You can even have your students create invitations for their own families.

Make sure the classroom looks especially attractive and neat. Bulletin boards should display the work of *all* children, not just a few.

If you want parents to sit in their children's seats, make sure there are name tags on the desks. Have your students write notes to their parents and leave them on their desks.

Greet parents at the door, introduce yourself, find out who they are, and show them where their child sits.

Make sure your presentation is succinct and well organized. Parents want to hear about your goals, plans, and philosophy, as well as the curriculum, schedules, and policies about homework and absences. Think about having a hand-out or an outline that parents can take home.

Inform parents of support staff (teachers' aides, basic skills instructors, special education teachers) who work in the classroom and introduce them if they are present.

If parents raise issues that are unique to their child, let them know in a sensitive way that the purpose of open house is to describe the general program. Indicate that you're more than happy to discuss their concerns during a private conference. You may want to have a sign-up sheet available for this purpose.

Listen carefully to questions that parents have. Provide an opportunity for parents to talk about *their* goals and expectations for their children in the coming school year. This can begin the two-way communication that is so crucial for family–school collaboration.

Provide a sign-up sheet for parents who are able to participate in classroom activities (e.g., as a teacher's aide, guest speaker, or chaperon on field trips).

If refreshments are being served after the class meetings, join in conversations with parents. Clustering with the other teachers separates you from parents and conveys the idea that there is a professional barrier.

Prepare a packet of materials (e.g., a statement of curriculum goals, class schedule, homework policies, etc.) for parents who were unable to attend back-to-school night. Send it home along with a note indicating how sorry you were that they had to miss the evening and how much you are looking forward to meeting them.

Given the hectic schedules of many parents, it may take some ingenuity to get a good turn out for back-to-school night. In Viviana's school, a sit-down dinner was held on back-to-school night this year in order to entice parents to come and to make them feel welcome. You might also consider holding a supplemental "back-to-school Saturday morning" for parents who work nights and may not be able to attend school functions scheduled on weekday evenings. (Providing coffee and doughnuts could also increase attendance!) Another idea was devised by a student teacher we know: She made a videotape of her class in action, recording two or three minutes of each major activity and making sure that every child in the class was included. She and her cooperating teacher publicized the fact that the video would be shown at back-to-school night, and they were rewarded by a substantially larger group than in previous years. Another benefit was that parents who were unable to attend could borrow the videotape to watch at home or at school. (Note that videotaping of children requires parental permission, so check with a school administrator about protocol.)

In addition to the regular back-to-school night, Ken has started having his own series of "parent evenings," each devoted to a different content area. On "science night," "social studies night," and "writing night," clusters of students make presentations about what they are doing in school in each subject. He reports that parents are extremely enthusiastic, but—take note—some of the other teachers in the building are unhappy with him.

Parent–Teacher Conferences

Schools generally schedule one or two formal parent–teacher conferences during the school year. (See Figure 6-6 for Calvin's reaction to the prospect of such a conference.) Interestingly, these meetings are often a source of frustration to both teachers and parents. Parents resent the formality of the situation and find the limited conference period frustrating. As one mother puts it, "Ten minutes is ridiculous, especially when other parents are waiting right outside the door. I need time to tell the teacher about how my child is at home, too" (Lindle, 1989, p. 14).

Teachers, too, are sometimes unhappy with these formal conferences. Many find the scheduling to be grueling. Ken observes, "It's hard to be pleasant, alert, sensitive, and productive when you're seeing families every 15 minutes for five or six hours in a row!" Moreover, teachers agree with parents that the brief time allotted often precludes

Calvin and Hobbes

by Bill Watterson

FIGURE 6-6. Parent–teacher conferences provide a way of communicating with families. *(Calvin and Hobbes* © Watterson. Dist. by Universal Press Syndicate. Reprinted with permission. All rights reserved.)

meaningful exchange. Finally, teachers complain about the lack of attendance: "The parents you *don't* need to see show up, while the ones you desperately *want* to talk with don't come."

Despite the problems, parent–teacher conferences are sometimes your only opportunity to have face-to-face interaction with members of a child's family, so it's important to encourage families to participate. Amazingly, all four teachers report that they generally have 100 percent attendance at parent–teacher conferences. This is obviously not an accident. By conference time, Viviana, Garnetta, Barbara, and Ken have already established a close relationship with families through notes, calls, and home visits. They schedule conferences when parents can come, even if this requires appointments before school begins or in the evening. If necessary, they use "incentives" to encourage attendance. Viviana, for example, enlists her children's aid by promising a surprise to each child whose family attends. She also distributes report cards at conferences, rather than sending them home with children.

All of our teachers stress the need to prepare carefully for conferences. Barbara tells us:

The first thing I do is collect samples of students' work and place them in individual folders. Using the report card as a model, I also prepare a profile of each student's academic progress and behavior. This helps to focus the conference and ensures that all important areas are discussed.

I try really hard to make the classroom particularly inviting. The students' work is displayed, and the room is neater than usual. I usually set up a table with adult-sized chairs so that we're both sitting on the same level. On the table I put a vase of flowers and a bowl of fruit or candies. Conference time is physically taxing. I need the refreshments, and I offer them to parents as a sign of hospitality.

Conferences can be tense—especially if you're meeting with family members for the first time—so all four teachers begin by trying to put parents at ease. They engage in small talk, offer candy or a cup of coffee, or share a funny incident that happened in school. They suggest leading with something positive: "Your son is a delight to have in class" or "Your daughter appears to be really interested in the topics we've been studying." They may share pictures of the student involved in various activities during the school day; this is especially helpful if family members have limited proficiency in English.

Next, they inform parents about the child's progress, pointing out both strengths and weaknesses. They document their reports by showing samples of students' work that they have collected for this purpose. They explain any strategies they are using to bring about improvements in academic work or behavior and try to enlist parents' support or assistance.

Although they try to provide parents with substantive information, our teachers emphasize the need to *listen.* They always allow time for parents to ask questions, and they solicit parents' suggestions. Remember, a conference should be a two-way conversation, not a monologue. *It's also critical not to assume that poor parents, uneducated parents, or parents with limited English proficiency have nothing of value to offer.* One mother in the study by Finders and Lewis (1994) expressed her frustration this way:

Whenever I go to school, they want to tell me what to do at home. They want to tell me how to raise my kid. They never ask what I think. They never ask me anything.

Kottler (1994) stresses the importance of encouraging families from non-English-speaking backgrounds to help you understand their children's educational and cultural background. For example, you might ask them about past educational experiences, if the child is experiencing any cultural conflicts, what their educational goals for the child are, whether English is used at home, and if there are any special needs or customs you need to take into consideration.

You also need to be sensitive to cultural differences in communication styles. Cultures shape the nature of verbal interaction, providing norms for who can initiate conversation, whether it's all right to interrupt, and how long to pause between a question and its answer (Swap, 1993). If these norms are not shared, partners may feel uncomfortable. The following example of conversation between Athabaskan Indians and whites in Alaska illustrates how misunderstanding can arise because of different communication styles:

[A] white speaker often will ask a question, then pause, waiting for the Indian speaker to reply; then, when it appears the listener has nothing to say, the white speaker will speak again. The Indian, who wishes to reply, but is accustomed to longer pauses between speakers, is not given an adequate opportunity to speak.

On the other hand, when Indian speakers do have the floor, they are interrupted frequently because they take what are perceived by whites to be "lengthy" pauses between thoughts. As an Athabaskan woman said to one of us, "While you're thinking about what you're going to say, they're already talking." Hence, Indian speakers often say very little and white speakers seem to do all the talking. (Nelson-Barber & Meier, 1990, p. 3, as cited in Swap, 1993, p. 91)

In addition, you need to recognize that different cultures hold different views about appropriate classroom behavior. For example, you may encourage students to participate actively in classroom discussions and to voice their opinions, while Hispanic parents may expect their children to be quiet and obedient. Table 6-2, adapted from Scarcella (1990) compares mainstream American teachers' expectations with those of Asian and Hispanic parents.

Regardless of the family's cultural background, Ken stresses the need to be as responsive as possible:

Sometimes parents have a particular request—for example, maybe they want to know immediately if a kid misses an assignment. Teachers sometimes resist requests like this and say, "That's not the way I do it. This is the policy in my class. The first time a child misses an assignment, I only give a

TABLE 6-2. Comparing the Expectations of Mainstream American Teachers with Asian and Hispanic Parents

Mainstream American Teachers' Expectations	Asian Parents' Expectations	Hispanic Parents' Expectations
Students should participate in classroom activities and discussion.	Students should be quiet and obedient.	Students should be quiet and obedient, observing more than participating.
Students should be creative.	Students should be told what to do.	Students should be shown what to do but allowed to organize the completion of the task creatively.
Students learn through inquiry and debate.	Students learn through memorization and observation.	Students learn through observation.
Students should state their own opinions, even when they contradict the teacher's.	Students should not contradict the teacher.	Students should not contradict the teacher.
Students need to ask questions.	Students should not ask questions.	Students should not ask questions.

Source: Adapted from Scarcella, 1990.

warning, the second time . . ." I tell parents, "If you want it that way, we'll do it that way." I try to understand what the situation is at home and to be accommodating. And, you know, it's the greatest feeling when a parent walks away from a conference and says thank you—*thank you for understanding and for being responsive, thank you for not telling me I'm a bad parent.*

If a parent is angry or upset with a particular approach or incident, our teachers also try hard not to respond with anger and defensiveness. As Viviana points out:

It's important to let the parents get it out of their system. Don't fight it. Let it go. Most times the parent is reacting to what was told to them by their child and that is not always accurate. Once the emotions are spent, find out what prompted the tirade. Gather information. Then you can tell parents how you see the situation.

Our teachers emphasize the importance of not closing doors to further communication. When a problem needs to be resolved, they try to reach consensus on possible solutions, determine who will be responsible for doing what, and schedule a follow-up meeting. If a conference is not going well, they might suggest another meeting, perhaps with the principal or guidance counselor on hand to mediate the discussion.

At the end of each conference, our teachers take a minute to summarize any decisions that have been made and to thank parents for coming. Sometimes, they follow up by

Name _____ Grade _____ Date _____

1 Select 3 pieces of work to share and tell why those were selected.

a _____

_____

_____

b _____

_____

_____

c _____

_____

_____

2 This year I'm most proud of:

3 I consider these to be my strengths:

4 A target area for improvement is:

5 Things I will do to try to improve are:

6 Overall, my fourth-grade experience has been:

7 Additional comments, if needed:

_____

Signature

FIGURE 6-7. Student conference organizer

sending a note home, expressing their appreciation for parents' attendance and reporting on children's subsequent progress.

Some schools offer three-way conferences that include the teacher, the parent or caretaker, and the child (Davies, Cameron, Politano, & Gregory, 1992; ASCD, 1997). Barbara, for example, provides parents with the option of having a regular two-way conference or a three-way conference, during which children can show pieces of work that they feel represent their best efforts and share the goals they have for the rest of the year. Barbara restricts three-way conferences to the spring, since students are more experienced by this time at setting goals and assessing their own work. If families opt to have a three-way conference, students must prepare for the conference by completing the organizer shown in Figure 6-7.

In addition to formally scheduled parent–teacher conferences, our teachers look for chances to have more casual face-to-face meetings. As we saw earlier, Viviana capitalizes on the fact that many of her children's parents bring their children to school on the first day. Other opportunities occur in the morning, when her parents walk their children to school, or at the end of the day, when they come to pick them up.

Interestingly, all of our teachers agree that if parents show up unexpectedly during the teaching day, they will meet with them on the spot. Sometimes they assign the class independent work or ask an aide, another teacher, or the principal to supervise the class while they speak with the parent. As Garnetta tells us:

> *If a parent felt it necessary and important to show up, you take care of it! They're not just coming in to chitchat. You cannot turn the parent away. If you do, there will be hurt feelings and anger. Parents need to feel you are accessible.*

Ken agrees, but offers a word of caution:

> *If a parent shows up angry or abusive, call the office and ask for assistance, or ask the teacher next door to cover your class so you escort the parent to the office to discuss the matter with the principal or an appropriate third party.*

Sending Home Student Work

Many teachers send students' work home so that families can see how their children are doing in school, but the work doesn't always arrive in very good condition. Sometimes it doesn't arrive at all! In order to avoid this problem, some teachers collect work over a week and then send it home in special envelopes that parents sign and return ("Friday folders"). If you're concerned that poor papers will be "lost" on the way, you can indicate on the envelope how many items should be inside. A parent response sheet might also accompany the work, to make it easier for parents to write back.

When you're sending home student work and tests, it's important to keep in mind that your written comments may be carefully scrutinized. Does children's work contain suggestions for improvement and specific praise for work well done, or is it so marked up with red slashes, zeros, and minus signs that it looks like an abstract painting? Remember, whatever you write on a paper is a communication to both child *and* parent.

You also need to think carefully about the kind of work you're sending home. Fill-in-the-blank worksheets are generally not products that children are proud to share, and they're unlikely to stimulate dinner conversation about what's happening in school. Social studies projects, science laboratory reports, and writing samples are not only more interesting, they're also more informative about what students have learned.

Ken believes strongly in the need to send home this kind of meaningful work. When students finish reading a novel, for example, he has them assemble a packet of the writing they've done about the story. He sits with each child, and together they evaluate the work as a whole. He might use items from the report card as a guide and ask students, "What grade would you give yourself for comprehension, for vocabulary, for making inferences?" Both the packet and the evaluation sheet are then sent home. Parents review the work and the evaluation, make their own comments on the sheet, and send it back so that Ken can see if everyone is in agreement.

Type 3: Family Involvement in School

Epstein's third type of family–school involvement refers to family members who come to school to attend student performances, athletic events, or other programs. It also refers to parents and other volunteers who assist in classrooms or in other areas of the school.

If you're teaching in a district where there has never been much parent involvement in school, special efforts may be needed to convince parents that you really want them to participate in the life of the school. When Bruce Davis (1995) became principal of an urban elementary school with no history of parent involvement, he immediately instituted a weekly awards assembly on Friday morning at 8:30 to which parents were invited. At the assembly, 44 students—two from each classroom—are honored as "students of the week" and "super readers of the week." Davis uses the assemblies as an opportunity to welcome parents to the school, to remind them about upcoming events, to make announcements of interest, and to encourage parents to become involved. He reports that about 50 parents attend each week, many with cameras and video recorders; some come *every* week, just to keep up with school news.

Classroom volunteer programs usually involve relatively few people, but even a few parents can provide considerable support. In Garnetta's classroom, for example, a mother comes in once a week to *assist with learning activities.* Depending on the day, she may work with small groups or individuals, read aloud, type stories into a computer, staff a learning center, or supervise the production of a puppet show. She also helps to carry out *clerical and housekeeping chores,* such as preparing bulletin boards, organizing games and toys, filing work samples, and collecting book club money. (Note that she does *not* tutor low-achieving children, who are most in need of the expertise of certified teachers.)

Parents can also enrich the curriculum by sharing information about their jobs, hobbies, and cultural backgrounds. When Barbara's class reads *In the Year of the Boar and Jackie Robinson* (Lord, 1984), a novel about a little girl who comes to the United States from China, Barbara has parents who have come from other countries discuss their immigration experiences.

If you decide to invite parents to participate in your classroom, you need to think carefully about how to recruit them. Sometimes parents don't volunteer simply because they're not sure what would be expected or how they could contribute. As we mentioned earlier, back-to-school night offers a good opportunity to make a direct, in-person appeal and to explain the various ways parents can assist. You might also send an invitation and a survey to families, soliciting their involvement. One kindergarten teacher we know periodically sends home "classified ads," listing specific jobs

CLASSIFIED NEWS

Help Wanted	Help Wanted	Help Wanted
Help needed on Thursday, October 31, for supervising cupcake decorating center in the morning.	Needed, parents to read "G" books during the week of October 28.	Wanted, parents to tape a Halloween book. Supplies included.
Parents wanted to read Halloween books to class on Thursday, October 31, morning or afternoon available.	Wanted! parents to read "G" books and record them on tape for our listening center. We will supply book, tape, and recorder. Please inquire.	Wanted! One parent to help make trick or treat bags on Monday, October 28.
One person needed for the Halloween Party to play pin the nose on the witch.	Help always wanted to help us in our math, art, and science centers every day!	Someone needed to help us paint our pumpkins on Thursday at 10:30 a.m.

THANK YOU!   THANK YOU!   THANK YOU!   THANK YOU!

I,_____, am replying to your ad in the classified news. I am very interested in helping our class with _____ on _____.

FIGURE 6-8. A Halloween appeal

that need to be done and requesting parents' help. (Figure 6-8 shows the appeal she sent home before Halloween.)

Using family members as volunteers in the classroom requires you to assess parents' strengths, interests, and availability and determine appropriate roles for them to play. You need to plan and coordinate activities, assign meaningful tasks, and provide direction and possibly even training. Despite these added responsibilities, the benefits can be substantial. Not only do you receive much-needed assistance in the classroom; parents obtain a better understanding of the classroom and become more comfortable in the school environment.

Parents of Youngsters with Special Needs

Since 1975, when Congress enacted Public Law 94–142 mandating that "all handi-capped children have available to them . . . a free appropriate public education which emphasizes special education and related services," parents of children with disabilities have had a legal mandate to participate in the planning of their children's educational program. Since then, P. L. 94–142 has been amended and renamed the Individuals with Disabilities Education Act (IDEA), but the essence of the law remains the same. Under IDEA, parents are required to be members of the team that creates the student's Indi-vidualized Education Plan (IEP), specifying *educational goals, services to be provided* (e.g., physical, occupational, or speech therapy, transportation, counseling), and *place-ment* (e.g., special school, self-contained special education class in the neighborhood school, general education class, etc.). Parents also have the right to see their children's records, to be informed prior to any change in placement or services, to initiate a due process hearing in the case of a disagreement with the school, and to appeal decisions through the court system.

The IDEA requires children with disabilities to be educated in the "least restrictive environment"—meaning that, whenever possible, they should be in classrooms with their nondisabled peers. In recent years, this principle has gained tremendous momen-tum. Advocates for "inclusion" have argued that the regular classroom benefits children with disabilities academically because they are held to higher expectations and are ex-posed to more stimulating content. Advocates also point to the social benefits that occur when students with disabilities can make friends with youngsters from their own neigh-borhoods and can observe peers behaving in a socially appropriate manner.

Given the trend toward inclusion and the fact that the IDEA mandates parental par-ticipation, you are likely to have contact with parents of children with disabilities and, hopefully, to be involved in the annual IEP meetings (at which a teacher must be pres-ent). For example, Barbara participated in the meetings for Stuart (the child in her class who has autism) and for Mark (the child with an emotional disorder). In Stuart's case, Barbara met with Stuart's mother, his caseworker (the school psychologist), his teacher-associate, his math teacher, the speech therapist, and Stuart himself to review his current IEP, discuss his academic and social goals, and consider strategies to fa-cilitate his progress. One reason the meeting was productive was that all members of the team had already interacted informally on numerous occasions. In fact, Barbara had invited Stuart and his parents to come over for dinner in *August—before school even began:*

> *When I have a child with a disability in my room, I don't wait for formal, mandated meetings or even for parent–teacher conferences. I know that Stuart's mother is anxious every time he gets a new teacher, so I wanted to give them the opportunity to get to know me in a less formal setting. I also wanted to get to know them a little. It's clear that Stuart and his mother have a very special bond. . . . I truly believe that the dialogue I'll have with her is a really important piece. She has a very clear view of Stuart and she can be my biggest help.*

In contrast, Mark's mother was not an active participant in his education because of her work schedule (she worked nights and slept days) and language (she spoke very little English, so she couldn't help him with reading). This didn't mean she didn't care; she just couldn't be as fully involved.

Type 4: Family Involvement in Learning Activities at Home

Epstein's fourth type of involvement refers to the ways families can assist their own children at home in learning activities that are coordinated with ongoing classwork. Interestingly, many parents say this is the kind of involvement they want most (Brandt, 1989). On the other hand, parental participation in learning activities at home may conflict with some families' beliefs and attitudes. For example, a mother in the study by Finders and Lewis (1994) explains why she stays out of her daughter's schooling:

It's her education, not mine. I've had to teach her to take care of herself. I work nights, so she's had to get up and get herself ready for school. I'm not going to be there all the time. She's gotta do it. She's a tough cookie . . . She's almost an adult, and I get the impression that they want me to walk her through her work. And it's not that I don't care either. I really do. I think it's important, but I don't think it's my place. (p. 52)

As Finders and Lewis (1994) comment, "This mother does not lack concern for her child. In her view, independence is essential for her daughter's success" (p. 52).

Since many children come from one-parent families or families in which both parents work outside the home, it is also important to think carefully about realistic ways that families can participate in learning activities at home. (Figure 6-9 provides a list of suggestions.) If you are working with children from very poor families, you might consider setting up a "family resource library" so that families can check out educational games, activities, materials, and books to use with their children at home (Gruber, 1983).

During one meeting, we asked our four teachers to describe the ways they try to involve families in learning activities. Their responses can be grouped into three categories.

Activities Involving Reading and Books

Often teachers of young children encourage parents to read aloud on a regular basis. This is a wonderful way to create a supportive literacy environment at home, but it can be a problem if parents aren't able to read. Viviana turns the tables: She gives her students books to read to their parents. She recalls how excited Eduardo's mother was the first time he read to her. She actually came to school the next day to tell Viviana how beautifully Eduardo had read, how he had translated each page, and how he had discussed the story with her in Spanish. Viviana tells us, "The parents are learning from the kids."

Activities Involving Joint Homework Assignments

In conjunction with *In the Year of the Boar and Jackie Robinson,* Barbara has students interview family members about their ethnic background. Students make a family scrapbook

READING

Read stories to your child.

Read the comics section of the newspaper with your child.

Listen to your child read.

Help your child get a library card from the public library.

Find out about special activities at the public library for your child.

Set aside a special place for your child to keep books.

Subscribe to a children's magazine in your child's name.

Bring books for your child to read in the car while he or she waits for you to run errands.

Bring books for your child to read while waiting in a doctor's or dentist's office.

Read road and street signs while you're walking, driving, or riding somewhere.

Show your child how to use the telephone directory.

WRITING

Make a mailbox for your child and leave notes in it.

Help your child write letters and notes to friends and relatives.

Help your child make a telephone/address directory of friends and relatives.

Help your child make birthday cards for friends and relatives.

Give your child a calendar to write down special events and mark off each day.

Help your child keep a scrapbook of his or her best school work.

Help your child make a journal or diary.

MATHEMATICS

Help your child use a yardstick, ruler, and tape measure for measuring objects around the house.

Show your child how to count change.

Help your child to tell time.

Help your child learn about measurement by following a simple recipe.

TELEVISION

Limit and screen your child's television watching.

Watch a television show together and discuss it.

Read a television guide and select a program to watch together.

Discuss and evaluate television commercials.

FIGURE 6-9. Suggestions for family involvement in learning activities at home
Source: Adapted from Gruber 1983, 1985.

with photographs, drawings, maps, and reports of interviews they've conducted. According to Barbara, "The really neat thing is that parents find out things they didn't know either. They have to call their parents and aunts and uncles and cousins to find out information."

A program called "Teachers Involve Parents in Schoolwork" (TIPS) developed by Joyce Epstein, colleagues, and teachers (1995), features homework assignments that require students to talk to someone at home about something interesting that they are learning in class. An example of a literacy assignment appears in Figure 6-10. Additional

TIPS LANGUAGE ARTS-ELEMENTARY

Student's Name_____ Date_____

TIPS: Hairy Tales

Dear Family Partner,
In language arts I am working on using information gathered from others to write explanations. For this assignment, I am comparing today's hairstyles with those of the past. I hope that you enjoy this activitiy with me. This assignment is due _____.

Sincerely,

_____
Student's signature

Family Interview

FIND A FAMILY MEMBER TO INTERVIEW.
Who is it?
Ask:
1) In what decade were you born? (1960s, 1970s, etc.)_____

2) What is one hairstyle that was popular when you were my age?

For boys:_____

For girls:_____

3) What hairstyle did you have when you were my age?_____

4) Did your family agree with your choice of hairstyle?_____

5) What is your favorite current hairstyle and why?_____

6) What is your least favorite current hairstyle and why? _____

Ask your family member to show you a picture of a hairstyle from the past. Draw a picture of the hairstyle here.

First Draft
Use the information from your interview to write a paragraph about hairstyles. Remember to:
• Give a paragraph a title
• Be sure all of your sentences related to your topic.
• Use descriptive words to help explain the ideas.
• If you compare hairstyles, tell how they are alike and how they are different.

Write your paragraph here

Title:_____

_____
_____
_____
_____
_____
_____
_____
_____

Read your paragraph aloud to your family partner. Revise or a sentences, as needed.

_____

Extension Activity

Select another topic for comparison—for example, clothing styl ways to have fun, or rules at home or school. What topic did ye choose?_____

Next to each "Q" line, write a questions about your topic. Use y questions to interview a family member. Write the family memb answer next to each "A" line.
1. Q: _____
   A: _____
2. Q: _____
   A: _____
3. Q: _____
   A: _____

Home -to-School Connection

Dear Parent/Guardian,
Your comments about your child's work in this activity are important. Please write YES or NO for each statement:
___My child understood the homework and was able to discus
___My child and I enjoyed this activity.
___This assignment helps me understand what my child is learning in language arts..
Other comments:_____
_____
_____

Epstein, J.L., Salinas, K.C., Jackson, V., & Van Voorhis, F.E. (revised 2000). Teachers Involve Parents in Scho (TIPS) Interactive Homework for the Middle Grades. Baltimore: Center on School, Family, and Com Partnerships, Johns Hopkins University. (Adapted for the elementary grades.)

FIGURE 6-10. TIPS language arts homework activity

examples can be found on the website for the National Network of Partnership Schools. (See the list of organizational resources at the end of the chapter.)

Supervising Homework

In interviews with 69 parents of first- through fifth-grade students, Hoover-Dempsey, Bassler, and Burow (1995) found that parents generally believed that involvement in homework was a "given" of parenthood. Many parents, however, expressed ambivalence about how much help they should provide and how independent their children should be. In addition, parents worried that they couldn't provide adequate help because they were unfamiliar with the topic being studied ("You would think I could do fourth-grade work, but sometimes I can't"); because they didn't understand the new way subjects were taught ("My [math] language was different, because that was 30 years' ago language"); or because competing demands on their time made it difficult to help as much as they felt they should (pp. 444–445). Despite their worries, parents did not want less involvement in their children's learning at home; they simply wanted "to know better how to be involved" (p. 447).

Helping children with their homework can be especially problematic for parents who are not fluent in English and have had little formal schooling themselves. In a study of six Mexican-American families in California, Concho Delgado-Gaitan (1992) found that all of the parents believed that it was their responsibility to assist with homework, but the parents of "novice" readers were unable to make sense out of the "reams of workbook pages and ditto sheets" that their children brought home (p. 510). Part of the problem was the "decontextualized drill and practice tasks [that] constituted most of the homework activities" (p. 511). Since these tasks depended on subject-matter knowledge covered in the classroom, they often caused a great deal of confusion and frustration.

You can support parents' desire to be involved by providing explicit information about your homework expectations and specific suggestions for working with children at home. Even simple suggestions such as "Read for 15 minutes most nights"; "Say 'Let's go over this together'"; or "Do about five math problems each night" are appreciated (Hoover-Dempsey, Bassler, & Burow, 1995).

You can also reassure parents by emphasizing the importance of simply monitoring their children's schoolwork, providing support and encouragement, and setting limits ("Doing math in front of the TV is not working" or "You have to do your homework before you go out to play"). In fact, parents can help simply by asking to see their children's papers; this prevents papers from going directly into the trash can from the bookbag. In Garnetta's class, for example, each student has a homework pad provided by the school. At the end of each school day, children copy the assignments listed on the chalkboard. Parents are required to review the homework pad each night and to sign it. When children come to school each morning, they put their homework and the pads on their desks for Garnetta to check. Garnetta remembers one boy who forged his father's signature. Since she had taught his brother, she knew what his father's signature looked like and she informed the boy that "the jig was up." As she puts it, "There was no use jumping all over the kid, but I wanted to make sure he took responsibility for getting the pad signed."

Concluding Comments

This chapter has described different ways that teachers can reach out to families. Our suggestions vary considerably in terms of how common they are and how much time and energy they demand. As you get to know your students and their family situations, you will be able to decide which practices are most appropriate and most feasible. Of course, you need to be realistic: As a beginning teacher, you may have to delay major efforts to facilitate communication and collaboration with families. Nonetheless, you need to remember that family involvement is key to children's success. This is an age of single parents; of mothers who work outside of the home; of grandparents, aunts, and neighbors who care for children; of increasing numbers of families whose cultural backgrounds differ from that of most teachers. Family–school collaboration has never been more difficult—but it has never been more essential.

Summary

This chapter began by discussing the benefits to working closely with families. We then examined the barriers to family–teacher cooperation and stressed that teachers' attitudes and practices—not the educational level, marital status, or workplace of parents—determine whether families become productively involved in their children's schooling. Finally, we presented strategies for overcoming the barriers and for fostering collaboration between families and schools.

Benefits of working closely with families:

- Knowing about a student's home situation provides insight into the student's classroom behavior.

- When families understand what you are trying to achieve, they can provide valuable support and assistance.

- Families can help to develop and implement strategies for changing behavior.

- Parent volunteers can make classroom management easier by assisting in the classroom.

Barriers to family–teacher cooperation:

- Teachers are sometimes reluctant to involve families in schooling because of
  The extra time and energy that are required.
  Their perceptions that families are too overburdened, apathetic and irresponsible, or that they lack the skills needed.
  The level of authority and autonomy teachers enjoy within their classrooms.

- Parents are sometimes reluctant to become involved in schooling because

They have competing demands from work.
They have unhappy memories of school.
They believe schooling should be left to the experts.
They feel guilty if their children are having problems.
They find schools intimidating and threatening places.

- The changing nature of the family means that

    The number of single–parent families has increased.
    The "stay–at–home" mother is vanishing.
    The significant adults in children's lives may not be parents, but grandparents, neighbors, aunts, or uncles.
    Many children come from non-English-speaking homes.

Fostering collaboration between families and schools:

- Schools can assist families in carrying out their basic obligations by providing parent education, establishing parent–support groups, and referring families to community and state agencies.
- Teachers need to communicate about school programs and students' progress through memos, e-mails, and notes, phone calls, report cards, progress reports, and face-to-face interactions (e.g., Back-to-School Night, parent conferences).
- Family members can serve as volunteers in classrooms.
- Families can assist their children at home on learning activities:

    Activities involving reading and books.
    Activities involving joint homework assignments.
    Supervising homework.
    Providing encouragement and support.
    Setting limits.

As a beginning teacher, you have to decide what you can realistically accomplish with respect to communication and collaboration with parents. Nonetheless, you need to remember that family involvement is critical to children's success. In this age of single parents, mothers who work outside the home, and children who come from diverse cultural backgrounds, meaningful family-school collaboration has never been more difficult, but it has never been more essential.

Activities

1. In getting ready for the school year, you have decided to send a letter to the family of each student in your class. The point of the letter is to introduce yourself, describe the curriculum, highlight a few upcoming projects, and provide information about what to expect the first day.

Select a grade level and write such a letter. As you write, think about the need to create a warm tone, to be clear and organized, to avoid educational jargon, and to stimulate interest and excitement about school.

2. Last week you conducted a parent conference with Mrs. Lewis, Joey's mother. During the conference you described his disruptive behaviors and what you've done to deal with them. You also explained that he is reading a half-grade below level. Mrs. Lewis seemed to accept and understand the information; however, the next day, an irate *Mr.* Lewis called. He told you that he had never seen his wife so upset and that he wants another conference as soon as possible to get to the bottom of the problem. He also intimated that the problem might be due to a personality conflict between you and his son. Although the phone call caught you off-guard, you scheduled the conference for two days later.
Consider the following questions:

   a. What will you do to prepare for the conference?

   b. How will you structure the meeting so that you can state your information in a productive way without being defensive?

   c. What sort of follow-up might you suggest?

3. Anita is extremely "forgetful" about doing homework assignments. She has received innumerable zeros and regularly has to stay for detention to make up the work. You have called her mother to report on this behavior and to ask for assistance, but her mother does not want to get involved. As she puts it, "I've got all I can do to handle her at home. What she does with schoolwork is your responsibility!"
   Interview two experienced teachers about what they would do in a case like this, and then formulate your own course of action based on what you learn.

4. In an effort to involve parents in their children's education, you planned a project that required students and their families to work together. The activity involved collecting 15 different leaves, identifying them, and creating a booklet or chart to display the collection in an interesting way. As you survey students about their progress, you realize that two of your students are not receiving any help from home. Identify four ways that you can help these children, either by trying to get the families involved or by providing alternative assistance.

✦ For Further Reading

Child Development Project (1994). *At home in our schools: A guide to schoolwide activities that build community.* Oakland, CA: Developmental Studies Center. (Contains activities that involve families, such as Family Read-Aloud, Family Film Night, and Family Heritage Museum.)

Davis, B. (1995). *How to involve parents in a multicultural school.* Alexandria, VA: Association of Supervision and Curriculum Development.

Epstein, J. L. (2001). *School, family, and community partnerships: Preparing educators and improving schools.* Boulder, CO: Westview Press.

Fuller, M. L., & Olsen, G. (1998). *Home–school relations: Working successfully with parents and families.* Boston: Allyn & Bacon.

Power, B., & Chandler, K. (1998). *Well-chosen words: Narrative assessments and report card comments.* Portland, ME: Stenhouse.

Swap, S. M. (1993). *Developing home–school partnerships: From concepts to practice.* New York: Teachers College Press.

✿ Organizational Resources

The National Network of Partnership Schools (Johns Hopkins University, Center on School, Family, and Community Partnerships, 3505 North Charles Street, Baltimore, MD 21218). Provides information on implementing school–family–community partnerships. Check out the interactive homework assignments (TIPS) and the "Promising Partnership Practices" at their website (www.csos.jhu.edu/p2000).

✿ References

Association for Supervision and Curriculum Development (December 1997). Student-involved conferences. *Education Update, 39*(8), 1, 6.

Becher, R. M. (1984). *Parent involvement: A review of research and principles of successful practice.* Washington, DC: National Institute of Education.

Brandt, R. (1989). On parents and schools: A conversation with Joyce Epstein. *Educational Leadership, 47*(2), 24–27.

Children's Defense Fund (1999). *The state of America's children yearbook.* Washington, DC: Children's Defense Fund.

Chrispeels, J. H., & Rivero, E. (April 2000). Engaging Latino families for student success: Understanding the process and impact of providing training to parents. Paper presented at the Annual Meeting of the American Educational Research Association, New Orleans.

Cushner, K., McClelland, A., & Safford, P. (2000). *Human diversity in education: An integrative approach* (3rd ed.). Boston, McGraw-Hill.

Davies, A., Cameron, C., Politano, C., & Gregory, K. (1992). *Together is better: Collaborative assessment, evaluation and reporting.* Winnipeg, MB, Canada: Peguis.

Davies, D. (1991). Schools reaching out: Family, school, and community partnerships for student success. *Phi Delta Kappan, 72*(5), 376–380, 382.

Davis, B. (1995). *How to involve parents in a multicultural school.* Alexandria, VA: Association for Supervision and Curriculum Development.

Delgado-Gaitan, C. (1992). School matters in the Mexican-American home: Socializing children to education. *AERJ, 29*(3), 495–513.

Epstein, J. L. (2001). *School, family, and community partnerships: Preparing educators and improving schools.* Boulder, CO: Westview Press.

Epstein, J. L. (1995). School/family/community partnerships: Caring for the children we share. *Phi Delta Kappan, 76*(9), 701–712.

Epstein, J. L., Clark, K. C., Jackson, V. E., with Language Arts, Science/Health, and Math Teachers (1995). *Manual for teachers: Teachers involve parents in schoolwork (TIPS), language arts, science/health, and math interactive homework in the middle grades.* Baltimore: Johns Hopkins University.

Epstein, J. L., & Becker, H. J. (1982). Teachers' reported practices of parent involvement: Problems and possibilities. *The Elementary School Journal, 83*(2), 103–113.

Epstein, J. L., & Dauber, S. L. (1991). School programs and teacher practices of parent involvement in inner-city elementary and middle schools. *The Elementary School Journal, 91*(3), 289–305.

Finders, M., & Lewis, C. (1994). Why some parents don't come to school. *Educational Leadership, 51*(8), 50–54.

Fuller, M. L., & Olsen, G. (1998). *Home–school relations: Working successfully with parents and families.* Boston: Allyn and Bacon.

Greenwood, G. E., & Hickman, C. W. (1991). Research and practice in parent involvement: Implications for teacher education. *The Elementary School Journal, 91*(3), 279–288.

Griffith, J. (1998). The relation of school structure and social environment to parent involvement in elementary schools. *The Elementary School Journal, 99*(1), 53–80.

Gruber, B. (1983). *Managing your classroom! An instant idea book.* Palos Verdes Estates, CA: Frank Schaffer.

Gruber, B. (1985). *Classroom management for elementary teachers. An instant idea book.* Palos Verdes Estates, CA: Frank Schaffer.

Gutman, L. M., & McLoyd, V. C. (2000). Parents' management of their children's education within the home, at school and in the community: An examination of African-American families living in poverty. *The Urban Review, 32*(1), 1–24.

Hodgkinson, H. (1985). *All one system: Demographics of education, 66 kindergarten through graduate school.* Washington, DC: Institute for Educational Leadership.

Hoover-Dempsey, K. V., Bassler, O. T., & Brissie, J. S. (1987). Parent involvement: Contributions of teacher efficacy, school socioeconomic status, and other school characteristics. *American Educational Research Journal, 24*(3), 417–435.

Hoover-Dempsey, K. V., Bassler, O. T., & Burow, R. (1995). Parents' reported involvement in students' homework: Strategies and practices. *The Elementary School Journal, 95*(5), 435–449.

Hoover-Dempsey, K. V., & Sandler, H. M. (1997). Why do parents become involved in their children's education? *Review of Educational Research, 67*(1), 3–42.

Kids Count Data Book (1999). Baltimore, MD: Annie E. Casey Foundation.

Kottler, E. (1994). *Children with limited English: Teaching strategies for the regular classroom.* Thousand Oaks, CA: Corwin Press.

Lightfoot, S. L. (1978). *Worlds apart: Relationships between families and schools.* New York: Basic Books.

Lindeman, B. (2001). Reaching out to immigrant parents. *Educational Leadership, 58*(6), 62–66.

Lindle, J. C. (1989). What do parents want from principals and teachers? *Educational Leadership, 47*(2), 12–14.

Lord, B. B. (1984). *In the year of the boar and Jackie Robinson.* New York: Harper & Row.

Menacker, J., Hurwitz, E., & Weldon, W. (1988). Parent–teacher cooperation in schools serving the urban poor. *Clearing House, 62*, 108–112.

Nelson-Barber, S., & Meier, T. (1990, Spring). Multicultural context a key factor in teaching. *Academic Connections,* Office of Academic Affairs, The College Board, 1–5, 9–11.

Olmsted, P. P. (1991). Parent involvement in elementary education: Findings and suggestions from the Follow Through Program. *The Elementary School Journal, 91*(3), 221–231.

Olson, L. (April 4, 1990). Parents as partners: Redefining the social contract between families and schools. *Education Week,* 17–24.

Power, B., & Chandler, K. (January/February 1998). Six steps to better report card comments. *Instructor, 107*(5), 76–78.

Scarcella, R. (1990). *Teaching language minority students in the multicultural classroom.* Upper Saddle River, NJ: Prentice Hall Regents.

Swap, S. M. (1999). *Developing home–school partnerships: From concepts to practice.* New York: Teachers College Press.

Vernberg, E. M., & Medway, F. J. (1981). Teacher and parent causal perceptions of school problems. *American Educational Research Journal, 18,* 29–37.

Walde, A. C., & Baker, K. (1990). How teachers view the parents' role in education. *Phi Delta Kappan, 72*(4), 319–320, 322.

Making the Most of Classroom Time

On the first day of school, the academic year seems to stretch out endlessly. If you're a beginning teacher, you may wonder how you'll ever fill all the hours of school that lie ahead (especially if you're not even certain what you're going to do *tomorrow*). And yet, as the days go by, you may begin to feel that there's never enough time to accomplish everything you need to do. With assemblies, fire drills, announcements over the intercom, recess, clerical tasks, and holidays, the hours available for instruction seem far fewer than they did at first. Indeed, by the end of the year, you may view time as a precious resource—not something that has to be filled (or killed), but something that must be conserved and used wisely. (Of course, your students may not share this view, as Figure 7-1 illustrates!)

This chapter focuses on the issues of time and time management. Guiding the chapter is the premise that the wise use of time will maximize opportunities for learning and minimize opportunities for disruption. First, we look at the amount of school time that is actually available for teaching and learning. Much of our discussion draws on the Beginning Teacher Evaluation Study (BTES; Fisher, et al., 1978), an influential project that examined how time is used in elementary schools and the relationship between time and

Calvin and Hobbes

by Bill Watterson

FIGURE 7-1 Calvin doesn't agree that time passes quickly in classrooms. (Calvin and Hobbes © Watterson. Dist. by Universal Press Syndicate. Reprinted with permission. All rights reserved.)

achievement. Our purpose here is to provide you with a set of concepts that you can use to think about the way time is used in your school and classroom. The second part of the chapter considers strategies for using classroom time efficiently. We discuss four complementary approaches—maintaining activity flow, minimizing transition time, holding students accountable, and limiting the disruption caused by students leaving the room for special instruction ("pull-outs").

How Much Time Is There, Anyway?

Although this seems like a straightforward question, the answer is not so simple. In fact, the answer depends on the kind of time you're talking about (Karweit, 1989). Most states mandate a school year of approximately 180 days, with a school day of six hours. This amounts to more than 1,000 hours of *mandated time* each year. But flu epidemics break out, and boilers break down; snowstorms cause delayed openings, and teacher workshops require early closings. Factors like these immediately reduce the time you have available for teaching.

Even when school is in session and students are present, only about five hours of the day are set aside for instruction, with the remaining time used for lunch, recess, and other breaks. Of these five hours, one is typically devoted to "specials"—art, music, and physical education—and four are allocated for instruction in academic areas—literacy, mathematics, science, and social studies.

The way the four hours of *academic time* are distributed among the content areas varies considerably from school to school and even from teacher to teacher. In one school in Maryland, for example, the time allocated to mathematics instruction ranged from 2 hours and 50 minutes per week in one classroom to 5 hours and 55 minutes per week in another (Karweit, 1989). This translates into a difference of more than 100 hours over the course of the school year! Variations like these may reflect differences in school policies and programs; however, in schools where teachers have autonomy to determine what topics to emphasize, these variations may also reflect individual teachers' priorities and preferences (Schmidt & Buchmann, 1983).

Not only do elementary teachers vary in the time they allocate to various subjects, they also vary in the *amount of allocated time they actually use for instruction.* In some classes, taking attendance, collecting lunch money, distributing materials, and reprimanding misbehaving students consume an inordinate amount of time. Karweit (1989) describes a "one-hour" math class, for example, in which the first 10 minutes were typically used to collect lunch money, and the last 10 were used to line up the students for lunch—leaving only 40 minutes for actual teaching and learning.

Situations like this are not unusual in the classrooms of teachers who lack efficient strategies for carrying out routine noninstructional tasks. Leinhardt and Greeno (1986) provide us with a glimpse into the difficulties encountered by one beginning teacher, Ms. Twain, as she attempted to check homework at the beginning of math. Ms. Twain had two goals—to identify who had done the homework and to correct it orally. She began by asking, "Who doesn't have their homework?" In response, students did one of three things: They held up their completed work, called out that they didn't have it, or walked over to the teacher and told her whether they had done it or not. Ms. Twain then talked about the importance of homework and marked the results of this check on a posted sheet of paper. Next, Ms. Twain chose students to give the correct answers to the homework problems:

> *She called out a set of problem numbers (1–10) and assigned a child to call out the answers as she called the problem number. The student slowly called out the answers in order. (The first child chosen was the lowest in the class, did not have her work done, and was doing the problems in her head.) Thus, for the first 10 problem answers, the teacher lost control of pace and correctness of answer; however, it was only when the child failed on the sixth problem that Twain realized the student had not done her homework. (p. 87)*

Ms. Twain continued to call on students to give the answers, while the rest of the class checked their work. The last child chosen went through the sequence of problems quickly, but gave both the problem number and the answer, a situation that caused some confusion (e.g., "24, 27; 25, 64"). Ms. Twain's entire homework check took six minutes—and it was clear to the observers that she was never certain which children had done their homework.

In contrast, Leinhardt and Greeno describe a homework check conducted by Ms. Longbranch, a successful, experienced teacher. Ms. Longbranch first gave a cue, "Okay, set 43," and then began to call the children's names. Children who had done the homework simply responded, "yes." Those who hadn't done the work got up and wrote their names on the chalkboard. In 30 seconds—with a minimum of fuss—Ms. Longbranch was able to determine who had completed the assignment.

The next goal was to correct the work:

The students took colored pencils out and responded chorally with the correct answer, a fraction in lowest terms. As the teacher called the problem, "1/12 + 1/12," they responded "2/12 or 1/6." Time to complete was 106 seconds. (p. 85)

We are not presenting Ms. Longbranch's homework check as a model to be copied in your classroom; her procedure may not be appropriate for your particular class. The important point is that Ms. Longbranch has established a routine that enables her to check homework efficiently, almost automatically, while Ms. Twain does not yet have a workable strategy. Although the difference in the time used by the two teachers is only about four minutes, it is probably symptomatic of the ways they managed class time in general.

As you can see, the answer to our question, "How much time is there, anyway?" depends on whether we are talking about the number of hours mandated by the state, the number of hours school is actually in session and students are in attendance, the time scheduled for instruction, or the time actually used for instruction. But even when teachers are actually teaching, students are not necessarily paying attention. We must consider still another kind of time—*engaged time* or *time-on-task.*

Let's suppose that while you are teaching, some of your students choose to pass notes about Halloween costumes, play with the latest action figures, or stare out the window. In this case, the amount of time you are devoting to instruction is greater than the amount of time students are directly engaged in learning. This is not an atypical situation. Research documents the fact that students tend to be "on-task" about 70 percent of the time (Rosenshine, 1980). Again, there are sizable variations from class to class. In the BTES study, some classes had an engagement rate of only 50 percent (i.e., the average student was attentive about one-half of the time), while in other classes the engagement rate approached 90 percent (Fisher, et al., 1980).

There are also substantial differences in engagement from activity to activity. During independent work, for example, engagement is usually about 70 percent, while discussions led by the teacher yield engagement rates of 84 percent (Rosenshine, 1980). Why should this be so? Paul Gump (1982) suggests that some classroom activities prod students to be involved and "push" them along, while others do not. In a class discussion, external events (i.e., the teachers' questions, the other students' answers, and the teacher's responses) press students to pay attention. In seatwork and silent reading, materials (e.g., worksheets, textbooks) are simply made available; students must depend on their own internal pacing to accomplish the task. In other words, students must provide their *own* push—and sometimes the push just isn't there.

Another type of time we need to consider is the *amount of time students spend on work that is meaningful and appropriate,* what Herbert Walberg (1988) calls *productive time.* We sometimes get so caught up ensuring that students are on task that we fail to select tasks that are educationally beneficial. An article in *Education Week* (October 24, 2001) provides a compelling example. Touring a high-poverty school that had received an international award for excellence in staff development, Mike Schmoker became puzzled, then astonished, as he went from room to room and observed children's activities. He was supposedly visiting during reading time, but *the activities he saw bore no relationship to reading.* Instead, students were *coloring.* Three hundred school tours later, Schmoker has concluded that the reason so many students reach the upper grades without reading skills is that they spend their time on the *"crayola curriculum."*

This chapter began by asking, "How much time is there, anyway?" Figure 7-2 depicts the answer to this question. The bar at the far left shows the number of hours in the typical *mandated* school year—1,080. For the sake of argument, we will assume that student absences and school closings reduce this figure by 10 days or 60 hours. Thus, the second bar indicates that *attended time* is 1,020. Since one hour of each day is generally spent in lunch and recess, only 816 hours are actually *available for instruction* (bar 3). Eighty percent or 652 of these hours are *allocated to academic instruction* (bar 4). Given the need to carry out clerical and administrative tasks, we have only 522 hours for *actual academic instruction* (bar 5). If students pay attention 80 percent of that time, *engaged time* is 417 hours (bar 6). And assuming that students work on meaningful, appropriate tasks for 80 percent of the time they are engaged, we see that *productive learning time* is only 333 hours—less than one-third of "mandated" school time.

Obviously, these figures are estimates. But the graph summarizes our fundamental point: *The hours available for learning are far more limited than they initially appear.*

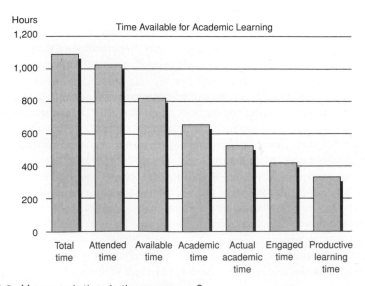

FIGURE 7-2. How much time is there, anyway?

Increasing Opportunity to Learn

The BTES data made time a popular topic for reform-minded educators. In 1983, for example, the National Commission on Excellence in Education declared that we were "a nation at risk" because of "a rising tide of mediocrity" in our educational system. The report advocated a variety of reforms, including recommendations to extend the school day to seven hours and to lengthen the school year to 200 or 220 days. A decade later, the National Education Commission on Time and Learning (1994) echoed these recommendations. Claiming that "learning in America is a prisoner of time," the Commission argued that "our time-bound mentality has fooled us all into believing that schools can educate all of the people all of the time in a school year of 180 six-hour days. The consequence of our self-deception has been to ask the impossible of our students."

Other educators contended that there was sufficient time for learning, but that it was used inappropriately. These educators urged teachers to increase time-on-task and to eliminate wasted time. They criticized teachers for allowing students to work on homework during class and for using Fridays as "film day" (Lowe & Gervais, 1988). In some districts, supervisors armed with clipboards and stopwatches visited classrooms to monitor students' engagement rates—and the results were used in evaluations of teaching effectiveness. We know teachers who became wary of doing anything that was not directly related to the standardized achievement tests given at the end of the year. They eliminated "frivolous" activities like reading aloud to children, creative writing, hands-on science experiments, sharing time, and arts and crafts in order to provide more time for the practice of basic skills.

It's easy to go overboard in this search for more hours. First, expecting students to be on-task 100 percent of the time is foolish. Total engagement is not easy for *anyone;* it is especially difficult for students who must work on tasks they have not selected and sometimes find tedious and irrelevant. Second, eliminating activities like science experiments and reading aloud results in a curriculum devoid of interest, vitality, and variety; this might actually cause a loss of engaged time, since students are likely to become bored or disruptive. Third, some loss of instructional time to activities like taking attendance, collecting and distributing materials, and lining up is unavoidable in the crowded, group setting of the classroom.

With these qualifications in mind, it is still essential to consider reasonable ways of increasing students' productive learning time. We will discuss four strategies for achieving this goal: *maintaining activity flow, minimizing transition time, holding students accountable,* and *managing "pullouts."* (See Table 7-1 for a summary.) Of course, these strategies not only maximize time for learning, they also help to create and maintain classroom order.

Maintaining Activity Flow

Good and Brophy (2000) observe, "four things can happen" when students must wait with nothing to do, and "three of them are bad: (1) students may remain interested and

TABLE 7-1. Strategies for Increasing Students' Learning Time

1. Maintain activity flow:	Avoid flip-flopping.
	Avoid "stimulus-bounded events": being pulled away from the ongoing activity by an event or object that doesn't really need attention.
	Avoid overdwelling and fragmentation.
2. Minimize transition time:	Prepare students for upcoming transition.
	Establish clear routines.
	Have clear beginnings and endings: bring first activity to a halt, announce the transition, monitor the transition, make sure everyone is attentive, begin second activity.
3. Hold students accountable:	Communicate assignments clearly.
	Monitor students' progress.
4. Manage "pull-outs":	Coordinate with special services to schedule pull-outs so they are not too disruptive:
	Create a schedule showing when various students are present and when the whole class is together. Establish a policy and procedures for having students who are pulled out complete work they missed.

attentive; (2) they may become bored or fatigued, losing interest and ability to concentrate; (3) they may become distracted or start daydreaming; or (4) they may actively misbehave" (p. 131). Given the three-to-one odds that waiting will result in undesirable behavior and a loss of valuable learning opportunities, it's essential for teachers to learn how to maintain the flow of classroom activities.

Once again, we turn for guidance to the classic work of Jacob Kounin (1970). Kounin investigated differences in teachers' ability to initiate and maintain activity flow in classrooms. He then looked for relationships between activity flow and students' engagement and misbehavior.

Kounin's research identified many differences in the ways teachers orchestrated classroom activities. In some classrooms, activities flowed smoothly and briskly, while in others activities were "jerky" and slow. Kounin even developed a special vocabulary to describe the problems he observed. For instance, he found that some ineffective managers would terminate an activity, start another, and then return to the first activity. Kounin called this *flip-flopping.* It is illustrated by the following situation: A teacher finishes reviewing math problems with the class and tells students to take out their reading books. She then stops and says, "Let's see now. How many got all the [math] problems right? . . . That's very good . . . All right, now let's get at our readers" (p. 94).

Kounin also observed *stimulus-bound events,* situations in which teachers are "pulled away" from the ongoing activity by a stimulus (an event or an object) that really doesn't need attention. Kounin describes the case of a teacher who is explaining a math problem at the board when she notices that a student is leaning on his left elbow as he works the problem. She leaves the board, instructs him to sit up straight, comments on his improved posture, and then returns to the board.

Sometimes, teachers slow down the pace of activity by *overdwelling*—continuing to explain when students already understand or preaching at length about appropriate behavior. Another type of slowdown is produced when a teacher breaks an activity into components even though the activity could be performed as a single unit—what Kounin called *fragmentation:*

> The teacher was making a transition from spelling to arithmetic as follows: "All right everybody, I want you to close your spelling books. Put away your red pencils. Now close your spelling books. Put your spelling books in your desks. Keep them out of the way." [There's a pause.] "All right now. Take out your arithmetic books and put them on your desks in front of you. That's right, let's keep everything off your desks except your arithmetic books. And let's sit up straight. We don't want any lazy-bones do we? That's fine. Now get your black pencils and open your books to page sixteen." (p. 106)

Flip-flops, stimulus-boundedness, overdwelling, fragmentation—these are all threats to the flow of classroom activities. Not only do they result in lost learning time, they can have a significant impact on children's behavior. When activities proceed smoothly and briskly, children are *more involved in work and less apt to misbehave.* Indeed, as Kounin concluded three decades ago, *activity flow plays a greater role in classroom order than the specific techniques that teachers use to handle misbehavior.*

During one visit to Garnetta's classroom, we watched the skillful way she maintained the flow of activity in her math class. Students were working in groups, using colorful cubes to solve division problems. For no apparent reason, there were innumerable interruptions that day. A messenger from the office wanted to know the number of children who had signed up for a special Saturday program; a child came to borrow an overhead projector for another teacher; and there was an announcement over the loudspeaker about after-school activities. All these interruptions occurred within a 15-minute period. Garnetta worked valiantly to keep the momentum going. She told the messenger from the office, "I'm in the middle of a lesson. I'll find out later and let the office know." When she turned to get the overhead projector, she first gave her class a task to do: "I'm going to give you a really tough problem while I take care of this business—88 divided by 2! Let's see if you can do that one!" The big number (88) bought Garnetta some additional time and created a special challenge for students. We heard murmurs like "That's not tough," and "Oh, that's easy," as they immediately began to manipulate the blocks to solve the problem.

Later, we talked with Garnetta about the way she had managed to keep activities moving. With a good deal of fervor, she told us:

> This can be a difficult group. If there's any "down time" at all, things can get out of hand. If students have to sit and wait while paper is being passed out, that provides an opportunity for trouble. If they have to wait until I've written problems on the board, they get fidgety. It's important to keep them

actively involved and participating. That's also why I tend to have them work in groups, rather than call on one student at a time.

Minimizing Transition Times

Kounin identified "flip-flopping" as one problem that can occur during transitions between activities. But transitions are vulnerable in other ways. An analysis by Paul Gump (1982, 1987) helps us to understand why transitions can be so problematic. First, Gump observes, there may be difficulty "closing out" the first activity—especially if students are deeply engaged. (Ironically, the very involvement that teachers strive to achieve makes it more difficult to get students to switch activities!) Second, transitions are more loosely structured than activities themselves (Ross, 1985). Since there's usually more leeway in terms of socializing and moving around the room, there is also more opportunity for disruption. In fact, in a study of 50 classes taught by student teachers, Arlin (1979) found that there was almost twice as much disruption during transitions (e.g., hitting, yelling, obscene gestures) as during nontransition time.

Third, students sometimes "save up" problems or tensions and deal with them during the transition time. They may seek out the teacher to complain about a neighbor, ask for permission to retrieve a book from a locker, or dump out the contents of their bookbags in search of a lost homework assignment. Although these behaviors are legitimate—and help to protect the adjacent activities from disturbance—they also make transitions more difficult to manage. Finally, there may be delays in getting students started on the second activity. Teachers may be held up because they are dealing with individual children's concerns or are busy assembling needed materials. Students may have difficulty settling down, especially if they are returning from physical education or recess.

Gump's analysis suggests that teachers can reduce the potential for chaos by *preparing students for upcoming transitions, by establishing efficient transition routines, and by clearly defining the boundaries of lessons* (Ross, 1985). These guidelines are especially important for children with attention-deficit/hyperactivity disorder, who have particular difficulty with transitions.

Advance Preparation

Arlin's (1979) research revealed that transitions were far more chaotic when student teachers failed to warn students about the imminent change of activity. This often occurred because student teachers didn't even realize the period was about to end:

The lesson was still continuing when the bell would ring. Not having reached any closure, the teacher, with some degree of desperation, would say something like "OK, you can go," and pupils would charge out of the room, often knocking each other over. (Sometimes, pupils did not even wait for the signal from the teacher.) The teacher might then remember an announcement and interject to the dispersing mob, "Don't forget to bring back money for the trip!" (p. 50)

In contrast, other student teachers in Arlin's study were able to prepare students for the upcoming transition. If they were about to dismiss the class to go to lunch, they made sure that desks were in order and that students were quiet and ready to leave. They made announcements while students were still seated and then lined children up in an orderly fashion.

Our four teachers are very skillful "clock watchers." They take care to monitor time and to inform students when an activity is drawing to a close. In the following scene, we see Garnetta warn her students that they will be changing activities in two minutes. We also see her spur them along by counting aloud, although she times her counting to match students' progress. Finally, she praises students for their cooperation:

10:15   *Ladies and gents, you have approximately two minutes to finish up whatever sentence you're working on. Then put your papers in your creative writing book and sit up straight to show me you're ready to go to Basic Skills.*

10:17   *OK, I'm starting to count. One. We've got one person ready, now two people, four people. Table 2 looks excellent; Table 1 is excellent. I'm on two. (She circulates, walking closer to those who are not yet ready and watching as more and more students sit up straight.) I'm up to three. Table 1 is good; table 2, beautiful. [At table 3, Robert is still putting things in his desk.] Almost everyone is ready to go. Robert, are you ready? [He sits up straight.] Table 3, lovely.*

10:18   *[She speaks in a very quiet voice] OK, everyone knows our hallway rules. . . . Are we going to talk in the hallway? [Kids murmur, "No . . ."] Table 2 line up, Table 3, Table 1 [Children all push in their chairs and line up quietly.] Table 1, I really like the way you lined up.*

10:19   *The class leaves the room in an orderly, quiet line.*

Not only do our teachers warn their students about upcoming transitions, they also prepare them for the activities that will occur after lunch, recess, or special classes. Here, we see Ken call his class together five minutes before they are to go to lunch. He reviews what the afternoon's activities will be and makes sure everyone has their materials out and ready:

KEN: Folks, I'd like everyone at their tables. [He pauses while students return to their seats from the various parts of the room where they have been working.] Now, before we go to lunch, I want to take five minutes so that you're all set for this afternoon. What are you going to need for this afternoon?

STUDENT: Page 39, page 40 [worksheets the students have been working on], and our newspapers.

KEN: Good. Take a minute to get those together and put them on your desks. What else?

STUDENT: We need our private journals with the answers to the questions.

KEN: Right. Get your private journals ready and on your desks.

STUDENT: We need our book reports.

KEN: Good. Is your book report on your desk?

STUDENT: We need our peer tutoring logs.

KEN: Yes. Get them out. I'm going to try to look at them this afternoon. We'll also watch the health video if we have time. Any problems? [Several students inform him about places they have to go that afternoon—to a second-grade class for peer tutoring, to band practice, to a yearbook meeting.] OK, folks, see you later. [Students get up, get their coats, and leave for recess.]

Since transitions and unpredictability are problematic for children with ADHD, it's helpful to tape a detailed schedule on their desks so they can keep track of what's going to happen when. In *Time to Teach, Time to Learn* (1999), Wood advises teachers to show the times *graphically,* so there is consistency between the schedule and the classroom clock. Wood also suggests that children have a watch that matches the clock (sweep hand or digital readout), so they are reading the time in the same way on their wrist and on the wall.

The Use of Routines

In Chapter 4 we talked about the need to have clear, specific routines in order to keep the classroom running smoothly. At no time is the use of routines more important than during transitions. Well-established routines provide a structure to transitions that helps to prevent confusion and lost time. Once again, this is particularly important for children who struggle with transitions. They can benefit from having a job to do, such as signaling the beginning and end of the transition, collecting papers, or timing the transition with a stopwatch. As Wood (1999) comments, "The point is not to control the child every minute . . . , but to give the transition some predictability and to give the child a sense of responsibility during the transition" (p. 259).

Barbara has instituted a routine for entering the room in the morning and settling in. This routine helps to ease the transition from home to school. When students come in, they immediately check the chalkboard to find out what they are to begin doing. Sometimes the board says "SQUIRT," and students know to begin Sustained, Quiet, UnInterrupted Reading Time. Sometimes the board says "JOURNALS":

It's 8:30. Students enter the room, glance at the board, go to their seats, and take out their journals. They quickly begin writing, as Barbara circulates. She gets the attendance form and silently notes attendance while students are working. Without a word, she hands the form to a boy who takes it to the office. He comes back in one minute. Barbara says, "Thank you, David." She continues to circulate, occasionally commenting to a child.

Viviana also has a well-established routine for beginning the school day:

Children begin arriving at 8:45. Viviana stands by the door. She greets each child with an enthusiastic "good morning" and a quick hug. The children go to the coat closet, hang up their coats, put their materials on the desks and then leave the room for a bathroom stop. When they return, they go to their desks and sit quietly, comparing homework, putting things away, and chatting.

At 8:57, Viviana moves to her stool in the center front of the room. "Good morning, children," she says.

The children respond chorally: "Good morning, Mrs. Love."

"How are you today, children?"

"Fine, thank you. How are you today?"

"Fine, thank you."

Then Viviana sings a good morning song to the students. When she is done, they sing the song to her. At 9:00 she instructs them to stand and say the Pledge of Allegiance. They do so and immediately move into "My country 'tis of thee." Then they turn to the calendar. Viviana asks a series of questions, all at a brisk pace: "What month is this?" "How many months are there?" "What are the months?" "What day is today?" "What day was yesterday?" "What day is tomorrow?" The children respond chorally to each question. At 9:10 they line up and leave for ESL class.

Viviana also has a routine that she uses whenever she erases boardwork in preparation for a new activity. The routine not only provides a structure to the transition that helps to keep children engaged, it also reinforces her first-graders' reading skills.

Children are creating sentences by unscrambling words written on the chalkboard. They come to the last set of words:

can   play   us   with   you

One child volunteers: "Can you play with us?" Viviana acknowledges that the sentence is correct and asks if children can think of any other. No one can. Viviana praises the children for their good work and tells them that they will do more scrambled words another day. Then she says, "Now let's erase the board." As she goes to erase each word, she pauses, and the children read it aloud. When all the words have been erased, Viviana begins the next part of her lesson. "OK children, now we're going to work a little bit with two vowel sounds."

Clear Beginnings and Endings

Arlin's (1979) study demonstrated that transitions proceed more smoothly if teachers bring the first activity to a halt, announce the transition, allow time to make sure that everyone is attentive, and then begin the second activity. In other words, smooth transitions are characterized by well-defined boundaries.

Sometimes, in an effort to maintain activity flow, teachers rush into the second activity without checking that students are "with them." Arlin (1979) writes: "Several times I noticed over 15 children continuing the previous activity while the teacher was giving directions for the new activity" (p. 50). Needless to say, those teachers then became exasperated when students asked questions about what to do.

In the following vignette, we see Viviana implement a transition with well-defined boundaries. Watch the way she gives explicit instructions for cleaning up, directs the orderly collection of materials, and pauses before beginning the second activity:

> *Children are working on a place value activity (10s and 1s). They are using wooden blocks to show two-digit numbers. They are supposed to place the appropriate number of blocks on a card divided into a 1s column and a 10s column. As they work, Viviana walks around, commenting on their work. After about 15 minutes, she is ready to change activities. She gives instructions in a very quiet voice: "OK, children. Put the cards together with a paper clip. Lesley collect the cards." [Children begin to yell, "Can I collect the ones blocks?" "Can I collect the 10s blocks?"] Viviana communicates her disapproval: "Too many people are talking to me at once. You need to be quiet and raise your hands." [The children quiet down.] "That's better. Okay, Alfredo collect the 10s blocks. Fernando collect the ones blocks." [They do so.] "Okay, children, sit straight facing me. One, two, and . . ." [Children rush to get into their seats and face forward.] Viviana scans the room, checking that students are paying attention. Then she begins the next activity: "Yesterday I asked you to think about all the things you could buy in the supermarket that you divide into parts . . . ."*

Our other three teachers also make certain that students are listening before they begin an activity. Often, they'll preface lessons with remarks designed to "grab" students' attention. Garnetta, for example, uses verbal cues like these:

"Let's get everything put away now. I want everybody with me 100 percent for this. It's important."

"Put everything else away. Now we're going to have some fun."

"We're doing this for the first time, so you all have to be quiet and listen very carefully."

"Please put your health books on your desks and look at me. Natasha, that's beautiful."

Although it's important to make sure that students are attentive before proceeding with a new lesson, Gump (1982) warns that waiting *too long* can cause a loss of momentum. He reminds us that a new activity will often "pull in" nonattending children. Gump writes: "Waiting for absolute and universal attention can sometimes lead to unnecessarily extended transition times" (p. 112). Clearly, teachers need to find the happy medium between rushing ahead when students are inattentive and waiting so long that momentum is lost. It's a delicate balancing act.

Holding Students Accountable

During a visit to Ken's class, we watched as Janice tried to get Monica to stop working on an assignment and do something with her. It wasn't clear exactly what Janice wanted to do, but Monica's reaction was unambiguous. "No," she responded firmly, "I want to do this *now.* I don't want to do it at recess, I don't want to do it at lunch time, and I don't want to do it for homework. I want to do it now."

Observing this interaction, we thought of Walter Doyle's (1983) comment that students tend to take assignments seriously only if they are held accountable for them. Your own school experiences probably testify to the truth of this statement. Even as adults, it takes a good deal of self-discipline, maturity, and intrinsic motivation to put your best effort into work that will never be seen by anyone. And elementary students are *children.* Unless they know that they will have to account for their performance, it is unlikely that they'll make the best use of class time.

Furthermore, students are *unable* to make good use of their time if they are confused about what they're supposed to be doing. Teachers sometimes tell students to "get to work" and are immediately bombarded by questions: "Can I use pen?" "Do I have to write down the problems or can I just put the answers?" "Do we have to reduce to lowest terms?" "Can I work on the rug?" When this happens, precious class time has to be spent clarifying the original instructions.

In order to help children use their time wisely, teachers must *communicate assignments and requirements clearly* and *monitor students' progress* (Evertson, Emmer, & Worsham, 2000). These practices minimize students' confusion and convey the message that school work is important. Let's see what our teachers and the research have to say about these two practices.

Communicating Assignments and Requirements

One finding of the BTES study (Fisher, et al., 1980) was that students were more likely to have success on assignments when teachers provided clear, thorough directions. Interestingly, the *number of explanations given in response to students' questions was negatively associated with high student success.* What could account for this curious finding? One possibility is that when many students have to ask questions about an assignment, it means that their teachers failed to provide sufficient preparation. In other words, the original instructions were not clear or thorough enough.

Before students begin to work, you should explain what students will be doing and why, how to get help, what to do with completed work, what to do when they're finished, and how long they'll be spending on the task. You also need to make sure that students are familiar with your work standards—for example, what kind of paper to use, whether they should use pencil or pen, how to number the page, and whether or not erasures are allowed. After giving instructions, it's a good idea to have students explain what they will be doing in their own words. Simply asking "Does everyone understand?" seldom yields useful information.

During one visit to Garnetta's classroom, we watched her explain to her class that they were going to read about the life of Martin Luther King, Jr., and then write summaries. She emphasized that the summaries should be brief, containing only the most important ideas. Moreover, she stressed that they needed to be written in the students' own words:

> *I don't want you to just copy the information from the story. You've got to use your . . . [points to head; children call out "BRAINS"]. That's right, your brains. You and your partner will read the story, decide what the important facts are, and then write them down in your own words. Let's make sure that everyone understands this. I'm going to read the beginning of one of the stories in our reader. [Garnetta opens the reader and reads a few paragraphs. The children are clearly familiar with this story. Then she closes the book.] In your own words, what is happening in this story? What did I just read? [Children raise their hands. Garnetta calls on individuals to tell the story.] Good. You are summarizing the story. You're not telling the whole thing— only the most important things. And you're not just copying the words from the book. You're picking out the most important information, discussing it with your partner, and then you're writing it down in your own words.*

It's often helpful to write the daily schedule and all work assignments on the chalkboard, so students can refer to them throughout the day. In Ken's class, the day's assignments are already on the chalkboard when students enter the classroom in the morning. A small chalkboard at the side of the room indicates how the morning will be structured. Each reading group is listed (by the title of the novel being read), along with its assignments and the time it will be meeting with Ken. After the morning meeting, Ken reviews the assignments with the class and checks that everyone knows what to do that morning. On the larger, front chalkboard is the schedule for the afternoon, along with due dates for the week's special assignments. For example, when Ken's students were studying the newspaper, the board read:

Newspaper Unit

Monday: Analysis of a comic strip character

Tuesday: Quotations from national/international news stories

Wednesday: Worksheet on New Jersey news articles

Thursday: Worksheet on local news articles

Friday: Newspaper folders due

Communicating assignments clearly is especially important if you are working with low-achieving students or students who have a history of "forgetting" work. Barbara has devised a homework procedure that she uses with her low math class. At the beginning of the month, she provides each student with a folder in which all the assignments for the month are stapled. On the cover of the folder is a calendar, showing exactly what homework students are to do each night. In this way, students can't claim they "didn't know what to do," and if they're absent (a common occurrence among low-achieving children), they still know what the assignment is. One of Barbara's calendars appears in Figure 7-3.

MARCH

SUN	MON	TUE	WED	THU	FRI	SAT
			1	2	3	4
5	6	7	8	9 Multiplication, Division Page 44	10 Word Problems Page 45	11
12	13 Fractions Pages 48–49	14 Symmetry Page 55	15 Subtraction Page 57	16 Multiplication, Division Page 59	17 Money Page 60	18
19	20 Word Problems Page 61	21 Check-up Page 64	22 Multiplication 2 Digit by 1 Digit Page 67	23 Multiplication Page 68	24	25
26	27 Subtraction Page 69	28 Bar Graph Page 74	29 Addition, Subtraction Page 78	30 Multiplication Page 87	31 Check-up Page 84	

FIGURE 7-3. Barbara Broggi's assignment calendar

Garnetta monitors students' progress on written work.

Monitoring Student Progress

Once you've given directions for an assignment and your class gets to work, it's important to monitor how students are doing. The BTES study found that teachers with high-
achieving classes circulated around the room while students were working at their seats
(Fisher *et al.*, 1980). This practice enables you to keep track of students' progress, to
identify and help with problems, and to verify that assignments are matched to students'
ability. Circulating also helps to ensure that students are using their time well.

Observations of our four teachers revealed that they rarely sit down, unless they're
working with a small group. In all four rooms, the teacher's desk is out of the way and
used for storage, rather than as a place to sit.

*Viviana's children are working with "Pattern Blocks," wooden blocks that
come in several different shapes—squares, triangles, diamonds, hexagons,
trapezoids. Each shape is a different color. The task is to use four blocks of
the same color and shape to cover outlined figures drawn on a worksheet.
Viviana introduces the activity: "Now this next page is not baby stuff. This
one you really have to think about and read the directions. Let's read the
first part out loud." [She calls on a child to read the first instruction: "Cover
each figure with four blocks of the same shape."] The children begin to
work. They are visibly excited, delighting in the ability to do the task: "This
is easy, this is baby stuff." While they work, Viviana circulates, checking
each child's paper: "You're supposed to use only one color. You're using
two." "These are not the same shape, are they?" "Good for you. You are
right!" When she sees that all of the children are done, she returns to the
front of the room and reviews what they did. "So you thought this first part
was easy, right? Who wants to tell me what you did? Alfredo?" [Alfredo tells*

her that he used four blocks of the same color and shape to cover each figure.] "Okay, so what color did you use for the first one?" [She continues to review the page and then introduces the next part of the activity.]

In classrooms where learning centers are prevalent, other forms of monitoring student performance and ensuring student accountability may be needed. A sign-in form by each learning center, for example, allows students to indicate that they have worked in a particular center; even kindergarten children can learn to check off or sign their names. The teacher can then pass by each center and readily determine which children have completed the centers. In addition, many teachers use response sheets that require students to perform some sort of written work associated with the center. These can be a simple fill-in-the-blank form, a small project, a review sheet, or a self-generated observation narrative. By requiring students to sign in and put something down in writing, the message is clear: The work done in centers is important and students are accountable.

In addition to monitoring how students do on short, daily assignments, it's essential to *keep track of progress on long-term assignments.* By establishing intermediate check points, you can help children develop a "plan of attack." For example, if students are writing a research paper, you can set due dates on which they have to submit each stage of the assignment (e.g., the topic; preliminary notes; a list of references; the first draft; the final draft). Not only does this allow you to monitor children's progress, it also helps to lessen the anxiety that young children sometimes feel when faced with a large assignment.

Ken uses this approach when he has students write stories. Although the final draft is not due for a month, Ken breaks the assignment down into components that are due every few days. First, students discuss characters in books they've already read and select one character to analyze (e.g., appearance, personality traits, mannerisms). Then they create a character of their own, following the format they used for their character analysis. This sequence of activities is repeated for the setting, the problem or conflict, and the resolution of the problem. By the end of three weeks, students have the ingredients necessary for a story. Only then do they actually begin writing.

In order to monitor if students are regularly completing assignments, it's important to *establish routines for collecting and checking classwork and homework.* Some teachers keep file folders for each child. These contain all of the worksheets and assignments for the day. Children complete their work and put it back in the file folders, which are then returned to the teacher's desk to await checking. Other teachers appoint student monitors to collect each assignment. If the monitors alphabetize the papers, it simplifies the task of noting whose work is missing. In some classes, students are assigned numbers, which they put at the top of every assignment. This enables the monitors to put the work in numerical order, another way of making it easy to scan assignments.

A very common system of collecting work is to have shallow boxes or baskets labeled for each subject; when students are done with an assignment, they simply drop it in the appropriate basket. Interestingly, neither Ken, Barbara, nor Garnetta like this system. Ken tells us, "Whenever I've used boxes like this, my kids begin to think that the only important thing is getting the work done as quickly as possible so they can throw it in the box." Garnetta points out another potential problem:

Boxes allow kids to slip by. I'd get home and find out that work wasn't there. I don't like to give zeroes; I'd rather have the work. So I try hard during the day to monitor who's turning in work and who's not, and I have kids finish their work during recess or some other free time. That way, when I got home at night, I have all the papers.

Some schools have moved toward portfolio assessment to document student progress. This form of assessment relies on the gathering of student work samples, selected by either the teacher or the student. Although portfolios provide an "authentic" record of students' growth over time, the collection and storage of work samples can create organizational problems. Teachers use a variety of systems—plastic milk crates with hanging file folders, pocket folders, cubbies labeled with the children's names, and file cabinets with specific drawers designated for portfolios. In developing a system that's right for you, keep in mind that the students need access to their work, either to revisit works in progress or to update their portfolios.

Finally, you need to *maintain records of what students are accomplishing.* In some districts, teachers can develop their own system for recording students' progress; others require teachers to follow a prescribed format. For example, Garnetta and Viviana have to keep grade books that reflect their weekly lesson plans and the "quarterly topic plans" they submit four times a year; following the district's objectives for their grade levels, these plans describe what they will be teaching day-by-day. For each marking period, Garnetta and Viviana must have two grades per week for homework and at least one test grade per objective. If five objectives are to be covered during a particular marking period, then Garnetta and Viviana would have to have at least five test grades.

Checking or grading all the work done each day is an arduous task. One student teacher recently wrote about "the looming mountain of paperwork that a teacher must perpetually climb":

Sometimes I'm not sure if I'm a teacher or certified [public] accountant! However, my experience . . . has enabled me to find ways to reckon with the ponderous load. Simple things like color coordinated folders . . . or writing the names of absent students on quiz sheets to keep track of make-up work, are "tricks" that I am extremely grateful to have been shown along the way.

Like this student teacher, you need to find ways to "make a molehill out of a mountain" (Shalaway, 1989). We asked our teachers how they handle the paperwork. Their ideas are listed in Figure 7-4.

Managing Pull-outs As Efficiently As Possible

With the movement toward inclusive education, children with special needs are increasingly served by special services personnel who are "pulled in" to the general education classroom. Nonetheless, "pull-outs" are still common. For example, students with learning disabilities may go to a resource room to work on reading and study skills; those who

Model your record keeping after the report card you use. In this way, you'll be sure to have sufficient documentation for each category of the report card. For example, if the report card reads: "Is able to grasp main idea," make sure that you have attended to this skill, that you have examples of each child's achievement in this area, and that you have recorded their progress.

Put some of the responsibility for keeping records on students. Teach them to keep track of their own progress. For example, they can construct a bar graph to record the number of spelling words they get right each week. Even kindergartners can date stamp their assignments.

Whenever possible, correct in-class work while students are doing it, or as a group immediately afterwards.

Collect in-class worksheets and then redistribute randomly for grading as a group. If students are assigned numbers, which they put at the top of their papers instead of their names, no one knows whose paper they're checking.

Monitor that students complete in-class worksheets (e.g., a set of math problems) and homework, but don't grade these. Grade only quizzes and tests.

Instead of correcting and grading every homework assignment, give periodic quizzes to check what students are learning.

Give quizzes with 5 questions instead of 25.

If you're drowning in paperwork, you're giving too much. Pare it down!

FIGURE 7-4. Ideas for handling paperwork

are "gifted and talented" may leave for an enrichment program; those with limited proficiency in English may receive instruction in English as a Second Language. In addition, the whole class may go to "specials" like art, music, and physical education. Given all these comings and goings, you may sometimes feel more like an air traffic controller than a teacher; furthermore, it may seem as though there is no time for whole-class instruction. One student teacher recently wrote about this problem in her journal:

I am so frustrated as of this journal entry!! Where is there any time in the day?!! My kids get pulled out for so many different things I rarely have a solid hour with them all together! How can anyone teach the subjects that all students are supposed to get? Three kids go out on three days at different times for compensatory education. One girl goes out four days a week at different times for a one-hour block of resource room. Three more students go out three days at different times for a HOTS (higher order thinking skills) program . . . Three-quarters of the class goes out once a week for chorus, band, and art club (and these are not even the specials, like music, gym, art, and library). Fourteen of my 24 kids go out of the room at scattered times throughout the entire week for music lessons. There is NO time in the day, and there is absolutely no consistency for the kids!!!

There is also no simple solution for this problem. All of our teachers face it to some extent, and all of them find it frustrating. The best approach is to try to have input into scheduling. If you can work closely with special services personnel, you can develop a schedule that will minimize the fragmentation and ensure that there are some time periods when you will be able to instruct the whole class or a small group without excluding somebody. For example, it can be helpful to schedule "G & T" (gifted and talented), basic skills, and ESL (English as a Second Language) all at the same time. In this way, a large number of children can be out of the room simultaneously, rather than scattered throughout the whole day. (At Barbara's school, these special services are now scheduled right before first period—8:00 to 8:40—so children do not have to be pulled out during the regular school day.) If you have students who require the maximum instruction possible in reading and math, make sure that you don't schedule your own instruction in these content areas while they are out of the room. On the other hand, if children go to a resource room *instead* of receiving regular class instruction in these areas, then it's a good idea to schedule your own literacy and math instruction at that time.

It's useful to create a daily schedule showing time blocks that are unlikely to be interrupted. An example of such a form appears in Figure 7-5.

Regardless of the scheduling, you need to find out the school's policy about requiring students who are pulled out to complete missed work. Consider another student teacher's journal entry:

It seems to me that my special ed students are confused about what is expected of them, where they are supposed to be, whose class they belong to, etc. I certainly know that I feel very confused in regard to teaching them. Basically, they are out of class almost half of the school day. When they return to the classroom from being in the Resource Room, I often don't know what to do with them . . . For example, is it fair to hold these children responsible for work that they weren't in class for? How fair is it to let them slide? Should I try to take them aside and explain what the class is doing? Amazingly, I have never been given a straight answer about whether or not these children are responsible for the work they missed. The "policy" seems to vary from week to week. This "laissez-faire" attitude is likely to doom students to always needing special services. It appears that there is little orchestration of objectives and material between the regular classroom teacher and special services personnel.

Usually, if children come into the class after being in the Resource Room, I have them simply join in with the class (or with their cooperative groups) wherever the class may be. But then it dawns on me that these are the children who are least likely to be able to pick up concepts in the middle of things and that a more effective routine needs to be established. Special needs children can get lost so easily!

Time	Monday	Tuesday	Wednesday
8:30-9:00	out: Mark Tanya _____ journal writing	out: Mark Tanya _____ journal writing	out: Mark Tanya _____ journal writing
9:00-9:30	out: Peter (Reading Group 2) _____ Reading Group 1	out: Terry (Reading Group 1) _____ Reading Group 2	out: Peter (Reading Group 2) _____ Reading Group 1
9:30-10:30	out: Bonnie (Reading Group 1) _____ Reading Group 2	out: Jean (Reading Group 2) _____ Reading Group 1	out: Bonnie (Reading Group 1) _____ Reading Group 2
10:30-11:15	Music	Phys Ed	Art
11:15-12:00	out: no one Math	out: no one Math	out: no one Math

FIGURE 7-5. A schedule indicating when children are available for instruction

If your school also has a "laissez faire" approach to this issue, you will have to establish your own policy. You will also need to think carefully about the procedures you want to implement to make children's leaving and reentry as smooth as possible. You might appoint a special "buddy" for each student who is pulled out; buddies are responsible for orienting the students upon their return to the regular classroom. It can also help to have a special folder or box for each child who is pulled out so that you don't forget to put aside assignments or materials for children who are out of the room.

Concluding Comments

Tracy Kidder's book, *Among Schoolchildren,* describes one year in the life of Chris Zajac, an elementary teacher who's feisty, demanding, blunt, fair, funny, and hard working. At the very end of the book, Kidder describes Chris's thoughts on the last day of school. Although she is convinced that she belongs "among schoolchildren," Chris laments the fact that she hadn't been able to help all her students—at least not enough:

> *Again this year, some had needed more help than she could provide. There were many problems that she hadn't solved. But it wasn't for lack of trying. She hadn't given up. She had run out of time.*

Like Chris, we all run out of time. The end of the year comes much too quickly, and some children's needs are much too great. Hopefully, the concepts and guidelines presented in this chapter will help you to make good use of the limited time you have.

Summary

In this chapter we discussed time as a "precious resource." First, we looked at the amount of school time that is actually available for teaching and learning. Then we discussed four strategies for increasing students' productive learning time. We reviewed research by Kounin demonstrating that activity flow plays a greater role in classroom order than specific techniques teachers use to handle misbehavior. We stressed the importance of minimizing transition times. We outlined ways of holding students accountable and helping them to use their time wisely. Finally, we talked about ways to cope with the managerial nightmare created by "pull-outs."

Types of Time

- Mandated time: the time the state requires school to be in session.
- Allocated time: the time the state, district, school, and teacher allocate for instruction in various content areas.
- Instructional time: the time that is actually used for instruction.

- Engaged time: the time a student spends working attentively on academic tasks.
- Productive time: the proportion of engaged time in which students are doing work that is meaningful and appropriate.

How to Increase Hours for Learning

Maintain activity flow by avoiding

Flip-flopping.
Stimulus-bound events.
Overdwelling.
Fragmentation.

Minimize transition time by

Defining boundaries to lessons.
Preparing students for transitions.
Establishing routines.

Hold students accountable by

Communicating assignments and requirements clearly.
Monitoring students' progress.
Establishing routines for collecting and checking classwork and homework.
Maintaining good records.

Manage pull-outs as efficiently as possible:

Try to have input into scheduling.
Create a schedule showing periods of time when various students are present and when the whole class is together.
Establish (or find out about) a policy regarding the responsibility of pulled-out students to complete work they missed.
Establish procedures for smooth transitions when students return to the classroom.

By using time wisely, you can maximize opportunities for learning and minimize occasions for disruption in your classroom. Think about how much time is being spent on meaningful and appropriate work in your room, and how much is being eaten up by business and clerical tasks. Be aware that the hours available for instruction are much fewer than they first appear!

Activities

1. Obtain a copy of the weekly schedule for the class you are observing. Analyze it to determine how much time is *allocated* each week to literacy (reading, language arts, creative writing, spelling, etc.), mathematics, science, social studies, art, music, and

physical education. Next, select one subject that is taught while you are visiting the class. Observe for one complete period, carefully noting how much of the allocated time is actually used for *instructional* purposes. For example, let's suppose you elect to observe a 50-minute mathematics class. The *allocated time* is 50 minutes. But while you are observing, you note that the first five minutes of the period are spent checking to see who does or does not have the homework (a clerical job). In the middle of the period, the teacher asks students to get into groups of four, and moving into groups takes up another five minutes that is not actually spent in instruction. Then an announcement comes on over the loudspeaker, and the class discusses the announcement for another three minutes. Finally, the teacher wraps up class five minutes before the end of the period and gives everyone free time. *Conclusion: Out of 50 minutes of allocated time, 18 minutes were spent on nonacademic or noninstructional activities, leaving 32 minutes of actual instructional time.*

2. Read the following vignette and identify the factors that threaten the activity flow of the lesson. Once you have identified the problems, rewrite the vignette so that activity flow is maintained OR explain how you would avoid the problems if you were the teacher.

Mrs. P. waits while her second-grade students take out their fraction circles to begin the math lesson. When most of the children have placed the circles on their desks, she begins to remind the class of the work they did on fractions the previous day. As she explains the tasks they are about to do, she notices that Jack doesn't have his circles.

"Jack, where are your circles?"

"I don't know."

"This is the third time you don't have your circles. You didn't have them last week, and you had to stay in at recess one day and you also lost free time. What did I tell you would happen if you lost your circles one more time?"

"You were going to call my mother."

"That's right. Now go and write your name on the board while I see if I have an extra pack for you to use."

Mrs. P. goes to the supply closet and pulls out a pack of fraction circles for Jack. She then instructs the class to place the bag of shapes on the top left side of their desks.

"Take out the blue circle and place it directly in front of you." She checks to see that all students have complied.

"Now take out one of the four red pieces and place it on the blue circle. Be careful not to drop it, and do this without talking to your neighbor."

Mrs. P. circulates to see if the children are following directions.

"Now take out another red piece and place it on the blue circle."

The children do so. Mrs. P. then directs them to take out two remaining red pieces and place them on the blue circle, "one at a time."

"How many red pieces did you use to cover the blue circle?"

The class responds, "Four."

"And what is one piece called?"

"One-fourth."

"I'd like everyone to say it together, please."

"One-fourth!"

"Did I hear the back table? I want everyone to repeat it with strong voices!"

"ONE-FOURTH!"

"Excellent. Now what are two pieces called?"

"Two-fourths."

"I still didn't hear everyone. Let's hear Rhonda's table. (Rhonda's table responds.) Okay, how about Shakia's table? (They respond.) And now Reggie's table. Good."

As she passes Rob's desk, she notices a pink slip of paper. "Class, I almost forgot. Those children who have permission forms for the zoo trip need to give them to me now, so I can get them to the office."

Children proceed to hunt through their desks. Several ask permission to go get their book bags. Once all the slips are collected, Mrs. P. returns to the lesson and goes on to talk about thirds. She directs the children to put away the red pieces, to take out the three green pieces, and to cover the blue circle with the green pieces. Mrs. P. checks that students know each green piece is "one-third." At the completion of this activity, Mrs. P. directs the students to put away the fraction circles and to take out their spelling books.

"Okay, children, turn to page 37 in your spellers and let's review the words for this week. Tanya, please read the first word and use it in a sentence."

As Tanya begins, Mrs. P. interrupts: "I'm sorry, Tanya, but I just realized that I forgot to tell you all what the math homework is. Everyone, take out your assignment pads and write down the assignment as I write it on the board." She takes a piece of chalk and writes, "Math—page 25, even problems only." The children copy the assignment. Mrs. P. scans the room to make sure everyone has written the assignment. When all the children are done, she directs them to return to their spellers. "All right, now where were we? Tanya, you were doing number one." When Tanya finishes, Mrs. P. has the class spell the word out loud and then moves on to the next word. The class is on the fourth word when the bell rings for lunch.

"Oh my, I don't know where the time went. OK, boys and girls, get ready for lunch. We'll continue with spelling when you get back."

3. Develop a routine or transition activity for each of the following situations. Remember, your goal is to use time wisely.

   a. Beginning of the school day.

   b. Snack time.

   c. Returning from gym.

   d. Moving from small group time to independent seatwork.

4. You want your fourth-grade students to do a research report on a famous inventor. They will also be creating their own inventions. As you plan this project, you will need to consider how to hold your students accountable. How will you

   a. Convey requirements clearly and thoroughly?

   b. Monitor student progress?

5. Interview two teachers about their policies and procedures with respect to pull-out instruction. Do they require students who are pulled out to complete the work they missed? If so, when do students do the work? How do they reorient students when they return to class? Do they see any alternatives to pull-out instruction?

✦For Further Reading

Adelman, N. E., Walking Eagle, K. P., & Hargreaves, A. (Eds.) (1997). *Racing with the clock.* New York: Teachers College Press.

National Education Commission on Time and Learning (1994). *Prisoners of time* [online]. Available at http://www.emich.edu/public/emu_programs/tlc/toc.html.

Wood, C. (1999). *Time to teach, time to learn: Changing the pace of school.* Greenfield, MA: Northeast Foundation for Children.

✦References

Arlin, M. (1979). Teacher transitions can disrupt time flow in classrooms. *American Educational Research Journal, 16,* 42–56.

Doyle, W. (1983). Academic work. *Review of Educational Research, 53*(2), 159–200.

Evertson, C. M., Emmer, E. T., & Worsham, M. E. (2000). *Classroom management for elementary teachers* (5th ed.). Englewood Cliffs, NJ: Prentice Hall.

Fisher, C. W., Filby, N. N., Marliave, R. S., Cahen, L. S., Dishaw, M. M., Moore, J. E., & Berliner, D. C. (1978). *Teaching behaviors, academic learning time and student achievement. Final report of Phase III-B, Beginning Teacher Evaluation Study.* San Francisco, CA: Far West Laboratory for Educational Research and Development.

Fisher, C. W., Berliner, D. C., Filby, N. N., Marliave, R., Cahen, L. S. & Dishaw, M. M. (1980). Teaching behaviors, academic learning time, and student achievement: An overview. In C. Denham & A. Lieberman (Eds.), *Time to learn.* Washington, DC: U.S. Department of Education, 7–32.

Good, T. L., & Brophy, J. E. (2000). *Looking in classrooms* (8th ed.). New York: HarperCollins.

Gump, P. V. (1982). School settings and their keeping. In D. L. Duke (Ed.), *Helping teachers manage classrooms.* Alexandria, VA: Association for Supervision and Curriculum Development, 98–114.

Gump, P. V. (1987). School and classroom environments. In D. Stokols & I. Altman (Eds.), *Handbook of environmental psychology.* New York: John Wiley & Sons, 691–732.

Karweit, N. (1989). Time and learning: A review. In R. E. Slavin (Ed.), *School and classroom organization.* Hillsdale, NJ: Lawrence Erlbaum Associates.

Kidder, T. (1989). *Among schoolchildren.* Boston: Houghton Mifflin.

Kounin, J. (1970). *Discipline and group management in classrooms.* New York: Holt, Rinehart and Winston.

Leinhardt, G., & Greeno, J. G. (1986). The cognitive skill of teaching. *Journal of Educational Psychology, 78*(2), 75–95.

Lowe, R., & Gervais, R. (1988). Increasing instructional time in today's classroom. *NASSP Bulletin,* 19–22.

National Commission on Excellence in Education (1983). *A nation at risk: The imperative for educational reform.* Washington, DC: Government Printing Office.

National Education Commission on Time and Learning (1994). *Prisoners of time* [online]. Available at http://www.emich.edu/public/emu_programs/tlc/toc.html.

Rosenshine, B. (1980). How time is spent in elementary classrooms. In C. Denham & A. Lieberman (Eds.), *Time to learn.* Washington, DC: U.S. Department of Education.

Ross, R. P. (1985). Elementary school activity segments and the transitions between them: Responsibilities of teachers and student teachers. Unpublished doctoral dissertation, University of Kansas.

Schmidt, W. H., & Buchmann, M. (1983). Six teachers' beliefs and attitudes and their curricular time allocations. *The Elementary School Journal, 84*(2), 162–171.

Shalaway, L. (1989). *Learning to teach . . . not just for beginners.* Cleveland, OH: Instructor Books, Edgell Communications.

Walberg, H. J. (1988). Synthesis of research on time and learning. *Educational Leadership, 45*(6), 76–85.

Wood, C. (1999). *Time to teach, time to learn: Changing the pace of school.* Greenfield, MA: Northeast Foundation for Children.

PART III

Organizing and Managing Instruction

Enhancing Students' Motivation

Midway through student teaching, a young woman in a fifth-grade placement came to seminar at her wits' end. "I give up with these kids," she told the group.

My cooperating teacher and I can threaten with zeroes, call their parents, keep them in at recess—nothing works. They just don't care, and I'm just about ready to quit! I want a placement in kindergarten, where kids still want to learn things!

As we talked further, it seemed as though she believed that motivation is entirely the student's responsibility; to be successful in school, students must arrive motivated, just as they must arrive with notebooks and pencils. She also seemed to think that motivation is a stable characteristic, like eye color. From this perspective, some individuals come to school wanting to learn, and some don't. This can be a comforting point of view: if motivation is an innate or unchangeable characteristic, then we don't have to spend time and energy figuring out ways to motivate students.

A contrasting view posits that motivation is an acquired disposition amenable to change. It can also be situation specific, varying with the nature of the particular activity. Thus, students can be enthusiastic about reading Judy Blume's novel, *Tales of a Fourth-Grade Nothing* (1972), but can appear bored and uninterested when it's time to do spelling sentences.

According to this latter perspective, teachers are responsible for trying to stimulate students' engagement in learning activities. It may be gratifying (and a lot easier) when students come to school already excited about learning; however, when this is not the case, teachers must redouble their efforts to create a classroom context that fosters students' involvement and interest (Hidi & Harackiewicz, 2000). Unfortunately, research indicates that this does not always happen. Skinner and Belmont (1993) found that teachers' actions actually "magnify" students' initial levels of motivation (p. 580). When children enter the classroom already motivated, teachers tend to respond positively and to provide additional support, affection, and encouragement. When children enter the classroom exhibiting a *lack* of motivation, however, teachers may respond negatively and become coercive and neglectful—thus exacerbating students' initial lack of interest.

This chapter focuses on ways to enhance students' motivation. We begin by reflecting on what is realistic and appropriate with respect to motivating students. We then examine the factors that give rise to motivation. Finally, we consider a variety of motivational strategies drawn from research, theory, and the practice of our four teachers.

What Is Realistic? What Is Appropriate?

Many of the teacher education students with whom we've worked believe that teachers motivate students *by making learning fun.* In fact, they frequently mention the ability to design activities that are enjoyable and entertaining as one of the defining characteristics of the "good teacher." Yet, as Jere Brophy (1998) reminds us, "schools are not day camps or recreational centers" (p. xviii), and teachers are not counselors or recreational directors. Given compulsory attendance, required curricula, class sizes that inhibit individualization, and the specter of high-stakes standardized testing, trying to ensure that learning is always fun is unreasonable and unrealistic. Bill Ayers (1993), a professor of education who has taught preschool through graduate school, is even more blunt. Characterizing the idea that good teachers make learning fun is one of the common myths that plague teaching, Ayers writes:

> *Fun is distracting, amusing. Clowns are fun. Jokes can be fun. Learning can be engaging, engrossing, amazing, disorienting, involving, and often deeply pleasurable. If it's fun, fine. But it doesn't need to be fun. (p. 13)*

Probably all of us can remember situations in which we were motivated to accomplish an academic task that was not fun, but that nonetheless seemed worthwhile and meaningful. The example that immediately comes to our own minds is learning a foreign language. Neither of the authors has ever been very good at languages, and we were anxious and self-conscious whenever we had to speak in language class. We found conversation and oral exercises painful; role-plays were excruciating. Yet, we each took 3 years of a foreign language in high school and 3 more in college, determined to communicate as fluently as possible when we were finally able to go abroad.

Brophy (1998) refers to this kind of drive as *motivation to learn*—the "tendency to find academic activities meaningful and worthwhile and to try to get the intended learning benefits from them" (p. 12). He distinguishes motivation to learn from *intrinsic motivation,* in which individuals pursue academic activities because they find them pleasurable. At times, of course, you may be able to capitalize on students' intrinsic interests so that the learning activities will be perceived as fun. But it's unlikely that this will always be the case. For this reason, teachers need to consider ways of developing and maintaining students' motivation to learn.

An Expectancy × Value Framework

It is helpful to think about stimulating motivation to learn in terms of an expectancy-value model (Brophy, 1998; Feather, 1982). This model proposes that motivation depends on *students' expectation of success* and *the value they place on the task* (or the rewards that it may bring—such as being able to speak fluent Spanish). The two factors work together like a multiplication equation (expectancy × value): If either one is missing (i.e., zero), there will be no motivation.

The expectancy × value model suggests that you have two major responsibilities with respect to motivation. *First, you need to ensure that students can successfully perform the task at hand if they expend the effort.* This means creating assignments that are well suited to students' achievement levels. This may also mean helping students to recognize their ability to perform successfully. Consider the case of Hopeless Hannah (Stipek, 1993). During math class, Hannah frequently sits at her desk doing nothing. If the teacher urges Hannah to try one of the problems she is supposed to be doing, she claims she can't. When the teacher walks her through a problem step by step, Hannah answers most of the questions correctly, but she insists that she was only guessing. Hannah considers herself incompetent, and she interprets her teacher's frustration as proof of her incompetence. She is a classic example of a student with "failure syndrome" problems (Brophy, 1998).

Fortunately, extreme cases like Hannah's are uncommon (Stipek, 1993). But we've probably all encountered situations where anticipation of failure has led to avoidance or paralysis. A lengthy term paper assignment is overwhelming, so we procrastinate until it's too late to do it really well. Calculus is daunting, so we take general mathematics instead. If failure is inevitable, there's no point in trying. And if we rarely try, we rarely succeed.

A second responsibility of teachers is to help students recognize the value of the academic work at hand. For example, Satisfied Sam (Stipek, 1993) is the class clown. He earns grades of C+ and B−, although he's clearly capable of earning As. At home, Sam spends hours at his computer, reads every book he can find on space, loves science fiction, and has even written a short novel. But he displays little interest in schoolwork. If assignments coincide with his personal interests, he exerts effort; otherwise, he simply sees no point in doing them.

In order to help students like Sam, you need to communicate the value of class activities or the value of the rewards that successful completion or mastery will bring. For example, students may see little value in learning decimals, but still recognize that a passing grade in math is required for promotion.

In accordance with the expectancy × value model, Brophy (1987, 1998) has reviewed relevant theory and research and derived a set of strategies that teachers can use to enhance students' motivation. The following sections of this chapter are based on Brophy's work. (See Table 8-1.) We begin with strategies that focus on the first variable in the model—students' expectations of success.

TABLE 8-1. Brophy's Strategies for Enhancing Motivation to Learn

---

Strategies for Increasing Expectation of Success
- Provide opportunities for success
- Teach students to set reasonable goals and to assess their own performance
- Help students recognize the relationship between effort and outcome
- Provide informative feedback
- Provide special motivational support to low achievers

Strategies for Increasing Perceived Value
- Relate lessons to students' own lives
- Provide opportunities for choice
- Model interest in learning and express enthusiasm for the material
- Include novelty/variety elements
- Provide opportunities for students to respond actively
- Allow students to create finished products
- Provide opportunities for students to interact with peers
- Provide extrinsic rewards

As you read, keep in mind *that none of these strategies will be very effective if you have not worked to create and sustain a safe, caring classroom environment* (Chapter 5). Before students can become motivated, they must feel safe from humiliation, understand that it's all right to take risks and make mistakes, and know that they are accepted, respected members of the class. In fact, Brophy considers a supportive environment to be an "essential precondition" for the successful use of motivational strategies (Good & Brophy, 2000, p. 221).

Strategies for Increasing Expectations of Success

Provide Opportunities for Success

If tasks appear too difficult, students may be afraid to tackle them. You need to make sure that instruction is on an appropriate level for each student. You may have to modify assignments for different students, make assignments open ended so that a variety of responses can be acceptable, allow extra time, or provide additional help. For example, when Garnetta reviews cursive writing, she gives some of her students an alphabet page that requires them to trace over dashed letters. Other students have to complete an alphabet in which every fourth or fifth letter is missing. Still others write most of the alphabet on their own, with just a few letters already present as cues. These differentiated assignments increase all children's chances of success.

Another example of differentiated assignments comes from Tomlinson (1999):

Today, [Ms. Cunningham's first-grade] students will work at a learning center on compound words. Students' names are listed at the center; one of four colors is beside each name. Each student works with the folder that matches the color beside his or her name. For example, Sam has the color red next to his name. Using the materials in the red folder, Sam must decide the correct order of pairs of words to make familiar compound words. He also will make a poster that illustrates each simple word and the new compound word they form. Using materials in the blue folder, Jenna will look around the classroom and in books to find examples of compound words. She will write them out and illustrate them in a booklet. Using materials in the purple folder, Tijuana will write a poem or a story that uses compound words she generates and that make the story or poem interesting . . . . In the green folder, Dillon will find a story the teacher has written. It contains correct and incorrect compound words. Dillon will be a word detective, looking for "villains" and "good guys" among the compound words. He will list [these] on a chart . . . and then write them correctly.

Teach Students to Set Reasonable Goals and to Assess Their Own Performance

Some children think anything less than 100 on a test is a failure, while others are content with a barely passing grade. You may have to help students set goals that are reasonable and obtainable. On the first day of school, Garnetta has her students write about their goals for third grade. These are discussed and posted on the front bulletin board, where they can serve as daily reminders: "I want to learn how to write in cursive." "I want to know times tables and divided by." "I will try to get strait [sic] A's." "I want to learn multiplication." And from a new child, "I want to make new friends." Similarly, on the first day of school, Ken gives his students their report cards from the previous year and copies of their standardized achievement test scores. He asks them "to sit and reflect and begin to set some goals." He encourages them to write these down. Then he distributes a blank report card to each student, telling them to "think about what you'd like to get in each subject." He stresses that this is "just the beginning" of the process and that they will continue to develop real objectives for the academic year.

Help Students Recognize the Relationship between Effort and Outcome

Like Hopeless Hannah, some youngsters proclaim defeat before they've even attempted a task. When they don't do well on an assignment, they attribute their failure to lack of ability, not realizing that achievement is often a function of effort. Other students may be overconfident—even cocky—and think they can do well without exerting much effort. In either situation, you have to make the relationship between effort and outcome explicit. Whenever possible, point out students' improvement and help them to see the role of effort: "See, you did all your math homework this week, and it really paid off. Look at how well you did on the quiz!"

Provide Informative Feedback

Sometimes turning in work to a teacher is like dropping it down a black hole. Assignments pile up in huge mounds on the teacher's desk, and students know that their papers will never be returned—graded or ungraded. From a student's perspective, it's infuriating to work hard on an assignment, turn it in, and then receive no feedback from the teacher. But a lack of academic feedback is not simply infuriating. It is also detrimental to students' motivation and achievement. The Beginning Teacher Evaluation Study (Fisher et al., 1980) documented the importance of providing feedback to students:

> *One particularly important teaching activity is providing academic feedback to students (letting them know whether their answers are right or wrong, or giving them the right answer). Academic feedback should be provided as often as possible to students. When more frequent feedback is offered, students pay attention more and learn more.* Academic feedback was more strongly and consistently related to achievement than any of the other teaching behaviors. *(p. 27; emphasis added)*

If you circulate while students are working on assignments, you can provide them with immediate feedback about their performance. You can catch errors, assist with problems, and affirm correct, thoughtful work. As Viviana comments:

I always correct papers as my children are doing them. That's the time to explain and correct mistakes. If children don't understand the first problem, they'll get all the rest wrong. This also allows students to take their work home every day, so parents can see how they're doing. Correcting work as students do it also means that I don't have to take home a huge stack of papers every night, and I can use that time for planning.

Sometimes you're unable to monitor and correct work while it's being done. In this case, you need to check assignments once they've been submitted and return them to students as soon as possible. You might also decide to allow your students to check their own work. Ken believes this has numerous educational benefits:

If I correct assignments, I'm doing all the important work—the editing, the problem solving, the analyzing of mistakes. That's what the kids should be doing, or at the very least, I should be doing it in front of them. They learn best by correcting their own mistakes, rather than reading somebody else's comments. And the most important stuff must be talked about. I prefer to have students discuss and correct work together, either in their small reading and math groups or as a whole class. I tell them, "Today at 2:00 you need to be ready to share your newspaper articles." We discuss what they've done, and the feedback session becomes an extension of the assignment.

Some teachers also encourage peer feedback, a practice that reinforces the idea that students can learn from one another and reduces the workload for teachers. If you choose to use peer feedback, be aware of some inherent problems (Latham, 1997). First, without proper training, students may not be able to provide high-quality feedback. Ching (1991), for example, notes that when providing feedback on written work, students may respond to "lower-order concerns," such as syntactic errors, rather than more substantive concerns, such as the development of ideas. Second, although Vygotsky (1978) argues that interactions with more able peers can help students work in their zone of proximal development, a classwide system of peer feedback inevitably requires some students to receive feedback from *less* able peers (DiPardo & Freedman, 1988). Finally, some students may not value feedback received from their peers. Zhang (1995) found that students whose native language was not English overwhelmingly preferred teacher feedback to student feedback.

Whether you correct work while it's being done, at home over a cup of coffee, or together with your students, the important point is that students *need to know how they are progressing.* It's also important to give feedback in terms of *absolute standards or students' own past performance rather than peers' performance* (Brophy, 1998). Thus, instead of saying, "Congratulations! You received the sixth-highest grade in the class," you could say, "Congratulations! You went from a 79 on your last quiz to an 87 on this quiz." Similarly, you can point out strengths and weaknesses and add a note of encouragement for further effort ("You've demonstrated a firm grasp of the perspectives of the slave-holders and the abolitionists, but not the slaves themselves. Check the chapter again, and add a paragraph to round out your presentation.")

Provide Special Motivational Support to Discouraged Students

For students with limited ability or learning disabilities, school may be a constant struggle to keep up with classmates and to maintain a sense of enthusiasm and motivation. Such students not only require instructional assistance (e.g., individualized activities, extra academic help, well-structured assignments, extra time), they may also need special encouragement and motivational support.

Unfortunately, teachers sometimes develop counterproductive behavior patterns that communicate low expectations and reinforce students' perceptions of themselves as failures. Table 8-2 lists some of the behaviors that have been identified.

As Brophy (1998) points out, some of these differences are due to the behavior of the students. For example, if students' contributions to discussions are irrelevant or incorrect, it is difficult for teachers to accept and use their ideas. Moreover, the boundary between *appropriate differentiated instruction and inappropriate differential treatment* is often fuzzy. Asking low achievers easier, nonanalytic questions may make instructional sense. Nonetheless, it's important to monitor the extent to which you engage in these behaviors and to reflect on the messages you are sending to your low-achieving or learning disabled students. If you find that you are engaging in a lot of

---

TABLE 8-2. Ways that Teachers May Communicate Low Expectations

1. Waiting less time for low achievers to answer a question before giving the answer or calling on someone else.
2. Giving answers to low achievers or calling on someone else rather than helping the students to improve their responses by giving clues or rephrasing questions.
3. Rewarding inappropriate behaviors or incorrect answers.
4. Criticizing low achievers more often for failure.
5. Praising low achievers less often for success.
6. Paying less attention to low achievers.
7. Seating low achievers farther away from the teacher.
8. Demanding less from low achievers than they are capable of learning.
9. Being less friendly in interactions with low achievers; showing less attention and responsiveness; making less eye contact.
10. Providing briefer and less informative answers to their questions.
11. Showing less acceptance and use of low achievers' ideas.
12. Limiting low achievers to low-level, repetitive curriculum with an emphasis on drill and practice tasks.

Source: Brophy, 1998.

the behaviors listed in Table 8-2, you may be "merely going through the motions of instructing low achievers, without seriously working to help them achieve their potential" (Brophy, 1998, p. 85).

Enhancing the Value of the Task

Recall that the students in the classes of our four teachers stressed the importance of teaching in a way that is stimulating. As one student wrote, "Not everything can be fun . . ., but there are ways teachers can make [material] more interesting and more challenging." (See Chapter 2.) This student intuitively understands that motivation to learn depends not only on success expectations, but also on students' perceptions of the value of the task or the rewards that successful completion or mastery will bring. Remember Satisfied Sam? Seeing no value in his course assignments, he invests little effort in them, even though he knows he could be successful. Since students like Sam are unlikely to respond to their teachers' exhortations to work harder, the challenge is to find ways to convince them that the work has (1) *intrinsic value* (doing it will provide enjoyment), (2) *utility value* (doing it will advance their personal goals), or (3) *attainment value* (doing it will affirm their self-concept or fulfill their needs for achievement, understanding, skill mastery, and prestige) (Brophy, 1998; Eccles & Wigfield, 1985). Let's consider some of the strategies that teachers can use to enhance the perception of value.

Relate Lessons to Students' Own Lives

A study by Newby (1991) of the motivational strategies of first-year teachers demonstrated that students are more engaged in classrooms where teachers provide reasons for doing tasks and relate lessons to students' personal experiences. Unfortunately, *he also found that first-year teachers use these "relevance strategies" only occasionally.* (See Figure 8-1.)

Observations of our four teachers provide numerous examples of attempts to link academic tasks to children's lives. In math class, for example, Barbara often creates word

SHOE   By JEFF MACNELLY

FIGURE 8-1. It's important to point out the relevance of learning activities. (© Tribune-Media Services, Inc. All rights reserved. Reprinted with permission.)

problems that incorporate her students' names and interests: "Mark collects baseball cards. His collection is worth $57.85. He purchases five new cards valued at $6.35. . . ." When Ken's class does writing, the topics come from the students' own lives. He asks them to write about what they're good at, what they can teach others, how they feel about school. Viviana and Garnetta teach map skills by having students make maps of the classroom and the neighborhood. Garnetta's students also play a game in which they write the directions to their houses. These are then read aloud and students try to guess whose house is involved.

When students are not from the dominant culture, teachers must make a special effort to relate academic content to referents from the students' own culture—what Gloria Ladson-Billings (1994) calls *culturally relevant teaching*. This practice not only helps to bridge the gap between the two cultures, it also allows the study of cultural referents in their own right. The case of Carter Forshay, an African American man in his late 20s, provides a compelling example (Ladson-Billings, 2001). As a first-year teacher, Carter was committed to fostering the literacy skills of his third-grade students, all African Americans. To his dismay, he discovered that his students "absolutely hated writing" (p. 19):

Every time Carter attempted to come up with an exciting and motivating topic on which to write, his students balked. . . ."Aww, Mr. Forshay, I don't want to do this." "Writin' is too hard." "I don't have nothin' to say; why are you makin' us write this stuff?" "Why can't you just give us some worksheets? We can do them!" (p. 19)

Knowing that his students loved music, Carter decided that "helping kids connect with music might be a way to help them connect with writing" (p. 20). He chose a CD by trumpeter Wynton Marsalis containing the song, *Blue Interlude: The Bittersweet Saga of Sugar Cane and Sweetie Pie*. As in *Peter and the Wolf,* various melodies in *Blue Interlude* reflect particular characters.

During the first lesson Carter played the CD and questioned the students about what they thought the action was and how they thought the characters were behaving and feeling. From there, Carter encouraged the students to take turns role-playing the characters and their interactions.

Although Carter's students were initially reluctant to do the role-plays, they eventually became more enthusiastic and more theatrical. Carter concluded the first lesson by having students record the traits of each character in the piece.

On subsequent days, students outlined the story they had created, developed dialogue, and wrote and illustrated their own drafts. As Ladson-Billings comments, "The students who no one thought would write had become writers" (21).

Provide Opportunities for Choice

One of the most obvious ways to ensure that learning activities connect to individuals' personal interests is to provide opportunities for choice. Moreover, research has shown that when students experience a sense of autonomy and self-determination, they are more likely to be intrinsically motivated (Ryan & Deci, 2000) and to "bond" with school (Roeser, Eccles, & Sameroff, 2000).

Mandated curricula and high-stakes standardized testing thwart opportunities for choice, but there are usually alternative ways for students to accomplish requirements. Think about whether students might (1) participate in the design of the academic tasks; (2) decide how the task is to be completed; and/or (3) decide when the task is to be completed (Stipek, 1993). (See Chapter 5 for additional ways of providing opportunities for choice.)

Model Interest in Learning and Express Enthusiasm for the Material

Before Barbara introduces students to the novel, *Mr. Popper's Penguins* (Atwater, 1966), she first discloses that "penguins are one of my favorite animals." Her enthusiasm for penguins is apparent—on the first day of school, students' name tags prominently feature a picture of a penguin; a five-foot-high, plastic penguin stands in the library corner; stuffed animal penguins perch on Barbara's desk; as days go by, dates on the class calendar are covered by paper penguins.

Include Novelty/Variety Elements

Garnetta's students play "Wheel of Fortune" to practice vocabulary. Barbara distributes the advertising flyers from supermarkets, assigns each child a designated amount of money, and has her students "go shopping." Viviana's students jump, hop, clap, and march when she's teaching them about verbs that depict action. When Ken's students learn about sampling procedures, they work with M&M's, extrapolating from a small bag in order to predict how many of each color would be contained in a half-pound bag.

Provide Opportunities for Students to Respond Actively

So often the teacher talks and moves, while students sit passively and listen. In contrast, when Ken's class studies probability, students work in small groups, gently tossing tacks and graphing how many land with the points up and how many land with the points down (and it's *not* 50–50!). Barbara's students make bubble solution, go outside to blow bubbles, and discuss what they saw, how the bubbles felt, and what they looked like. Then they come back in and write poems, essays, or stories about the experience.

Allow Students to Create Finished Products

Too much school time is devoted to exercises, drills, and practice. Students practice writing, but rarely write. They practice reading skills, but rarely read. They practice mathematical procedures, but rarely do real mathematics. Yet, creating a finished product gives meaning and purpose to assignments and increases students' motivation to learn. After Garnetta's students finish their research on the solar system, each child constructs an eight-foot mural of the planets that they can take home. When Viviana's students learn about seeds, they construct displays for the district's Academic Fair. Barbara's students participate in the "Invention Convention": they define a problem (e.g., scratching your back in an out-of-the-way place) and then construct an invention to solve the problem.

Garnetta's students carry out a science experiment.

In addition, students write ads for their inventions, which are compiled in a book that resembles a Sears catalog. When Ken's students have a writing assignment, the due date is called the "publication date." At that time, they "celebrate authorship" by reading and discussing their work (and, of course, by sharing some treats).

Provide Opportunities for Students to Interact with Peers

All four teachers allow students to work in small groups to accomplish tasks (a topic that will be explored further in Chapter 10). For example, Viviana's students work in pairs during math, manipulating Unifix cubes to demonstrate two-digit numbers. In Ken's class, students form simulation teams to experience firsthand the hardships of pioneer life. Garnetta's class divides into "food groups" when they are studying nutrition. Barbara's students have spelling partners because "spelling can be tedious."

Provide Extrinsic Rewards

Some effective managers find it useful to provide students with rewards for engaging in the behaviors that support learning (such as paying attention and participating) and for academic achievement. The use of rewards in classrooms is based on the psychological principle of *positive reinforcement:* Behavior that is rewarded is strengthened and is therefore likely to be repeated. Although rewards do not increase the perceived value of the behavior or the task, they link performance of the behavior or successful completion of the task to attractive, desirable consequences.

Rewards can be divided into three categories: social rewards, activity rewards, and tangible rewards. *Social rewards* are verbal and nonverbal indications that you recognize and appreciate students' behavior or achievements. A pat on the back, a smile, a thumbs-up signal—these are commonly used social rewards that are low in cost and readily available.

Praise can also function as a social reward. In order to be effective, however, praise must be *specific and sincere*. Instead of "Good paper," you can try something like this: "Your paper shows a firm grasp of the distinction between metaphor and similes." Instead of "You were great this morning," try, "The way you came into the room, took off your baseball caps, and immediately got out your notebooks was terrific." Being specific will make your praise more informative; it will also help you to avoid using the same tired, old phrases week after week, phrases that quickly lose any impact (e.g., "good job"). If praise is to serve as a reinforcer, it also needs to be *contingent on the behavior you are trying to strengthen*. In other words, it should be given only when that behavior occurs, so that students understand exactly what evoked the praise.

> *Viviana's students sit quietly while she speaks with a visitor by the door. When she turns back to the class, she tells them: "Thank you for being so quiet just now. It was so helpful. I was able to talk to Mrs. Johnson without being interrupted. By being quiet you helped the teacher."*

In addition to pats on the back and verbal praise, some teachers institute more formal ways of recognizing accomplishment, improvement, or cooperation. For example, they may display student work, provide award certificates, nominate students for school awards given at the end of the year, or select a "Student of the Week." Ken has developed an interesting variation of this program. Instead of deciding on the student of the week by himself, he and his students work together to develop the criteria (see Figure 8-2), and students vote each week to choose the recipient (another way of sharing responsibility and decision making with students). We asked Ken how he made sure that the weekly vote didn't degenerate into a popularity contest. Here's his response:

> *Every Friday afternoon we sit in a circle and nominate people. Nominations have to be supported with references to the criteria. For example, "I nominate Paul. He helped me in math this week," or "I nominate Leah. She shared her snack with me," or "she helped a new student." When the list of nominees is complete, each child gets a ballot and we vote. The winner receives a certificate to take home, and we all write a note to the student giving three reasons why they deserved it.*
>
> *The class created the rule that you can win twice, but you can't win a third time until everyone in the class has won. Now maybe a kid who hasn't been picked begins to feel uncomfortable. I think that's okay. Maybe he'll think about not getting picked and begin to modify his own behavior. Maybe he'll hold a door for the other kids or stack chairs. I'll talk privately to a kid who isn't selected: Why do you think you haven't been chosen? What do you think you could do in order to be chosen as student of the week? When I see him begin to change his behavior, I make sure to point that out: "I want to thank Robert for holding the door for all of us." It's funny, I*

THE STUDENT OF THE WEEK IS A PERSON WHO

1. is neat in work.
2. does homework.
3. is friendly to all classmates.
4. can be trusted and can be reliable.
5. helps others.
6. listens to the teacher's instructions.
7. respects other people's property.
8. is kind to people.
9. is responsible.
10. shares with other people.
11. treats eveyone equally.
12. cooperates with students and teachers.
13. has self-control.
14. doesn't curse or doesn't talk back.
15. doesn't give up and always tries his or her hardest.
16. doesn't hurt others' feelings.
17. helps people with work.
18. uses gifts and talents well.

FIGURE 8-2. Criteria for student of the week

thought maybe this year I wouldn't do student of the week, but the class really wanted it . . . And they do choose well.

In addition to social rewards, teachers sometimes use *special activities* as rewards for good behavior or accomplishment. (Table 8-3 lists activities that may be reinforcing.) In fact, Fredric Jones (2000) believes that the activities students enjoy are the best overall incentives. He recommends that teachers allow students to have "preferred activity time" (PAT) if they act responsibly. Students can also earn "bonus PAT" by saving time during transitions and "being in the right place at the right time with the right stuff" (p. 261). (See Jones's book, *Tools for Teaching,* for detailed advice about instituting a PAT incentive program.)

Finally, teachers can use *tangible, material rewards* for good behavior—cookies, stickers, award certificates, candy, baseball cards, pencils. For example, Barbara's math class has particular difficulty remembering to bring in homework. In order to encourage this behavior, Barbara gives out stickers that can then be traded for special privileges. Garnetta's students all have sticker folders they made out of cardboard, and Garnetta dispenses cats, pumpkins, stars, and hearts of every conceivable size, texture, and smell. In addition to the rewards she distributes in class, there is a schoolwide recognition program called GISMOS: Grand Incentive System for McKinley's Outstanding Students. By following established school rules, students earn purchasing power in the form of GISMOS points that can be used at the school store to purchase novelty items.

TABLE 8-3. Possible Reinforcers

Being first in line
Choosing a game to play with a friend
Choosing a game for the class to play
Choosing a story for the teacher to read to the class
Having 10 minutes of free time
Taking care of the class pet
Taking home the class pet for the weekend
Keeping a favorite stuffed animal on your desk for a day
Having breakfast or lunch with the teacher
Reading a story to a class in a lower grade
Reading a story to the principal
Using the computer alone or with a friend
Listening to music through earphones
Working with special art materials
Leading a game
Removing lowest test grade
Being excused from a homework assignment
Chewing gum at a specified time
Keeping score during a class game
Creating a bulletin board display
Checking out a classroom game to take home
Having a private, three-minute talk with the teacher

Problems with Rewards

The practice of providing extrinsic rewards has been the focus of considerable controversy. In particular, educators have debated the legitimacy and ultimate value of *material* rewards. Even among our four teachers, there is disagreement. While Ken, Garnetta, and Barbara all use material rewards to some extent, Viviana does not, preferring to rely on praise and recognition.

One objection is that giving students material rewards in exchange for good behavior is tantamount to bribery. Proponents of this position argue that students should engage in appropriate behavior and activities for their own sake: They should be quiet during independent work time because that is the socially responsible thing to do; they should do their homework so that they can practice skills taught during class; they should learn multiplication tables because they need to know them. Other educators acknowledge the desirability of such intrinsic motivation, but believe that the use of rewards is inevitable in situations where people are not completely free to follow their own inclinations. Even Ryan and Deci (2000), two psychologists who strongly endorse the importance of self-determination and autonomy, acknowledge that teachers "cannot always rely on intrinsic motivation to foster learning" since "many of the tasks that educators want their students to perform are not inherently interesting or enjoyable" (p. 55).

Another objection to the use of rewards is the fact that they are attempts to control and manipulate people. When we dispense rewards, we are essentially saying, "Do this, and you'll get that"—an approach not unlike the way we train our pets. Indeed, Alfie Kohn, author of *Punished by Rewards: The Trouble with Gold Stars, Incentive Plans, A's, Praise, and Other Bribes* (1993) contends that rewards and punishments are "two sides of the same coin" (p. 50). Although rewards are certainly more pleasurable, they are "every bit as controlling as punishments, even if they control by seduction" (p. 51). According to Kohn, if we want youngsters to become self-regulating, responsible, caring individuals, we must abandon attempts at external control and provide students with opportunities to develop competence, connection, and autonomy in caring classroom communities.

Another major concern is that rewarding students for behaving in certain ways actually *undermines their intrinsic motivation to engage in those behaviors.* This question was explored in an influential study conducted by Lepper, Greene, and Nisbett (1973). First, the researchers identified preschoolers who showed interest in a particular drawing activity during free play. Then they met with the children individually. Some children were simply invited to draw with the materials (the "no-reward" subjects). Others were told they could receive a "good-player" award, which they received for drawing (the "expected-reward" subjects). Still others were invited to draw and were then given an unexpected reward at the end (the "unexpected-reward" subjects). Subsequent observations during free play revealed that the children who had been promised a reward ahead of time engaged in the art activity half as much as they had initially. Children in the other two groups showed no change.

The study by Lepper, Greene, and Nisbett stimulated a great deal of research on the potentially detrimental effects of external rewards. Although the results were not always consistent, this research led educators to conclude that *rewarding people for doing something that is inherently pleasurable decreases their interest in continuing that behavior.* A common explanation for this effect is the *overjustification hypothesis.* It appears to work like this: Individuals being rewarded reason that the task must not be very interesting or engaging, since they have to be rewarded (i.e., provided with extra justification) for undertaking it.

The detrimental effect of extrinsic reward on intrinsic motivation has been—and continues to be—hotly debated. In fact, reviews of the research (Cameron & Pierce, 1994; Deci, Koestner, & Ryan, 1999) have reached contradictory conclusions about the effects of expected tangible rewards. According to Cameron and Pierce, it's all right to say, "If you complete the assignment accurately, you'll get a coupon for something at the school store at the end of the period" (reward contingent on completion and level of performance), but it's *not* all right to say, "Work on the assignment and you'll get a coupon for something at the school store at the end of the period" (noncontingent reward). In contrast, Deci, Koestner, and Ryan contend that expected "tangible rewards offered for engaging in, completing, or doing well at a task" are *all* deleterious to intrinsic motivation (p. 656). With respect to verbal rewards and unexpected tangible rewards, the two reviews are more consistent: Both sets of researchers conclude that verbal praise can enhance intrinsic motivation and that unexpected tangible rewards have no detrimental effect.

At the present time, caution in the use of external rewards is clearly in order. As you contemplate whether or not to use rewards in your classroom, keep in mind the following suggestions:

Use verbal rewards to increase intrinsic motivation for academic tasks. It seems clear that praise can have a positive impact on intrinsic motivation, especially if it is specific, sincere, and contingent on the behavior you are trying to strengthen. But remember that individual public praise may be embarrassing to older students and to those from cultures that value the collective over individual achievement.

Save tangible rewards for activities that students find unattractive. When students already enjoy doing a task, there's no need to provide tangible rewards. Save tangible rewards for activities that students tend to find boring and aversive.

If you're using tangible rewards, provide them unexpectedly, after the task perform-ance. In this way, students are more likely to view the rewards as information about their performance and as an expression of the teacher's pleasure, rather than as an attempt to control their behavior.

Be extremely careful about using expected tangible rewards. If you choose to use them, be sure to make them contingent upon completion of a task or achieving a specific level of performance. If you reward students simply for engaging in a task, regardless of their performance, they are likely to spend less time on the task once the reward is removed.

Make sure that you select rewards that students like. You may think that animal stickers are really neat, but if your sixth-graders do not find them rewarding, their behavior will not be reinforced.

Keep your program of rewards simple. An elaborate system of rewards is impos-sible to maintain in the complex world of the classroom. The fancier your system, the more likely that you will abandon it. Moreover, if rewards become too salient, they overshadow more intrinsic reasons for behaving in certain ways. Students become so preoccupied with collecting, counting, and comparing that they lose sight of why the behavior is necessary or valuable.

Think about ways to provide recognition without rewards. Although rewards and recognition are often used interchangeably, in fact they are very different. Rewards are based on criteria set by teachers to control students' behavior and motivate learning. Recognition, on the other hand, involves noticing, validating, describing, or acknowledging. For example, instead of handing out stickers or points for "good work," you can provide time each day for students to reflect on, record, and share their accomplishments. (See Cameron, Tate, MacNaughton, & Politano, 1997, for ideas on how to provide recognition without rewards.)

Motivating Underachieving and Disaffected Students

Finding ways to enhance students' motivation is particularly daunting when students are disaffected, apathetic, or resistant. As Brophy (1998) observes, such students find academic tasks relatively meaningless and resist engaging in them although they know that they could be successful. Some may even be fearful that school learning "will make them into something that they do not want to become" (p. 205). This fear is apparent in some African Americans and other students of color who equate academic achievement with "acting white." In a now classic paper, Fordham and Ogbu (1986) describe how bright black students may "put brakes" on their academic achievement by not studying or doing homework, cutting class, being late, and not participating in class:

> *This problem arose partly because white Americans traditionally refused to acknowledge that black Americans are capable of intellectual achievement, and partly because black Americans subsequently began to doubt their own intellectual ability, began to define academic success as white people's prerogative, and began to discourage their peers, perhaps unconsciously, from emulating white people in academic striving. . . . (p. 177)*

Motivating resistant, underachieving, or apathetic students requires "resocialization" (Brophy, 1998, p. 203). This means using the strategies described in this chapter in more sustained, systematic, and personalized ways. Extrinsic rewards may be especially useful in this regard (Hidi & Harackiewicz, 2000). By triggering engagement in tasks that students initially view as boring or irrelevant, "there is at least a chance" that real interest will develop (p. 159).

Barbara remembers a student who "didn't want to do much of anything," but who was an avid skateboarder. She tells us what happened when she paired him up with a high school student who also loved to skateboard:

> *I called the high school student and asked him who his English teacher was, and she and I were able to coordinate. The tenth-grader worked with my student on a "How to Skateboard" book. I worked after school with them and helped them to put the book together. Three things made this a successful intervention. First, working with a tenth-grader was a real kick for my student. Second, they were able to use technology, and that in itself is a real motivator. Finally, he knew I had paid attention to him, that I cared enough about him to do this. He began to demonstrate more willingness to do other work.*

Concluding Comments

A while back, a professor of educational psychology told us that learning about classroom management would be unnecessary if prospective teachers understood how to enhance students' motivation. Although we thought his argument was naive and unrealistic, we understood—and agreed with—its underlying premise; *namely, that students who are interested and involved in the academic work at hand are less likely to daydream, disrupt, and defy.* In other words, management and motivation are inextricably linked.

As you contemplate ways to increase your students' expectations for success and the value they place on academic tasks, remember that motivating students doesn't happen accidentally. You need to make the topic of motivation an integral part of every lesson plan. Fortunately, the motivational strategies discussed in this chapter are consistent with current thinking about good instruction, which emphasizes students' active participation, collaborative groupwork, and the use of varying assessments (Brophy, 1998).

Finally, remember the suggestions in Chapter 5 for creating a safer, more caring classroom. Rogers and Renard (1999) contend that "students are motivated when they believe that teachers treat them like people and care about them personally and educationally" (p. 34). Research by Kathryn Wentzel (1997, 1998) confirms this assertion. In two recent studies, Wentzel demonstrated that when middle-school students perceive their teachers as caring and supportive, they are more likely to be academically motivated, to engage in classroom activities, and to behave in prosocial, responsible ways. As Brophy (1998) observes: "You can become your own most powerful motivational tool by establishing productive relationships with each of your students" (p. 254).

Summary

Although teachers are responsible for enhancing motivation, this chapter began by questioning the belief that "good teachers should make learning fun." We argued that such a goal is unrealistic and inappropriate given the constraints of schooling—compulsory attendance, required curricula, class sizes that inhibit individualization, and the specter of high-stakes standardized testing. A more appropriate, realistic goal is to stimulate students' *motivation to learn,* whereby students pursue academic activities because they find them meaningful and worthwhile.

An expectancy × value framework

- Motivation depends on (1) students' expectation of success and (2) the value they place on the task (or the rewards that it may bring).
- If either factor is missing, there will be no motivation.

Strategies for increasing expectations of success

- Provide opportunities for success.
- Teach students to set reasonable goals and to evaluate their own performance.
- Help students recognize the relationship between effort and outcome.
- Provide informative feedback.
- Provide special motivational support to discouraged students.

Strategies for enhancing the value of the task

- Relate lessons to students' own lives.
- Provide opportunities for choice.
- Model interest in learning and express enthusiasm for the material.
- Include novelty/variety elements.
- Provide opportunities for students to respond actively.
- Allow students to create finished products.
- Provide opportunities for students to interact with peers.
- Provide extrinsic rewards, including social rewards, special activities, and tangible rewards. However,

  Be aware that rewarding people for doing something they already like to do may decrease their interest in continuing that behavior.
  Think carefully about when and how to use rewards:
    Use verbal rewards to increase intrinsic motivation for academic tasks.
    Save tangible rewards for activities that students find unappealing.
    Provide tangible rewards unexpectedly (after task performance).
    Provide expected tangible rewards only for completion of a task or for achieving a specific level of performance.
    Select rewards that your students like.
    Keep your reward program simple.

Motivating underachieving and disaffected students

- Be sensitive to the possibility that students of color may fear accusations of "acting white" if they strive to achieve academically.
- Recognize that resistant, apathetic students require "resocialization"—using the strategies described in this chapter in more sustained and systematic ways.
- Extrinsic rewards may be especially useful for motivating resistant, apathetic students.

By working to ensure that students are engaged in learning activities, you can avoid many of the managerial problems that arise when students are bored and frustrated. Management and motivation are closely intertwined.

✄ Activities

1. Design an assignment that will enable students of varying achievement levels to experience success. For example, the task might vary in complexity or the amount of scaffolding you provide; it might be open ended, allowing a variety of acceptable responses; it might require the use of different reference materials; or it might allow students to choose the format in which they demonstrate their understanding (e.g., a report, poster, or role-play). (Refer to the example from Tomlinson (1999) presented earlier in the chapter.)

2. Select a topic in a content area of your choice and design a lesson or activity that incorporates at least one of the strategies for enhancing perceived value. For example, you might relate the material to students' lives, provide opportunities for choice, allow students to work with peers, or produce a final product.

3. In the following two vignettes, the teachers have directed the activity. Think about ways they could have involved students in the planning, directing, creating, or evaluating. Rewrite each vignette to show this more student-centered approach.

   a. Mrs. Peters felt that the unit her fourth-grade class completed on folk tales would lend itself to a class play. She chose Paul Bunyan and Pecos Bill as the stories to dramatize. The students were excited as Mrs. Peters gave out parts and assigned students to paint scenery. Mrs. Peters wrote a script and sent it home for the students to memorize. She asked parents to help make the costumes. After three weeks of practice, the play was performed for the lower-grade classes and the parents.

   b. Mr. Wilkins wanted his sixth-grade class to develop an understanding about ancient civilizations. He assigned a five-part project. Students had to research four civilizations (Egyptian, Mesopotamian, Indus Valley, and Shang); write a biography of Howard Carter, a famous archaeologist; describe three pyramids (step, Great Pyramid, Pyramid of Sesostris II); outline the reigns of five kings (Hammurabi, Thutmose III, Ramses II, David, and Nebuchadnezzar); and make a model of a pyramid. He gave the class four weeks to complete the projects and then collected them, graded them, and displayed them in the school library.

4. Interview an experienced, effective teacher about the motivational strategies he or she finds particularly effective with disaffected, resistant students.

✄ For Further Reading

Brophy, J. (1998). *Motivating students to learn.* Boston: McGraw-Hill.

Burden, P. R. (2000). *Powerful classroom management strategies: Motivating students to learn.* Thousand Oaks, CA: Corwin Press.

Cameron, C., Tate, B., MacNaughton, D., & Politano, C. (1997). *Recognition without rewards: Building connections.* Winnipeg, Manitoba: Peguis Publishers.

Ginsberg, M. B., & Wlodkowski, R. J. (2000). *Creating highly motivating classrooms for all students: A schoolwide approach to powerful teaching with diverse learners.* San Francisco: Jossey-Bass.

Jones, F. (2000). *Tools for Teaching.* Santa Cruz, CA: Fredric H. Jones & Associates.

Kohn, A. (1993). *Punished by rewards: The trouble with gold stars, incentive plans, A's, praise, and other bribes.* Boston: Houghton Mifflin.

Stipek, D. J. (1993). *Motivation to learn: From theory to practice* (2nd ed.). Boston: Allyn and Bacon.

Tomlinson, C. A. (1999). *The differentiated classroom: Responding to the needs of all learners.* Alexandria, VA: Association for Supervision and Curriculum Development.

✸ References

Atwater, R. & F. (1966). *Mr. Popper's Penguins.* New York: Scholastic.

Ayers, W. (1993). *To teach: The journey of a teacher.* New York: Teachers College Press.

Blume, J. (1972). *Tales of a fourth grade nothing.* New York: Dell.

Brophy, J. (1998). *Motivating students to learn.* Boston: McGraw-Hill.

Brophy, J. (1987). Synthesis of research on strategies for motivating students to learn. *Educational Leadership, 45,* 40–48.

Cameron, C., Tate, B., MacNaughton, D., & Politano, C. (1997). *Recognition without rewards: Building connections.* Winnipeg, Manitoba: Peguis Publishers.

Cameron, J., & Pierce, W. D. (1994). Reinforcement, reward, and intrinsic motivation: A meta-analysis. *Review of Educational Research, 64,* 363–423.

Ching, C. L. P. (1991). Giving feedback on written work. *Guidelines, 13*(2), 68–80.

Deci, E. L., Koestner, R., & Ryan, R. M. (1999). A meta-analytic review of experiments examining the effects of extrinsic rewards on intrinsic motivation. *Psychological Bulletin, 125*(6), 627–668.

DiPardo, A., & Freedman, S. W. (1988). Peer response groups in the writing classroom: Theoretical foundations and new directions. *Review of Educational Research, 58*(2), 119–149.

Eccles, J., & Wigfield, A. (1985). Teacher expectations and student motivation. In J. Dusek (Ed.), *Teacher expectancies* (pp. 185–226). Hillsdale, NJ: Erlbaum.

Feather, N. (Ed.) (1982). *Expectations and actions.* Hillsdale, NJ: Erlbaum.

Fisher, C. W., Berliner, D. C., Filby, N. N., Marliave, R., Cahen, L. S., & Dishaw, M. M. (1980). Teaching behaviors, academic learning time, and student achievement: An overview. In C. Denham & A. Lieberman (Eds.), *Time to learn.* Washington, DC: U.S. Department of Education, 7–32.

Fordham, S., & Ogbu, J. U. (1986). Black students' school success: Coping with the "burden of 'acting white.'" *The Urban Review, 18*(3), 176–206.

Good, T. L., & Brophy, J. E. (2000). *Looking in classrooms* (8th ed.). New York: Addison Wesley Longman.

Hidi, S., & Harackiewicz, J. M. (2000). Motivating the academically unmotivated: A critical issue for the 21st century. *Review of Educational Research, 70*(2), 151–179.

Jones, F. (2000). *Tools for Teaching.* Santa Cruz, CA: Fredric H. Jones & Associates.

Kohn, A. (1993). *Punished by rewards: The trouble with gold stars, incentive plans, A's, praise, and other bribes.* Boston: Houghton Mifflin.

Ladson-Billings, G. (1994). *The dreamkeepers: Successful teachers of African American children.* San Francisco: Jossey-Bass.

Ladson-Billings, G. (2001). *Crossing over to Canaan: The journey of new teachers in diverse classrooms.* San Francisco: Jossey-Bass.

Latham, A. S. (1997). Learning through feedback. *Educational Leadership, 54*(8), 86–87.

Lepper, M., Greene, D., & Nisbett, R. E. (1973). Undermining children's intrinsic interest with extrinsic rewards: A test of the "overjustification" hypothesis. *Journal of Personality and Social Psychology, 28,* 129–137.

Newby, T. (1991). Classroom motivation: Strategies of first-year teachers. *Journal of Educational Psychology, 83,* 195–200.

Roeser, R. W., Eccles, J. S., & Sameroff, A. J. (2000). School as a context of early adolescents' academic and social–emotional development: A summary of research findings. *The Elementary School Journal, 100*(5), 443–471.

Rogers, S., & Renard, L. (1999). Relationship-driven teaching. *Educational Leadership, 57*(1), 34–37.

Ryan, R. M., & Deci. E. L. (2000). Intrinsic and extrinsic motivations: Classic definitions and new directions. *Contemporary Educational Psychology, 25,* 54–67.

Skinner, E. A., & Belmont, M. J. (1993). Motivation in the classroom: Reciprocal effects of teacher behavior and student engagement across the school year. *Journal of Educational Psychology, 85*(4), 571–581.

Stipek, D. J. (1993). *Motivation to learn: From theory to practice* (2nd ed.). Boston: Allyn and Bacon.

Tomlinson, C. A. (1999). *The differentiated classroom: Responding to the needs of all learners.* Alexandria, VA: Association for Supervision and Curriculum Development.

Vygotsky, L. (1978). *Mind in society: The development of higher psychological processes.* (Eds. M. Cole, V. John-Steiner, S. Scribner, & E. Souberman). Cambridge: Harvard University Press.

Wentzel, K. R. (1997). Student motivation in middle school: The role of perceived pedagogical caring. *Journal of Educational Psychology, 89*(3), 411–419.

Wentzel, K. R. (1998). Social relationships and motivation in middle school: The role of parents, teachers, and peers. *Journal of Educational Psychology, 90*(2), 202–209.

Zhang, S. (1995). Reexamining the effective advantage of peer feedback in ESL writing class. *Journal of Second Language Writing, 4*(3), 209–222.

Managing Independent Work

Chapter 1 discussed the assumption that the tasks of classroom management vary across different classroom situations. We pointed out that the classroom is not a "homogenized glob" (Kounin & Sherman, 1979), but is composed of numerous "subsettings," such as sharing time, guided reading groups, transitions, whole-class discussions, and cooperative learning. What constitutes order in each of these subsettings is likely to vary. During transitions, for example, students may be allowed to sharpen pencils, talk with friends, and use the water fountain, but these same behaviors may be prohibited during a whole-group discussion or a teacher presentation.

Variations in behavioral expectations are understandable, given the fact that subsettings have different goals and pose different challenges in terms of establishing and maintaining order. To be an effective manager, you must consider the unique characteristics of your classroom's subsettings and decide how you want your students to behave in each one.

While Ken meets with a small group, the rest of the class works independently.

This chapter focuses on the subsetting known as *independent work,* the situation in which the majority of children work independently on tasks while the teacher meets with individuals or small groups. We devote an entire chapter to this subsetting because independent work can be particularly difficult for beginning teachers to manage; even for experienced teachers, independent work poses a challenging set of "built-in hazards" (Carter, 1985) that must be well understood if they are to be overcome.

To be honest, this chapter almost didn't get written. Independent work is also referred to as *seatwork,* and this term has very negative connotations, particularly among educators who promote students' active participation and collaboration. Indeed, when we sat down with Viviana, Garnetta, Barbara, and Ken to discuss their views on independent work, we found heated differences of opinion. On one hand, Ken told us he used seatwork every day: "I teach both mathematics and reading in small groups. I can't see any other way to do it, especially given the heterogeneity of my class. That means the rest of the class *has* to work on their own. If you want to individualize instruction, seatwork is inevitable." Ken thought a chapter on the topic would be "invaluable, even fascinating, for new teachers."

On the other hand, Barbara—normally so soft-spoken and gentle—was vehemently negative: "I *hate* seatwork," she told us, "and I make a point to avoid it whenever possible. I don't know why you'd ever want to have a chapter like this in the book." Similarly, Garnetta and Viviana claimed they never used seatwork, so they couldn't really contribute to the chapter. As Garnetta asserted, "If you write a chapter like this, it won't be about us." To these three teachers, seatwork clearly meant "filling in the blanks." The term itself conjured up images of bored, passive children, sitting alone at their desks, doing repetitive, tedious worksheets.

We debated, we moralized, and we shared anecdotes about the awfulness or the usefulness of seatwork. Eventually, we came to realize that there was no fundamental difference of opinion among us. We all agreed that teachers sometimes need to assign independent work so they can meet with an individual or a small group (although the four teachers differ considerably in the amount of time they do this). We agreed that seatwork is too often busywork, that it frequently goes on for too long, and that too many teachers use it as a substitute for active teaching.

This chapter examines the ways that Ken, Barbara, Garnetta, and Viviana work to make independent assignments worthwhile and engaging. We also discuss the unique challenges that seatwork poses—for both teachers and students—and provide suggestions for meeting these challenges. To set the stage for this discussion, we begin by considering three questions: (1) What does research say about the amount of time students spend doing seatwork? (2) What do they generally do during this time? and (3) What are the purposes of seatwork? Throughout the discussion, the two terms—*independent work* and *seatwork*—are used interchangeably.

Seatwork: How Much, What, and Why?

The amount of time that elementary students spend doing seatwork has long been a cause of concern among educators. One widely cited statistic comes from the BTES study (Fisher *et al.,* 1978), which found that seatwork sometimes constitutes as much as *70 percent of instructional time.* More recent research on mathematics instruction in the United States, Japan, and Taiwan provides an interesting cross-cultural perspective on independent seatwork. Stigler, Lee, and Stevenson (1987) found that first- and fifth-grade children in the United States typically spent 51 percent of their mathematics time working alone, compared with 9 percent in Taiwan and 26 percent in Japan. Furthermore, American children spent only 46 percent of their class time in activities led by the teacher; in Taiwan and Japan, the comparable figures were 90 percent and 74 percent. With some dismay, the investigators concluded that classes in the United States "were organized so that American children were frequently left to work alone at their seats on material in mathematics that they apparently did not understand well . . ." (p. 70).

Figures like these prompted Linda Anderson (1985) to ask, "What are students doing when they do all that seatwork?" The answer is that in many classrooms seatwork time is spent completing workbook pages and worksheets. Indeed, it has been estimated (Anderson, Hiebert, Scott, & Wilkinson, 1984) that in the course of a school year, an elementary child might complete a thousand workbook pages and skill sheets in reading alone! The vast majority of worksheets focus on discrete skills that students are to practice and foster learning only at low cognitive levels. A typical first-grade reading worksheet, for example, might ask a child to circle all the pictures that begin with a particular consonant. In mathematics, a first-grade worksheet might have students do basic addition problems printed inside balloons and then color the balloons according to a key (e.g., color the balloon red if the sum is 6; color the balloon blue if the sum is 8). Figure 9-1 compares the time spent in three kinds of seatwork tasks in Germany, Japan, and the United States.

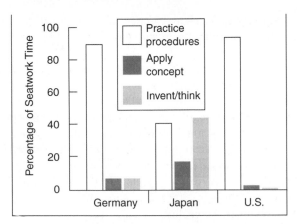

FIGURE 9-1. Average percentage of seatwork time spent in three kinds of tasks
Source: U.S. Department of Education, NCES (1998).

Why do American children engage in so much seatwork? What purpose does it serve? The answer to these questions depends on whether we look at seatwork from an instructional perspective or a managerial perspective (Anderson, 1985; Anderson, Brubaker, Alleman-Brooks, & Duffy, 1985). From an *instructional perspective,* the purpose of seatwork is to give students an opportunity to practice skills, synthesize and apply new knowledge, and develop independent work habits (such as learning to pace themselves and to check their work). Seatwork can also serve as a diagnostic tool for the teacher, providing a check on students' understanding (Chilcoat, 1990). From a *managerial perspective,* the purpose of seatwork is to keep students involved for a predictable period of time in quiet tasks that do not require close teacher supervision. As Ken pointed out, this way of organizing the class enables teachers to work with individuals and small groups and—theoretically at least—to tailor instruction to students' diverse needs. In other words, seatwork helps teachers deal with the heterogeneity of their classrooms.

The Challenges for Teachers

Independent work poses unique managerial and instructional problems for the teacher. (These are summarized in Table 9-1.) *The first challenge is to coordinate the instructional and managerial purposes of seatwork—namely, to select or create tasks that promote students' academic achievement, yet can be done independently.* This is easier said than done. If tasks are simple enough for students to complete on their own (fulfilling the managerial purpose), they may present minimal cognitive demands. If tasks are more academically demanding (achieving the instructional purpose), students may need considerable support from teachers.

TABLE 9-1. The Challenges of Seatwork

For the Teacher	For the Students
1. Selecting or creating seatwork that promotes academic achievement, yet can be done independently	1. Completing assigned work on their own
2. Matching seatwork to students' varying levels of achievement	2. Understanding how and when to obtain the teacher's help
3. Keeping track of what the rest of the class is doing	3. Understanding the norms for assisting peers
4. Keeping students on task	4. Learning how to be effective in obtaining help from peers
5. Dealing with the varying paces at which students work ("ragged" endings)	
6. Collecting, correcting, recording, and returning seatwork assignments	

Unfortunately, research suggests that too many of the worksheets assigned to students satisfy the managerial function of seatwork at the expense of the instructional function (Anderson, 1994). An analysis of reading workbooks, conducted by the National Academy of Education's Commission on Reading, concluded that many workbook exercises drill students on skills that have little value in learning to read. Consider the following task, cited in the Commission's report, *Becoming a Nation of Readers* (Anderson, Hiebert, Scott, & Wilkinson, 1985):

Read each sentence. Decide which consonant letter is used the most. Underline it each time.

1. My most important toy is a toy train.
2. Nancy, who lives in the next house, has nine cats.
3. Will you bring your box of marbles to the party?

As the report's authors point out, if children can already read the sentences, it is unlikely that their reading ability will be improved by asking them to underline consonants. On the other hand, if they *cannot* read the sentences, it is difficult to see how underlining consonants will help.

A second challenge for teachers is to ensure that seatwork is matched to students' varying levels of achievement. Anderson and her colleagues (Anderson, Brubaker, Alleman-Brooks, & Duffy, 1985) observed two high-achievers and two low-achievers in six first-grade classrooms. They also talked with students about what they were doing and why. They found that children were often unable to complete successfully the tasks they were given:

Randy (Student 8) could not read all of the words used in the standard board assignment, which involved copying sentences with blanks and selecting a word from a list of options. Every time observers noted him doing this type of assignment, he became "stuck" (his word) because he could not decode the key words to make the choice and proceed.

Beth (Student 9) could only read about a third of the key words in a Weekly Reader *article that students read in order to answer questions that they copied from the board. She could not read all of the questions either.*

On a ditto with nine pictures of seasonal activities, Sean (Student 1) was to cut out and paste on the name of the season that matched the picture. After he quickly completed the assignment, the observer questioned him about it. He had matched only two out of eight correctly, he could not read any of the seasons' names, and he was not sure in what season one sledded, flew a kite, went camping in a tent, or went swimming outdoors.

Aaron (Student 13) was to compose sentences with new vocabulary words listed on the board. He could not read some of the words, he could not spell most of the words he wanted to write, and he soon bogged down and stopped attending to the task. (Anderson, Brubaker, Alleman-Brooks, & Duffy, 1985, p. 130)

Third, you need to keep track of what the rest of the class is doing when you are work-ing with an individual or a small group. Careful monitoring requires the ability to "over-lap" (Kounin, 1970)—to deal with simultaneous situations without becoming so im-mersed in one that you ignore the other. Overlapping can be a challenge for even the most experienced teachers. Ken honestly admits that's he's been concerned about this for years:

I've had people observe my classes to determine if students doing seatwork are really working. They generally say that the kids are on-task and that the talk I hear centers on work. But if you're working with a small group on the other side of the room, and kids are encouraged to help each other, how can you ever really be certain?

Fourth, you need to ensure that students stay engaged and do not lose interest and be-come uninvolved, especially if the seatwork period is long. As we mentioned in the last chapter, seatwork requires students to pace themselves through assignments. Since there are no external signals (such as teachers' questions) to push students along (Gump, 1982), children may begin to doodle, pass notes, comb their hair, and sharpen pencils—until the teacher reminds students to get back to work. In fact, research has shown that engagement in seatwork often follows a predictable cycle (deVoss, 1979): Students be-gin their assignments; attention wanes; the noise level increases; the teacher intervenes; the children return to the assignment. This cycle can repeat several times, until a final spurt when students rush to complete their tasks before seatwork time is over.

A fifth challenge that faces teachers is to accommodate the varying pace at which students work. They may *begin* seatwork at the same time, but they never *finish* at the same time. Viviana observes that "it's common for some students to be on the second problem, while others are on number 10." Garnetta tells us that "Maria finishes everything in a minute—and if she doesn't have anything to do she'll create havoc." Ken contrasts Dana and Jessica:

> *Dana races to get everything done, and then she lords it over the others who are still working. Jessica is always ready to cry because she's the slowest; even if you gave her 10 times as much time as everybody else, she still wouldn't finish.*

You need to plan carefully in order to deal with ragged endings like these. On one hand, you need to plan activities for the Marias and Danas who complete their work earlier than you expected; if they must sit and wait with nothing to do, they'll inevitably distract students who are still working. On the other hand, you need to decide what to do about students like Jessica, who simply cannot complete assignments in the allotted time. Will you have them stay in at recess to complete their work? Will you provide an opportunity later in the day? May they do it for homework? Will you shorten the assignment or prioritize tasks making some required and some optional? And what will you do about students who are *capable* of finishing work in the allotted time, but do not?

Finally, *a sixth challenge is to collect, correct, record, and return all the paperwork assigned as seatwork—or to use activities that rely less on workbooks and skill sheets.* We once observed second graders complete eight language arts worksheets during an hour-and-a-half of seatwork time. Since there were 27 students in this class, a quick calculation told us that this teacher would have *216* worksheets to grade that evening—in this one content area alone! This much paperwork can be unbearably tedious for both teachers and students, and we had to wonder about the educational value of all these worksheets. Ken also thinks about the issue of paperwork from an *environmental* point of view: "It's easy to use reams of paper, and if the work isn't really necessary—if it's really just busywork and you end up throwing a lot of it out—then you feel terribly guilty."

The Challenges for Students

We sometimes get so caught up in the problems that seatwork poses for *teachers* that we overlook the problems for *students.* In this section of the chapter, we consider four of the special challenges that students must confront when doing independent seatwork. (See Table 9-1.)

First, since the teacher is often unavailable, students have to complete assigned work on their own. This statement may seem obvious, but it has several not-so-obvious

Calvin and Hobbes

by Bill Watterson

FIGURE 9-2. Calvin's response to seatwork that is too difficult for him (Calvin and Hobbes © Watterson. Dist. by Universal Press Syndicate. Reprinted with permission. All rights reserved.)

implications. In order to complete assignments, students must maintain an internal push even when tasks are boring and personally irrelevant. They must remain free from distraction amid the crowded social environment of the classroom. They must decipher directions that are sometimes unclear. They must monitor their comprehension and recognize when they understand and when they do not.

The study by Anderson and her colleagues (Anderson, Brubaker, Alleman-Brooks, & Duffy, 1985) reveals that children often develop elaborate strategies that allow them to finish their work even when they don't understand it. (Figure 9-2 depicts Calvin's rather special strategy.) For example, they may mark answers by matching the length of the word to the length of the blank, use pictures as cues for the correct answers, or simply ask others for answers.

Randy (Student 8) could not read some of the words on the board assignment. Even when he did read some, he tried to decide on a word to go in the blank as soon as he came to the blank in the sentence, even if it was the second or third word. That is, he did not read the entire sentence to provide a context for the choice. When he did not figure out the answer immediately, he asked another child for the answer. In this manner, he often received most of the answers from others and completed this assignment without learning to read the new vocabulary words (ostensibly the purpose of the task).

Beth (Student 9), unable to read enough of the Weekly Reader *articles necessary to answer the questions, simply copied the questions and wrote answers that seemed logical to her, without consulting the articles. In the one instance when she did look, she searched for a number word to answer "How many legs does a grasshopper have?" She came to the phrase "five eyes" in the article and copied the number five. (Anderson, Brubaker, Alleman-Brooks, Duffy, 1985, pp. 131–132)*

Students like Randy and Beth define success in terms of putting down an answer and finishing the assignment, even if the work makes no sense to them. As Richard, one of the target students, gleefully commented, "I don't know what it means, but I did it" (Anderson, Brubaker, Alleman-Brooks, Duffy, 1985, p. 132).

A second challenge that independent work poses for children is understanding how and when to obtain the teacher's help. Since the teacher is generally interacting with an individual or with a small group, gaining the teacher's attention is a lot like trying to get the attention of a store clerk who is busy with another customer (Cazden, 1988). Students must learn the appropriate ways to obtain assistance: Do they simply raise their hands and hope the teacher notices? May they call the teacher's name? Are they allowed to get out of their seats and walk over to the teacher? Must they wait until the teacher is finished with a particular group before asking their question? Unless procedures for obtaining the teacher's help are explicit, students who encounter problems with their work may become frustrated, unengaged, and disruptive.

In addition to learning the appropriate ways to obtain the teacher's help, *students must meet a third challenge—understanding and accepting the norms for assisting peers.* In some classes, teachers encourage students to work collaboratively, while in other classes giving or receiving help is tantamount to cheating (Rizzo, 1989). This latter situation can present a real dilemma for students. On one hand is their need to follow the teacher's directions— and to stay out of trouble. On the other hand is their need to complete the assignment successfully and to assist friends who are having difficulty (Bloome & Theodorou, 1988).

Students' understanding and acceptance of the norms for helping peers can also be influenced by culture. Providing assistance may be especially valued by children with cultural roots in collectivist societies (e.g., African, Asian, Hispanic, and Native American). In collectivist cultures, people assume responsibility for one another's welfare, and the focus is on working toward the common good (Cartledge with Milburn, 1996). Thus, children from these cultures may resist teachers' directives to work independently. In contrast, children from individualistic cultures (e.g., English-speaking countries) may value individual effort and self-sufficiency; they may resist teachers' efforts to encourage peer assistance.

Finally, *a fourth challenge for students is learning how to be effective in obtaining help from peers.* It is important to recognize that even in situations where helping peers is permitted or encouraged, not all students are able to gain assistance. For example, students who are low in social status may be ignored or actually rejected when they seek help. A study conducted by Elizabeth Cohen (1984) illustrates this phenomenon. Cohen observed children in grades two through four working at learning centers. Students were told they had the right to ask for help and that they also had the duty to assist anyone who asked for help. Cohen found that children's social status was positively related to the amount of peer interaction. Moreover, the more children talked and worked together, the more they learned from the curriculum. She concludes: "Those children with high social status have more access to peer interaction that, in turn, assists their learning. In other words, the rich get richer" (p. 184).

Children's ability to obtain peer assistance also depends on their ability to be "effective speakers." Research by Louise Wilkinson and her colleagues (Wilkinson & Calculator, 1982) indicates that students are more likely to get appropriate responses from their peers if their requests are *direct, made to a specific, designated listener, and perceived as sincere* (i.e., the listener believes that the speaker really wants the information and does not already know the answer). Furthermore, effective speakers are flexible and persistent: If initially unsuccessful in obtaining help, they can *revise* and *repeat* their request.

These characteristics are illustrated in the following example (Wilkinson & Calculator, 1982, p. 97). Three first-grade students, Amy, Joe, and Dave, have been instructed to help each other on their reading work. In this excerpt, Amy first turns to Joe for assistance. When he refuses, she turns to Dave. Dave hesitates at first, but Amy persists, and he eventually provides the answer:

> AMY: Ok, what, what's that word?
> JOE: Don't ask me.
> AMY: I'll ask him. What's that word (to Dave)?
> JOE: Dave, do you know what we should write, like here?
> AMY: Right here. (Several seconds elapse.)
> I want you to look at my paper. (Several seconds elapse.)
> Listen to this.
> I've got these words.
> I keep gettin mixed up, Dave.
> Dave, I keep gettin . . .
> The words requested by Amy are provided by Dave.

In this very brief example, we can see why Amy is an "effective speaker." She directly frames her requests for help ("What's that word?" "I want you to look at my paper."); she requests help from a specific person (Dave); and she is obviously persistent. Unfortunately, not all children are as successful as Amy. In order to ensure that everyone benefits from working with peers, you will need to observe children's patterns of interaction and provide special assistance for those who are less effective speakers.

Implications for Practice

The research on seatwork sheds light on the special challenges or "hazards" associated with this particular subsetting of the classroom. How can you avoid—or at least minimize—these hazards? In this section of the chapter, we propose seven guidelines derived from both the research on seatwork and the collected wisdom of our four teachers. (See Table 9-2.)

Assign Work That Is Clear and Meaningful

During one visit to Barbara's classroom we saw her assign some dictionary skill sheets to her students. Later, when we discussed the assignment, Barbara told us what she had thought about when she selected and screened the pages:

TABLE 9-2. Guidelines for Independent Work

1. Assign work that is clear and meaningful.
2. Match the work to varying achievement levels.
3. Make sure oral directions are clear.
4. Monitor behavior and comprehension.
5. Teach children what to do if they get stuck.
6. Plan for ragged endings.
7. Find alternatives to workbook pages (e.g., authentic reading and writing, listening activities, working on ongoing projects, learning center tasks).

I wanted to provide students with work they could do without me, so I could work with individuals who needed help on the ads for their inventions [a special language arts/science project they were working on]. First, I looked at whether the skills on these pages meshed with the objectives of the fourth-grade curriculum. Then I made sure that the material had been previously presented by the librarian or by me, so that the pages would be practice and reinforcement—not instruction. We've worked on dictionary skills before—at the library, in spelling—so there was nothing new in these workbook pages. Then I checked the format to make sure it was familiar and understandable, and I checked that the directions were clear. If the pages had been confusing, that would have defeated the whole purpose.

As Barbara's comment illustrates, it is essential to evaluate the tasks you give students to complete during class. Here are some of the questions that Viviana, Garnetta, Barbara, and Ken ask themselves before they assign independent work:

What is the purpose of the task?

Does the task relate to current instruction? Are students likely to see the connection?

Are students likely to see the task as something worth doing or something boring and unrewarding?

Are the directions unambiguous and easy to follow?

Does the task provide students with an opportunity to practice important skills or to apply what they are learning?

Does the task provide students with the opportunity to think critically or to engage in problem solving?

Does the task require reading and writing, or does it simply ask students to fill in the blank, underline, or circle?

Does the task require higher-level responses or does it emphasize low-level, factual recall and "drill and kill" practice of isolated subskills?

Is there a reason the task should be done in school (e.g., the need for coaching by the teacher) rather than at home?

Will students be able to accomplish the task without assistance? If not, how will assistance be provided?

Match the Work to Varying Achievement Levels

When your classroom contains children who vary in ability and achievement level, it's necessary to differentiate independent work assignments. Tomlinson (1999) advises teachers to think in terms of differentiating *content* (what students will learn and the materials that represent that learning), *process* (the activities that students will do), *product* (how students will demonstrate what they understand and can do), and/or *learning environment* (the conditions that set the tone and expectations of learning). For example, in order to teach classification, you might take your first-graders on a nature walk to gather objects that they will all classify as living or nonliving. Then they will classify by other attributes, such as shape, size, color, and type of object. Some children will classify the actual objects, while others—those who are early readers—will have both objects and cards with the objects' names. Some of the early readers will have one or two cards, while others have many. Since students are using different materials, this is an example of *differentiating by content.*

In addition to classification, first-graders often learn about patterns. In this case, you might read your students *The Important Book* by Margaret Wise Brown (1949), which uses the following pattern:

> *The important thing about _____ is that it is _____. It is _____. It is _____.*
> *And it is _____. But the important thing about _____ is that it is _____.*

For example: "The important thing about night is that it is dark. It is quiet. It is creepy. And it is scary. But the important thing about night is that it is dark." After reading the book, you might have students work in groups of varying sizes to write their own "Important" book. Students who need more assistance and support will work with you in a small group. They will work together to choose a topic and to describe what's important about it. You will write their statements on chart paper (later transferring it to the same size paper that other students are using). Others will work in pairs to complete a "template" page that you have created (like the one above). More advanced students will create a page for the book on their own. Eventually, all of the pages will be bound, and the book will be added to the class library. The content of this lesson is the same for all children, but the *process varies* in terms of the support or scaffolding you provide. (See Tomlinson, 1999, for additional examples.)

Make Sure Oral Directions Are Clear

Once assignments have been selected or created, it is important to explain them clearly before sending children off to work. Unfortunately, research indicates that this does not always occur. The study by Emmer, Evertson, and Anderson (1980), for example, indicated that less effective managers often gave unclear directions. They stated instructions vaguely and did not check to see whether the children understood the tasks. Not surprisingly, this resulted in off-task behavior, considerable talk as children tried to figure out what to do, and frequent interruptions of the teacher.

Furthermore, Linda Anderson's (1985) research on seatwork revealed that even when teachers provided introductory explanations, they rarely focused on the purpose of the seatwork or the strategies to be used. Instead, they emphasized procedural directions. Anderson recommends that teachers explain *why students are doing what they're doing, describe the strategies to be used, and do a few examples.* Indeed, studies of effective instruction (Rosenshine, 1980) demonstrate that students make fewer errors on seatwork when teachers provide "guided practice" before allowing students to work independently. As Viviana comments, "If I can catch students making a mistake on the first problem, I can prevent them from making that mistake all the way through the assignment!"

During one visit to Garnetta's classroom, we watched her introduce a letter-writing activity that was to be done as independent work while Garnetta met with individuals who needed additional support. She began by reminding students about a visitor who had come the previous week:

> *Last week, we had a visitor, Miss Kinsey, who came and brought us all ice cream. I think we should thank her in some way. Think about the things we could do for Miss Kinsey. Could we hug her? ["No-o-o."] Could we shake her hand? ["No-o-o."] Could we write her a note? ["Yes."] Could we give her something? ["Yes."] Yes, we could send her thank you notes, and we could send her pictures of us eating the ice cream.*

After the students enthusiastically recalled the ice cream (vanilla with chocolate-covered almonds), Garnetta reviewed with the class the format for writing letters:

GARNETTA: OK, what's the first thing that goes on our letter?
STUDENT: The heading.
GARNETTA: What goes in the heading? Edwin?
EDWIN: Dear . . .
GARNETTA: No, that's in the greeting. [Pauses. No one volunteers.] I'll give you a hint. [She writes the number 35 on the board.]
STUDENT: The address!
GARNETTA: Good. [She writes the school's address on the board.] What's next. Something really important comes next.
STUDENT: The date!
GARNETTA: Yes. [She writes the date.] Okay, we've got the heading now. What comes next?
STUDENT: The greeting.

In this manner, Garnetta continued to review the format for letters. She left the model format on the chalkboard so that students could refer to it as they wrote their letters. She then instructed students that their letters had to contain at least five sentences (*not* five lines) and explained that the letter was to be written *independently*. She explained what to do if they were not sure how to spell a word. She answered students' questions and told them that after they had finished their first draft they should have another student check it. Then they were to write the final letter and draw the picture they would send. She showed them the paper to use for their final copies and put out paper and markers for their pictures.

There is an interesting postscript to this episode. About 10 minutes into the letter writing, a student went over to Garnetta to show her his letter. She quickly scanned the page. Then she threw her hands up, gave a rueful laugh, and held a quiet but intense conference with him. He got a clean sheet of paper and returned to his desk to start again.

We were curious. The directions had been so clear. What could have possibly gone wrong? During a free moment, Garnetta came over and told us what had happened. Instead of a thank you note to Ms. Kinsey, the boy had written a letter to a substitute who had been there the week before, apologizing for his poor behavior! We learned a good lesson: Even the most clear and thorough directions don't ensure that everyone will carry out the assignment as you intended!

Interestingly, a similar situation occurred a few days later, when we watched Ken explain a writing assignment that students were to do while he worked with small reading groups:

This assignment is going to be a challenge, so listen carefully. Instead of the usual book report, you're going to do something different. [He draws three intersecting circles on the chalkboard.] I want you to write about three different books of your choice. The first circle here represents a book I've read out loud to the class. What's one book I've read? [He calls on a student who responds.] Good. What's another? [He continues calling on students until about eight books have been named.] The next circle is a book you've read in your reading group. [He notices that Charles has his hand up.] Okay, Charles, you look like you can tell me all the books you've read in reading group. Go ahead. [Charles names six books.] Good for you. [He continues to call on students from various reading groups who recite the titles of five or six books.] Okay, so everyone's got about six books from reading group to choose from. Now this last circle is for any book you've read on your own. I'd suggest the most recent.

Now, take out the worksheet I gave you for evaluating pieces of literature. [This is a page that lists various "areas of criticism and analysis"—e.g., adventure, imagination, humor, emotion, illustrations, mystery and suspense, characters, pace, theme.] Your book report is going to be about one-and-one-half pages, so you obviously can't hit all these items. I want you to pick one of these categories and write a book report that compares the three books on this one category.

Let's practice this now and see how to think about it. Let's take one book I read to the class, say Johnny/Bingo, and for the reading group book, let's choose The House of Dies Drear. *[He writes those names in two of the circles.] Okay, somebody suggest a topic for comparison. [Girl responds that both books have adventure.] Good. What would you say about the adventure in each book? [Boy describes some adventurous episode in each book.] Excellent. You guys are ready to become literary critics. Okay, let's change this circle to* The Trial of Anna Cottman. *What topic from this sheet would you use now? [Boy volunteers: Theme—good versus bad.] Good! How would you discuss the theme of good versus bad? Give me an example from each book. [Students volunteer examples.] All right. In your book report, you would need to write examples of this theme from each book. If you just say "there's the theme of good versus bad in each book" I won't really see it, but if you explain that in* Anna Cottman, *Anna was fighting the Yellow Lord, and in* Johnny/Bingo, *Johnny and Bingo were fighting the bank robbers, then I can understand what you mean. [The conversation continues with more examples of categories on which to compare the books they select.]*

Okay, we've got seven minutes before gym. Jeff, give everyone a white sheet of paper. Start thinking of the three books you're going to choose. I want the list of the three books before we go to gym. When you've gotten your three books, decide on the category you're going to use to compare them, and start jotting down some ideas. Remember, I'm expecting your report to be about one and one-half pages. My goal here is not for you to tell me about one book, but to compare *three books.*

Just like Garnetta's instructions for the letter-writing activity, Ken's instructions were clear and thorough. He had explained what students were to do, suggested a strategy for beginning (i.e., select the three books, choose a category), and had modeled how to think about the comparisons. Yet a few minutes after Ken finished giving directions, a student raised her hand and said she was finished with her report. Incredulously, Ken went over to see what she had written. She had drawn the three circles and simply filled in the names of three books. She thought she was done. Once again we were reminded that although clear directions are necessary, they are not a surefire guarantee that students will know what to do!

Monitor Behavior and Comprehension

Chapter 7 discussed the fact that engagement rate during independent seatwork is often lower than engagement rate during teacher-directed activities. When children have to work on their own, without close teacher supervision and interaction, it's not uncommon for them to become distracted and lose the momentum needed to complete their assignments. For this reason, it is particularly important for you to monitor students' behavior.

In the following examples, we see the way Barbara and Ken are able to "overlap" (Kounin, 1970)—to monitor the behavior of students doing seatwork, while continuing to work with an individual or a small group. As if they had "eyes in the back of their heads," both teachers manage to deal with simultaneous situations:

Barbara is working at her desk with two children. She glances over at two girls who are whispering. "Sarah, are you helping Jessica?" [The girl says no.] "Then you're not to be talking." She asks the two children at her desk to check their papers for punctuation errors. While they are focused on their papers, she again scans the room and sees another person talking. "Louis, do you need help?" He shakes his head no and stops talking.

Ken is working with a small reading group. He calls on a girl to read the question she has prepared. While the other students are answering her question, Ken scans the room. He silently signals a boy to come over and quietly tells him to leave his neighbor alone. The boy returns to his seat and begins to work. A few minutes later, Ken calls another boy's name and motions him over. He directs him to collect his materials and go work alone at a separate desk.

In addition to monitoring behavior, it's essential to monitor students' *understanding of their assignments.* Recall the distinction between *engaged time* and *productive time* discussed in Chapter 7. Clearly, it's not enough for students to remain busy and on task. They must also understand what they are supposed to do and carry out their tasks successfully.

Monitoring comprehension can be particularly difficult when you're also involved with a small group of students. One hint is to spend the first five minutes of independent work time circulating throughout the room. Once you've checked that students understand what to do, you can convene your first small group. It's also a good idea to circulate in the time between small-group sessions, checking on students' progress and helping with problems.

Garnetta has explained a reading/writing assignment that the class will carry out in pairs while she meets with individuals. Before she sits down, she circulates throughout the room. She notices Jason signaling another boy. "Jason, what's the problem?" She moves over to Jason, quietly discusses what he is supposed to do, and tells him she will return in a little while to see how he is progressing. Garnetta moves to the small round table to work with a few children who need special help. When she is finished, she again moves around the room. As she approaches one cluster of children, a girl calls for her: "Ms. Chain, tell him what to do. He says he don't know what to do." Garnetta responds, "You tell him. He's your partner. And I'll listen." The girl explains the assignment. She asks: "Get that?" The boy shakes his head no. The girl tells Garnetta, "He says he don't get what I'm saying!" "OK, let's see if I can help." Garnetta clears up the confusion. She then continues to circulate, making sure to check in with Jason, before moving back to the small table.

Standing at the front of the room, Barbara gives instructions for a writing assignment and announces that she will be working with individuals at her desk. Slowly, she makes her way to her desk, stopping at various students' desks to see that they have begun to work. At Larry's desk, she crouches down: "You need to begin writing. Put these things away [the remnants from an earlier snack and a game he brought from home]. Now, what memory are you going to write about? [She discusses various ideas for the writing assignment.] Yes, those would be good memories to write about. OK, you've got a bunch of ideas. Now get started." She circulates some more and then sits down at her desk and begins to confer with two students who need help on a project. When she finishes with them, she walks over to a student who had been whispering. Barbara instructs her to turn her desk around so she is not facing other students. She checks the girl's work and quietly discusses her progress on the assignment. She does another loop through the room, glancing at students' papers, answering questions, and providing assistance. Then she returns to her desk, where another child is waiting to discuss her work.

Watching Garnetta and Barbara monitor seatwork, we were struck by the very quiet, discreet way they interacted with each child. This kind of discretion appears to be important for students' achievement. Helmke and Schrader (1988) found that contact with individual students during seatwork was positively related to achievement only if it was private and discreet. They speculate on two reasons for this finding. First, audible comments may disturb everyone's concentration and progress; second, loud, public comments may be embarrassing and may have a negative effect on students' motivation or willingness to ask questions.

Fredric Jones (2000) offers additional advice for giving help to individual students during seatwork: "Be *clear.* Be *brief.* Be *gone*" (p. 54). According to Jones, teachers should give help in 20 seconds or less for each student. Instead of questioning students ("What did we say was the first thing to do?") and providing individual tutoring, teachers should praise something the student has done correctly ("Good job up to here"), give a straightforward prompt ("Follow the model on the chalkboard"), and leave. In this way, teachers can circulate quickly and efficiently and minimize the time that students spend waiting for assistance.

Teach Children What to Do if They Get Stuck

When children encounter problems with seatwork assignments, they need to know what to do. In particular, students need to understand how and when they can obtain your help. Effective managers often establish the rule that they cannot be interrupted during their time with small groups; however, they make it clear that they will be available for help in between group meetings. They tell students to skip tasks that are causing problems and to work on something else in the meantime.

Some teachers devise special systems that students can use to indicate their need for assistance. They may give children a "help" sign or a small red flag to keep on top of their desks. A child who needs help turns the help sign up or raises the red flag. In some classrooms, students sign up for help on the chalkboard or on a clipboard.

Systems like these allow you to scan the room periodically to determine who needs assistance and to provide help at an appropriate time. This practice is far preferable to allowing children to come up to your desk or small group meeting area whenever they need help. We've seen classrooms where long lines of children were allowed to form by the teacher's desk. Not only is this distracting to other students, it's also a waste of time for the children waiting in line.

In addition to teaching children the procedures for obtaining the teacher's help, you need to make it clear whether or not students can ask peers for assistance. Most of the time, our four teachers not only *allow* peer assistance, they *direct* students to help one another. This allows our teachers uninterrupted time to conduct small group instruction or work with individual students. Garnetta tells us:

> *I believe that students learn from other students. Sometimes students understand the concept* better *when other students are teaching it. I try to have students work together as much as possible in order to avoid having students sitting there not knowing what to do or interrupting my work with small groups.*

In order to promote peer assistance, Barbara teaches her students, "Ask three, then me." Explicit encouragement like this may be necessary, since students are often reluctant to ask peers for help. A study of third-, fifth- and seventh-graders' attitudes toward seeking help (Newman & Schwager, 1993) sheds light on this reluctance: Across all grade levels, students saw the teacher as not only more likely to facilitate learning, but also less likely to think they were "dumb" for asking questions.

It's also important to note that all of the teachers work hard to explain what "helping" really means. They take pains to explain to students that simply providing the answer is not helping, and they stress the futility of copying (a practice that often irritates more diligent students, as Figure 9-3 illustrates). As Barbara tells us:

> *In the beginning of the year we talk a lot about what is helping and what is doing it for the other person. We role play different situations. For example, we look at a page in the math book, and I pretend I don't know how to do a*

Calvin and Hobbes

by Bill Watterson

FIGURE 9-3. Sometimes students don't like to help classmates who haven't tried to do the assignment on their own. (Calvin and Hobbes © Watterson. Dist. by Universal Press Syndicate. Reprinted with permission. All rights reserved.)

problem. I ask someone for help. Then I ask the class, "Was that good help? Was that explaining *or was that doing the work* for *me?"*

Although all our teachers firmly believe in the value of peer assistance, there are also times when they do *not* allow students to help one another. In these situations, they are careful to explain that the ground rules are different:

It is almost the end of the school year. Barbara is explaining that students will be writing an essay that will go into their writing folders. These will then be given to the fifth-grade teachers so they can see the progress that students made in fourth grade. Barbara emphasizes the fact that students must work alone: "The only thing that is different about today's assignment is that it is to be done independently. What does independently mean?" [Boy responds, "Alone."] "Yes. You may not help one another. You may not have anyone edit or proofread your essay. I don't want to hear any peer conferencing today. This is to be a silent *activity."*

Plan for Ragged Endings

Since students finish seatwork at varying times, they need to know what to do when they're done. Activities should be provided that are educational, but enjoyable. If students learn that they'll only be given more work to do, there's a danger that they'll learn to dawdle. Jones and Jones (1986) report the following anecdote:

During a visit to a second-grade classroom, a student in one of our courses reported observing a child who was spending most of his time staring out the window or doodling on his paper. The observer finally approached the child and asked if she could be of any assistance. Much to her surprise, the child indicated that he understood the work. When asked why he was staring out the window rather than working on his assignment, the boy pointed to a girl several rows away and said, "See her? She does all her work real fast and when she's done she just gets more work." (p. 234)

In the classrooms of our four teachers, there are numerous activities for students who finish before others. They can work on a computer; they can do free reading, extra-credit assignments, or journal writing; they can tackle brainteasers and puzzles; they can work with manipulative materials, such as Tangrams (seven plastic shapes that form a square when positioned properly) or Pattern Blocks. Finishing early also means that students can resume work on long-term, ongoing projects, such as social studies reports, science experiments, or book reviews.

Find Alternatives to Workbook Pages

Reliance on commercially prepared workbooks can lead to boredom and off-task behavior. In *Becoming a Nation of Readers,* Richard Anderson and his colleagues (Anderson, Hiebert, Scott, & Wilkinson, 1985) recommend that children spend less time completing workbooks and skill sheets:

Workbook and skill sheet activities consume a large proportion of the time allocated to reading instruction in most American classrooms, despite the fact that there is little evidence that these activities are related to reading achievement. Workbook and skill sheet activities should be pared to the minimum that actually provide worthwhile practice in aspects of reading. (p. 119)

Our four teachers provide students with innumerable alternatives to "filling in the blank." Viviana seems to speak for them all when she states:

I rarely give my children worksheets to fill out. I really dislike them. Most of them don't make the children think. They're not challenging; they become tedious. Some of those skill sheets make children do so many problems— many more than they need. If they can do the first 5 right, why give them 95 more? That's when children get bored and tired. I try to give my children work that will challenge them to think and to express themselves.

We asked Viviana, Ken, Barbara, and Garnetta to share some of their ideas for meaningful assignments that students can do while teachers are working with individuals or small groups. Here are some of their suggestions.

Authentic Reading Activities

All four teachers encourage students to do silent reading, and Viviana and Garnetta also encourage children to do paired or partner reading. This emphasis on reading is consistent with educational research. In fact, studies suggest that the amount of independent, silent reading children do in school is significantly related to gains in reading achievement (Anderson et al., 1985).

Sometimes teachers are reluctant to use reading as independent work because they are convinced their students "won't just sit there and read!" (Cunningham, 1991). One fourth-grade teacher put it this way:

> *I know reading is important and I know they need to do more of it but they just won't! Oh, some of them would, of course, and they'd love it but a lot of them wouldn't take it seriously. They'd read a page or two, then they'd get fidgety and start talking or cleaning out their desks. When a few started this, the others would stop reading too. They have to have something to complete and turn in and know that they are accountable for it or they just won't do it! (Cunningham, 1991, p. 188)*

In order to avoid this problem, Cunningham (1991) suggests that teachers explain that since people learn to read better by reading, it's important to take time each day just to read. You can also support authentic reading activities by making sure that students have access to a variety of genres (including comic books, magazines, and newspapers) and to books on a variety of topics, including sports and cars. (See Chapter 3.)

Authentic Writing

In addition to requiring and encouraging children to read, our four teachers create assignments that call for *real* writing (instead of simply filling in blanks). When Ken is teaching punctuation, for example, he has students pair up and have a conversation. They have to write it down and then punctuate it correctly. He also uses independent seatwork time to have students write reports for science, health, and social studies. And students always have writing to do in connection with the literature they are reading. Typically, students read a chapter or two in their novels, and then write questions (and answers) to ask other students during the small-group meeting.

Since Ken teaches sixth grade, it's easy to see how his students can do independent writing, but these kinds of activities should go on at all grade levels. We've observed Viviana's first-graders eagerly tackle writing assignments of all kinds. Sometimes Viviana gives them a set of pictures and they choose one on which to write. At other times, they "write" their favorite nursery rhymes by drawing pictures of the events in correct sequence. Viviana manages to incorporate writing in all subject areas—even mathematics. During one math lesson, for example, we watched students write "story problems." First, Viviana reviewed what a mathematics story problem was. Then she had a child create one for the class to solve. Finally she had children work independently to create their own:

VIVIANA: I'm going to give you one second to think of a story problem. [She pauses.] Okay, Luis.

LUIS: Anita has four dolls. Her sister has three fewer dolls. How many dolls does her sister have?

VIVIANA: Good. What information is his problem giving us?

STUDENT: That Anita has four dolls.

VIVIANA: What else?

STUDENT: That her sister has three fewer.

VIVIANA: And what do we have to do?

STUDENT: Find out how many dolls her sister has.

VIVIANA: Who wants to illustrate this problem? Pedro? [He goes to the chalkboard and draws four little squares.]

VIVIANA: What do these represent?

CLASS: Ones.

VIVIANA: Now, how are you going to illustrate what the sister has? [He crosses out three of the squares.] Why did he cross them out?

STUDENT: Because fewer means less.

VIVIANA: Very good. Now, who wants to translate this illustration into numbers? Stephen? [He writes $4 - 3 = 1$ on the chalkboard.] And what does the one stand for?

STUDENT: The number of dolls that her sister has.

VIVIANA: Okay, so how will you answer the question? Andres? [Andres goes to the board and prints: "Her sister has one doll?"] It's a beautiful sentence, Andres, but is it an asking sentence or a telling sentence? [He changes the question mark to a period.] You were thinking about how story problems ask a question, right? Let's read this together, children. [They read the sentence aloud.] You know, you have become so proficient at this, I'm going to give you all a chance to make up some story problems now. I'm going to give you some paper, folded in half. On each side, write a story problem. Illustrate it with 1s and 10s and translate it into numbers. Then you can draw a picture to go with your problem. [The children cheer.] When you're finished, let me know and I'll check your problems while the rest are finishing. [She gives out paper. The class works quietly. Viviana meets with individuals at a small round table. As she checks children's papers, she not only looks at their mathematics, she also has them correct spelling and punctuation.]

While the students worked, we circulated through the room to see what children were writing. One boy turned to us and exclaimed, "I *love* story problems!" We asked why, and he responded, "Because I love to write!" (Figure 9-4 shows a story problem written by one of Viviana's first-grade students.)

In addition to content area assignments that require students to write, some teachers have students keep notebooks that they use "just for writing" on a daily basis. Teachers may specify a designated length of time for the writing (e.g., 10 minutes) or a designated amount (e.g., "about a page"). In Ken's class, for example, students have private journals. To ward off students' complaints that they "don't know what to write about," Ken lists one or two suggested topics on the chalkboard every morning: What are some things

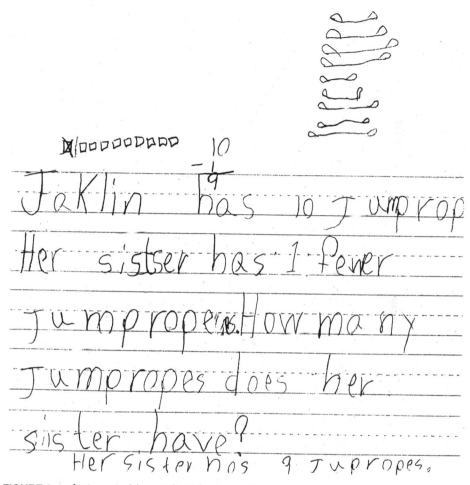

FIGURE 9-4. A story problem written by one of Viviana's first-graders

that glow? How would your life be different if you didn't need to sleep? If these questions don't appeal to students, they may write on any topic they wish. Ken responds in writing in students' journals.

Some teachers we know have students brainstorm topics they know about—dogs, baseball cards, soccer—and topics they'd like to learn more about and list these ideas in their individual writing folders (e.g., "Topics I Can Write About"). This way they have ready topics at hand when it is writing time or when they have free time. You can also encourage students to record interesting language they come across in literature or snippets of conversation. These can then be used as resource material for their independent writing. Have available samples of various kinds of writing for students to use as models (e.g., plays, newspaper editorials, letters, biographies). If using writing workshop, students may work on their current pieces, continuing where they left off in the writing process (planning, drafting, revising, editing, or publishing).

Listening

This is an often-ignored aspect of language arts, but listening activities are ideal alternatives to workbook pages. By providing students with books on tape, either commercial or teacher made, even less confident readers can follow along in the text and enjoy more complex books. Some teachers have more competent readers create listening tapes for other children in the class to use. Others encourage their less able readers to create book tapes for use in younger classes.

Ongoing Projects

Independent work time can be viewed as an opportunity for students to continue work on long-term projects. In Garnetta's class, for example, students were studying a health unit on drugs. Students were responsible for mastering a particular part of the chapter in the textbook and teaching it to the rest of the class. Garnetta also encouraged them to do additional research, using resources from the library.

In Viviana's class, children studied "work." They drew pictures of people doing different kinds of physical work (lifting, pulling, carrying, pushing) and pasted them on cardboard so they could stand. Then they made a milk carton city, populated with their "workers." Although projects like these may begin as whole-class lessons, seatwork time provides a chance for students to make progress on their own individual tasks.

Learning Centers

Originally found only in early childhood classes, learning centers are increasingly used in elementary classrooms as alternatives to paper-and-pencil seatwork. Centers can be simple, containing commercially produced activities in a folder, or more complex, incorporating science experiments, math problem solving, or story writing. Many teachers use centers to integrate a theme across content areas. Children are able to explore different aspects of the theme as they circulate, individually or in groups, among the learning centers. (See Table 9-3 for suggestions.) The critical point is that the work must be meaningful and connected to the curriculum.

When using centers, you need to think about how your students will know which centers to go to and how many children will be allowed in each center. Fountas and Pinnell (1996) advise teachers to create "workboards"—charts that list children's names and pictorial representations of the centers they are to visit. It's also essential to reflect on how students will be held accountable. Will you collect written work from students at each center? Will students report on their accomplishments at the end of center time? Will students initial a record sheet at the center?

You also need to design activities that can be done by students with varying ability or to differentiate instruction in some way. At curriculum-based learning centers, for example, you can color-code activities according to different achievement levels. Students can self-select the level of difficulty or the teacher can direct students to different col-

TABLE 9-3. Suggestions for Learning Centers

Science
Doing experiments
Recording observations
Drawing or charting experimental results
Conducting research about animal life on the Internet

Social Studies
Drawing or adding to maps
Creating charts or graphs of population trends
Using the computer to create a timeline
Comparing methods of communication using two different time periods and cultures
Writing a dialogue between an abolitionist and a slaveholder

Mathematics
Creating and solving math problems
Using dice or number cubes to reinforce concepts
Finding math applications in newspapers and magazines
Doing paired fact practice
Working on the computer to strengthen a math concept

Art
Illustrating a story
Creating a holiday-related craft
Drawing scenes depicting life in another country

Literacy
Doing shared reading
Listening to books on tape
Making words with letter tiles
Handwriting
Rereading familiar texts
Creating stories on the computer
Working with poems and chants
Comparing three different cultural versions of Cinderella

ored activities (e.g., blue: single digit addition; yellow: double digit addition without regrouping; red: double digit addition with regrouping).

A computer station can make an ideal learning center. In Ken's class, for example, computers are an integral part of the science curriculum. Students identify acid rain patterns around the world using a National Geographic Society computer network and learn about marine environments with *A Field Trip to the Sea* (1999). According to Ken, software packages like these not only help his students learn about important science topics, they also teach students to use the computer as a research tool. There's also a social benefit: Since two to three students can work at each computer (one to work the mouse or keyboard, one to keep notes and record information, and one to help with decisions and to serve as timekeeper), they have to learn to collaborate.

Barbara and Garnetta also make extensive use of the computer. In fact, the computers stay on all day so that students can work on stories, conduct research, and prepare presentations. In Barbara's classroom, students use bookmarked websites for science and social studies, and they do PowerPoint and HyperStudio presentations. In Garnetta's classroom, students enjoy using Inspiration Software to create graphic organizers for creative writing.

Cross-Age Tutoring

This year, Ken began a program of cross-age tutoring with the primary classes in his school. Students went to a kindergarten, first- or second-grade classroom where they tutored students in reading, writing, and social studies. They also helped the younger children do research on topics like seashells, spiders, and sharks. Tutors kept tutoring logs in which they entered mini-lesson plans and the results of each day's lesson.

Concluding Comments

In this chapter, we have tried to provide you with an understanding of the pitfalls and problems associated with independent seatwork, as well as suggestions for avoiding, or at least minimizing, these problems. We hope you will keep these in mind as you decide on the kinds of activities students will do during seatwork time, the way you will introduce seatwork assignments, and the rules and procedures you will establish to guide behavior.

As you plan seatwork tasks, remember that even young children are capable of doing activities that are challenging and thought provoking. We recently observed a kindergarten class, for example, where students circulated through various learning centers during independent work time. They visited a literacy center where they listened to taped stories; they carried out scientific observations at a "cocoon center"; they discovered how many cups were in a pint by pouring water at a "liquid measurement center"; they used teddy bear counters and Pepperidge Farm goldfish to solve addition problems at a math center. As you can see, these "seatwork" activities don't even require students to be at their seats!

The extent to which you will use independent seatwork in your classroom will depend on a number of factors—the heterogeneity of your class, the grade level you teach, district policy, the ability of your students to work without close teacher supervision, and your beliefs about the appropriateness of whole- or small-group instruction. Indeed, Viviana, Garnetta, Barbara, and Ken vary greatly in their use of independent seatwork. For example, Ken always teaches reading in small groups, since he has concluded that this practice best allows him to match students' interests with pieces of literature. The inevitable consequence is daily seatwork for those not meeting in the small group. In contrast, Barbara prefers to teach reading as a total class, selecting a piece of literature that children at varying levels of achievement can read together. Thus, she has less need to plan independent seatwork assignments for her students.

Similarly, both Garnetta and Viviana use whole-group instruction for reading, a practice that is mandated by their district. Both teachers form small groups only as needed (e.g., to work on a skill with which a small number of students are having difficulty). Viviana tells us:

> *I always introduce lessons to the whole group, but when I see a need I work with individuals. There are always some children who can move ahead quickly—children who swim. Others have trouble—they'll sink—and we have to rescue them. Then the teacher has to sit and work with them in a group. During those times, I'll have my children work independently on seatwork. But it's not a regular part of the day.*

As you decide on the extent to which you'll use seatwork, keep in mind the trade-off that is involved. The primary advantage of seatwork is that it allows you to work with children in a small group and to tailor instruction to individual needs. The primary disadvantage is that children not in the small group must work on their own, without close teacher supervision and interaction. Fortunately, this disadvantage can be alleviated by using *groupwork*—the topic of our next chapter.

Summary

If you plan to work with students individually or in small groups, you will need to use some form of independent work or seatwork. In this chapter we discussed some of the challenges seatwork presents to teachers and students. We also offered some suggestions for creating meaningful, appropriate assignments that students can do instead of traditional worksheets and workbook pages.

Challenges of seatwork (for the teacher)
- Assigning work that promotes students' achievement but that can be done independently.
- Matching seatwork to varying levels of achievement.
- Monitoring the class.
- Assigning work that maintains students' interest.
- Coping with "ragged" endings.
- Handling the paperwork.

Challenges of seatwork (for the students)
- Completing work on their own.
- Understanding how and when to get the teacher's help.
- Understanding norms for assisting peers.
- Learning how to be effective in obtaining help from peers.

Implications for practice

- Check workbook pages for clarity and meaningfulness.
- Match work to varying achievement levels.
- Present seatwork assignments clearly.
- Monitor behavior and comprehension.
- Teach children what to do if they get stuck.
- Plan for ragged endings.
- Use alternatives to traditional seatwork assignments.

Ideas for meaningful and appropriate seatwork assignments

- Reading.
- Writing.
- Listening.
- Ongoing projects.
- Learning centers.
- Computer activities.
- Cross-age tutoring.

Think about how much time your students spend working independently, with peers, and with you. As you decide on time allocations for various kinds of groupings, remember the trade-off that is involved: Seatwork allows you to work with children in small groups and to tailor instruction to individual needs, but it also means that children *not* in the small group must work on their own. Also keep in mind the limitations of commercially prepared seatwork, and choose seatwork assignments carefully. Find alternatives to workbook pages whenever possible. Many sources of quality seatwork are available—you don't have to create it all yourself. Seatwork does not have to mean busywork!

Activities

1. Since we all need to use independent seatwork at some time, it's useful to explore alternatives to a worksheet. All of the following skills or concepts could be reviewed with a worksheet. Select four, and for each one, think of a more active, engaging independent activity that would also provide an opportunity for review and reinforcement.

For example, teach letter formation in first grade by tracing letters in sand or salt, using finger paints, or making letters from clay.

Grade Level	Skill/Concept	Worksheet Alternative
Kindergarten	The number "4"	
1st grade	Recognizing sight words	
2nd grade	Double-digit addition	
3rd grade	The sequence of events in a story	
4th grade	Using quotation marks	
5th grade	The parts of a flower	
6th grade	Geography terminology	
7th grade	French vocabulary	
8th grade	Character analysis in a short story	

2. Select a workbook page or a worksheet from your class or a class you are observing. Examine it, using the following questions as a guide. Suggest ways to improve the page or suggest alternative ways of reviewing the same skill or concept.

Question	Response	Suggested Improvement
Are the directions clear?		
Does the page organization facilitate students' understanding of the task?		
Does the activity reinforce the intended skill?		
Is the task meaningful?		
Are the pictures a help or a distraction?		

3. Analyze the weekly schedule of the class you are teaching or observing. Determine how much time is allocated to independent work. During that seatwork period, observe three "target" students. (Try to select a high-, average-, and low-achieving student.) Note what activities each child is required to do during seatwork time. (Are the activities the same across achievement levels?) Every five minutes, record if the children are on-task or off-task. If possible, ask the children to explain what they are doing and why.

4. Interview two to four elementary students to learn their perceptions of seatwork. If possible, select students who vary in terms of achievement level. Include the following questions in your interview:

In what subject is seatwork used most? least?
When is seatwork useful/useless? interesting/boring?
What does your teacher generally do when the class is doing seatwork?
Are you generally allowed to ask for help from peers or do you have to work alone?
Are your peers willing to help you? Are they able to help you?

5. Design three learning centers for a content area of your choice. For each center, provide the following information:

The curriculum connection and objective.
How many students can use the center at one time.
How much time students will stay at the center.
How the center provides for differentiated instruction.
How students will be held accountable.
How you will evaluate student work.

For Further Reading

Anderson, L. M. (1994). Assignment and supervision of seatwork. *The International Encyclopedia of Education,* 5359–5363.

Jones, F. H. (2000). *Tools for Teaching.* Santa Cruz, CA: Fredric H. Jones & Associates.

Tomlinson, C. A. (1999). *The differentiated classroom: Responding to the needs of all learners.* Alexandria, VA: Association for Supervision and Curriculum Development.

References

A field trip to the sea (1999). Pleasantville, NY: Sunburst Communications.

Anderson, L. (1985). What are students doing when they do all that seatwork? In C. W. Fisher & D. C. Berliner (Eds.), *Perspectives on instructional time.* New York: Longman, 189–202.

Anderson, L. (1994). Assignment and supervision of seatwork. International Encyclopedia of Education (2nd ed.). Oxford: Pergamon Press, 5359–5363.

Anderson, L., Brubaker, N., Alleman-Brooks, J., & Duffy, G. (1985). A qualitative study of seatwork in first-grade classrooms. *Elementary School Journal, 86,* 123–140.

Anderson, R., Hiebert, E., Scott, J., & Wilkinson, I. (1985). *Becoming a nation of readers: The report of the Commission on Reading.* Washington, DC: National Institute of Education.

Bank Street College Project in Science and Math (1985). *Voyage of the Mimi.* New York: Holt, Rinehart & Winston.

Bloome, D., & Theodorou, E. (1988). Analyzing teacher–student and student–student discourse. In J. E. Green & J. O. Harker (Eds.), *Multiple perspective analyses of classroom discourse.* Norwood, NJ: Ablex, 217–248.

Brown, M. W. (1949). *The important book.* New York: Harper and Row.

Carter, K. (March–April 1985). Teacher comprehension of classroom processes: An emerging direction in classroom management research. Paper presented at the annual meeting of the American Educational Research Association, Chicago, IL.

Cartledge, G., with Milburn, J. F. (1996). *Cultural diversity and social skills instruction: Understanding ethnic and gender differences.* Champaign, IL: Research Press.

Cazden, C. B. (1988). *Classroom discourse: The language of teaching and learning.* Portsmouth, NH: Heinemann.

Chilcoat, G. W. (1990). How to make seatwork more meaningful. *Middle School Journal, 21*(4), 26–28.

Cohen, E. G. (1984). Talking and working together: status, interaction, and learning. In P. L. Peterson, L. C. Wilkinson, & M. Hallinan (Eds). *The social context of instruction.* New York: Academic Press, 171–188.

Cunningham, P. M. (1991). Making seatwork work. *Reading Horizons, 31*(4), 286–298.

deVoss, G. G. (1979). The structure of major lessons and collective student activity. *The Elementary School Journal, 80,* 8–18.

Emmer, E. T., Evertson, C. M., & Anderson, L. M. (1980). Effective classroom management at the beginning of the school year. *The Elementary School Journal, 80*(5), 219–231.

Fisher, C. W., Filby, N. N., Marliave, R. S., Cahen, L. S., Dishaw, M. M., Moore, J. E., & Berliner, D. C. (1978). *Teaching behaviors, academic learning time and student achievement. Final report of Phase III-B, Beginning Teacher Evaluation Study.* San Francisco, CA: Far West Laboratory for Educational Research and Development.

Fountas, I. C., & Pinnell, G. S. (1996). *Guided reading: Good first teaching for all children.* Portsmouth, NH: Heinemann.

Gump, P. V. (1982). School settings and their keeping. In D. L. Duke (Ed.), *Helping teachers manage classrooms.* Alexandria, VA: Association for Supervision and Curriculum Development.

Helmke, A., & Schrader, F. W. (1988). Successful student practice during seatwork: Efficient management and active supervision not enough. *Journal of Educational Research, 82*(2), 70–75.

Jones, F. H. (2000). *Tools for Teaching.* Santa Cruz, CA: Fredric H. Jones & Associates.

Jones, V. F., & Jones, L. S. (1986). *Comprehensive classroom management. Creating positive learning environments.* Boston: Allyn and Bacon.

Kounin, J. S. (1970). *Discipline and group management in classrooms.* New York: Holt, Rinehart & Winston.

Kounin, J. S., and Sherman, L. (1979). School environments as behavior settings. *Theory into Practice, 14,* 145–151.

Newman, R. S., and Schwager, M. T. (1993). Students' perceptions of the teacher and classmates in relation to reported help seeking in math class. *The Elementary School Journal, 94*(1), 3–17.

Rizzo, T. A. (1989). *Friendship development among children in school.* Norwood, NJ: Ablex.

Rosenshine, B. (1980). How time is spent in elementary classrooms. In C. Denham and A. Lieberman (Eds.). *Time to learn.* Washington, DC: U.S. Department of Education.

Stigler, J. W., Lee, S., & Stevenson, H. W. (1987). Mathematics classrooms in Japan, Taiwan, and the United States. *Child Development, 58,* 1272–1285.

Tomlinson, C. A. (1999). *The differentiated classroom: Responding to the needs of all learners.* Alexandria, VA: Association for Supervision and Curriculum Development.

U. S. Department of Education, National Center for Education Statistics (NCES). (March 13, 1998). *Third international math and science study* (TIMSS). Online: <http://nces.ed.gov/timss/video/finding3.htm>.

Wilkinson, L. C. & Calculator, S. (1982). Effective speakers: Students' use of language to request and obtain information and action in the classroom. In L. C. Wilkinson (Ed.), *Communicating in the classroom.* New York: Academic Press, 85–100.

Managing Groupwork

Keep your eyes on your own paper.

Don't talk to your neighbor.

Pay attention to the teacher.

If you need help, raise your hand.

Do your *own* work.

These are the norms of the traditional classroom, a setting in which children have little opportunity to interact, assist one another, and collaborate on tasks. (See Figure 10-1). In the last two decades, however, educators have begun to recognize the benefits of groupwork. According to a review in the *Harvard Education Letter* (Walters, 2000),

> *hundreds of studies . . . show a positive correlation between cooperative learning [a form of groupwork] and achievement. Research has been done in every subject, at all grade levels, in all kinds of schools. And there is widespread consensus that students benefit when they can help one another learn instead of having to work apart from—or against—one another. (pp. 3–4)*

One reason for the benefits is that cooperative learning allows students to take an active role in their own learning—to ask questions, to allocate turns for speaking, to evaluate the work of others, to provide encouragement and support, to debate, and to explain—and some of these behaviors have clear academic payoffs. For example, research has consistently demonstrated that providing explanations to peers is beneficial to achievement (Webb & Farivar, 1994); in other words, the more students explain, the more they learn.

"This class will stimulate your ideas and thoughts. And remember — no talking."

FIGURE 10-1. In the traditional classroom, students are rarely allowed to work together. (Reprinted with permission.)

Opportunities for interaction also have social payoffs. When children work in heterogeneous groups, they can develop relationships across gender, racial, and ethnic boundaries (Manning & Lucking, 1993; Slavin, 1991). Groupwork can also help to integrate children with disabilities into the general education classroom (Johnson & Johnson, 1980; Madden & Slavin, 1983). As our school-age population becomes increasingly diverse, fostering positive intergroup relationships grows more and more important.

Given all these benefits, why are some teachers still reluctant to use groupwork in elementary classrooms? Part of the answer has to do with the teacher's responsibility for keeping order and covering curriculum. In the crowded, complex world of the classroom, it's easier to keep order and cover curriculum when teachers do the talking and students do the listening. Furthermore, if the school culture equates orderly classrooms with quiet classrooms, teachers may feel uncomfortable when groupwork raises the noise level. Consider this student teacher's journal entry:

> *Every time I read about groupwork it sounds so great I'm ready to use it every day. Then I attempt it in the classroom and I start having second thoughts. I love the learning that comes out of it, but I never feel in control when it is happening. The part that really upsets me is that I really do not mind if the class gets loud. It's the other teachers and the principal I worry about. There have been a few times when I was using cooperative learning and someone has come in to ask if I need any help or they will take it upon themselves to tell my class to be quiet. This really makes me angry. I feel like the only acceptable noise level is no noise at all.*

Finally, like seatwork, groupwork has its own set of "built-in hazards" (Carter, 1985) that can make it particularly difficult for teachers to manage. In this chapter, we examine those special pitfalls. Then we discuss ways they can be minimized, drawing on the experiences of our four teachers, as well as the research and scholarly literature on groupwork. In the last section of the chapter, four specific approaches to groupwork are described—STAD, Jigsaw and Jigsaw II, Group Investigation, and the structural approach to cooperative learning.

The Pitfalls of Groupwork

Let's begin by considering the recent experience of a student teacher named Tom. During an evening seminar for student teachers, Tom told us about his first attempt to use groupwork with his fourth-grade class:

> *I couldn't wait to get my students into small groups. I didn't want to be like my cooperating teacher—she does all the talking and students are never allowed to work together. They seem so passive and so isolated from one another. Although she wasn't particularly enthusiastic about small-group work, she*

gave me her blessing. I was really excited. I was sure that the kids would respond well if they were given the chance to be active and to interact.

I decided to use small groups in science, since my cooperating teacher has given me the most freedom in this area. (I think she doesn't like science and doesn't think it's all that important, so she lets me do whatever I want.) I told the kids that they could choose their own groups. I figured that being allowed to work with friends would be really motivating.

Well, just getting into groups was chaotic. First we had to move the desks from rows into clusters. Then there was lots of shouting and arguing about who was going to be in which group. The whole process took about 10 minutes and was really noisy. My cooperating teacher was not pleased, and I was really upset when I saw what happened. My class is real heterogeneous—I've got Blacks, Whites, Hispanics, Asian Americans. Well, the groups turned out really segregated. They also tended to be just about all boy or all girl. Even worse—I have a boy in my class who has a learning disability and is real hyperactive, and nobody wanted to work with him at all. I ended up making a group take him, and they were pretty nasty about it. And there's another kid who's real shy and quiet; I had to get her into a group too. It was really embarrassing for both of them.

Finally, I got everyone settled down and they started to work on the assignment. We've been talking about seeds and plants, and each group was supposed to plan an experiment that they would actually carry out to demonstrate what plants needed in order to grow. I emphasized that they were supposed to work together and make sure everyone contributed to the plan.

Well, it was a real mess. A couple of the groups worked out OK, but one group argued the whole time and never got anything written. In another group—all boys—they decided to just let the kid who was smartest in science plan the experiment. He kept coming up and complaining that no one else would do any work. And it was true. The rest just sat and fooled around the whole time. Another group had three girls and one boy. The boy immediately took charge. He dominated the whole thing; the girls just sat there and let him tell them what to do.

I had pictured everyone cooperating, helping one another, contributing ideas. But it didn't work out that way at all. And the noise—it just kept getting louder and louder. I kept turning off the lights and reminding them to use their "indoor voices." For a few minutes, they'd get quieter, but then it would get loud again. Finally, my cooperating teacher stepped in and yelled at everybody. I was really humiliated. I just couldn't control them.

Right now I'm pretty turned off to using cooperative groups. I think maybe she's right. Maybe these kids just can't handle working together. Maybe I should just go back to having everyone sit and listen to me explain the lesson.

Unfortunately, Tom's story is not unusual. It illustrates all too vividly what can happen when teachers don't understand the problems associated with groupwork and don't work to prevent them from occurring. Let's take a closer look at four of these problems.

First, as Tom discovered, allowing children to form their own groups often leads to segregation among students in terms of gender and ethnicity. Have you ever had lunch in the cafeteria of a desegregated school? One glance is enough to see that members of each ethnic and racial group tend to sit together (Slavin, 1985). Similarly, at the elementary level, it is typical for boys to prefer sitting with boys, and girls with girls. It is important to recognize that strong forces operate against the formation of cross-ethnic, cross-gender friendships; left to their own devices, most children will choose to be with those they perceive as similar (Webb, Baxter, & Thompson, 1997). An even greater barrier to friendship exists between children with disabilities and their nondisabled peers. Public Law 94-142, passed in 1975 and reauthorized as the Individuals with Disabilities Education Act (IDEA), encourages the inclusion of children with disabilities in regular mainstream classrooms, but mere physical presence is not enough to ensure that these children will be liked, or even accepted.

A second problem of groupwork is the *unequal participation of group members.* Sometimes, this is due to what Garnetta calls the "freeloader" phenomenon, where one or two children in the group end up doing all the work, while the others sit back and relax. We saw this occur in Tom's class, when one group decided to have the best science student design the group's experiment. Although this might be an efficient approach to the task, it's not exactly a fair distribution of responsibility. And those who are freeloading are unlikely to learn anything about designing science experiments.

Unequal participation can occur for other, more poignant, reasons as well. In a study of students' perceptions of doing mathematics in a cooperative learning group (King, Luberda, Barry, & Zehnder, 1998), Brett, an average achiever, reported that he often failed to understand the task; consequently, he either withdrew from participation or engaged in distracting, off-task behavior. Similarly, Peter, a low achiever, "was aware that the other students seldom asked for his ideas and if he suggested ideas they never listened to him" (p. 8). In order to save face, he engaged in "silly," "weird" behaviors.

Brett and Peter are good examples of the "discouraged" and "unrecognized" categories in Catherine Mulryan's (1992) typology of passive students (outlined in Table 10-1). It is worth keeping these categories in mind. Although a desire to freeload may be at the root of some students' passivity, it is also possible that uninvolved students are feeling discouraged, despondent, unrecognized, bored, or superior.

Just as some individuals may be passive and uninvolved in the group activity, others may take over and dominate the interaction (Cohen, 1994a, 1994b). Frequently, the dominant students are those with high academic status in the classroom—those who are rec-

TABLE 10-1. Six Categories of Passive Students

Category	Description	Typical Achievement Level
Discouraged student	The student perceives the group task to be too difficult and thinks it better to leave it to others who understand.	Mostly low achievers
Unrecognized student	The student's initial efforts to participate are ignored or unrecognized by others, and he/she feels that it's best to retire.	Mostly low achievers
Despondent student	The student dislikes or feels uncomfortable with one or more students in the group and does not want to work with them.	High or low achievers
Unmotivated student	The student perceives the task as unimportant or "only a game," with no grade being assigned to reward effort expended.	High or low achievers
Bored student	The student thinks the task is uninteresting or boring, often because it is seen as too easy or unchallenging.	Mostly high achievers
Intellectual snob	The student feels that peers are less competent and doesn't want to have to do a lot of explaining. Often ends up working on the task individually.	High achievers

Source: C. Mulryan, 1992.

ognized by their peers as successful, competent students. At other times the dominant students are those who are popular because they are good athletes or are especially attractive. And sometimes dominance simply reflects the higher status our society accords to those who are white and male. Indeed, research has shown that in heterogeneous groups, males often dominate over females (Webb, 1984), while whites dominate over African Americans and Hispanics (Cohen, 1972; Rosenholtz & Cohen, 1985).

A third pitfall of groupwork is *lack of accomplishment*. In Tom's class, a significant amount of instructional time was wasted while children formed groups, and some groups didn't get anything done even when they had finally formed. The unproductive groups seemed to view the opportunity to interact as an opportunity to socialize. (Mulryan, 1992, calls these the "social opportunists.") Their behavior undoubtedly distracted students who were trying to work. Furthermore, the noise and disruption was of particular concern to Tom's cooperating teacher and upsetting to Tom, who repeatedly asked students to use their "inside" voices—without success.

Finally, a fourth problem associated with groupwork is children's *lack of cooperation* with one another. Tom tells us that "one group spent the whole time arguing." Although this kind of behavior is disappointing, it should not be surprising. Tom's students had apparently had little experience in cooperative groups, and they had clearly not internalized the norms for successful groupwork (Cohen, 1994a):

> Ask peers for assistance.
>
> Help one another.
>
> Explain material to other students.
>
> Check that they understand.
>
> Provide support.
>
> Listen to your peers.
>
> Give everyone a chance to talk.

Children who are used to keeping their eyes on their own papers may find it difficult to follow these new norms. Those who are used to asking the teacher for help may be reluctant to turn to their peers, perhaps because they don't want to appear "dumb" (Newman & Schwager, 1993). Some may have trouble giving clear, thorough explanations to their peers (O'Donnell & O'Kelly, 1994; Webb & Kenderski, 1984). Those who are not "effective speakers" may lack the skills needed to obtain assistance (Wilkinson & Calculator, 1982; refer back to Chapter 9 for the characteristics of "effective speakers"). Students whose cultural backgrounds have fostered a competitive orientation may have difficulties functioning in cooperative situations (Kagan, Zahn, Widaman, Schwarzwald, & Tyrrell, 1985). And students who are used to being passive may be unwilling to assume a more active role (Lazarowitz, Baird, Hertz-Lazarowitz, & Jenkins, 1985). As Elizabeth Cohen (1994a) reminds us, it is a mistake to assume that individuals (children *or* adults) know how to work together in a productive, collegial manner.

Lack of cooperative behavior—and a cooperative *ethic*—is especially problematic when teachers rely on groupwork as a strategy for promoting inclusion and accommodating the needs of children with disabilities. O'Connor & Jenkins (1996) observed 22 children with mild disabilities as they worked in cooperative learning reading lessons with their nondisabled peers. The investigators classified only 40 percent of the disabled students as successfully participating in cooperative groups. The following scenario illustrates an unsuccessful interaction. Here, Jake, a fifth-grader with a learning disability, has been paired with a nondisabled peer for partner reading. Then they rejoin two other members of their group to work on a set of literacy tasks:

> *The teacher cajoled the pair into starting, then listened to the first few exchanges before walking away. Jake read unevenly, hesitating before multisyllable words and making long pauses between phrases. His partner played with papers and rocked back in his chair when he should have been*

following Jake's reading and correcting his errors. When Jake stopped reading, his partner knocked softly on Jake's head, saying: "Jake, anybody in there?". . . . By the time they finished their reading and returned to the group of four, the other two group members had proceeded through the first few tasks without them. Jake noted their progress and sighed. He pounded the back of the list of questions with his ballpoint pen, making many small perforations. His partner asked the group, "What are we supposed to do, anyway? Aren't we supposed to work as a team?" The other two ignored the partner and Jake, who continued to jam his pen through the paper more vehemently. (pp. 40–41)

The next section of this chapter considers some general strategies for managing groupwork. Remember, *successful groupwork will not just happen.* If you want your students to work together constructively, you must plan the groups and the tasks carefully, teach students the new norms, and provide opportunities for them to practice the behaviors that are required. This takes time, and you may want to heed Ken's words of caution:

If you want to do it right, you have to allot sufficient time to teach students how to work together. And in some schools, this could be viewed as taking time away from "covering the curriculum." It's a good idea to get administrative support before launching cooperative groupwork. That way, when your principal comes in to observe, he or she will understand what you're doing and why. You won't get asked, "Where is this in the curriculum guide?"

Designing and Implementing Successful Groupwork

Decide on the Type of Group to Use

Students can work together in a variety of ways. Susan Stodolsky (1984) has identified five different types of groupwork: helping permitted, helping obligatory, peer tutoring, cooperative, and completely cooperative. The first three types of groups can be considered "collaborative seatwork" (Cohen, 1994a). All of them involve children assisting one another on individual assignments. In a *helping permitted* group, children work on their own tasks, and they are evaluated as individuals; however, they are allowed—but not required—to help one another. *Helping obligatory* situations differ only in that children are now *expected* to offer mutual assistance. In *peer tutoring,* the relationship between the students is not equal: An "expert" is paired with a student who needs help, so assistance flows in only one direction. In recent years, peer tutoring has been recommended as a particularly useful way of meeting the needs of students from culturally and linguistically diverse backgrounds (Webb & Palincsar, 1996).

Cooperative groups differ from these helping situations in that children now share a common goal or end, instead of working on completely individual tasks. In a simple *cooperative group,* some division of responsibilities may occur. For example, a group researching the Civil War might decide that one child will learn about the causes of the War, while another learns about famous battles, and a third learns about important leaders. Tasks are carried out independently, but everyone's assignment has to be coordinated at the end in order to produce the final joint product.

More complex is a *completely cooperative group.* Here, students not only share a common goal, there is little or no division of labor. All members of the group work together to create the group product. This was the type of groupwork that Tom used when he directed his fourth-grade students to plan an experiment demonstrating what plants need in order to grow.

It is important to keep these distinctions in mind as you plan groupwork. *Different types of groups are suitable for different types of activities, and they require different kinds of skills.* (See Table 10-2.) In helping situations, for example, students are ultimately responsible for completing individual tasks. Although these students need to know how to ask for help, how to explain and demonstrate (rather than simply providing the right answer), and how to provide support and encouragement, they do not need the more complex skills required in truly cooperative situations where they share a common goal. For this reason, helping situations are particularly useful when working with young children or those who are new to groupwork. Educators of young children often

TABLE 10-2. Different Types of Groups

Type of Group	Skills Required	Example of an Activity

Helping permitted
Helping obligatory
	How to ask for help
	How to explain
	How to provide support
	   and encouragement
		Using newspapers to learn
		   about geography and current
		   events; students help one
		   another, but complete an
		   individual worksheet

Peer tutoring	How to ask for help
	How to explain
	How to provide support
	   and encouragement
		Tutor helps tutee to complete a
		   set of math problems

Cooperative group	Divide group task into
	   individual tasks
	Coordinate individual efforts
	   to produce final group
	   product
		M&M™ activity: students
		   count the number of candies
		   in individual bags and then
		   pool figures

Complete cooperative
  group
	Take turns
	Listen to one another
	Coordinate efforts
	Share materials
	Collaborate on a single task
	Solve conflicts
	Achieve consensus
		Building a landfill that doesn't
		   leach toxins into the ground

recommend Think-Pair-Share (F. Lyman, 1993, cited in L. Lyman, Foyle, and Azwell, 1993), in which students work on a question or problem individually and then pair up with another student to share responses and report to the teacher. "Sidework" like this, followed by interaction, may be more appropriate for very young children than full collaboration (Dowrick, 1993).

As an example of a helping situation, let's consider the following activity that we observed in Ken's class:

Ken's students have been using newspapers to learn about geography and current events. Today, each student is to look through the newspaper and find five articles from cities in the state (other than their hometown), five articles from other states, and five articles from countries other than the United States. Students are expected to help one another, but each student is to complete an individual worksheet on which the geographical location, page number, and title of each article are to be listed. Then each student is to select an article to read in more depth and to write about how he or she "relates" to it; for example, what ideas does it trigger? What else do I know about the topic? Why is the article particularly interesting to me?

Students have the newspapers spread out all over their tables and on the floor. As we watch, we see lots of discussion about the assignment. Much of the talk is simple commentary on the articles students are finding: "Look, there's a flower show coming soon." "Penn State played Rutgers." "James Brown is singing in Los Angeles." "Guys, look at the top of page 11 . . ." But there are also requests for assistance: "I can't find a fifth article on a New Jersey city." "Is Franklin in New Jersey?" "I don't know how to relate to this article. Relating is hard. How do you think I should relate to this?"

In contrast to helping situations, cooperative groups require skills beyond requesting and giving appropriate assistance. Students must be able to develop a plan of action; they must be able to coordinate efforts toward a common goal; they must be able to evaluate the contributions of their peers and give feedback in a constructive way; they must monitor individuals' progress toward the group goal; they must be able to summarize and synthesize individual efforts.

During one visit to Garnetta's classroom, we observed a good example of a cooperative activity. The class was divided into groups of four or five to do "experimental math." Although students were required to carry out individual tasks, they had to coordinate their individual efforts if the groups were to be successful:

Garnetta introduces the math activity by explaining that each student is going to receive a bag of M&Ms.™ The first task is to predict how many of each color are in the bag. Predictions are to be recorded on a "Candy Facts" page; a bar graph is then to be constructed and colored with the appropriate M&M colors. Once predictions have been made, students are to open their bags and count the actual number of M&Ms™ of each color. This information is also to be recorded and then graphed.

Garnetta also explains that once each student in the group is finished with the actual count, their figures are to be pooled. In other words, students are to find out the total number of each color in the group. This information is to be entered on a large "group graph" taped to the chalkboard. Each group member is to color at least one of the bars with the appropriate color.

As students set to work, Garnetta reminds them of the rules: "You are to stay in your seats and work with your group. You cannot get up and go to another group. Use indoor voices. If you have a problem, ask someone in your group. And remember, if you eat the M&Ms™ you'll ruin the experiment. You've got to wait until the very end."

There is subdued excitement as group members begin to make predictions and color their graphs. Predictions vary tremendously. Some children guess that there will be 8 or 10 of every color, while others guess that there will be 25 or 30. There are lots of comments on each other's predictions: "That's way too high. There couldn't be that many!" "You think that's all the reds? No way!"

When children begin to open their bags, the excitement mounts. Some students go about the counting task very methodically. They separate each color into little clusters and then count each cluster. Some students line up each color and compare the length of the lines. Others are far more haphazard and have difficulty keeping track of which M&Ms™ they've counted. Again, there is lots of comparing and commenting: "You got hardly any oranges!" "I got more light browns than anyone at the table!" "You should line yours up like I did."

When it's time to pool the individual numbers of each color, students call out their totals. In some groups, one person does the addition for everyone. In other groups, every group member writes down the numbers and does the addition. There are quite a few discrepancies: "I got 65 light browns." "Uh-oh, I got 58." Garnetta offers each group a calculator so they can check their work.

In the final step of this activity, the results of different groups are compared and also pooled. Under Garnetta's direction, the class works together to find out which color was most common and which color was least common.

In this experimental math lesson, students were required to carry out an individual task. We can consider this a division of labor, since each student counted the M&Ms™ in only one bag. In order for the group to complete the entire assignment, however, each member needed to do the task correctly. This structure provided an incentive for group members to monitor everyone's progress and to help one another. Moreover, students had to coordinate their individual efforts in order to produce a joint product—the group tally of each M&M color.

Completely cooperative groups with no division of labor present even greater challenges. Not only must students be able to take turns, listen to one another carefully, and coordinate efforts, but they must also be able to share materials, collaborate on a single task, reconcile differences, compromise, and reach a consensus. Consider the following activity observed in Barbara's class, part of a science unit on the environment:

Barbara's class has been studying the environmental problems associated with garbage. Today's lesson is about landfills. Barbara explains what each group of five is to do: "The objective for today's activity is to build a landfill that doesn't leach toxins into the ground. On your lab tray are most of the materials you will need. You have a plastic container [a two-liter bottle from soda, with the top and bottom cut off]. You also have clay, cheesecloth, raisins, leaves, and plastic. All these can be used in your landfill. You'll also have to get soil from the big bucket on the side of the room, and a beaker of water from the water bucket. The only thing you can't use are the three little pieces of sponge. When you have built your landfill and you're satisfied that it won't leak, I'll come around and put red food coloring—the "toxin"—on each sponge. Then you'll put the three sponges on the top of the landfill and make it rain by pouring water from your beaker. We'll watch to see if the toxin comes through. If it doesn't, then your group has made a state-of-the art landfill. You'll have 15 minutes to work."

Before the groups begin to work, Barbara reviews the roles for each group member. The materials *person gets the lab tray, the dirt, and the water for the group; the* timekeeper *keeps track of the time; the* recorder *writes down what the group decides to do and draws a diagram of the group's landfill; the* facilitator *makes sure that everyone has a chance to participate; and at the end of the lesson, the* reporter *will tell the class what happened.*

In this activity, students had different roles to play, but they still needed to work together on the building of the landfill. They had to develop one plan, explain the reasons for their ideas, listen respectfully to one another, reject ideas without being destructive, reach consensus on which ideas to try, and take turns building the landfill. These are not easy skills to learn—even for adults.

As these three examples illustrate, the more interdependent students are, the more skills they need to cooperate successfully. In Tom's case, we can see that he began with the most complex kind of groupwork. He set up a situation in which students who were not even used to helping one another were expected to cooperate completely. Moreover, he assigned an intellectually demanding task that required creativity and problem solving. His students not only had to contend with an unfamiliar social situation, they also had to grapple with an unusually challenging academic task.

It's a good idea to use simpler types of groups when you are just starting out, but don't get stuck there. If you use students' achievement, maturity, or behavior to justify never trying more complex structures, you eliminate the possibility that students will ever learn to work productively in cooperative settings. But remember, you need to introduce more complex structures in a deliberate, systematic way, modeling expected behaviors and providing opportunities for practice and feedback.

Decide on the Size of the Group

To some extent, the size of the group you use depends on the task you assign. Pairs are appropriate when students are revising or editing writing or assessing each other's open-ended responses to a math problem using a rubric. Groups of two are also easier for beginning teachers to manage (Johnson, Johnson, Holubec, & Roy, 1984), and teachers of younger students often prefer pairs over larger groups that require more elaborate social skills (Edwards & Stout, 1989/90).

This is definitely true of Viviana, who frequently has "neighbors" work together on tasks. In the following example, notice how Viviana provides step-by-step directions for her students; she doesn't simply put them in pairs and tell them to get to work.

> *Viviana's students are working on place value. She gives each child a worksheet that is divided into a 10s column and a 1s column. She explains: "Now children, we're going to play a game. I'm going to give each pair of students a set of number cards. Put the cards between you and your partner." [She distributes the cards and checks to see that everyone has a partner.] Now, one person take the two top cards and put them side by side so that you make a two-digit number. Now, form the number on your worksheet using the 10s blocks and the 1s blocks. I want you to work individually and then check with your partner to see how your partner has made the number."*

> *As the children work, Viviana walks around and checks what they are doing. Each partner makes the number on the place value worksheet by placing blocks in the appropriate columns. Then the partners confer. Sometimes they have represented the numbers exactly the same way. Sometimes, they discover that they have represented the numbers differently; for example, one child makes 67 with 6 10s and 7 1s; her partner has made 67 with 5 tens and 17 ones. They discuss the difference. Viviana helps them to see that they have each created 67 but in different ways. When pairs have completed the first number and checked their work*

with their partner, Viviana instructs them to reverse the two digits. She tells them: "Now remember, you don't have the same number, even though you are using the same cards. With a six and a seven you can make 67 or you can make 76."

In situations where the academic task requires a division of labor (e.g., the unit on the Civil War), it makes sense to form groups larger than two. Groups of three are still relatively easy to manage, but you need to make sure that two students don't form a coalition, leaving the third isolated and excluded (Cohen, 1986).

In general, educators recommend cooperative groups of four or five (Cohen, 1986), and six is usually the upper limit (Johnson, et al., 1984). Keep in mind that as group size increases, the "resource pool" also increases; in other words, there are more heads to think about the task and more hands to share the work. It is also true, however, that the larger the group, the more difficult it is to develop a plan of action, allocate turns for speaking, share materials, and reach consensus.

Assign Students to Groups

In addition to deciding on the type and size of your groups, you must think carefully about group composition. As we mentioned earlier in this chapter, groupwork allows children to develop relationships with those who differ in terms of gender and ethnicity. Groupwork can also help to integrate children with disabilities into the general education classroom. For these reasons, groups should be heterogeneous with respect to gender and ethnicity, and children with disabilities should be included in groups with their nondisabled peers.

You also need to consider whether groups will be homogeneous or heterogeneous with respect to ability level. At times, homogeneous groups can be useful; for example, you may want to form a group of several children who are all having difficulty with a particular mathematics concept, or you may want to structure opportunities for children who are gifted and talented to work together on more advanced material (Robinson, 1990). In general, however, educators recommend the use of heterogeneous groups (Cohen, 1994a; Johnson, et al., 1984; Slavin, 1991). One reason is that they provide more opportunities for asking questions and receiving explanations (Johnson, et al., 1984; Webb, 1985).

Just how heterogeneous your groups should be is still not clear. Research by Noreen Webb and her colleagues has shown that in groups composed of high-, medium-, and low-achieving students, those of medium ability tend to get left out of the interaction. In fact, Webb (1985) argues that two-level groups (high-medium or medium-low) are most beneficial for all students. In contrast, other proponents of cooperative learning (e.g., Slavin, 1991) recommend that four-person teams consist of a high achiever, a low achiever, and two average achievers.

Another variable you need to consider when deciding on group composition is social skill. Some children have unusual leadership abilities; others are particularly adept at resolving conflicts; still others are especially alert to injustice and can help to ensure that everyone in the group has a chance to participate. When forming groups, it makes sense to disperse children like these, so that each group has the benefit of their talents.

On the other hand, some children have extreme difficulty working with others. It makes sense to disperse *these* students too. As Garnetta points out:

> *Some children are really volatile—they come to school angry and disrupt whatever group they're in. Some children freeload and don't do anything; they just want to play. Some kids dominate. Some kids prefer to work indi-vidually. You have to be really careful who you place these kinds of kids with—and you certainly don't want to put them all together in one group!*

Since group composition is so important, it is risky to allow students to select their own groups. We saw what happened in Tom's class: Students segregated themselves ac-cording to gender and ethnicity; friends elected to be together—and did more socializ-ing than work; the student with a learning disability and the social isolate were excluded. Experiences like this lead Ken to believe that students should rarely be allowed to select their own groups. As he puts it,

> *If you allow children to select their own groups without carefully structuring the situation, the pitfalls are really there. You're inviting problems—espe-cially if you're a beginning teacher. Just about the only time I allow my students to choose their own groups is when they're selecting novels to read. [See Chapter 5.] In that case, the groups are built upon the selection of the novel; it's not just "I want to work with this person," although that certainly enters into it.*

Interestingly, Garnetta and Barbara allow their students to choose their own groups more frequently than Ken does, but not until the students have had substantial experi-ence working in various kinds of groups with almost everyone in the class.

Teachers develop different systems for assigning students to groups. When Barbara forms heterogeneous groups, for example, she first writes each student's name on a note card, along with information about achievement and interpersonal relationships (e.g., with whom the student doesn't get along). Then she ranks students in terms of achieve-ment level and assigns a top-ranked student and a bottom-ranked student to each of the groups. Next, the average students are distributed, keeping in mind the need to balance the groups in terms of gender, ethnicity, and social skill. Having each student's name on a note card allows her to shuffle students around as she tries to form equivalent groups that will work well together. Barbara comments, "It's impossible to form perfect groups, but at least this system gives me a fighting chance!"

Barbara pays special attention to the group assignment of children with disabilities. For example, when placing Stuart (the child with autism) in a group, she also includes one of his "student advocates," as well as a child who needs extra help and can benefit from the presence of Stuart's teacher associate. When she assigns Mark (the child who is classified as emotionally disturbed) to a group, she is extremely careful to put him with children who are unlikely to "set him off" and become involved in volatile interactions. She also allows Mark to "opt out of groupwork if he's having a really bad day. But it's always his choice."

Structure the Task for Positive Interdependence

If you want to ensure that students cooperate on a task, you have to create a situation in which they need one another in order to succeed. This is called positive interdependence, and it's one of the essential features that transforms a groupwork activity into true cooperative learning (Antil, Jenkins, Wayne, & Vadasy, 1998).

One simple strategy for promoting interdependence is to require group members to *share materials* (Johnson, et al. 1984). If one member of a pair has a page of math problems, for example, and the other member has the answer sheet, they need to coordinate (at least a little) if they are both to complete the problems and check their answers. By itself, however, sharing materials is unlikely to ensure meaningful interaction.

Another way to create interdependence is to create a *group goal*. For example, you might have each group produce a single product, such as a report, a science demonstration, a puppet show, or a story. Near the end of the year, when Viviana's students learn about "school helpers" (e.g., the nurse, the principal, a counselor, the librarian), she divides her class into groups. Each group interviews a different helper, and each member of the group has to ask a different question (e.g., "What is your job?" "How do you help people in the school?"). After the interviews, the group creates a poster about their school helper, with each student writing one sentence. (Notice that Viviana structured the task so that every child in the group had to participate in order to produce the group product. If she hadn't done this, one person in the group could have done all the work while the others remained uninvolved.)

Another way to stress the importance of collaborating is to give a *group grade* or *group reward*. For example, suppose you want to encourage students to help one another with spelling words. You can do this by rewarding groups on the basis of the total number of words spelled correctly by all the members of the group (Johnson, et al., 1984). Similarly, you can give bonus points to every math group in which all students reach a predetermined level of achievement. Some teachers give each group member a number (e.g., one to four) at the beginning of class, and then spin a numbered spinner or toss a die to select the number of the group member whose homework or classwork paper will be graded (Webb & Farivar, 1994). Then everyone in the group receives that score. Such a practice clearly increases the pressure on group members to make sure that everyone's homework or classwork is complete and well done.

Another way of promoting collaboration is to structure the task so that students are dependent on one another for *information* (Johnson, et al., 1984). In Garnetta's M&Ms™ math lesson, for example, group members had to pool their individual data to get a group count of the M&Ms™ of each color. They needed each other in order to produce the group graph.

You can also foster interdependence by creating rich, complex tasks that require *multiple abilities* (e.g., reading, writing, computing, role playing, building models, spatial problem solving, drawing, creating songs, public speaking). By convincing your students that *every* member of the group is good at *some* of these and that *no* member of the group is good at *all* of them, you can reduce the differences in participation between high- and low-status students and enable those who are often left out to contribute (Cohen, 1994a, 1994b, 1998). Listen to Ken:

When ecosystem teams work on A Field Trip to the Sea, *everyone has to pitch in to carry out the research and create a poster presenting their information. Some have special leadership ability, and they can organize the group for the library research. Some people are really good at spelling and handwriting, but they're terrible artists. Others have terrible handwriting, but they're great artists. Some people can design the layout, while others are the speakers.*

Finally, you can assign *different roles* to group members, requiring each role to be fulfilled if the group is to complete the task. In the landfill lesson that Barbara conducted, each group contained a materials person, a timekeeper, a recorder, a facilitator, and a reporter. In *Heritage,* a social studies simulation that Ken uses (Wesley, 1976), students form three-person racing teams that plot a course of travel from San Diego, California, to Bangor, Maine, stopping along the way at 15 important historical sites. Each team member plays a specific role—the driver, the navigator, or the leader. In each round of play, students change roles. The leader rolls the dice at the beginning of each round of play and selects a "fate card," which adds or subtracts miles that the team "travels." The driver computes the number of points the team earns each day and the miles gained or lost; he or she also moves the team's car symbol along the plotted course of travel on a large class map and writes a "diary entry" for the day. The navigator keeps a "daily travel log," recording the number of miles gained or lost during the round of play, the number of hours traveled, the road and weather conditions, and other important information.

Even very young children can learn to carry out roles like these. One way of reminding them about their individual responsibilities is to place a different symbol on each person's desk. For example, you can give each student a star of a different color (Edwards & Stout, 1989/90). The child with the red star reads the instructions, the blue star records what the group does, the yellow star gets the materials, and the green star monitors the noise level. Recently, one student teacher we know used this strategy in a cooperative learning activity on spiders. After dividing her class into four-person groups, she gave each member of the group a different aspect of spiders to research (e.g., the structure of spiders; what they eat; how they construct webs). She also gave each group member a marker of a different color to use in recording his or her findings on poster board. This student teacher reports: "[Using the different colors] made it visually easy for me to see if they did their part of the research, and the different colors . . . reminded them of the specific tasks they were to be engaged in."

Ensure Individual Accountability

As we discussed earlier in the chapter, one of the major problems associated with groupwork is unequal participation. Sometimes children refuse to contribute to the group effort, preferring to freeload. Sometimes more assertive children dominate, making it difficult for others to participate. In either case, lack of participation is a genuine problem. Those who do not actively participate will not learn anything about the academic task; furthermore, the group is not learning the skills of collaboration.

One way to encourage the participation of all group members is to make sure that everyone is held responsible for his or her contribution to the goal and that each student's learning is assessed individually. *Individual accountability* is the second essential feature of cooperative learning—and it is one that teachers most often neglect (Antil, et al., 1998).

There are several ways to establish individual accountability. You can require students to take individual quizzes on the material and receive individual grades; you can have each student complete an identifiable part of the total group project; or you can call on one or two students from each group to answer a question, explain the group's reasoning, or provide a demonstration. When Garnetta did the M&Ms™ lesson, for example, all students had to complete their own set of worksheets with their individual predictions and actual counts, as well as the group tally.

Ken's *Heritage* simulation (Wesley, 1976) provides another good example of a task that fosters individual accountability as well as group cooperation. The number of miles that each team travels during a round of play is determined by the number of points the team accumulates. Team members earn points by carrying out the specific responsibilities associated with their particular roles; for example, the daily travel log is worth 10 points, and diary entries are worth 20 points. The better these are, the more miles the team is allowed to travel. In addition, each team member also has to complete three research reports on a historical site. Each research report is worth 40 points, so there is substantial pressure to do a good job. *Heritage* is structured so that the team will suffer if individuals do not participate or if they fail to do acceptable work; in other words, the success of the team depends on each person's contribution. This structure allows teachers to assign individual grades and to provide a group goal—being the first team to reach Bangor, Maine.

In addition to planning tasks so that individuals are held accountable, you need to monitor students' efforts and progress during groupwork time. Our four teachers continually circulate throughout the room, observing each group's activity. In this way they can note problems, provide assistance, and keep students on task. They are also careful to build in progress checkpoints. For example, Barbara occasionally stops the groups' activity and asks each group to report, either verbally or in writing, on what they've accomplished. Similarly, Ken divides large assignments into components that are due every few days (see the section on monitoring student progress in Chapter 7). This allows him to keep track of how well groups are functioning.

If your groups include children with disabilities or those who have limited proficiency in English, you may have to modify the group task so that everyone can participate and everyone can succeed. Ann Nevin (1993) describes several cooperative learning situations in which teachers have made adaptations for students with especially challenging educational needs. For example, one teacher developed a science lesson so that Bobby, who was visually impaired and nonverbal, could be included:

In a lesson in which the objective was for all students to identify different fruits by their seeds (color, size, shape, and number), each group was to complete a poster and, as a group, present it to the rest of the class. Posters were expected to include four or five different fruits and their seeds. Bobby's objective was to tactually explore each fruit and to stay with the group. The objective was explained to the students, and they were asked what other things Bobby could do to be part of the group's activities. The students suggested that Bobby paste some materials on to the poster instead of drawing them. Once all the groups had completed and corrected their posters as necessary, each made and ate a fruit salad. (Nevin, 1993, p. 52)

Similarly, a social studies activity on the countries of Africa was modified to address the needs of an eighth-grader with memory deficits, as well as limited reading and spelling skills:

The teacher asked each of six groups of four students to develop a memory aid, or mnemonic, to represent each of three sets of African countries being studied. The student with memory deficits was held accountable for one of the sets (a reduced assignment). All of the groups were successful in creating mnemonics that enabled them to remember both the names of the nations and their locations. (Nevin, 1993, p. 53)

Teach Students to Cooperate

David and Roger Johnson (1989/90), two experts on cooperative learning, warn teachers not to assume that students know how to work together. They write:

People do not know instinctively how to interact effectively with others. Nor do interpersonal and group skills magically appear when they are needed. Students must be taught these skills and must be motivated to use them. If group members lack the interpersonal and small-group skills to cooperate effectively, cooperative groups will not be productive. (p. 30)

As the classroom teacher, *it is your responsibility to teach students to work together.* This is not a simple process; students do not learn to cooperate in one 45-minute lesson. Indeed, we can think about the process in terms of three stages: learning to value cooperation, developing group skills, and evaluation. Let's consider each of these briefly.

Valuing Cooperation

Before students can work together productively, they must understand the value of cooperation. This is especially important for high achievers who may prefer to work alone, without having to assist others they perceive to be less able. Similarly, when cooperative learning is used to facilitate the inclusion of students with disabilities, nondisabled peers may not be inclined to provide support for children with disabilities (O'Connor & Jenkins, 1996).

If students are going to work in the same groups over a period of time, it's often helpful to have them engage in a nonacademic activity designed to build a team identity and to foster a sense of group cohesion. For example, when Barbara forms cooperative groups that will work together for several weeks, she begins by instructing them to decide on a team name. They then create a banner displaying the team name and an appropriate logo. Sometimes, Barbara gives each member of a team a marker of a different color; individuals can only use the marker they have been given, but the banner must contain all the colors. In this way, everyone has to participate in its creation.

Another activity that is useful for team building (particularly at the primary level) is making a "Things the _____ Team Likes" book (Graves & Graves, 1990). Each group gets a stack of pictures, and each student gets a turn to select a picture for the book. No picture can be included, however, unless all teammates agree that they like the picture. Once there's agreement, pictures are pasted on tagboard or construction paper, and team members provide labels or captions. This activity can be extended by having teams create "Things the _____ Team Likes to Do" books—or even "Things the _____ Team Hates to Do" books.

Group Skills Training

Recently, a student teacher wrote in her journal:

> *After my first disaster with working in groups, I decided I needed to write out a lesson plan for teaching my class how to participate in cooperative learning. I taught it just as I would a math lesson. I realized I could not expect them to know how to do something successfully if I had never taught them how. I would never expect them to be able to add two-digit numbers without training and practice; groupwork is the same thing.*

This student teacher has learned an important lesson: Group skills training requires systematic explanation, modeling, practice, and feedback. *It's simply not enough to state the rules and expect students to understand and remember.* And don't take anything for granted: Even basic guidelines like "don't distract others" and "use indoor voices" may need to be taught.

A particularly important skill to teach and encourage is asking for help. In Chapter 9, we discussed the difficulty that some students have in obtaining assistance. (See the section on effective speakers.) But even if students are effective communicators, they may be reluctant to turn to their peers. For example, Newman and Schwager's (1993) study of students' attitudes toward seeking help found that third-, fifth-, and seventh-grade students generally preferred to seek help from the teacher rather than from classmates. Students saw the teacher as not only more likely to facilitate learning, but also less likely to think they were "dumb" for asking questions. To counteract attitudes like these, you may need to give explicit instructions about when, to whom, and how to ask questions (Farivar & Webb, 1991). You can also encourage this behavior by reminding students that asking other group members can help them learn, by stressing that they're not alone in needing help, or by not responding to requests unless they're unsuccessful in obtaining help from their peers. (Remember Barbara's phrase: "Ask three, then me.") Keep in mind that low achievers—those most in need of academic help—are likely to be the most passive in seeking it (Newman & Schwager, 1993).

Let's see what teaching a group skill might look like in action. During a visit to Garnetta's classroom early in the school year, we observed a science lesson on the solar system. Students were working in pairs, researching information on the planet they had selected. Before the lesson began, Garnetta told us that students had not worked well together during the last science class: "Some people were guarding their work, not letting anybody else see. I knew I'd have to stress the importance of cooperation before we could work again in groups."

GARNETTA: Ladies and gents, there are a few things we need to discuss before we begin. Last time we did science, you were supposed to be working with a partner. Sometimes in school we don't always work with partners. For example, on a spelling test. What if you worked together on a spelling test and looked at someone else's paper?

STUDENT: You might get the answer wrong if the other person had it wrong.

GARNETTA: True. But what do we call it if you look at someone else's paper during a spelling test?

STUDENT: Copying.

GARNETTA: Yes. And that is what?

STUDENT: Cheating.

GARNETTA: Right. During a spelling test, you're supposed to work alone. But what do you have to do when you're working on your projects? What's the big word we use to describe that? The "C" word.

STUDENTS: Cooperation! (choral response)

GARNETTA: Right! We're going to use this big word today in science. Let's say you're working on . . . Johnny, what's your planet?

JOHNNY: Venus.

GARNETTA: OK, *you're* working on Venus, and *he's* working on Venus. [She points to a boy sitting across from Johnny.] If Johnny finds some really good information about Venus's atmosphere, should he hide it and not tell Raymond? [She mimes a child hiding his work.]

STUDENT: No. He should help him.

GARNETTA: Why?

STUDENT: Because he might not know the answer and they're supposed to work together.

GARNETTA: OK. Let's say they're trying to find the answers to questions one and two, but the books they're using are written differently. Johnny doesn't have the answer to number one, and Raymond doesn't have the answer to number two. If they *share* the information, they can *both* do better. They can *both* answer one and two. And they'll probably both get good grades because they . . . what?

STUDENTS: Cooperated!

GARNETTA: Yes! OK, I want to talk about one other thing that's important for today's science lesson. When people are working, I sometimes see this [she pretends to be a child whispering to another child]:

          "Hey, did you see so-and-so, he was down at the office, 'cause he got in trouble . . ." Are you going to get your work done if you're doing this?

STUDENTS: No.

GARNETTA: Right. If you're whispering like this, you're not sticking to the task, and you're not going to get your work done, and you're not going to . . .

STUDENTS: Learn!

GARNETTA: You got it. OK, so I want you to remember these two things today. To *cooperate* by sharing your information and to *stick to the task,* not playing around with your neighbor or talking about other stuff. And that way you will . . .

STUDENTS: Learn!

It's helpful to begin by analyzing the groupwork task you have selected in order to determine the specific skills students need to know (Cohen, 1994a). Will students have to explain material? Will they have to listen carefully to one another? Will they have to reach a consensus? Once you have analyzed the task, select one or two key behaviors to teach your students. Resist the temptation to introduce all the required group skills at once; going too far too fast is sure to lead to frustration.

Next, explain to your students that they will be learning a skill necessary for working in groups. Be sure to *define terms, discuss rationales, and provide examples.* Johnson and Johnson (1989/90) suggest that you construct a "T-chart" on which you list the skill and then—with the class—record ideas about what the skill would look like and what it would sound like. Figure 10-2 shows a T-chart for "sharing."

Finally, you need to provide opportunities for students to practice the skill and to receive feedback. You might have students role play; you might pair the skill with a familiar academic task so that students can focus their attention on using the social skill (Carson & Hoyle, 1989/90); or you might have students engage in exercises designed to teach particular skills.

Sharing	
Looks Like	**Sounds Like**
Leave the markers in the middle of the table where all can reach	Here's the marker.
Offer the markers to somebody else when finished using	Thanks for handling me the marker.
Return markers to middle of the table	I'm done with the marker; does anybody want it?
Take turns with the markers	Anybody need the red marker?

FIGURE 10-2. A T-chart for sharing

Regardless of the type of practice you provide, you need to give students feedback about their performance. They need to know how often and how well they have engaged in the new behavior. As Ken observes:

Social skills need to be constantly reinforced. I have to tell my kids every day that I appreciate the way they're cooperating, or that I saw some groups doing a terrific job of explaining problems. As far as I'm concerned, teaching these skills is as important as teaching the math or the language arts.

In addition to providing feedback himself, Ken has found it effective to designate a "process person" for each group. This individual is responsible for keeping track of how well the group is functioning; for example, he or she may monitor how many times each person speaks. At the end of the groupwork session, the process person is able to share specific data that the group can use to evaluate its ability to work together.

Evaluation

In order to learn from their experiences, students need the chance to discuss what happened and to evaluate how successful they were in working together. Ross (1995) demonstrated the power of feedback in a study that audiotaped seventh-grade mathematics students in cooperative learning groups, gave students edited transcripts of their discussions, and trained them in how to interpret them. Students then devised an improvement plan to increase the frequency of requesting help, giving help, and being on task. According to Ross, after the feedback, both the frequency and quality of help seeking and help giving improved. For example, students became more aware of the needs of lower-ability students and felt more obligated to help. Consider the following exchange, recorded before the feedback. Here, Sharon has fallen behind the other members of her group, but they will not wait, and they exclude her from the discussion of the answers:

> SHARON: Hey, what about me?
> CURTIS: You're not in it.
> SHARON: Hey, you guys, what about me? . . . How come you guys won't let me do none?
> GWEN: Because you're not even here yet.
> SHARON: I'm on number 15.
> GWEN: Yeah, I know, but we're on number 16. (p. 135)

In a session recorded after the feedback, group members continue to treat Sharon rather impatiently when she has fallen behind; nonetheless, they are now more willing to wait for her:

> CURTIS: We have to wait for her. We have to wait for her.
> GWEN: Come on, Sharon. You know we are waiting.
> SHARON: You guys were going ahead and you weren't supposed to.
> GWEN: I know; we won't. We won't do the answers.
> CURTIS: We won't look at the answers. We'll wait for you. (p. 135)

Obviously, it's impossible to provide this kind of elaborate, detailed feedback on a regular basis. But an extensive evaluation session can be instructive when norms for groupwork are first being established.

A far simpler approach to evaluation is to ask students to name three things their group did well and one thing the group could do better next time (Johnson & Johnson, 1989/90). You can also have students consider more specific questions, such as

Did you use "indoor voices"?

Did you take turns?

Did everyone carry out his or her job?

Did everyone get a chance to talk?

Did you listen to one another?

What did you do if you didn't agree?

For young children, a simple checklist, like the one in Figure 10-3, can be helpful.

After individual groups have talked about their experiences, it is often helpful to have groups report to the whole class. You can encourage groups to share and compare their experiences by asking, "Did your group have a similar problem?" "How many groups agree with the way they solved their problem?" "What do you recommend?"

Unfortunately, there are times when teaching group skills and providing for practice and evaluation are just not enough to get particular children to cooperate. Some youngsters are so troubled, volatile, or hostile that they cause conflict no matter where they're placed. When this occurs, you may have no recourse but to exclude them from the activity and devise an individual assignment for them. In cases like this, Barbara tells students, "If you absolutely can't work with the group, then you'll just have to carry the whole load by yourself." (Then she makes sure that the individual activity is *less* enjoyable and *more* onerous than the group activity!)

Name_____		Date_____	
How was I in group today?			
Did I . . .			
	YES		NO
1. Share ideas?			
2. Encourage others?			
3. Let others speak?			
4. Listen to others?			
5. Do my job?			

FIGURE 10-3. A checklist for evaluating group skills

Monitor Learning, Involvement, and Cooperative Behavior

During cooperative learning activities, Viviana, Garnetta, Barbara, and Ken constantly circulate throughout the room, listening, assisting, encouraging, prodding, questioning, and in general, ensuring that students are involved, productive, and working collaboratively. Research confirms that teacher monitoring helps to promote a high level of student involvement in group activities (Emmer & Gerwels, 1998). Monitoring also helps to promote the successful participation of children with disabilities. In their study of cooperative learning as an inclusion strategy, O'Connor and Jenkins (1996) found that monitoring allowed teachers to make public statements validating the contributions of students with disabilities—what Cohen (1998) calls "assigning competence." Consider this example from Viviana's class:

> *Viviana stops to listen to Jorge's cooperative group as they work on a math assignment to create four story problems using money. The students were outlining a story in which three items were being bought, and they wanted to know how much change would be received from one dollar. Viviana overhears Jorge, a low-ability student, point out that the three items add up to more than one dollar. She remarks, "Jorge's discovery is a good one. I know he goes to the store for his mom and has experience with this." After Viviana leaves, we notice Jorge taking a more active role in the group. Viviana's comment appears to have validated Jorge's contribution and raised his status in the group. Even though his writing skills and knowledge of number facts are poor, his group now looks to him for his knowledge about spending.*

In addition to circulating throughout the room, all four teachers have a signal for gaining students' attention. This allows them to provide needed instructions to the whole class or to bring the activity to a close. A study of 13 elementary teachers in six urban schools (Emmer & Gerwels, 1998) found a variety of group attention signals (e.g., "Stop, look, and listen," "Clap if you can hear me," "Fold your hands," "Thumbs up if you can hear me," "Hands on head," and rhythmic clapping). Signals requiring an overt student response were more effective than those that simply asked for students' attention.

Four Specific Approaches to Cooperative Learning

Several structured programs of cooperative learning have been developed to avoid the problems characteristic of groupwork and to encourage norms of effort and mutual support. Designed for use at any grade level and in most school subjects, all of these cooperative learning strategies are characterized by heterogeneous groups working together to achieve a common goal (Slavin, 1985). In this section of the chapter, we briefly examine four of these programs: STAD, Jigsaw and Jigsaw II, Group Investigation, and the structural approach to cooperative learning. You can learn more about these programs by referring to the references listed in "For Further Reading."

Barbara checks in with a cooperative learning group.

Student Teams-Achievement Divisions (STAD)

STAD is a cooperative learning method developed and studied at Johns Hopkins University by Robert Slavin and his colleagues. STAD is particularly appropriate for content areas where there are "right answers," such as mathematics, spelling, and grammar.

In STAD, the teacher presents a lesson, and students then work within their teams on an academic task. In other words, students help one another with the assignment instead of doing it as individual seatwork. Suppose the task is to complete pages in a spelling workbook. Students may take turns quizzing one another on the spelling words, do the exercises individually and then compare answers, or work together on each exercise. Their objective is to ensure that all team members master the material. Team members are told that they are not finished studying until everyone on the team feels confident about knowing the material.

Following team practice, students take individual quizzes on which they receive individual scores. In addition, a *team score* is calculated, based on team members' *individual improvement over their own past performance.* This is an extremely important feature: Using improvement scores prevents low-achieving students from being rejected because they cannot contribute to the team. In STAD, the student whose quiz scores go from 57 to 67 contributes as much as the student whose scores go from 85 to 95. Finally, teams that earn a designated number of points receive certificates or other rewards.

As you can see, STAD clearly reflects the two conditions essential to cooperative learning. Positive interdependence and individual accountability are induced by having students receive a group reward based on every member's individual quiz score.

Jigsaw and Jigsaw II

In Jigsaw, one of the earliest cooperative learning methods (Aronson, Blaney, Stephan, Sikes, & Snapp, 1978), heterogeneous teams work on academic material that has been divided into sections. Jigsaw is particularly appropriate for narrative material, such as a social studies chapter, a biography, or a short story. Each team member reads only one section of the material. The teams then disband, and students meet in "expert groups" with other people who have been assigned the same section. Working together, they learn the material in these expert groups and then return to their home teams to teach it to their teammates. Since everyone is responsible for learning all the material, successful task completion requires students to listen carefully to their peers. Jigsaw also includes team-building activities and training to improve communication and tutoring skills.

Jigsaw II (Slavin, 1985) is a modification developed by the researchers at Johns Hopkins. It differs from the original Jigsaw in that all students on a team read the entire assignment. Then they are assigned a particular topic on which to become an expert. Like STAD, Jigsaw II uses individual quizzes and team scores based on individual improvement.

Group Investigation

Group Investigation, developed by Shlomo Sharan and his colleagues at the University of Tel Aviv (Sharan & Sharan, 1976, 1989/90) places students in small groups to investigate topics from a unit being studied by the entire class. Each group further divides their topic into individual subtopics and then carries out the research. Students work together to find resource materials, to collect and analyze information, and to plan and present a report, demonstration, play, learning center, or exhibition for the class. Evaluation focuses on both learning and effective experiences; assessment procedures may include comments from peers, students' self-evaluations, and questions submitted by groups for a common test, as well as evaluation by the teacher.

The Structural Approach to Cooperative Learning

The structural approach was developed by Spencer Kagan, a former psychology professor at the University of California, Riverside, and director of Kagan Publishing and Professional Development. According to Kagan (1989/90), teachers can make cooperative learning a part of any lesson by using "structures"—content-free ways of organizing social interaction among students. Structures usually involve a series of steps, with prescribed behavior at each step. A traditional classroom structure, for example, is the "whole-class question-answer" situation. In this structure, the teacher asks a question, children raise their hands to respond, and the teacher calls on one student. If that student answers the question incorrectly, the other children get a chance to respond and to win the teacher's praise. Thus, children are often happy if a classmate makes a mistake, and they may even root for one another's failure.

Kagan has developed a number of simple cooperative structures that can be used at a variety of grade levels and in many content areas. He emphasizes the need for teachers to select the structures that are most appropriate for their specific objectives. Some structures are useful for team building or for developing communication skills; others are most suitable for increasing mastery of factual material or for concept development.

"Numbered Heads Together" is a good example of a structure that is appropriate for checking on students' understanding of content. (It also provides a cooperative alternative to "whole-class question-answer.") In Numbered Heads, students "number off" within teams (e.g., one through four). When the teacher asks a question, team members "put their heads together" to make sure that everyone on the team knows the answer. The teacher then calls a number, and students with that number may raise their hands to answer. This structure promotes interdependence among team members: If one student knows the answer, everyone's chance of answering correctly increases. At the same time, the structure encourages individual accountability: Once the teacher calls a number, students are on their own.

Another structure is "Timed Pair Share," in which students pair up to share their responses to a question posed by the teacher. First Student A talks for a minute, and then Student B has a turn. As Kagan points out, this simultaneous interaction allows all students to respond in the same amount of time that it would have taken for just two students if the teacher had used the more traditional "whole-class question-answer" structure (Walters, 2000).

Some of Kagan's other structures are listed in Figure 10-4.

Concluding Comments

Although this chapter is entitled "Managing Groupwork," we have seen that there are actually a number of different groupwork situations, each with its own set of uses, procedures, requirements, and pitfalls. As you plan and implement groupwork in your classroom, it's important to remember these distinctions. Too many teachers think that cooperative learning is putting students into groups and telling them to work together. They select tasks that are inappropriate for the size of the group; they use heterogeneous groups when homogeneous groups would be more suitable (or vice versa); they fail to build in positive interdependence and individual accountability; they fail to appreciate the differences between helping groups and cooperative learning. The following example, taken from O'Donnell and O'Kelly (1994), would be funny—if it weren't true:

> *One of our colleagues recently described an example of "cooperative learning" in his son's school. The classroom teacher informed the students that [they] would be using cooperative learning. His son was paired with another student. The two students were required to complete two separate parts of a project but were expected to complete the work outside of class. A grade was assigned to each part of the project and a group grade was given. In this instance, one child received an "F" as he failed to complete the required part of the project. The other child received an "A." The group grade was a "C," thus rewarding the student who had failed to complete the work, and punishing the child who had completed his work. In this use of "cooperative learning," there was no opportunity for the students to*

Name	Purpose	Description	Functions
Round-Robin	Team building	Each student in turn shares something with teammates.	Expressing ideas and opinions. Getting acquainted.
Match Mine	Communication	Students try to match the arrangement of objects on a grid of another student using oral communication only.	Vocabulary building. Communication skills. Role-taking ability.
Three-Step Interview	Concept Development	Students interview each other in pairs, first one way, then the other. Students then share information they learned with the group.	Sharing personal information such as hypotheses, reactions to a poem,conclusions from a unit. Equal participation. Listening.
Inside-Outside Circle	Multifunctional	Students stand in pairs in two concentric circles.The inside circle faces out; the outside circle faces in. Students use flash cards or respond to teacher questions as they rotate to each new partner.	Checking for understanding. Review. Tutoring. Meeting classmates. Sharing.

FIGURE 10-4. Some of Spencer Kagan's cooperative structures
Source: Adapted from Kagan, S. (1989/90). The structural approach to cooperative learning. *Educational Leadership, 47*(4) p. 14.

interact, and the attempt to use a group reward (the group grade) backfired. Although this scenario is not recognizable as cooperative learning to most proponents of cooperation, the classroom teacher described it as such to the students' parents. (p. 322)

This example illustrates the need for teachers to acquire an understanding of the intricacies of groupwork in general and cooperative learning in particular. No three-hour class, no one-shot in-service workshop, and no chapter can adequately meet this need. Groupwork is an extremely challenging subsetting of the classroom, and successful management requires unusually careful planning and implementation. It is especially challenging for beginning teachers who are not yet experienced classroom managers.

Despite the potential pitfalls, we believe that groupwork should be an integral part of elementary classrooms. As was the case with independent work, Barbara, Ken, Viviana, and Garnetta use groupwork to varying degrees, but all of them believe that students must learn to work together and that students can learn from one another.

After a meeting with our four teachers, during which we discussed the topic of small groups, Ken wrote us a brief note. In it, he reflected on the impact of groupwork on learning:

> *The real advantage with small groups, at least from my angle, is increased learning. When kids interact with each other, when they speak to and listen to others, there is a greater level of involvement and increased support for learning. It is, of course, difficult to verify or assess this increase, yet I often hear kids talking about how they answered their questions and how the group affected their final product. Sometimes a child will say, "See you guys, I was right and you talked me out of it!" Sometimes no one is really sure who came up with the answer; they all sort of pieced it together. For my kids, having to work alone on an assignment is a punishment.*

Ken's reflections focus on the academic benefits of groupwork. But as we mentioned at the beginning of the chapter, groupwork has social payoffs as well. It's important to remember that the classroom is not simply a place where students learn academic lessons. It's also a place where students learn *social lessons*—lessons about the benefits or the dangers of helping one another, about relationships with students from other ethnic groups, about accepting or rejecting children with disabilities, and about friendship. As a teacher, you will determine the content of these lessons. If planned and implemented well, groupwork can provide students with opportunities to learn lessons of caring, fairness, and self-worth.

Summary

We began this chapter by talking about the potential benefits of groupwork and about some of the special challenges it presents. Then we suggested strategies for designing successful groupwork. Finally we described some structured programs of cooperative learning.

Benefits of groupwork
- Less idle time while waiting for the teacher to help.
- Enhanced motivation.
- More involvement in learning.
- Greater achievement.
- Decreased competition among students.
- Increased interaction across gender, ethnic, and racial lines.
- Improved relationships between mainstreamed students and their peers.

Some common pitfalls
- Segregation in terms of gender, ethnicity, and race.
- Unequal participation.
- Lack of accomplishment.
- Lack of cooperation among group members.

Challenges of groupwork
- Maintaining order.
- Achieving accountability for all students.
- Teaching new (cooperative) behavioral norms.
- Creating effective groups.

Designing and implementing successful groupwork
- Decide on the type of group to use (helping permitted, helping obligatory, peer tutoring, cooperative, completely cooperative).
- Decide on the size of the group.
- Assign students to groups.
- Structure the task for interdependence.
- Ensure individual accountability.
- Teach students to cooperate.
- Monitor learning, involvement, and cooperative behavior.

Structured programs of cooperative learning
- STAD.
- Jigsaw I and II.
- Group Investigation.
- The Structural Approach to Cooperative Learning.

Groupwork offers unique social and academic rewards, but it is important to understand the challenges it presents and not to assume that, just because a task is fun or interesting, the lesson will run smoothly. Remember to plan groupwork carefully, prepare your students thoroughly, and allow yourself time to develop experience as a facilitator of cooperative groups.

✦ Activities

1. For each of the following cases, choose the type of groupwork you would use (helping permitted, helping obligatory, peer tutoring, cooperative group, completely cooperative group) and briefly describe your reasons.

   a. You are teaching your heterogeneous math class how to tell time. Eight of the 17 students pick up the concept quickly, but the remaining students are having some difficulty.

   b. Your third-grade class is divided into three literature groups. Each group is reading a different novel, but each group has to define 10 vocabulary words you have drawn from its book. Your main goal is for each child in each group to have the definitions correctly written to use as a study guide for a future quiz.

   c. In your homogeneous fifth-grade math class you are reviewing the decimal equivalents of fractions. You want children to use flash cards to assist them in memorizing the equivalents.

   d. In sixth grade, your science class is studying rocks and minerals. You would like the students to work in groups of three to study the three types of rocks (igneous, metamorphic, sedimentary). Each group is to create a large poster showing the characteristics and examples of each type of rock.

   e. Your fourth-grade class just read tall tales in their literature anthology. To capitalize on their enthusiasm you have them form groups to write and perform (complete with scenery and costumes) a play or puppet show based on one of the tall tales. You would like each member of the group to enjoy the many aspects of this project, from writing to acting.

2. You want your class to work on editing and peer conferencing skills with the mystery stories they've been writing. It is important to you that students be able to give and receive constructive criticism and feedback. You have decided to have the students work in groups of three. How will you model the skills you want them to practice? What roles might you assign to facilitate the objective? What forms of accountability will you build in? How will you monitor the groupwork?

3. Choose two of the topics listed below. For each one, select an approach discussed in this chapter (STAD, Jigsaw, Group Investigation, or one of Kagan's cooperative structures). Describe briefly how you would use the cooperative learning strategy you selected. Use a different strategy for each topic.

   a. Inventors and their inventions.

   b. Uses of plants.

   c. Linear measurement.

    d. Pioneer life.

    e. Character analysis.

    f. Using a thesaurus.

    g. Dinosaurs.

    h. Systems of the body.

    i. Nutrition.

4. Observe a cooperative learning activity. In what ways has the teacher tried to promote positive interdependence and individual accountability?

For Further Reading

Cohen, E. G. (1986). *Designing groupwork: Strategies for the heterogeneous classroom.* (2nd ed.) New York: Teacher College Press.

Johnson, D. W., Johnson, R. T., Holubec, E. J., & Roy, P. (1993). *Circles of learning: Cooperation in the classroom.* 4th ed. Edina, MN: Interaction.

Kagan, S. (1990). *Cooperative learning: Resources for teachers.* San Juan Capistrano, CA: Resources for Teachers.

Slavin, R. (1995). *Cooperative learning: Research, theory, and practice.* (2nd ed.). Boston: Allyn and Bacon.

Webb, N. M., & Palincsar, A. S. (1996). Group processes in the classroom. In D. Berliner and R. C. Calfee (Eds.), *Handbook of Educational Psychology.* New York: Macmillan, 841–876.

References

Antil, L. R., Jenkins, J. R., Wayne, S. K., & Vadasy, P. F. (1998). Cooperative learning: Prevalence, conceptualizations, and the relation between research and practice. *American Educational Research Journal, 35*(3), 419–454.

Aronson, E., Blaney, N., Stephan, C., Sikes, J., Snapp, M. (1978). *The Jigsaw classroom.* Beverly Hills, CA: Sage.

Carson, L., & Hoyle, S. (1989/90). Teaching social skills: A view from the classroom. *Educational Leadership, 47*(4), 31.

Carter, K. (March–April 1985). Teacher comprehension of classroom processes: An emerging direction in classroom management research. Paper presented at the annual meeting of the American Educational Research Association, Chicago, Illinois.

Cohen, E. G. (1972). Interracial interaction disability. *Human Relations, 25,* 9–24.

Cohen, E. G. (1994a). *Designing groupwork: Strategies for the heterogeneous classroom* (2nd ed.). New York: Teachers College Press.

Cohen, E. G. (1994b). Restructuring the classroom: Conditions for productive small groups. *Review of Educational Research, 64*(1), 1–35.

Cohen, E. G. (1998). Making cooperative learning equitable. *Educational Leadership, 56*(1), 18–21.

Dowrick, N. (1993). Talking and learning in pairs: A comparison of two interactive modes for six- and seven-year-old pupils. *International Journal of Early Years Education, 1*(3), 49–60.

Edwards, C., & Stout, J. (1989/90). Cooperative learning: The first year. *Educational Leadership, 47*(4), 38–41.

Emmer, E. T., & Gerwels, M. C. (April 1998). Classroom management tasks in cooperative groups. Paper presented at the annual meeting of the American Educational Research Association, San Diego, CA.

Farivar, S., & Webb, N. (1991). *Helping behavior activities handbook: Cooperative small group problem solving in middle school mathematics (Report to the National Science Foundation).* Los Angeles: University of California, Los Angeles.

Gerleman, S. L. (1987). An observational study of small-group instruction in fourth-grade mathematics classrooms. *The Elementary School Journal, 88,* 3–28.

Goodlad, J. I. (1984). *A place called school.* New York: McGraw-Hill.

Graves, T., & Graves, N. (1990). Things we like: A team-building/language development lesson for preschool–grade 2. *Cooperative Learning, The Magazine for Cooperation in Education, 10*(3), 45.

Graybeal, S. S., & Stodolsky, S. S. (1985). Peer work groups in elementary schools. *American Journal of Education, 93,* 409–428.

Johnson, D. W., & Johnson, R. T. (1980). Integrating handicapped students into the mainstream. *Exceptional children, 47*(2), 90–98.

Johnson, D. W., & Johnson, R. T. (1989/90). Social skills for successful groupwork. *Educational Leadership, 47*(4), 29–33.

Johnson, D. W., Johnson, R. T., Holubec, E. J., & Roy, P. (1984). *Circles of learning: Cooperation in the classroom.* Alexandria, VA: Association for Supervision and Curriculum Development.

Kagan, S. (1989/90). The structural approach to cooperative learning. *Educational Leadership, 47*(4), 12–15.

Kagan, S., Zahn, G. L., Widaman, K. F., Schwarzwald, J., & Tyrrell, G. (1985). Classroom structural bias: Impact of cooperative and competitive classroom structures on cooperative and competitive individuals and groups. In R. Slavin, S. Sharan, S. Kagan, R. Hertz-Lazarowitz, C. Webb, & R. Schmuck (Eds.), *Learning to cooperate, cooperating to learn* (277–312). New York: Plenum Press.

King, L., Luberda, H., Barry, K., & Zehnder, S. (1998). A case study of the perceptions of students in a small-group cooperative learning situation. Paper presented at the Annual Conference of the American Educational Research Association. San Diego, CA.

Lazarowitz, R., Baird, J. H., Hertz-Lazarowitz, R., & Jenkins, J. (1985). The effects of modified jigsaw on achievement, classroom social climate, and self-esteem in high-school science classes. In R. Slavin, S. Sharan, S. Kagan, R. Hertz-Lazarowitz, C. Webb, & R. Schmuck (Eds.), *Learning to cooperate, cooperating to learn* (231–253). New York: Plenum Press.

Lyman, L., Foyle, H. C., & Azwell, T. S. (1993). *Cooperative learning in the elementary classroom.* Washington, DC: National Education Association.

Madden, N. A., & Slavin, R. E. (1983). Cooperative learning and social acceptance of mainstreamed academically handicapped students. *Journal of Special Education, 17,* 171–182.

Manning, M. L., & Lucking, R. (1993). Cooperative learning and multicultural classrooms. *The Clearing House, 67*(1), 12–16.

Mulryan, C. M. (1992). Student passivity during cooperative small groups in mathematics. *Journal of Educational Research, 85*(5), 261–273.

Nevin, A. (1993). Curricula and instructional adaptations for including students with disabilities in cooperative groups. In J. W. Putnam, *Cooperative learning and strategies for inclusion: Celebrating diversity in the classroom* (41–56). Baltimore, MD: Paul H. Brookes.

Newman, R. S., & Schwager, M. T. (1993). Students' perceptions of the teacher and classmates in relation to reported help seeking in math class. *The Elementary School Journal, 94*(1), 3–17.

O'Connor, R. E., Jenkins, J. R. (1996). Cooperative learning as an inclusion strategy: A closer look. *Exceptionality, 6*(1), 9–51.

O'Donnell, A., & O'Kelly, J. (1994). Learning from peers: Beyond the rhetoric of positive results. *Educational Psychology Review, 6*(4), 321–349.

Robinson, A. (1990). Cooperation or exploitation? The argument against cooperative learning for talented students. *Journal for the Education of the Gifted, 14*(1), 9–27.

Rosenholtz, S. J., & Cohen, E. G. (1985). Status in the eye of the beholder. In J. Berger & M. Zelditch, Jr. (Eds.), *Status, rewards, and influence.* San Francisco: Jossey Bass.

Ross, J. A. (1995). Effects of feedback on student behavior in cooperative learning groups in a grade 7 math class. *The Elementary School Journal, 96*(2), 125–143.

Sharan, S. (1990). The group investigation approach to cooperative learning: Theoretical foundations. In M. Brubacher, R. Payne, & K. Rickett (Eds.), *Perspectives on small group learning.* Oakville, Ontario: Rubicon.

Sharan, S. & Sharan, Y. (1976). *Small-group teaching.* Englewood Cliffs, NJ: Educational Technology Publications.

Sharan, Y., & Sharan, S. (1989/90). Group investigation expands cooperative learning. *Educational Leadership, 47*(4), 17–21.

Slavin, R. (1985). An introduction to cooperative learning research. In R. Slavin, S. Sharan, S. Kagan, R. Hertz-Lazarowitz, C. Webb, & R. Schmuck (Eds.), *Learning to cooperate, cooperating to learn.* New York: Plenum Press, 5–15.

Slavin, R. E. (1991). *Student team learning: A practical guide to cooperative learning* (3rd ed.). Washington, DC: National Education Association.

Stodolsky, S. S. (1984). Frameworks for studying instructional processes in peer work groups. In P. L. Peterson, L. C. Wilkinson, & M. Hallinan (Eds.), *The social context of instruction.* (107–124). New York: Academic Press.

Walters, L. S. (2000). Putting cooperative learning to the test. *Harvard Education Letter, 16*(3), 1–6.

Webb, N. M. (1984). Sex differences in interaction and achievement in cooperative small groups. *Journal of Educational Psychology, 76,* 33–44.

Webb, N. M. (1985). Student interaction and learning in small groups: A research summary. In R. Slavin, S. Sharan, S. Kagan, R. Hertz-Lazarowitz, C. Webb, & R. Schmuck (Eds.), *Learning to cooperate, cooperating to learn* (147–172). New York: Plenum Press.

Webb, N. M., Baxter, G. P., & Thompson, L. (1997). Teachers' grouping practices in fifth-grade science classrooms. *The Elementary School Journal, 98*(2), 91–113.

Webb, N. M., & Farivar, S. (1994). Promoting helping behavior in cooperative small groups in middle school mathematics. *American Educational Research Journal, 31,* 369–395.

Webb, N. M., & Kenderski, C. M. (1984). Student interaction and learning in small group and whole class settings. In P. L. Peterson, L. C. Wilkinson, & M. Hallinan (Eds.), *The social context of instruction.* New York: Academic Press, 153–170.

Webb, N. M., & Palincsar, A. S. (1996). Group processes in the classroom. In D. Berliner and R. C. Calfee (Eds.). *Handbook of Educational Psychology* (841–876). New York: Macmillan.

Wesley, D. (1976). *Heritage.* Lakeside, CA: Interact Company.

Wilkinson, L. C., & Calculator, S. (1982). Effective speakers: Students' use of language to request and obtain information and action in the classroom. In L. C. Wilkinson (Ed.), *Communicating in the classroom.* New York: Academic Press, 85–100.

Chapter Eleven

Managing Recitations and Discussions

Much of the talk that occurs between teachers and students is unlike the talk you hear in the "real world." Let's consider just one example (Cazden, 1988). In the real world, if you ask someone for the time, we can assume that you really need to know what time it is and will be grateful for a reply. The conversation would probably go like this:

    "What time is it?"

    "2:30."

"Thank you."

In contrast, if a teacher asks for the time during a lesson, the dialogue generally sounds like this:

"What time is it?"

"2:30."

"Very good."

Here, the question is not a request for needed information, but a way of finding out what students know. The interaction is more like a quiz show (Roby, 1988) than a true conversation: The teacher asks a question, a student replies, and the teacher evaluates the response (Mehan, 1979). This pattern of interaction (initiation-response-evaluation or I-R-E) is called *recitation,* and several studies (e.g., Stodolsky, 1988) have documented the substantial amount of time that students spend in this subsetting of the classroom.

The recitation has been frequently denounced as a method of instruction. Critics object to the active, dominant role of the teacher and the relatively passive role of the student. They decry the lack of interaction among students. They condemn the fact that recitations often emphasize the recall of factual information and demand little higher-level thinking. (See Figure 11-1 for an example of this kind of recitation.)

An additional criticism focuses on the public evaluation that occurs during recitation. When the teacher calls on a student, everyone can witness and pass judgment on the response. In fact, as Phil Jackson (1968) comments, classmates "frequently join in the act":

Sometimes the class as a whole is invited to participate in the evaluation of a students' work, as when the teacher asks, "Who can correct Billy?" or "How many believe that Shirley read that poem with a lot of expression?" (p. 20)

Questions like these exacerbate the "negative interdependence" among students that recitations can generate (Kagan, 1989/90). In other words, if a student is unable to respond to the teacher's question, the other students have a greater chance to be called on and to receive praise; thus, students may actually root for their classmates' failure.

Finally, critics observe that the format of the recitation is incompatible with the cultural background of some students. For example, recitation generally follows a "passive-receptive" discourse pattern: Students are expected to listen quietly during teacher presentations and then respond individually to teacher-initiated questions. African American students, however, may be accustomed to a more active, participatory discourse pattern ("call-response"). When they demonstrate their engagement by calling out prompts, comments, and reactions, European American teachers may interpret the behavior as rude and disruptive (Gay, 2000).

Another illustration comes from Susan Philips (1972), who wondered why children on the Warm Springs Indian Reservation in Oregon were so reluctant to participate in classroom recitations. Her analysis of life in this Native American community disclosed a set of behavioral norms that conflict with the way recitations are conducted. As we

Mr. Lowe's fourth-grade students have been reading some of *Aesop's Fables*. Today, they are focusing on "Androcles and the Lion." In this well-known fable, an escaped slave named Androcles earns a lion's gratitude for removing a large thorn stuck in one of the lion's toes. Later, Androcles is recaptured and is to be thrown to the lion, who has also been captured. When the lion's cage is opened, he rushes with a great roar toward his victim. At the last moment, however, he recognizes his friend and treats Androcles with gentleness and gratitude.

MR. LOWE:	OK, let's start at the very beginning. What is the name of the slave?
STUDENT:	Androcles?
MR. LOWE:	Right. Now how was Androcles treated by his master?
STUDENT:	Cruelly.
MR. LOWE:	Good. So what did Androcles do?
STUDENT:	He escaped.
MR. LOWE:	Ah, yes. He escapes and he heads for the forest. He's wandering around and he meets a . . . a what, Jane?
JANE:	A lion.
MR. LOWE:	Yes, a lion. And something's wrong with the lion. What's wrong, Ari?
ARI:	He has a cut on his paw.
MR. LOWE:	Not exactly a cut. Tasheika?
TASHEIKA:	A thorn is stuck in his paw.
MR. LOWE:	Absolutely. A thorn. And this moaning, whimpering, distressed lion holds out his paw for Androcles, and Androcles does what?
STUDENT:	Takes the thorn out.
MR. LOWE:	Good, he takes the thorn out. Now the lion is so grateful that he leads Androcles to his cave, and they live in the forest together. But one day, when Androcles and the lion went out together, what happened?
STUDENT:	They were captured.
MR. LOWE:	Yes, and then what?
STUDENT:	Androcles is going to be thrown to the lion.
MR. LOWE:	Very good. Yes. And the lion is purposely starved for several days so that he will be even more ferocious. The Emperor and his court all come to the arena to see Androcles face the lion. They expect that the lion will do what, Billy?
STUDENT:	Kill Androcles.
MR. LOWE:	Yes, they think the lion will tear him to shreds. But what happens, Sivan?
SIVAN:	He recognizes Androcles and doesn't kill him.
MR. LOWE:	Right—because the lion is . . . what, class?
STUDENTS:	[Silence.]
MR. LOWE:	How does the lion feel toward Androcles?
STUDENTS:	[Students murmur a variety of responses.] Grateful. Happy. He likes him. Loving.
MR. LOWE:	Good, he is grateful to him for pulling out the thorn so he does not kill him.

FIGURE 11-1. An example of a poor recitation: *Aesop's Fables* as quiz show

have noted, recitations permit little student–student interaction, but Warm Springs children are extremely peer oriented. During recitations, the teacher decides who will participate, while Warm Springs traditions allow individuals to decide for themselves if and when to participate in public events. Recitations involve public performance and public evaluation—even if a student has not yet mastered the material—but Warm Springs children are used to testing their skills in private before they choose to demonstrate them in public. Understanding these disparities helps us to see why the children would find recitations unfamiliar and uncomfortable.

Despite the validity of these criticisms, the recitation remains an extremely common feature of elementary classrooms. What is there about this instructional strategy that makes it so enduring in the face of other, more highly touted methods (Hoetker & Ahlbrand, 1969)?

We thought hard about these questions during one visit to Barbara's classroom, and our observation of a recitation she conducted provided some clues. The students had just read the first few chapters in their new novel, *The Cay* (Taylor, 1969). Barbara asked them to take out their books and to get ready to talk about what they had read. She perched on her stool in the front of the room.

BARBARA: Let's review what you read last night. First of all, what is a cay? [One girl raises her hand.] Only one person? [She pauses and a few more hands go up. Barbara calls on a volunteer.] Maggie?

MAGGIE: An island.

BARBARA: Any particular kind of island?

STUDENT: A very small island.

BARBARA: OK. What did you find out about where the island was? [A boy raises his hand, but then lowers it.] Ben, you put your hand down, but you wanted to say something?

BEN: It's near Aruba.

BARBARA: Good. What else? [Barbara calls on a nonvolunteer.]

STUDENT: In the Caribbean.

BARBARA: OK. [Barbara directs students to look at their individual maps and locate the island. When she is satisfied that everyone has located the island, she continues.] This story takes place in what time in history?

STUDENT: 1942.

BARBARA: Good. What important thing was happening then?

STUDENT: It was the middle of World War II.

BARBARA: Right. Where did most of the fighting take place in World War II?

STUDENT: Europe.

BARBARA: OK, but are they in Europe? [She calls on a nonvolunteer.]

STUDENT: No.

BARBARA: Then why are they affected? [Barbara sounds very puzzled.]

STUDENT: It's a world war, so it affects a lot of places.

BARBARA: True, but why *this* place?

STUDENT: Because there are three submarines there.

> BARBARA: But *why?*
> STUDENT: Because of a supply of oil that was there.
> BARBARA: So what? Why is oil important?
> STUDENT: It's worth a lot of money.
> BARBARA: Why?
> STUDENT: Because it's rare and we need it.
> BARBARA: Okay, it's an important natural resource that's not plentiful every-where.

Barbara's recitation helped us to identify five very useful functions of classroom recitations. First, the recitation allowed Barbara to review some basic facts about the story and to check on students' comprehension. Second, by asking intellectually demanding questions (e.g., why the war affected people in the Caribbean), Barbara was able to prod her students beyond low-level factual recall to higher levels of thinking. Third, the recitation permitted Barbara to involve students in the presentation of material—what Roby (1988) calls "lecturing in the interrogatory mood." Instead of telling students where the island was located, for example, or why it was affected by the war, Barbara brought out the information by asking questions. Fourth, the recitation provided the chance to interact individually with students, even in the midst of a whole-group lesson. In fact, our notes indicate that Barbara made contact with 12 different students in just the brief interaction reported here. Finally, through her questions, changes in voice tone, and gestures, Barbara was able to maintain a relatively high attention level; in other words, she was able to keep most of her students "with her."

Later, Barbara reflected aloud on her use of recitation in this lesson:

Obviously, this was a teacher-directed lesson: One of my major goals was to get specific information to everyone without standing there and telling them. Because of this, all the talk was filtered through me. This was real different from a true discussion, when I'd encourage students to talk directly with one another and I'd pretty much stay out of things. Yet one of the interesting things about this kind of lesson is that even though I'm directing it, my kids don't really think of this as teaching. They see it more like a personal conversation with me, and don't realize that it's a "lesson."

One of the things I like about recitations is that I can push my kids to give more complete responses than they would in writing. Fourth graders are more comfortable talking than writing, so their oral responses tend to be more complete than their written ones. During a recitation, I can encourage them to expand on what they're saying, to substantiate their positions. I can also use their verbal responses as a model for the kind of answers that I'd expect on a written test or in a paper.

The recitation also allows me to find out what they don't have straight and to clear up misconceptions that they have about the material. I can also find out what they bring to the lesson. For example, in this lesson, I was really impressed by how much they had learned about geography in their social studies class. Since they go to another teacher for social studies, I didn't realize they knew so much about maps and climate. And they also knew more about World War II than I had anticipated.

As we can see, Barbara's recitation session was hardly a "quiz show" in which passive students mindlessly recalled low-level, insignificant facts. On the other hand, both the pattern of talk (I-R-E) and the primary intent (to assess students' understanding of the reading) set it apart from another type of verbal interaction—the *discussion*. (Table 11-1, adapted from Dillon, 1994, summarizes the differences between recitation and discussion.)

In contrast to recitation, discussion is a form of verbal interaction in which individuals work together to consider an issue or a question. The discussion is intended to stimulate a variety of responses, to encourage students to consider different points of view, to foster problem solving, to examine implications, and to relate material to students' own personal experiences (Good & Brophy, 2000). In a discussion, individuals may offer their understandings, relevant facts, suggestions, opinions, perspectives, and experiences. These are examined for their usefulness in answering the question or resolving the issue (Dillon, 1994).

In order to make the distinction between recitation and discussion clear, let's consider another example, this time from Ken's class.

TABLE 11-1. Differences between Recitations and Discussions

Dimension	Recitation	Discussion
1. Predominant speaker	Teacher (2/3 or more)	Students (half or more)
2. Typical exchange	Teacher question, student answer, teacher evaluation (I-R-E)	Mix of statements and questions by mix of teachers and students
3. Pace	Many brief, fast exchanges	Fewer, longer, slower exchanges
4. Primary purpose	To check students' comprehension	To stimulate variety of responses, encourage students to consider different points of view, foster problem solving and critical thinking, examine implications
5. The answer	Predetermined right or wrong; same right answer for all students	No predetermined right or wrong; can have different answers for different students
6. Evaluation	Right/wrong, by teacher only	Agree/disagree, by student and teacher

Source: Adapted from Dillon, 1994

Eight students are sitting at the reading table with Ken, about to discuss the book they have been reading, George Washington's Socks *by Elvia Woodruff (1991). They roll a die to see who goes first. A "two" comes up; thus, the second person from the end, Eric, goes first. Eric asks the other students an analysis question that he has prepared on the reading assignment. [Analysis questions require students to go beyond simple recall or comprehension to a deeper examination of the meaning.]*

> Eric: Should Adam Hibbs have returned the General's cape instead of Matt?
>
> Suzanne: In a way, yes . . . because he was the soldier and Matt wasn't the soldier.
>
> Charlene: I don't think so. Adam Hibbs should not have returned it because he could get in a lot of trouble for leaving his post.
>
> Lauren: I think Adam should have returned it because he was older and then he wouldn't have fallen on the bayonet.

The interaction becomes heated; several students speak at the same time. Ken looks at Eric and quietly murmurs: "You might want to get some control of this discussion."

> Eric: OK, hold on. Jamie, what do you think?
>
> Jamie: For me, it's kind of in the middle . . .
>
> Neil: Yeah, for me too, it's right smack in the middle. In a way I think he should have left it there, because he returns the cape and then—
>
> Suzanne: [interrupting Neil] The captain says, "You're in the war."
>
> Neil: And it's just a cape. What's the big deal? Somebody else could've given him a cape.

The discussion continues for a few more minutes. Then Ken asks Eric to read the answer he has prepared to his own question.

> Ken: Comments about Eric's answer?
>
> Charlene: If Adam Hibbs hadn't let Matt go, then maybe he wouldn't have gotten hurt.
>
> Lauren: Some of your answer goes along with the question, but then in the end, I think you were talking about something else . . .

A few more comments are made on Eric's answer.

> Ken: What a great analysis question! You saw all the debate, discussion it generated. I don't even have to judge the question; you can judge for yourself from the reaction. OK, let's hear another question. Suzanne?
>
> Suzanne: Why did Matt return George Washington's cape?
>
> Eleanor: He didn't want the general to be cold.

> Mark: Yeah, he would have frozen.

There's silence.

> Jessica: I think this is a comprehension question, not an analysis question.
> Ken: Yes, it can be. But you can also answer it like an analysis question. When we want to figure out really why somebody does something, it's rarely so simple. Let's examine this more deeply. Let's take a look at page 47. Read it to yourselves and then let's continue. [Discussion continues about the reasons for Matt's returning the cape.]

As we can see from this excerpt, the predominant pattern in this interchange was not I-R-E (teacher initiation, student response, and teacher evaluation), but initiation (by a student in the teacher's role) followed by multiple responses (I-R-R-R). Ken essentially stays out of the interaction, except for making sure that students have an opportunity to speak when the interaction gets excited and pushing students to probe more deeply. In contrast to the recitation, students speak directly to one another. They comment on one another's contributions; they question; they disagree; and they explain.

Recitation and discussion are often confused. Teachers often say that they use discussion a great deal, when in fact they are conducting recitations. In a provocative article entitled "What teachers do when they say they're having discussions of content area reading assignments," Alvermann, O'Brien, and Dillon (1990) found that although 24 middle school teachers reported using discussion, only 7 could actually be observed doing so; the others were using recitation and lecture with question-answer. These findings are consistent with observations of 1,000 elementary and secondary classrooms across the country, in which discussion was seen only *4 to 7 percent of the time* (Goodlad, 1984). It is clear that real discussion is very rarely used in classrooms.

James Dillon (1994) suggests three major reasons for the infrequency of classroom discussion. First, discussion does not come naturally; it has to be learned, and it is difficult—for both students and teachers. Second, teachers themselves have had few experiences with classroom discussions and may not have received training and guidance in leading them. Finally, school culture is generally not supportive of discussion. If teachers feel pressured to "cover the curriculum" and to have students do well on standardized tests, they may consider discussion a luxury they cannot afford. In addition, providing opportunities for discussions means that teachers have to give up their role as *leader* and assume the role of *facilitator.* This can be difficult for teachers who work in schools that emphasize control and who are used to dominating or at least directing the conversation.

Educational critics frequently decry the use of recitation and promote the use of discussion, but both types of interaction have a legitimate place in the elementary classroom—if done well. As Good and Brophy (2000) write: "The operative question about recitation for most teachers is not whether to use it but when and how to use it effectively" (p. 387).

This chapter begins by examining the managerial problems associated with recitations. Like independent work and groupwork, this subsetting has its own set of "built-in hazards" (Carter, 1985): unequal participation; loss of pace, focus, and involvement; and the difficulty of monitoring comprehension. Next, we consider what our teachers and the research have to say about minimizing these problems. We then turn to a consideration of discussions and offer some guidelines for managing this pattern of interaction.

The Pitfalls of Recitations

Unequal Participation

Imagine yourself in front of a class of 25 children. You've just asked a question. A few children are wildly waving their hands, murmuring "ooh, ooh," and clearly conveying their desire to be called on. Others are sitting quietly, staring into space, their expressions blank. Still others are slumped down as far as possible in their seats; their posture clearly says, "Don't call on me."

In a situation like this, it's tempting to call on a child who is eager to be chosen. After all, you're likely to get the correct response—a very gratifying situation! You also avoid embarrassing children who feel uncomfortable speaking in front of the group or who don't know the answer, and you're able to keep up the pace of the lesson. But selecting only those who volunteer or those who call out may limit the interaction to a handful of students. This can be a problem. Students tend to learn more if they are actively participating (Morine-Dershimer & Beyerbach, 1987). Furthermore, since those who volunteer are often high achievers, calling only on volunteers is likely to give you a distorted picture of how well everyone understands. Finally, restricting your questions to a small number of students can communicate negative expectations to the others (Good & Brophy, 2000): "I'm not calling on you because I'm sure you have nothing to contribute."

Losing It All: Pace, Focus, and Involvement

A popular television program of the 1960s (revived in the 1990s) capitalized on the fact that "Kids Say the Darndest Things." The title of the show aptly describes what can happen during a recitation. When you ask your question, you might receive the response you have in mind. You might also get answers that indicate confusion and misunderstanding, ill-timed remarks that have nothing to do with the lesson (e.g., "There's gum on my shoe" or "I forgot my lunch money"), or unexpected comments that momentarily throw you off balance. All of these threaten the smooth flow of a recitation and can cause it to become sluggish, jerky, or unfocused.

Threats like these require you to make instantaneous decisions about how to proceed. It's not easy. If a student's answer reveals confusion, for example, it's essential to provide feedback and assistance. On the other hand, staying with that student can cause the lesson to become so slow that everyone else begins to daydream and fidget. During recitations, you are frequently confronted with two incompatible needs: the need to stay with an individual to enhance that child's learning and the need to move on to avoid losing both the momentum and the group's attention.

At one point in Barbara's lesson on *The Cay,* we saw a good illustration of this tension. Students had been talking about the problems faced by the main character, when Jessica suddenly raised her hand and asked, "If I got stranded on an island in the Caribbean, would it be possible for me to live?" The question was clearly out of sequence, but Barbara allowed it to stand. In fact, she responded, "*I* don't know." Turning to the class, she asked, "What do *you* think? Could Jessica survive?" That initiated a long interchange on the relevant factors: presence of food, water, shelter, temperature, animals, and so on. Eventually, Barbara returned students' attention to the book:

> BARBARA: Okay, we've been talking about Jessica's being stranded on an island and whether she could survive. How does this relate to the book?
>
> STUDENT: Philip gets stranded on the island.

When we discussed this incident with Barbara after her lesson, she explained why she decided to pursue Jessica's question:

Jessica's question really floored me, and I was tempted to go on. We had been moving at a nice clip, and I didn't want to lose the flow. I also didn't want to lose the focus of the discussion. But she seemed sincere—it didn't seem like a ploy to get us off the topic—and she hardly ever participates. This book is really a challenge for her. I decided to let the question stand because I wanted to bring her into the conversation, to "move her up" in the eyes of the other kids, and to give her some credibility. Also, I decided I could use the question to bring up some of the problems that Philip, the character in the book, has to face. But I was taking a risk. It's so easy for a lesson to get way off target. When you're standing up there, it can get really scary. Sometimes, you don't have a clue what they're going to bring up when you ask a question. It's hard to tell a child we can't talk about that now, but if you follow every tangent someone brings up, you'll never get anywhere. If I decide not to talk about a question or a comment a child brings up, I try to write it on the board and remember to talk about it later, maybe during free time or lunch.

When "kids say the darndest things" during a recitation, it's easy to lose the pace of the lesson. But questioning sessions can also become bogged down if the teacher has not developed a set of verbal or nonverbal signals that communicate to children when they are to raise their hands and when they are to respond chorally. Without clear signals, students are likely to call out when the teacher wants them to raise their hands, or to remain silent and raise their hands when the teacher wants them to call out in a choral response.

Sometimes, questioning sessions get sluggish because ambiguity in the teacher's question makes it difficult for students to respond. For example, Farrar (1988) analyzed a social studies lesson in which the teacher asked a yes–no question: "Did you read any-where in the book that Washington's army was destroyed?" When students responded, "No," and "Uh-uh," he rejected their answers. The result was confusion and a momen-tary breakdown of the recitation. In retrospect, it appears that the teacher was not really expecting a yes or no answer, but wanted a restatement of information that had appeared in the reading. Students responded to his *explicit* question, while he was waiting for the answer to his *implicit* question: "What happened to Washington's army?"

Difficulties in Monitoring Students' Comprehension

Recitations provide an opportunity for teachers to check students' comprehension, but doing so is not always easy. Recently, a fifth-grade teacher told us about a lesson taught by her student teacher, Rebecca. The class had been studying the human body, and halfway through the unit, Rebecca planned to give her students a quiz. On the day of the quiz, she conducted a brief review of the material by firing off a series of questions on the respiratory and circulatory systems. Satisfied with the high percentage of correct an-swers, Rebecca then asked, "Before I give out the quiz, are there any questions?" When there were none, she added, "So everybody understands?" Again, there was silence. Re-becca told the students to close their books and distributed the quiz papers. That after-noon, she corrected the quiz. The results were an unpleasant shock; a large number of students received Ds and Fs. During a post-lesson conference with her cooperating teacher, she wailed, "How could this happen? They certainly knew the answers during our review session!"

This incident underscores the difficulty of gauging the extent to which all members of a class really understand what is going on. As we mentioned earlier, teachers sometimes get fooled because they call only on volunteers—the students most likely to give the cor-rect answers. In this case, Rebecca's cooperating teacher had kept a "map" of the verbal interaction between teacher and students and was able to share some revealing data: Dur-ing a 15-minute review, Rebecca had called on only 6 of the 19 children in the class, and all of these had been volunteers. Although this allowed Rebecca to maintain the smooth flow of the interaction, it led her to overestimate the extent of students' mastery. More-over, as Rebecca's cooperating teacher pointed out to her, questions that try to assess com-prehension by asking "Does everyone understand?" are unlikely to be successful. There's no accountability built into questions like this; in other words, they don't require students to demonstrate an understanding of the material. In addition, students who do not under-stand are often too embarrassed to admit it. (They may not even realize they don't under-stand!) Clearly, you need to find other ways to assess if your class is "with" you.

Strategies for Managing Recitations

Recitations pose formidable challenges to teachers. You need to respond to each indi-vidual's learning needs, while maintaining the attention and interest of the group; to dis-tribute participation widely, without dampening the enthusiasm of those who are eager to volunteer; to assess students' understanding without embarrassing those who don't know the answers; to allow students to contribute to the interaction, while remaining "on course."

In this section of the chapter, we suggest five strategies for meeting these challenges. As in previous chapters, research on teaching, discussions with our four teachers, and observations of their classes provide the basis for our suggestions. Although there are no foolproof guarantees of success, these strategies can reduce the hazards associated with recitations. (Table 11-2 provides a summary of our suggestions.)

Distributing Chances to Participate

Early in the school year, we watched Ken conduct a recitation using his "coffee cup system" of calling on students. (This was described briefly in Chapter 4, when we discussed interaction routines.) The lesson involved "summer maps" the students had created a few

TABLE 11-2. Strategies for Managing Recitations

Strategy	Example
Distribute chances to participate	Pick names from a cup. Check off names on a seating chart. Use patterned turn-taking.
Provide time to think	Extend wait time to three seconds. Tell students you don't expect an immediate answer. Allow students to write a response.
Stimulate and maintain interest	Inject mystery and suspense. Inject humor and novelty. Challenge students to think. Incorporate physical activity.
Provide feedback to students	When answer is correct and confident, affirm briefly. When answer is correct but hesitant, provide more deliberate affirmation. When answer is incorrect, but careless, make a simple correction. When answer is incorrect but student could get answer with help, prompt or backtrack to simpler question. If student is unable to respond, don't belabor the issue.
Require overt responses	Have students hold up response cards, physically display answers with manipulative materials, respond chorally.
Use a steering group	Observe the performance of a sample of students (including low-achievers) in order to know when to move on.

days earlier. Each student had selected a key word to represent a highlight of the summer and had printed it in the middle of a large piece of paper. Around the key word, students had placed related words, drawing lines among the words to indicate relationships. Ken used the summer maps in a variety of lessons and activities. He introduced students to the thesaurus, for example, by having them find synonyms for a word that appeared on their maps. The recitation we watched him conduct was based on this synonym activity:

Ken stands toward the front of the room, a coffee mug in his hand. In the mug are popsicle sticks, each one containing a letter of the alphabet.

Ken:	When I call your letter, tell me what word you found a synonym for and then give the synonyms. Remember, the cup knows . . . [He pulls a stick from the cup. On it is printed the letter B.] Banana, give me a word.
Banana:	[He is caught off guard.] I didn't finish yet.
Ken:	Aha, see, the cup knows . . . [He pulls another stick from the cup: I.] All right, Iceberg, give me a word.
Iceberg:	Fun.
Ken:	What are the synonyms?
Iceberg:	Amusement, play, sport, good time, pleasure, entertainment, enjoyment.
Ken:	[He turns to the class.] Did you hear that? I heard seven words for fun. How many people had fun somewhere on their summer map? [Students raise their hands. He acknowledges their hands with a nod.] Great job, Iceberg. [He pulls a new letter from the cup.] Obedient.
Obedient:	Pain. Hurt. I just started, so I only have one.
Ken:	You have your thesaurus? [The boy nods.] Okay, keep working. [He pulls a new letter.] Lucky.
Lucky:	Mission.
Ken:	That's a real space word. What's his key word, anyone remember?
Class:	Space Camp.
Ken:	Good memory. Okay, Lucky, what are your synonyms for mission?
Lucky:	Errand, task, job, assignment, duty.
Ken:	He got five synonyms. What do we know about five?
Student:	It's a Fibonacci number.
Ken:	Right. Well done, Aaron.

When we discussed this lesson with Ken, we asked him about the use of the cup to select students and what he had meant when he said, "The cup knows . . ." We also commented on his students' strange "names." Ken explained:

Using the cup helps me to make sure that I get around to everyone. Once a person's letter is called, I keep that stick out of the cup so everyone gets a chance. I find that unless I use a system like this, I have trouble keeping track of who's gotten a chance to talk and who hasn't. And some kids are so eager to volunteer that they'd probably monopolize the whole lesson.

I tell the kids that the cup is going to call on people who are not ready. It's amazing, but it often works out that the first few people the cup calls aren't ready. I've had kids convinced that the cup really knows. In one class, we used to chant, "Cup, cup, wake someone up." This system works well for me. The kids know that I'm not looking around the room, hoping to catch someone who doesn't know the answer or who's not ready. It's purely random, but it serves to keep them on their toes.

About the strange names, I used to list the kids' names in alphabetical order and give them each a number. This way, things like taking attendance can go real quickly. The kids simply count off. A while back, I got the idea of giving students a letter of the alphabet instead of a number, and letting them choose a word that begins with that letter. When I take attendance, they "count off" in alphabetical order by saying their word. It's more personal than numbers. And it makes whole class lessons more fun when you call on "Obedient," "Knowledgeable," and "Vacuum Cleaner," instead of Susan or Mark.

Ken doesn't use the coffee mug for every recitation, and we are certainly not suggesting that you should do so. There are times when you won't want to call on students randomly, preferring to select particular individuals for particular questions. Nonetheless, the cup system helps Ken to sustain students' attention and to distribute participation widely and fairly. It also enables him to keep the pace moving, since he doesn't have to deliberate each time he calls on someone. Watching him, we recalled a study by McDermott (1977) of first-grade reading groups. McDermott found that turn taking in the high-achievement group proceeded efficiently in round-robin fashion, with little time lost between readers. In the low-achievement group, however, the teacher allowed the students to bid for a turn, and so much time was devoted to deciding who would read next that students spent only one-third as much time reading as students in the top group.

Instead of a coffee mug, some teachers use a list of names or a seating chart to keep track of who has spoken, placing a tick mark by the name of each child who participates. Other teachers use "patterned turn taking," calling on students in some designated order. The research evidence on the usefulness of this practice is inconclusive. Many educators (e.g., Kounin, 1970) argue that patterned turn taking leads to inattention, since children know exactly when they will be called on. But research by Brophy and Evertson (1976) found that the use of patterned turn taking in small reading groups leads to higher achievement. One explanation for this finding is that patterned turn taking allows more reading to occur, as in the McDermott study we just cited. Another explanation is that the use of a pattern ensures that everyone has an opportunity to interact with the teacher.

Whichever system you choose, *the important point is to make sure that the interaction is not dominated by a few volunteers.* Some children are just not comfortable speaking in class and seek to avoid the risk of appearing foolish or stupid. Jones and Gerig (1994) examined verbal interaction between teachers and students in four sixth-grade classrooms. They identified *32 percent of the students as "silent."* During interviews, these students typically described themselves as shy (72 percent) and lacking in self-confidence (50 percent). Karen explained her silence by referring to an incident that happened *four years earlier:*

> I talk just a little in class. I'm afraid that what I say, someone won't like. When I was in the second grade, we were going to have a Thanksgiving dinner thing and students were going to be Pilgrims. I raised my hand and said I would like to be an Indian and would wear my hair in braids. Nobody said anything, and the teacher just went "Um hum," and it was embarrassing. (p. 177)

Our four teachers are well aware of the need to encourage shy students to participate. Listen to Barbara:

> It's your job to keep everyone involved and to bring in the kids who are not talking. I generally ask, "What do you think?" or "Do you agree with what Peter said?" If a kid isn't comfortable talking, I may not call on them as frequently, and when I do, I try to be especially gentle. I'll ask something I know they know, or I'll call on them as soon as I see any gesture that indicates they're thinking about raising their hand. I also try to validate what the kid said, something like, "Peter just told us . . ." But however I do it, I eventually get to everyone, and my kids know that.

"Getting to everyone" can be a daunting task, especially in a large class. One useful strategy is to use *response cards*—small chalkboards or dry erase boards—on which students write one- or two-word responses to your questions. Response cards not only increase the rate of active student response; they also seem to improve students' academic achievement and engagement (Narayan, Heward, Gardner, Courson, & Omness, 1990).

Another strategy is to allow several students to answer a question instead of "grabbing" the first answer and moving on. In the following interaction, we see Garnetta increase participation by following this practice:

GARNETTA: What do you do when you experiment?

STUDENT: Invent things.

GARNETTA: OK, what else? (There's silence.) I'm going to put two letters on the board as a hint. (Writes IN.)

STUDENT: Investigate!
GARNETTA: Good! That's a big word. We traded one big word—experiment—
for another—investigate. What does investigate mean?
STUDENT: When you be trying to find something out.
STUDENT: When you be a detective and try to find something out.
STUDENT: Finding out the facts—looking and finding out.
GARNETTA: Out of sight! (Writes on board: look at something, find out the facts,
be a detective.)

At times, distributing participation is difficult not because children are reluctant to speak and there are too *few* volunteers, but because there are too *many*. The more teachers stimulate interest in a particular lesson, the more students want to respond. This means greater competition for each turn (Doyle, 1986), and "bidding" for a chance to speak can become loud and unruly. During one visit to Garnetta's class, we watched her deal with this situation. She and the students were talking about a movie they had just seen, *A Connecticut Yankee in King Arthur's Court.* The children were incredibly excited about the movie and were eager to share their reactions:

GARNETTA: Let's think about the ways people lived at the time of King Arthur.
What did you see in the movie that was the same as the way we live
now? [There are lots of "oohs," and calls of "Ms. Chain" as children compete for a chance to respond.] So many people want to
talk, let's just go around, and hear one from everybody. Aleesha,
you start.
ALEESHA: They rode horses and we ride horses. [Garnetta continues to call on
students in order.]

Garnetta was able to use a "round robin" pattern of turn taking because her class is small (15 students). This approach might not work as well in a larger class, where children seated at the "end of the line" sometimes feel cheated because they have nothing new to add. An alternative strategy is to have each child write a response and share it with one or two neighbors. This allows everyone to participate actively. You might then ask some of the groups to report on what they discussed.

It's also important to make sure that males and females have equal opportunity to participate. A review of the literature (Grossman & Grossman, 1994) reports that "teachers demonstrate a clear bias in favor of male participation in their classes":

*Teachers are more likely to call on a male volunteer when students are
asked to recite; this is also true when they call on nonvolunteers. When
students recite, teachers are also more likely to listen to and talk to males.
They also use more of their ideas in classroom discussions and respond to
them in more helpful ways. (p. 76)*

Similarly, *How Schools Shortchange Girls* (1992), a study commissioned by the American Association of University Women (AAUW), reports that males often demand—and receive—more attention from teachers. In one study of elementary and middle school students, Sadker, Sadker, and Thomas (1981) found that boys called out answers eight times more often than girls did. Furthermore, when the boys called out, teachers typically listened to the comment. In contrast, when girls called out, they were usually told to "Please raise your hand if you want to speak." In another study, Sadker and Sadker (1985) found that, even when boys do not volunteer, the teacher is more likely to solicit their responses.

Why would teachers allow male students to dominate classroom interaction by calling out? Morse and Handley (1985) suggest three possible reasons: (1) the behavior is so frequent that teachers come to accept it; (2) teachers expect males to be aggressive; and (3) the call-outs may be perceived by teachers as indicators of interest. Whatever the reasons, teachers need to be sensitive to gender differences in participation and use strategies to ensure that both males and females have opportunities to participate.

One final thought: While you're thinking about ways to distribute participation widely, keep in mind the suggestions we made in Chapter 3 when we talked about the action zone phenomenon: (1) move around the room whenever possible; (2) establish eye contact with students seated farther away from you; (3) direct comments to students seated in the rear and on the sides; and (4) periodically change students' seats so that all students have an opportunity to be up front.

Providing Time to Think without Losing the Pace

Envision this scenario: You've just asked a well-formulated, carefully worded, higher-level question designed to stimulate critical thinking and problem solving. And you're met with total silence. Your face begins to feel flushed, and your heart beats a little faster. What to do now?

One reason silence is so uncomfortable is that it's hard to interpret: Are students thinking about the question? Are they asleep? Are they so muddled they're unable to respond? Silence is also troubling to teachers because it can threaten the pace and momentum of the lesson. Even a few seconds of silence can seem like eternity. This helps to explain why many teachers wait less than *one second* before calling on a student (Rowe, 1974). Yet research demonstrates that if you extend *"wait time"* to *three or four seconds,* you can increase the quality of students' answers and promote participation. In fact, Garnetta finds it helpful to count silently to 10.

Sometimes, it's helpful to indicate to students that you don't expect an immediate answer. This legitimates the silence and gives students an opportunity to formulate their responses. During Barbara's recitation lesson on *The Cay,* we saw her indicate to children that she wanted everyone to think for a while before responding:

> BARBARA: What's one survival technique that CT used? [Children raise their hands.] Jim? [He had not raised his hand.]
>
> JIM: Using a carved twig for fire.
>
> BARBARA: Show us on the board how the twig was carved. While he's drawing, the rest of you think of another. [He draws a twig that has been carved.

> Barbara turns to the class.] Why would that burn more easily? [A few students raise their hands.] Everyone put your hands down and think for a minute. [There's a long pause. Then a few hands go back up; then some more. Finally Barbara nods to a student.]
>
> GIRL: Because there are more places to burn?
>
> BARBARA: Right.

Allowing children to write an answer to your question is another way of providing them with time to think. Written responses also help to maintain students' engagement, since everyone has to construct a response. In addition, students who are uncomfortable speaking extemporaneously can read from their written papers. We observed an example of this strategy when Barbara's class began their study of *Sarah, Plain and Tall* (MacLachlan, 1985). Barbara gave them the following directions:

> BARBARA: Read the first chapter silently. While you do that, I'm going to give each of you a piece of paper. Write down just a little bit about each of the characters you meet. [When students have finished reading and writing, Barbara regains their attention.] OK, you met Sarah. What did you learn about her?

Once you have selected someone to respond, it's also important to provide that student with an opportunity to think. This is another kind of wait time, and research has documented that here, too, teachers often jump in too soon (Rowe, 1974). Sometimes they provide the answer themselves or call on another child. This is particularly tempting if other students are frantically waving their hands. Watch the way Ken deals with this situation during a lesson on number sequences:

> KEN: What is Sequence C? Robin? [Robin is silent. Other children in the class are waving their hands to answer and murmuring "ooh, ooh, Mr. K. . . ."] Let her take her time. This is tricky. Give her a chance. . . .
>
> ROBIN: It's adding on every odd number, 1, 3, 5. . . .
>
> KEN: Hmmm, I wonder if that continues. . . .

Stimulating and Maintaining Interest

In previous chapters, we have discussed Kounin's classic study (1970) of the differences between orderly and disorderly classrooms. One finding of that study was that children are more involved in work and less disruptive when teachers attempt to involve non-reciting children in the recitation task, maintain their attention, and keep them "on their toes." Kounin called this behavior "group alerting." Observations of our four teachers reveal that they frequently use group-alerting strategies to stimulate attention and to maintain the pace of the lesson. For example, watch how Garnetta creates interest in her upcoming lesson by beginning with mystery and suspense:

> GARNETTA: I need everyone to look up here while I draw something on the board. You know I'm not an artist, so this won't be perfect. [Students all murmur, "Amen." Slowly and deliberately, Garnetta draws

a pattern of triangles and squares on the board. As she draws, students call out, "It's curtains." "It's a baseball field." "It's congruent shapes."] Now that I have your attention, I'm going to tell you what we're going to do. These are like pieces of a . . .

STUDENTS: Puzzle!

GARNETTA: Right. We're going to do a puzzle. I'm going to give you seven pieces of plastic. They're called Tangrams. You need to make a square with the pieces. You need to use *all* the pieces. You may work with a partner. The person next to you would be best.

Ken also injects suspense into recitations that could be dry and boring. For example, in a lesson on number sequences, students were to compare the rate at which "Fibonacci" numbers increase (1, 1, 2, 3, 5, 8, 13, 21, . . .) in comparison with sequences that square (1, 4, 9, 16, 25, . . .) or add 10 (10, 20, 30, 40, 50, . . .):

KEN: Look at this. It's round 12 and Fibonacci and Squares are neck and neck. Which is going to win?

STUDENTS: [Chorally] Fibonacci.

KEN: Are you sure? Fibonacci started off so *slow* and it's going to get *higher* than squares? [With real amazement in his voice.]

STUDENTS: Yeah!

KEN: So . . . all you people who told me Fibonacci was going to come in last were wrong! They came in what?

STUDENTS: Second.

KEN: What came in last?

STUDENTS: Tens.

KEN: Yeah, all you hot shots who told me yesterday that my team was going to come in last, just look at the chalkboard. Tens came in last!

Children's interest can also be maintained if you inject some humor or novelty into the recitation itself. During an observation of Viviana's math class, she was discussing "story problems":

VIVIANA: I'm going to give you a few seconds to think of a story problem. [Pause while children think.] Luis?

LUIS: Anita has four dolls. Her sister has three fewer dolls. How many dolls does her sister have?

VIVIANA: What information is the problem giving us?

STUDENT: That Anita has four dolls.

VIVIANA: What else?

STUDENT: Her sister has three fewer.

VIVIANA: Three fewer what? Cats? [The children laugh.]

CLASS: [Choral response] Dolls.

Challenges to students can also be a way of keeping them on their toes. During another math lesson, for example, Viviana told her students, "This next one is not baby stuff. This one you really have to think about and read the directions." The excitement in the room was almost palpable, and afterwards we heard students murmuring, "This is easy, this is baby stuff, I can do this." Viviana's challenge is reminiscent of the behavior of "Teacher X," one of the subjects in Hermine Marshall's (1987) study of three teachers' motivational strategies. Marshall found that Teacher X frequently used statements designed to challenge students to think: "I'm going to trick you, " "Get your brain started . . . You're going to think," "Get your mind started," "Look bright-eyed and bushy-tailed" (stated, according to Marshall, "with enthusiasm and a touch of humor"). This frequent use of statements to stimulate and maintain student attention was in sharp contrast to the statements made by the other two teachers in the study. In fact, Teacher Y and Teacher Z *never* used the strategy of alerting students to pay attention, and they rarely challenged students to think. The vast majority of their directives were attempts to return students to the task *after* attention and interest had waned.

Another day, we observed Viviana teach her students about action verbs. Although this can be deadly dull, the room was alive with excitement because Viviana allowed her children to engage in the actions they were studying:

> VIVIANA: Let's stand up. Run in place. Run, run, run, run. Don't stop until I tell you to. [All the children run in place by their desks.] You are doing something. What are you doing?
>
> STUDENTS: We're running.
>
> VIVIANA: So run is an action. Something you are doing. Okay, stop. Let's . . . hop. [Children begin to hop in place.] Are you doing something?
>
> STUDENTS: Yes.
>
> VIVIANA: What are you doing?
>
> STUDENTS: We're hopping.
>
> VIVIANA: So hop is an action, something you are doing. [The pattern repeats as children jump and then skip around the room back to their desks.]

All too often, incorporating physical activity in a lesson leads to chaos rather than involvement. Viviana can use this strategy because she has established herself as the classroom leader. She tells us:

You have to know your class first. I'd never do this the first week of school. You have to have the rules and routines well established and make sure the children know exactly what you expect. I tell them, "This will be fun, but you have to listen carefully to my directions so that we can all learn." It's really important to wait until you know your class and your class knows you.

Providing Feedback without Losing the Pace

As we discussed in Chapter 7, the Beginning Teacher Evaluation Study (Fisher et al., 1980) documented the importance of providing feedback to students:

When more frequent feedback is offered, students pay attention more and learn more. Academic feedback was more strongly and consistently related to achievement than any of the other teaching behaviors. (p. 27)

But how can you provide appropriate feedback while maintaining the pace and momentum of your lesson? Barak Rosenshine (1986) has reviewed the research on effective teaching and has developed a set of guidelines that may be helpful. According to Rosenshine, when students give correct, confident answers, you can simply ask another question or provide a brief verbal or nonverbal indication that they are correct. If students are correct but hesitant, however, a more deliberate affirmation is necessary. You might also explain *why* the answer is correct ("Yes, that's correct, because . . .") in order to reinforce the material.

When students provide an incorrect answer, the feedback process is trickier. If you think the child has made a careless error, you can make a simple correction and move on. If you decide that the student can arrive at the correct answer with a little help, you can provide hints or prompts. Sometimes it's useful to backtrack to a simpler question that you think the child can answer, and then work up to your original question step by step.

There are times when students are simply unable to respond to your question. When that happens, there's little point in belaboring the issue by providing prompts or cues; this will only make the recitation sluggish. Ken allows students in this situation to "pass," and both he and Garnetta permit children to call on a friend to help. These practices not only help to maintain the pace, they also allow students to "save face." Meanwhile, the teachers make a mental note that they need to reteach the material to the individuals having difficulty.

We saw a good example of this situation in Viviana's class when she was introducing the concept of thirds. Her students had been working on "halves" with Cuisenaire rods. After seeing that two yellow rods were equivalent to one orange rod, and that each yellow rod was one-half of the orange, Viviana asked the children to take the blue rod (the "nine" rod):

> VIVIANA: Everyone have the blue rod? Okay, divide it into equal parts. [A boy yells out, "Three greens." Viviana tells him that by yelling out he is not being fair to other children, not giving them a chance to figure out the answer. She scans the room and sees that everyone has three greens lined up with one blue.] How many greens equal one blue?
>
> STUDENTS: Three.
>
> VIVIANA: If you give one green to your friend, how many are left?
>
> STUDENTS: Two.
>
> VIVIANA: Good. If you give one green to your friend, what *fraction* have you given away? [There is silence. Children look puzzled. A few children try a guess: 1/2? One? Two? Noting the extreme confusion, Viviana provides the answer.] You have given away one-third. And

you kept two-thirds. We'll talk about this more tomorrow. Now we have to clean up and go to lunch. We need to collect the blocks. I want to see neat tables.

Afterwards, we spoke with Viviana about what had happened during the lesson. She told us why she had decided to "give up" on her question about thirds:

There was just too much confusion, and I didn't want the children to get frustrated. It was also too close to lunch time to start reteaching about thirds; when they're hungry it's hard to think. It was better to just tell them the answer. Tomorrow I can pick up from where we left off.

We also talked with Viviana about how to provide appropriate feedback when children's answers are clearly incorrect. She was very emphatic as she talked about the need to be honest and clear. We think her perspective is worth remembering:

I strongly believe that teachers should not sugarcoat their responses to children's answers for fear of hurting children's feelings. If the answer is wrong, the child needs to know it's wrong. You can reject an answer without rejecting a child. But you have to explain why the answer is wrong. I often ask other children to help out. When I get the right answer from another child, I go back to the first child and check to see if they now understand. It's important not to leave kids hanging.

Monitoring Comprehension: Requiring Overt Responses

A simple way to determine how well your students understand the material is to have them respond overtly to your questions. For example, you might give children cards reading "yes" or "no," colored red or green, or depicting a happy face or a sad face, which they then hold up in response to your yes/no questions. As we mentioned earlier, students can also use small chalkboards or dry-erase boards to write one- or two-word responses (Narayan, et al., 1990). In mathematics, students can use number cards or operation sign cards to show you the correct answer. "Number fans" (Rief, 1993) are also useful for whole group responses; they can be used to indicate "strongly agree" (1), "I kind of agree" (2), or "I disagree" (3). (See Figure 11-2.) Barbara often uses "thumbs up" or "thumbs down" signals to check on students' comprehension:

> BARBARA: Who can show us what I showed you yesterday about fractions? Let's say I have the fraction 1/4. Okay, Brenda, take the chalk and go for it. [Brenda takes the chalk and goes to the board. She writes 1/4, referring to the top number as the numerator and the bottom number as the denominator and explaining what each number represents.] How many people agree with that? Put your thumbs up if you agree, thumbs down if you disagree. [Barbara scans the room.] Okay, Brenda, we have total agreement.

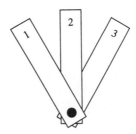

FIGURE 11-2. Number fans (from Rief, 1993)
Number fans can be made by writing numerals on cardboard cards. Punch a hole in one end and attach with a metal fastener. Students hold up a card to answer a question.

You can also have children manipulate some material at their seats and physically display their work. During one visit to Garnetta's class, she was reviewing division with her students. She had students work with colored blocks at their desks, while one student did the division problem at the chalkboard:

> GARNETTA: Okay, now count out 48. I see most of you have taken four ten blocks and eight ones blocks. Put the other ones away. We're going to divide the 48 by four. [There's a gasp, as if the children think that's too hard.] You're going to divide the 48 blocks into four groups. [One child murmurs, "Oh, that's easy!"] Rashad, you come to the board and do the problem while everyone else works with the blocks. Okay, let's see how many you put in each group. [She scans the room to see how the students did on the problem.] I want only hands.
>
> STUDENT: 12.
> GARNETTA: Everyone, look up here at the problem on the board. Rashad, what did you get?
> RASHAD: 12.
> GARNETTA: Okay, so we agree. Now let's do this problem. [She writes $2\overline{)28}$ on the chalkboard.]

Another way of assessing students' comprehension is by having them respond chorally rather than individually. This allows you to scan the room and see who's having difficulty. Let's watch Viviana, who frequently uses this strategy. She is seated behind a large abacus with 100 brightly colored beads. As she moves each bead across the rod, the children count out loud in unison.

> VIVIANA: We have 100 beads here. It took us a long time to count by ones, didn't it? Now let's count by twos and see which way is faster. [The children count out loud by twos.] Which was faster?
> STUDENTS: [Choral response.] By twos.

VIVIANA: What's another way to count? [She shoots her hand into the air, indicating that children should raise their hands.] José?

JOSÉ: By fives.

VIVIANA: OK, let's go. [The class counts by fives.] Now which way should we . . . [Students start yelling out "by 5s," "by 10s."] Wait a minute, wait . . . wait . . . wait . . . You're not letting me ask the question. You're getting ahead of me."

Monitoring Comprehension: Using a Steering Group

Another way of checking on students' understanding is to observe a "steering group." This is a sample of students whose performance is used as an indicator that the class is "with you" and that it's all right to move on to a new topic. Be careful, however, about choosing students for the steering group. If you select only high achievers, their performance may lead you to overestimate the comprehension of the class as a whole.

During one discussion with Garnetta, she indicated that Joelle, a low-achieving student, was a key member of her mathematics steering group. She shared this example of how Joelle helps her to monitor the class's understanding:

We were working on place value, and I wrote 382 on the board. I asked Joelle to tell us which number was in the ones column, which was in the tens column, and which was in the hundreds column and what that meant. He got it! That was a clue that the lesson was successful, and I confirmed it by sampling a couple of the other students.

Moderating Discussions

Thus far, the chapter has examined three major problems associated with recitations and has provided some suggestions for avoiding these problems. Now we turn to the second type of verbal interaction, the discussion. As we said earlier, although the terms *recitation* and *discussion* are often used interchangeably, it is important to distinguish clearly between the two. (Refer again to Table 11-1).

Let's consider this example of a discussion, witnessed in Garnetta's class early in the school year. Here, students are working on a set of riddles designed to foster critical thinking—specifically, the ability to make inferences. Garnetta has chosen a convergent task, rather than something more open ended (e.g., a literature discussion). Although the answer in this situation is a predetermined right or wrong (more characteristic of a recitation than a discussion), Garnetta has decided that this is more appropriate for her students since they have had little experience with student-centered discussions. She also structures the interaction by instructing the children to begin their comments with the words, "I agree" or "I disagree." Before opening the discussion, Garnetta first has the students put their desks in a circle so that they can make eye contact. Then she reviews expectations for behavior:

GARNETTA: Now remember our rules for discussions. Talk in a normal tone of voice; don't scream at anyone. Use the words, "I agree with so-and-so," or "I don't agree with so-and-so." And one person speak at a time. All right? OK, Aleesha, would you like to read the first riddle?

ALEESHA: [She reads.] "It eats insects. It has more than two legs. Is it a spider, dog, or bird?"

GARNETTA: [Nods.] Now the person who made up this riddle has provided some sentences with blanks to help you figure out the answer. The first one says, "It isn't a blank because it eats insects." The second one says, "It isn't a blank because it has more than two legs." We have to figure out what it is. Aleesha, what do you think goes in the first blank?

ALEESHA: Spider. [She reads, filling in the blank.] It isn't a spider because it eats insects.

VICTOR: I disagree because a spider eats insects.

TANAYA: I agree with Victor, because a dog don't eat insects.

VICTOR: Yeah. A bird don't eat insects, he eats worms.

JOSÉ: I disagree with Victor. It says it has more than two legs, so it can't be a bird or a dog.

VICTOR: It *could* be a dog, because a dog has more than two legs, and a dog don't eat insects. And a bird has two legs.

LUCIA: It says it has more than two legs, so it isn't a dog, and it isn't a bird because it eats insects.

SHENEIKA: But it says it *isn't* a bird because it has more than two legs.

EDWARD: I agree with Sheneika. [He reads.] "It isn't a bird because it has more than two legs," and a bird only has two legs.

GRANDON: Yeah, and it isn't a dog because a dog doesn't eat insects, but a dog has more than two legs.

LUCIA: [Vehemently] It says, "It *isn't* a bird because it eats insects."

GARNETTA: I think some people are getting mixed up by the "its." You need to remember that "it" refers to the animal we're looking for, not the animal that is named in the sentence.

LUCIA: I think it should be "It isn't a bird because it eats insects. It isn't a dog because it has more than two legs." So it's a spider.

VICTOR: I agree it's a spider, but it should be like this: It isn't a dog because it eats insects. It isn't a bird because it has more than two legs."

GARNETTA: Lucia, you still don't agree, do you?

LUCIA: No.

GARNETTA: Can someone help Lucia to understand?

As we can see, the predominant pattern here is not the I-R-E characteristic of a recitation. Once Garnetta reminded students of the rules for conducting discussions and focused them on the task at hand, she generally stayed out of the interaction, allowing the students to comment on the contributions of their peers. In fact, Garnetta intervened only to clarify Lucia's reasoning and to explain the referent for *it*. Furthermore, the purpose of the interaction was not to "go over material," but to engage in a problem-solving activity.

Several months later, we observed another discussion in Garnetta's classroom. This time, since her students had more experience with discussions, Garnetta chose an open-ended question about a story they had just read, *Buford, the Little Bighorn,* by Bill Peet (1993). Buford, "a scrawny little runt of a mountain sheep," has a huge pair of horns that cause him considerable difficulty throughout the story. At the very end, however, Buford discovers that his horns have some use after all. Using them as skis, he is able to escape from hunters and becomes a "star attraction" at a winter ski resort.

Garnetta's students are considering a question written on the chalkboard: "Suppose a vet offered to trim Buford's horns to a normal size. Do you think Buford would agree to that? Why or why not?" Once again, their desks are arranged in a circle, and Garnetta begins by reviewing the expectations for behavior:

GARNETTA: My ladies and gents, let's review how to behave in a discussion. If someone's talking, we don't cut them off, right? Raise your hand, and I'll recognize you. Remember, you can't just say "I agree" or "I disagree"—you have to be able to *defend* your answer. What does that mean? Sheneika?

SHENEIKA: You have to try to convince people you're right.

GARNETTA: OK, you have to give reasons why you think what you think. You have to explain. Luis, read the question for us. [He does so.] Thank you. Luis, you want to start us off, tell us what you think, and give us some supporting arguments?

LUIS: Yes.

GARNETTA: Yes, he should get his horns trimmed? [Luis nods.] Why do you say yes?

LUIS: Cause they're too long, and if he fall down he can get hurt. [Victor's hand shoots up. Garnetta calls on him.]

VICTOR: I disagree. In the story, when he fell, he ended up hanging on a tree. So the horns help him.

TANAYA: I disagree 'cause the horns made him fall in the first place. He should take off his horns so the hunters won't get to him.

GRANDON: I agree with Luis. If Buford don't get his horns cut, he'll trip and get hurt.

ALEESHA: Yeah, I agree with Luis too. He'll fall if he don't get them cut.

SHENEIKA: I disagree, because Buford, when he was walking, he fell, and his horns saved him.

VICTOR: Yeah, and if he get his horns cut off, then the folks from all over the world won't come and he won't be a big star.

GARNETTA: Do you want to say something, James?

JAMES: I don't want him to get his horns cut off because then he won't be able to ski.

LUCIA: What if there's that big pole sticking up out of the snow, and then there's the wires across, he could use his horns to hang on and go across the mountain. But he can't do that if he gets his horns cut.

GARNETTA: Are you talking about the ski lift?

LUCIA: Yeah. He can go on the ski lift if his horns are long.

EDWARD: Yeah. How could he ski on his horns if they're cut? And he can't *roll* down.

GARNETTA: Grandon, you look like you're trying to say something.

GRANDON: If Buford get his horns off, they might just grow back. So why bother?

RASHAD: But what if they get bigger and bigger?

GRANDON: So he'll just go back to the vet.

RASHAD: But the vet will just keep charging and charging!

VICTOR: But it says the vet *offered* to trim his horns. That means he would be doing it for free.

GARNETTA: Hmm, that's an interesting point. Julio, we haven't heard from you. You want to say something?

JULIO: He was sad.

GARNETTA: Yes, he was sad. What do you think he should do about his horns?

JULIO: Cut them off.

LUCIA: I disagree, cause if someone's chasing him, he can get away fast. [The discussion erupts in disagreement. Around the circle, there are lots of small debates going on.]

GARNETTA: Ladies and gents. Ladies and gents. I think I have to remind you about the rules. We need to have one person talk at a time, and you need to listen to that person and not start talking with the people sitting next to you. OK, now, Tanaya, what did you want to say? [Order restored, the class continues the discussion.]

Later that day, Garnetta talked with us about the discussion and the differences that she observed from the beginning of the year:

It used to be that two or three students dominated everything, and the others would not join the discussion. Victor used to jump on anybody who disagreed with him, and the other children actually seemed afraid to speak up. Now he's beginning to realize that other people are entitled to their opinions. Instead of just Victor and Lucia doing all the talking, just about everyone is willing to express an opinion. Sometimes I still have to intervene to make sure people get a chance to speak, but not as much. Like with Julio today. He's new, and he's real quiet; he needs an "invitation" to speak. But I'm pleased by the way people are willing to participate.

One of the problems we still have is that little subgroups develop around the circle, especially when the discussion heats up. We saw that today:

Somebody would make a comment and then children turned to their neighbors and began debating among themselves. I had to keep pulling them back together. But that's OK. It takes time to learn how to participate in a discussion. They've made a lot of progress since the beginning of the year, but they still need the teacher to make sure they stick with the topic and listen to each other. If we want them to be problem solvers and to develop critical thinking skills, we've got to let them practice. *And it takes* practice *on the part of the teacher too. We've got to learn to* guide *the discussion without taking over.*

As Garnetta's comments suggest, it's not easy to conduct a good discussion, particularly for teachers who are used to dominating verbal interaction in the classroom. Keep in mind three basic suggestions (Gall & Gillett, 1981). First, it may be wise to *limit the size of the group.* It's difficult to have a student-centered discussion with a large number of participants. One option is to use the "fishbowl" method, in which five or six students carry on the discussion in the middle of the room, while the rest of the class sits in a large circle around them and acts as observers and recorders. Another solution is to divide the class into small discussion groups of five, with one student in each group acting as a discussion leader.

Second, *arrange students so they can make eye contact.* It's hard to speak directly to someone if all you can see is the back of a head. If at all possible, students should move their desks into an arrangement that allows them to be face to face.

Finally, *prepare students for participating in a student-centered discussion by explicitly teaching* the prerequisite skills:

- Talk to each other, not just to the moderator.
- Don't monopolize.
- Ask others what they think.
- Don't engage in personal attack.
- Listen to others' ideas.
- Acknowledge others' ideas.
- Question irrelevant remarks.
- Ask for clarification.
- Ask for reasons for others' opinions.
- Give reasons for your opinions.

Since some students have difficulty taking turns, you can use a prop (e.g., a special pen, a wand, or a toy) to designate the speaker. The prop is passed from child to child. This encourages turn taking and helps children remember not to call out.

James Dillon (1994) also provides some extremely helpful guidelines for preparing and conducting discussions (see Figure 11-3). Note that Dillon advises against asking questions during a student-centered discussion (guideline number 6) for fear of turning the discussion into a recitation. Although his concern is well-founded, other discussion experts believe that questions can be an appropriate and effective way to keep conversation going. In fact, Brookfield and Preskill (1999) identify several kinds of questions that are especially helpful in maintaining momentum:

Questions that ask for more evidence:

How do you know that?

What data is that claim based on?

What does the author say that supports your argument?

Where did you find that view expressed in the text?

What evidence would you give to someone who doubted your interpretation?

---

1. Carefully formulate the discussion question (making sure that it is not in a form that invites a yes–no or either–or answer), along with subsidiary questions, embedded questions, follow-up questions, and related questions.

2. Create a question outline, identifying at least three subquestions and at least four alternative answers to the main question.

3. Present the discussion question to the class, writing it on the chalkboard, an overhead transparency, or paper distributed to the class. After reading the question aloud, go on to give the sense of the question, identifying terms, explaining the relevance of the question, connecting it to a previous discussion or class activity, and so on. End with an invitation to the class to begin addressing the question.

4. Initially, help the class focus on the question, rather than giving answers to it. For example, invite the class to tell what they know about the question, what it means to them.

5. DO NOT COMMENT AFTER THE FIRST STUDENT'S CONTRIBUTION. (If you do, the interaction will quickly become I-R-E.) In addition, do not ask, "What does someone else think about that?" (If you do, you invite statements of difference or opposition to the first position, and your discussion turns into a debate.)

6. In general, do not ask questions beyond the first question. Use instead nonquestion alternatives: statements (the thoughts that occurred to you in relation to what the speaker has just said); reflective statements that basically restate the speaker's contribution; statements indicating interest in hearing further about what the speaker has just said; statements indicating the relationship between what the speaker has just said and what a previous speaker has said; signals (sounds or words indicating interest in what the speaker has said); even silence. (Dillon acknowledges that deliberate silence is the hardest of all for teachers to do. To help teachers remain quiet, he recommends silently singing "Baa, baa, black sheep" after each student's contribution.)

7. Facilitate the discussion by

   Locating: "Where are we now? What are we saying?"

   Summarizing: "What have we accomplished? agreed on?"

   Opening: "What shall we do next?"

   Tracking: "We seem a little off track here. How can we all get back on the same line of thought?"

   Pacing: "Just a minute, I wonder whether we're not moving a little too fast here. Let's take a closer look at this idea . . ."

8. When it is time to end the discussion, help students to summarize the discussion and identify the remaining questions.

FIGURE 11-3. Guidelines for leading discussions
Source: Dillon, 1994.

Questions that ask for clarification:

> Can you put that another way?
>
> What do you mean by that?
>
> What's an example of what you are talking about?
>
> Can you explain the term you just used?

Linking or extension questions:

> Is there any connection between what you've just said and what Rajiv was saying a moment ago?
>
> How does your comment fit in with Neng's earlier comment?
>
> How does your observation relate to what the group decided last week?
>
> Does your idea challenge or support what we seem to be saying?

Hypothetical questions:

> What might have happened if Joey hadn't missed the school bus?
>
> In the video we just saw, how might the story have turned out if Arnold had caught the ball?
>
> If the author had wanted the teacher to be a more sympathetic figure, how might he have changed this conversation?

Cause-and-effect questions:

> What is likely to be the effect of the name calling?
>
> How might the rumor affect the school play?

Summary and synthesis questions:

> What are the one or two most important ideas that emerged from this discussion?
>
> What remains unresolved or contentious about this topic?
>
> What do you understand better as a result of today's discussion?
>
> Based on our discussion today, what do we need to talk about next time if we're to understand this issue better?
>
> What key word or concept best captures our discussion today?

Concluding Comments

This chapter has focused on two different patterns of verbal interaction—recitations and discussions. It's important not to get them confused—to think that you're leading a discussion when you're actually conducting a recitation. Also keep in mind the criticisms that have been leveled against recitations, and reflect on how frequently you dominate the verbal interaction in your classroom. Ask yourself whether you also provide opportunities for student-centered discussion, during which you serve as a facilitator (rather than a questioner) and encourage direct student–student interaction. Reflect on the level of thinking that you require from students. The classroom recitation can serve a number of useful functions, but *overuse* suggests that your curriculum consists largely of names, dates, facts, and algorithms (Cazden, 1988).

Summary

This chapter began by examining some of the major criticisms of recitation, as well as the useful functions it can serve. It then distinguished recitations from discussions. Next, the chapter considered the hazards that recitations present to teachers and suggested a number of strategies for avoiding the problems. Finally, we looked at an example of a discussion, reflected on reasons for the infrequent use of discussion, and briefly considered a number of guidelines for managing this type of verbal interaction.

Characteristic pattern of a recitation

- I-R-E (teacher initiation, student response, teacher evaluation).
- Quick pace.
- To review material, to elaborate on a text.

Criticisms of recitation

- Gives the teacher a dominant role, the student a passive one.
- Lacks interaction among students.
- Emphasizes recall over higher-level thinking skills.
- Promotes public evaluation, which can lead to negative interdependence.
- Format sometimes conflicts with students' cultural background.

Five functions of recitation

- Provides opportunity to check on students' comprehension.
- Involves students in presentation of material.
- Allows for contact with individuals in a group setting.
- Helps to maintain attention level.
- Offers an opportunity to push students to construct more complete responses.

Characteristics of a discussion

- I-R-R-R.
- Student-initiated questions.
- Student comments on contributions of peers.
- Slower pace.
- Intended to stimulate thinking, to foster problem solving, and to examine implications.

Three hazards of recitations

- Unequal participation.
- Losing the pace and focus.
- Difficulty in monitoring comprehension.

Strategies for successful use of recitations

- Distribute chances for participation by

  Using patterned turn taking.
  Using names in a jar.
  Using a checklist.
  Gently encouraging silent students to participate.
  Ensuring that males and females have equal opportunity to participate.

- Provide time to think about answers before responding.
- Stimulate and maintain interest by

  Injecting mystery/suspense elements into your questions.
  Using humor, novelty.
  Incorporating physical activity.

- Provide feedback without losing the pace.
- Monitor comprehension by requiring overt responses.
- Monitor comprehension by observing a steering group.

Moderating Discussions

- Limit group size.
- Arrange students so they have eye contact.
- Teach discussion skills.
- Act as facilitator rather than questioner.
- Plan discussion questions (and subsidiary questions) and outline.
- At the beginning of the discussion, focus on the question, not on answers.

- After the initial question, use nonquestion alternatives to keep discussion going (or use questions very judiciously).
- Manage the discussion by locating, summarizing, opening, tracking, and pacing.

When planning your lessons, think about the extent to which you use recitations and discussions in your classroom. Think about the level of the questions that you ask: Are all of your questions low-level, factual questions that can be answered with a word or two, or are your questions designed to stimulate thinking and problem solving? Ask yourself if you consistently dominate the interaction, or if you also provide opportunities for real discussion among students.

Activities

1. Visit a classroom and observe a recitation. On a seating chart, map the verbal interaction by placing a check in the "seat" of each child who participates. Analyze your results and draw conclusions about how widely and fairly participation is distributed in this class.

√ = question/comment
X = response to a question

2. Your colleague has asked you to help him figure out why his students are not paying attention in class. He would like you to observe him and offer feedback. What follows is a session you observed. Using what you know about distributing participation, stimulating and maintaining interest, and monitoring comprehension, identify the trouble spots of his lesson and provide three specific suggestions for improvement. When you enter the class, Mr. B. is perched on a stool in front of the room with the science book in his hand.

MR. B. Who remembers what photosynthesis is? [No response.] Do you remember yesterday when we looked at green plants and we discussed how a plant makes its own food? [Mr. B. notices that Thea is nodding.] Thea, do you remember about photosynthesis?

THEA: Yeah.

MR. B. Well, can you tell the class about it?

THEA: It has something to do with light and chlorophyll.

MR. B. Good. Tom, can you add to this? [Tom was drawing in his notebook.]

TOM: No.

MR. B. Tom, Thea told us that photosynthesis had to do with light and chlorophyll. Do you recall our discussion from yesterday when we defined photosynthesis?

TOM: Sort of.

MR. B. What do you mean? Didn't you write down the definition with the rest of the class? Look in your notebook and tell me the definition. [Tom starts to page through his notebook. Many of the students have begun to whisper and snicker. Some are looking in their notebooks.] How many of you have found the page where we defined photosynthesis? [Seven students raise their hands.] Good. Would somebody read to me that definition? Thea.

THEA: Photosynthesis is the process of forming sugars and starches in plants from water and carbon dioxide when sunlight acts upon chlorophyll.

MR. B. Excellent. Does everyone understand? [A few students nod.] Good. Tomorrow we will be having a quiz about plants and photosynthesis. Tom, will you be ready for the quiz?

TOM: Sure, Mr. B.

MR. B. Okay, now let's all turn to page 135 in our science texts and read about the uses of plants.

3. Monitoring students' comprehension is sometimes problematic. Choose one of the following topics and suggest two different ways a teacher could elicit overt participation in order to determine student understanding.

a. Main characters and their traits.

b. Fractional parts.

c. Greater than and less than symbols.

d. Syllabication.

e. Spanish vocabulary words.

f. State capitals.

g. Types of clouds.

4. We know that recitations and discussions are often confused. Observe and record 10 minutes of a class "discussion." Then, using the following checklist, see if the verbal interaction actually meets the criteria for a discussion or if it is more like a recitation.

   • Students are the predominant speakers.
   • The verbal interaction pattern is not I-R-E, but a mix of statements and questions by a mix of teacher and students.
   • The pace is longer and slower.
   • The primary purpose is to stimulate a variety of responses, to encourage students to consider different points of view, to foster problem-solving, and the like.
   • Evaluation consists of agree/disagree, rather than right/wrong.

For Further Reading

Brookfield, S. D., & Preskill, S. (1999). *Discussion as a way of teaching: Tools and techniques for democratic classrooms.* San Francisco: Jossey-Bass.
Dillon, J. T. (1994). *Using discussion in classrooms.* Philadelphia: Open University Press.

References

The AAUW Report: How schools shortchange girls. (1992). Washington, DC: The AAUW Educational Foundation and National Education Association.
Alvermann, D., O'Brien, D., & Dillon, D. (1990). What teachers do when they say they're having discussions of content area reading assignments. *Reading Research Quarterly, 25,* 296–322.
Bossert, S. T. (1979). *Tasks and social relationships in classrooms. A study of instructional organization and its consequences.* Cambridge: Cambridge University Press.
Brookfield, S. D., & Preskill, S. (1999). *Discussion as a way of teaching: Tools and techniques for democratic classrooms.* San Francisco: Jossey-Bass.
Brophy, J. E., & Evertson, C. (1976). *Learning from teaching: A developmental perspective.* Boston: Allyn & Bacon.
Carter, K. (March–April 1985). Teacher comprehension of classroom processes: An emerging direction in classroom management research. Paper presented at the annual meeting of the American Educational Research Association, Chicago, Illinois.
Cazden, C. B. (1988). *Classroom discourse: The language of teaching and learning.* Portsmouth, NH: Heinemann.
Dillon, J. T. (1994). *Using discussion in classrooms.* Philadelphia: Open University Press.
Doyle, W. (1986). Classroom organization and management. In M. C. Wittrock (Ed.), *The handbook of research on teaching,* (3rd ed.). (392–431). New York: Macmillan.

Farrar, M. T. (1988). A sociolinguistic analysis of discussion. In J. T. Dillon (Ed.), *Questioning and discussion—A multidisciplinary study.* Norwood, NJ: Ablex.

Fisher, C. W., Berliner, D. C., Filby, N. N., Marliave, R., Cahen, L. S., & Dishaw, M. M. (1980). Teaching behaviors, academic learning time, and student achievement: An overview. In C. Denham & A. Lieberman (Eds.), *Time to learn.* Washington, DC: U.S. Department of Education, 7–32.

Gall, M. D., & Gillett, M. (1981). The discussion method in classroom teaching. *Theory into Practice, 19*(2), 98–103.

Gay, G. (2000). *Culturally responsive teaching: Theory, research, and practice.* New York: Teachers College Press.

Good, T., & Brophy, J. E. (2000). *Looking in classrooms.* (8th ed.). New York: Harper/Collins.

Goodlad, J. (1984). *A place called school.* New York: McGraw-Hill.

Grossman, H., & Grossman, S. H. (1994). *Gender issues in education.* Boston: Allyn and Bacon.

Hoetker, J., & Ahlbrand, W. P. Jr. (1969). The persistence of the recitation. *American Educational Research Journal, 6,* 145–167.

Jackson, P. W. (1968). *Life in classrooms.* New York: Holt, Rinehart and Winston.

Jones, M. G., & Gerig, T. M. (1994). Silent sixth-grade students: Characteristics, achievement, and teacher expectations. *The Elementary School Journal, 95*(2), 169–182.

Kounin, J. (1970). *Discipline and group management in classrooms.* New York: Holt, Rinehart & Winston.

Lundgren, U. (1972). *Frame factors and the teaching process.* Stockholm: Almqvist and Wiksell.

MacLachlan, P. (1985). *Sarah, Plain and Tall.* New York: Harper & Row Junior Books.

Marshall, H. H. (1987). Motivational strategies of three fifth-grade teachers. *The Elementary School Journal, 88*(2), 135–150.

McDermott, R. P. (1977). Social relations as contexts for learning in school. *Harvard Educational Review, 47,* 198–213.

Mehan, H. (1979). *Learning lessons: Social organization in a classroom.* Cambridge, MA: Harvard University Press.

Morine-Dershimer, G., & Beyerbach, B. (1987). Moving right along . . . . In V. Richardson-Koehler (Ed.), *Educators' handbook, A research perspective* (207–232). New York: Longman.

Morse, L. W., & Handley, H. M. (1985). Listening to adolescents: Gender differences in science classroom interaction. In L. C. Wilkinson & C. B. Marrett (Eds.), *Gender influences in classroom interaction.* Orlando, FL: Academic Press.

Narayn, J. S., Heward, W. L., Gardner, III, R., Courson, F. H., & Omness, C. K. (1990). Using response cards to increase student participation in an elementary classroom. *Journal of Applied Behavior Analysis, 23*(4), 483–490.

Peet, B. (1993). Buford, the little bighorn. In R. C. Farr & D. S. Strickland (senior authors), *A most unusual sight. HBJ Treasury of literature.* Orlando, FL: Harcourt Brace Jovanovich.

Philips, S. (1972). Participant structures and communicative competence: Warm Springs children in community and classroom. In C. Cazden, V. John, & D. Hymes (Eds.), *Functions of language in the classroom.* New York: Teachers College Press.

Rief, S. F. (1993). *How to reach and teach ADD/ADHD children.* West Nyack, NY: The Center for Applied Research in Education.

Roby, T. W. (1988). Models of discussion. In J. T. Dillon (Ed.), *Questioning and discussion—A multidisciplinary study* (163–191). Norwood, NJ: Ablex.

Rosenshine, B. V. (1986). Synthesis of research on explicit teaching. *Educational Leadership, 43*(7), 60–69.

Rowe, M. B. (1974). Wait-time and rewards as instructional variables, their influence on language, logic, and fate control: Part 1: Wait time. *Journal of Research in Science Teaching, 11,* 291–308.

Sadker, D., Sadker, M., & Thomas, D. (1981). Sex equity and special education. *The Pointer, 26,* 33–38.

Sadker, D., & Sadker, M. (1985). Is the OK Classroom OK? *Phi Delta Kappan, 55,* 358–367.

Stodolsky, S. S. (1988). *The subject matters: Classroom activity in math and social studies.* Chicago: University of Chicago Press.

Taylor, T. (1969). *The cay.* New York: Doubleday.

Woodruff, E. (1991). *George Washington's socks.* New York: Apple Paperback, Scholastic.

PART IV

Coping with the Challenges

Chapter 12

When Prevention Is Not Enough: Protecting and Restoring Order

Failure to Do Homework

Concluding Comments

Summary

Not too long ago, we spoke with Cheryl, a first-year teacher whose class was giving her a hard time. It was only October, but she was close to tears as she talked about the disrespectful and disruptive behavior of her fifth-graders. "I'm more like a cop than a teacher," she told us, and she was both surprised and dismayed by the antagonism she felt toward her students. She had always "loved children so much." What had gone wrong?

As we talked, it became clear that Cheryl's problem was not due to an absence of clear rules and routines or to boring, tedious instruction:

It's not like they don't understand what I want. On the first day of school, we talked a lot about the rules. You know, whisper quietly, don't interrupt, raise your hand to speak. . . . I thought we were off to such a great start. They were so well-behaved! But now they just don't seem to care. I'll remind them about a rule, like listening when the teacher is giving a lesson, and for a few minutes they're OK, but then they start shouting out, getting up to sharpen pencils, throwing erasers back and forth. I get so frustrated, I just start yelling—something I said I'd never do. I don't know . . . I just don't understand how to get them to follow all those great rules I set up. Sometimes I tell them that we're not going to do any interesting things anymore, and I'm just going to give them worksheets to do every day. But that's not the kind of classroom I always dreamed of. I want my classroom to be exciting. I want my kids to love coming to school.

This first-year teacher had learned a sad fact of classroom life: Having clear, reasonable rules and routines doesn't automatically mean that everyone will follow them. At the beginning of the school year, students work hard at "figuring out the teacher"—determining teachers' expectations and requirements, the amount of socializing they will tolerate, and how far they can be pushed. Most students will pursue their agendas within the limits the teacher sets, but they need to know those limits. This underscores the importance of communicating your behavioral expectations to students (the topic of Chapter 4)—and then *enforcing those expectations*. In other words, just as it's part of the students' role to push, it's part of the teacher's role to communicate that students can't push too far. During our discussions on misbehavior, Garnetta, Ken, Barbara, and Viviana repeatedly stressed the importance of following through on the rules and routines that you've planned and taught to your students. As Barbara put it, "If you tell kids to do something, then you have to make sure they do it. Otherwise, you're communicating that you don't really mean it."

In this chapter, we consider ways of responding to the problems that you may encounter—from minor, nondisruptive infractions to chronic, more serious misbehaviors.

Principles for Dealing with Inappropriate Behavior

There is little research on the relative effectiveness of disciplinary strategies (see Emmer and Aussiker, 1990), but four principles guide our discussion. First, *disciplinary strategies must be consistent with the goal of creating a safe, caring classroom environment.* You need to achieve order, but you also need to choose strategies that support your relationship with students, help them to become self-regulating, and allow them to save face in front of their peers. Curwin and Mendler (1988), authors of *Discipline with Dignity,* put it this way:

> *Students will protect their dignity at all costs, even with their lives if pushed hard enough. In the game of chicken, with two cars racing at top speed toward a cliff, the loser is the one who steps on the brake. Nothing explains this bizarre reasoning better than the need for peer approval and dignity. (p. 27)*

In order to protect students' dignity, it is important to avoid power struggles that may cause students to lose face with their peers. Our four teachers speak with misbehaving students calmly and quietly. They don't bring up past sins. They take care to separate the child's *character* from the specific *misbehavior;* instead of attacking the child as a person ("You're lazy"), they talk about what the child has done ("You have not handed in the last two homework assignments"). When more than a brief intervention is necessary, they try to meet with students privately.

On the second day of school, we witnessed a good example of disciplining with dignity in Garnetta's classroom. Even though it was so early in the school year, Tanya was already displaying the behaviors that had contributed to her notorious reputation:

> *During the first hour of the morning, Tanya breaks down in tears, refuses to participate in a class activity, punches two children passing by her desk, and creates a fuss about her place in the bathroom line. She gets little work done without individual supervision, constantly asks Garnetta for assistance, and pouts if immediate help is not forthcoming. At 10:00, when Tanya is again in tears, Garnetta tells her class they have five minutes of free time. She goes over to Tanya and speaks quietly with her. The two of them go into the hallway. After a few minutes, Garnetta comes back alone; Tanya follows shortly. She sits down at her desk and begins to work on the assignment that Garnetta has just given. After about 10 minutes, Garnetta asks Tanya to go on an important errand to the office. We are astounded by*

the smile on Tanya's face as she leaves the room. She returns shortly, and there are no problems for the rest of the morning.

Later, we ask Garnetta to reveal what happened in the hallway. She tells us that she began by asking Tanya what was bothering her. Tanya reported that the boy next to her had said her shoes were ugly. "Do you think they're ugly?" Garnetta asked. "No," Tanya replied. They spoke for a few minutes about her shoes and how it feels when somebody says something bad about the way you look. Although this clearly had not been the cause of Tanya's problems all morning, Garnetta let it go, assuring Tanya that she would talk to the boy about his comment. Garnetta then talked about how glad she was that Tanya was in her class, pointed out good things Tanya had done that morning as well as the things that had been problematic, and encouraged her to work hard for the rest of the morning. She told her to go to the bathroom, wash her face, get a drink, and then return to the room. "When I saw her working so well, I wanted to give her an immediate reward. Children like Tanya often don't get to go on errands, because teachers are sure they'll misbehave in the hallways. So I sent her on an errand to let her know that I trusted her and that I liked her and that I knew she had been working well."

In this vignette, we see how Garnetta tried to avoid embarrassing Tanya by speaking with her privately; how she demonstrated concern for Tanya's feelings about the boy's nasty comments; how she focused on the appropriate behavior Tanya had demonstrated that morning rather than her misbehavior; and how she attempted to reinforce Tanya's on-task behavior and increase her feelings of self-importance by sending her on an errand. This encounter was not a magical cure. Although Garnetta was able to bring about definite improvements in Tanya's behavior, the child's problems were deep-rooted and persistent. Nonetheless, this vignette demonstrates the way Garnetta worked to communicate her expectations for appropriate behavior while preserving Tanya's dignity.

Another way of disciplining with dignity is to structure opportunities for students to assume some responsibility for regulating their own behavior. In Chapter 5 we talked about gaining students' cooperation by sharing responsibility and decision-making authority. This chapter continues that theme by discussing strategies that involve students in solving the problems that arise in classrooms.

Second, when dealing with misbehavior, it is essential to *keep the instructional program going with a minimum of disruption.* Achieving this goal requires a delicate balancing act. On one hand, you cannot allow inappropriate behavior to interrupt the teaching–learning process. On the other hand, you must realize that disciplinary strategies themselves can be disruptive. As Doyle (1986) comments, interventions are "inherently risky" because they call attention to misbehavior and can actually pull students away from a lesson (p. 421). In order to avoid this situation, you must try to anticipate potential problems and head them off; if you decide that a disciplinary intervention *is* necessary, you need to be as unobtrusive as possible.

Watching our four teachers in action, it is clear that they recognize the importance of protecting the instructional program. In the following incident, Viviana sizes up a potentially disruptive situation and is able to maintain the flow of her lesson:

It is Halloween time, and Viviana's students have just returned from art class, where they made masks. They enter the room wearing the masks, obviously excited and proud of the way they look. Viviana stands at the chalkboard, about to begin a language arts lesson. She takes a long look at her students and waits for them to get settled. Then, she moves to her desk, takes out a mask, and puts it on. She moves back to the chalkboard and announces, "Since you have your masks on, I will wear one too. We will do language arts with our masks on." Later, she tells us: "I had only two choices. It was clear that if I made them take their masks off, I'd be fighting with them the whole period; my lesson would go down the drain. If I let them wear the masks, and even put one on myself, I could keep the lesson going and get them involved. I couldn't let my lesson fall apart.

The third principle is that *whether or not a particular action constitutes misbehavior depends on the context in which it occurs* (Doyle, 1986). There are obvious exceptions to this notion—punching another child and stealing property are obvious violations that always require a teacher response. But other behaviors are not so clear cut. For example, in some classes, wearing a hat, sitting on your desk, chewing gum, and talking to neighbors are all misbehaviors, while in other classes these are perfectly acceptable. What constitutes misbehavior is often a function of a particular teacher's tolerance level or the standards set by a particular school (Cairns, 1987). When determining a course of action, you need to ask yourself, "Is this behavior disrupting the ongoing instructional activity? Is it hurtful to other children? Does it violate established rules?" If the answer to these questions is no, disciplinary interventions may not be necessary.

"I'm a fidgeter," Barbara tells us. "When I first went for an interview for a teaching position, my mother told me not to wear any jewelry, because she knew that I'd play with it while I talked. Because of this, I'm sympathetic to the fidgeters in my class. If a kid has trouble sitting still and crawls all over his or her chair, I don't do anything—unless it's bothering other people. Sometimes I hear a child singing softly while working. I'll check to see if other people seem to be disturbed before doing anything. For me, that's the most important question: Is the behavior affecting others and denying them the right to instruction? If not, it's usually OK with me."

Considering the context has become more important as the home lives of many children have become more unstable and unsupportive. Sometimes teachers excuse the inappropriate behavior of certain students because "these kids can't help it." We hear teachers say, "What can you expect, with a family situation like that?" or "These poor kids are going through so much at home, I hate to make their lives more difficult by enforcing rules." As well intentioned as these teachers may be, not holding students accountable for inappropriate behavior rarely helps. Children may protest limits, but they crave consistency, predictability, and structure—particularly when they live inconsistent, unpredictable, and unstructured lives out of school. Garnetta tells this vignette:

I have one girl in my class with serious behavior problems. Her mother is in and out of jail, and the child is shunted around to different relatives and friends. She's thin and frail, prone to tantrums, and very sensitive. She can't stand to be yelled at and needs a lot of TLC [tender, loving care]. I have to be more mellow with her than with the other kids. For example, when I tell her she has to do her work, she'll say, "OK, I'll be good, Mrs. Chain. Just give me a hug. Do you still love me?" I tell her, "I love you, and I'll hug you, but you still have to do your work."

Despite the need to enforce expectations for appropriate behavior, we do think that teachers need to be sensitive to conditions at home that make some children's lives a constant struggle. We recently learned about a second-grader who was frequently late to school because he had to get himself up, wake his younger brother (a kindergartner), prepare breakfast, and get them both to school. When he would appear at the door of his classroom 15 minutes late, his teacher would harshly berate him and send him to the office. It's true that the child was violating the school rule about not being tardy, but we think a more humane response would have been to welcome him to school with a warm hello, while working with the school social worker to see what could be done to improve the situation. After all, the fact that he got to school at all was quite an accomplishment.

Finally, the fourth principle emphasizes the importance of *making sure the severity of the disciplinary strategy matches the misbehavior you are trying to eliminate.* Research (e.g., Pittman, 1985) has indicated that some teachers think about misbehavior in terms of three categories: *minor misbehaviors* (noisiness, socializing, daydreaming); *more serious misbehaviors* (arguing, failing to respond to a group directive); and *never tolerated misbehaviors* (stealing, intentionally hurting someone, destroying property). They also consider whether the misbehavior is part of a pattern or an isolated event.

When deciding how to respond to a problem, it is useful to think in terms of these categories and to select a response that is congruent with the seriousness of the misbehavior. This is easier said than done, of course. When misbehavior occurs, teachers have little time to assess its seriousness, decide if it's part of a pattern, and select an appropriate response. And too often, the situation is ambiguous: Since misbehavior often occurs when the teacher is looking somewhere else, it may not be absolutely clear who is doing what to whom. Nonetheless, you don't want to ignore or react mildly to misbehavior that warrants a more severe response; nor do you want to overreact to behavior that is relatively minor.

With these four principles in mind—preserving a safe, caring classroom environment, protecting the instructional program, considering the context, and selecting a disciplinary strategy that matches the misbehavior—we turn now to specific ways of responding to inappropriate behavior.

Dealing with Minor Misbehavior

As we mentioned in Chapter 4, Jacob Kounin's (1970) classic study of orderly and disorderly classrooms gave research support to the belief that successful classroom managers have eyes in the back of their heads. Kounin found that effective managers knew what was going on all over the room; moreover, *their students knew they knew* because the teachers were able to spot minor problems and "nip them in the bud." Kounin called this ability "withitness," a term that has since become widely used in discussions of classroom management.

How do "with it" teachers deal with minor misbehavior? How do they succeed in nipping problems in the bud? This section discusses both nonverbal and verbal interventions and then considers the times when it may be better to do nothing at all. (Suggestions are summarized in Table 12-1.)

Nonverbal Interventions

A while back, an 11-year-old we know announced that she could be a successful teacher. When we asked why she was so confident, she replied: "I know how to make *the look.*"

TABLE 12-1. Dealing with Minor Misbehavior

Strategy	Advantages
1. Nonverbal interventions:	Allow you to prompt appropriate behavior without
Facial expressions	disrupting lesson
Eye contact	Encourage students to assume responsibility for
Hand signals	changing behavior
Proximity	
2. Verbal interventions:	
Nondirect	
Stating student's name	Brief, unobtrusive
Incorporating name into lesson	Gets student back on task without even citing the
Calling on child to participate	misbehavior; maintains lesson flow
Use of gentle humor	Prompts a smile along with appropriate behavior
I-message	Minimizes negative evaluations and preserves
Direct	relationships
Command	Straightforward
Rule reminder	Reinforces desired behavior
Giving choice between behaving	Points out consequences of behavior
appropriately or receiving penalty	Promotes students' autonomy and responsibility for
	actions
3. Ignoring the misbehavior	Unobtrusive; protects the flow of the lesson

She proceeded to demonstrate: her eyebrows slanted downward, her forehead creased, and her lips flattened into a straight line. She definitely had "the look" down pat.

The "teacher look" is a good example of an unobtrusive, nonverbal intervention. Making eye contact, using hand signals, and moving closer to the misbehaving student are other nonverbal ways of communicating disapproval. According to Fredric Jones (2001), the proper use of body language is one of the most effective disciplinary interventions available to teachers. It requires a good deal of practice, however, before you can "look students back to work" (p. 178). Jones provides detailed instructions on turning "regally" toward misbehaving students and "staring them down" (p. 190).

Nonverbal strategies are most appropriate for behaviors that are minor but persistent: frequent or sustained whispering, staring into space, calling out, walking around the room, playing with a toy, and passing notes. Nonverbal interventions not only allow you to deal with these misbehaviors, they enable you to protect and continue your lesson.

> *It's a few days after Christmas vacation, and we are observing in Garnetta's classroom. During a creative writing activity, two boys seated across the room from each other begin a "shooting match," using their pencils as "guns." They make convincing gun noises. Garnetta is working with another child; she stops and looks hard and long at both boys. They look back, immediately stop what they're doing, and get back to work. Garnetta finishes her conversation and begins to circulate around the room. She stops at both boys' desks and checks their work.*

As this anecdote illustrates, a nonverbal cue is sometimes all that's needed to stop a misbehavior and get a student back on task. In fact, a study of six middle school teachers (Lasley, Lasley, & Ward, 1989) found that the *most successful responses to misbehavior were nonverbal.* These strategies stopped misbehavior 79 percent of the time; among the three "more effective managers," the success rate was even higher—an amazing 95 percent.

The obvious advantage of using a nonverbal cue is that you don't distract other students while dealing with the misbehavior. As Barbara comments:

> *Whenever you're involved in a verbal confrontation with one child, the others are "free-timing it." They're listening to you instead of doing their work. If a child is playing with a car, it's much more effective to simply walk over and take it. That way it's gone, and you don't have to worry about it anymore.*

Placing a hand on a student's shoulder or physically guiding a child to pick up a pencil and get to work are also unobtrusive, nonverbal interventions that teachers have found helpful. Remember the cautions expressed in Chapter 5, however, about physical contact with students. We know a student teacher who tried to get a student on task by taking the child's head in her hands and directing it away from the window toward the chalkboard. Later, the child complained about a stiff neck and accused the student teacher of "jerking" her head around. The student teacher immediately notified her cooperating teacher and principal about what had happened, and a phone call to the parents fortunately headed off further trouble. Incidents like these, however, point to the importance of avoiding any physical interventions that could be interpreted as abusive.

Verbal Interventions

Sometimes you find yourself in situations where it's just not possible to use a nonverbal cue. Perhaps you can't catch the student's eye, or you're working with a small group and it would be too disruptive to get up and walk across the room to the misbehaving child. Other times, you're able to use a nonverbal cue, but it's unsuccessful in stopping the misbehavior.

In cases like this, you can use a *nondirective verbal intervention.* These allow you to prompt the appropriate behavior, while leaving the responsibility for figuring out what to do with the misbehaving student. For example, *simply saying the student's name* might be enough to get the student back on task. Sometimes it's possible to *incorporate the child's name* into the ongoing instruction. We witnessed Ken use this unobtrusive strategy during a small-group discussion:

> *Brian is slouching down in his seat and appears inattentive. Ken is praising the comment of another student: "Did you see the way Joey made that into an analysis question? He didn't just say, 'Brian is slouching in his seat,' he said . . ." Brian immediately sits up, with a small smile on his face and begins to participate in the discussion.*

If the misbehavior occurs while a group discussion or recitation is going on, you can *call on the child to answer a question.* Consider the following example:

> *Viviana is conducting a whole-group reading lesson—"The Hen and the Bread." She asks the class, "What is make believe in this picture and what is real?" The children scrutinize the illustration, and one by one hands go up into the air. She calls on a nonvolunteer who appears to be daydreaming. "Fernando, what is make believe in this picture?" He is brought back to the task, looks at the picture, and slowly responds.*

Calling on a student allows you to communicate that you know what's going on and to capture the student's attention—without even citing the misbehavior. But keep in mind what we said earlier about preserving students' dignity. If you are obviously trying to "catch" students and to embarrass them, the strategy may well backfire by creating resentment (Good & Brophy, 2000). One way to avoid this problem is to alert the student that you will be calling on them to answer the *next question:* "Sharon, what's the answer to number 18? Taysha, the next one's yours."

The *use of humor* can provide another "gentle" way of reminding children to correct their behavior. Used well, humor can show students that you are able to understand the funny sides of classroom life. But you must be careful that the humor is not tinged with sarcasm that can hurt students' feelings.

Garnetta instructs her students to clean off their desks in anticipation of the next activity. One boy takes a paper, crumples it up into a ball and sticks it in his desk. Garnetta makes big eyes and says "I saw that paper go squish into your desk." The boy and the class laugh. He takes the paper ball and puts it in the wastebasket.

Viviana sees a few students playing with toys inside their desks when they're supposed to be paying attention to the lesson. Very dramatically, she warns them: "You're going to make me mad, and when I get mad I make an ugly face. You don't want to see my ugly face, do you?" The children "shiver" with the thought of seeing her ugly face, put the toys away, and return to work.

An *"I-message"* is another way of verbally prompting appropriate behavior without giving a direct command. I-messages generally contain three parts. First, the teacher *describes the unacceptable behavior in a nonblaming, nonjudgmental way*. This phrase often begins with "when": "When people talk while I'm giving directions . . ." The second part describes the *tangible effect on the teacher:* "I have to repeat the directions and that wastes time . . ." Finally, the third part of the message states the *teacher's feelings* about the tangible effect: "and I get frustrated." Barbara used a three-part I-message like this when her class failed to clean up after a particularly messy art activity: "When you leave the room a mess, I have to clean it up, and I may not want to do an activity like this again."

These are some other examples of I-messages:

"When you come to class without your supplies, I can't start the lesson on time, and I get really irritated."

"When you leave your skateboard in the middle of the aisle, I can trip over it, and I'm afraid I'll break a leg."

Although I-messages ideally contain all three parts in the recommended sequence, I-messages in any order, or even with one part missing, can still be effective (Gordon, 1974). We've witnessed our teachers use "abbreviated" I-messages. For example, Viviana communicates the importance of not laughing at people's mistakes when she states: "If you laugh at me when I make a mistake then I'll feel bad." And Barbara honestly tells her class: "When you guys do that, it drives me up the wall."

There are several benefits to using this approach. In contrast to typical "you-messages" (e.g., "You are being rude," "You ought to know better," "You're acting like a baby"), I-messages minimize negative evaluations of the student. For this reason, they foster and preserve a positive relationship between people. Since I-messages leave decisions about changing behavior up to students, this approach is also likely to promote a sense of responsibility and autonomy. In addition, I-messages show students that their behavior has consequences and that teachers are people with genuine feelings. Unlike you-messages, I-messages don't make students defensive and stubborn; thus, students may be more willing to change their behavior.

Most of us are not used to speaking this way, so I-messages can seem awkward and artificial. With practice, however, using I-messages can become natural. We once heard a four-year-old girl (whose parents had consistently used I-messages at home) tell her nursery school peer: "When you poke me with that pencil, it really hurts, and I feel bad 'cause I think you don't want to be my friend."

In addition to these nondirective approaches, there are also *more directive strategies* you can try. Indeed, these may be particularly appropriate for African American students from low socioeconomic backgrounds. Lisa Delpit, African American author of *Other People's Children: Cultural Conflict in the Classroom* (1995), observes that framing directives as questions (e.g., "Would you like to sit down now?") is a particularly mainstream, middle-class (and female) way of speaking, designed to foster a more egalitarian and nonauthoritarian climate. According to Delpit,

> *Many kids will not respond to that structure because commands are not couched as questions in their home culture. Rather than asking questions, some teachers need to learn to say, "Put the scissors away" and "Sit down now" or "Please sit down now." (Valentine, 1998, p. 17)*

As Delpit suggests, the most straightforward approach is to *direct students to the task at hand* ("Get to work on that math problem"; "Your group should be discussing the first three pages"). You can also *remind the student about the rule* or behavioral expectation that is being violated (e.g., "When someone is talking, everyone else is supposed to be listening"). Sometimes, if inappropriate behavior is fairly widespread, it's useful to review rules with the entire group. This is often true after a holiday, a weekend, or a vacation.

Another strategy is to *give students a choice between behaving appropriately or receiving a penalty* for continued inappropriate behavior (e.g., "If you can't handle working in your group, you'll have to return to your seats"; "You either choose to raise your hand instead of calling out, or you will be choosing not to participate in our discussion"). Statements like these not only warn students that a penalty will be invoked if the inappropriate behavior continues, they also emphasize that students have real choices about how to behave and that penalties are not imposed without reason. Ken often uses this strategy. For example, when a boy in his class repeatedly called out during a spelling test, despite nonverbal cues and nondirective reminders, Ken told him: "Barry, you either choose to be quiet, or you will lose the opportunity to play soccer with the rest of the class." Barry protested in a shocked tone: "What am I doing?" In response, Ken calmly described his behavior and its effects: "You're calling out and disturbing people in the room, including me."

Sometimes, Ken also gives students a choice about the particular penalty that will be imposed if they choose to continue their inappropriate behavior. When Evan disregarded Ken's warning not to disrupt a social studies game the class was playing, Ken told him: "Evan, you leave me no choice—to bench you [i.e., exclude him from the game] or to give your whole team a penalty. Which one do you want the next time you call out improperly?"

Deliberately Ignoring the Misbehavior

If misbehavior is extremely brief and unobtrusive, the best course of action may be *in-action*. For example, during a discussion a student may be so eager to comment that she forgets to raise her hand; or someone becomes momentarily distracted and inattentive; or two boys quietly exchange a comment while you're giving directions. In cases like these, an intervention can be more disruptive than the students' behavior.

One risk of ignoring minor misbehavior is that students may conclude you're unaware of what's going on. Suspecting that you're not "with-it," they may decide to see how much they can get away with, and then problems are sure to escalate. You need to monitor your class carefully to make sure this doesn't happen.

Another problem is that occasional ignoring can turn into full-fledged "blindness." This was vividly demonstrated in a study of a student teacher named Heleen (Créton, Wubbels, & Hooymayers, 1989). When Heleen was lecturing, her students frequently became noisy and inattentive. In response, Heleen talked more loudly and looked more at the chalkboard, turning her back on her students. She did not allow herself to see or hear the disorder—perhaps because it was too threatening and she didn't know how to handle it. Unfortunately, Heleen's students seemed to interpret her "blindness" as an indication that noise was allowed, and they became even more disorderly. Heleen eventually recognized the importance of "seeing" and responding to slight disturbances in order to prevent them from escalating.

Dealing with More Serious Misbehavior: Using Penalties

Sometimes, nonverbal cues or verbal reminders are not enough to convince students that you're serious about the behavioral expectations that you've established. And sometimes misbehavior is just too serious to use these kinds of low-level responses. In cases like these, it may be necessary to impose a penalty in order to enforce your expectations for appropriate behavior.

The importance of enforcing expectations was clearly demonstrated in Emmer, Evertson, and Anderson's (1980) study of effective classroom management. When rule violations occurred in the classrooms of ineffective classroom managers, they often issued reminders and warned students of penalties, but they didn't act on their warnings. Inevitably, behavior problems increased in frequency and severity. In contrast, effective classroom managers dealt both quickly and predictably with rule violations. When they warned students that a penalty would result if the misbehavior didn't stop, the teachers made sure to follow through on the warning.

Emmer, Evertson, and their colleagues also found that effective classroom managers planned their penalties ahead of time. In some cases, teachers discussed penalties when they taught rules and procedures so students understood the consequences of violating a rule from the very beginning. We saw Garnetta do this with her students in Chapter 4. This practice prevents unpleasant "surprises" and hopefully minimizes protests of blissful ignorance: "But you didn't *tell* me that would happen!"

Selecting Penalties

It's often difficult for beginning teachers to decide on appropriate penalties. One frustrated student teacher told us:

> *I can't keep kids after school because they have to catch the school bus. I don't like keeping them in from recess or lunch because that's the only time I have for myself, and I've got to use it for preparation. My cooperating teacher says I'm not allowed to keep kids from going to "specials," because art, music, and physical education are legitimate, valuable parts of the curriculum. I was told by other teachers not to send kids to the office, because then the principal and my cooperating teacher will think I can't handle problems by myself. And my professors have told me never to use extra work as a penalty because kids will come to see schoolwork as punishment.* So what's left?!

During one meeting, we posed this question to our four teachers and learned about the types of penalties that they typically use. The penalties fall into seven categories:

EXPRESSIONS OF DISAPPOINTMENT. We normally don't think of this as a penalty, but since students in these classes really like their teachers, they feel bad when their teachers are upset. In serious, almost sorrowful tones, our teachers express their disappointment and surprise at the inappropriate behavior and direct students to think about the consequences of their actions.

LOSS OF PRIVILEGES. In Barbara's, Garnetta's and Ken's classes, students who consistently misbehave may lose the highly valued privilege of free time. If they have "forgotten" to do their homework, they need to do it during this time. Ken tells us that for his students being eligible for the "student of the week" is extremely important; thus, losing eligibility for the week is also viewed as a serious penalty.

TIME-OUT. In all four classes, students who distract other students or fail to cooperate with their peers must move to another part of the room until they are ready to rejoin the group. Viviana tells her students: "You decide when you can come back." When Ken has a student who constantly talks too much, he and the student agree upon a pleasant, quiet, and isolated place for the child to go if needed. They work out a signal that Ken uses to send the child to the agreed-upon spot if a verbal warning is ineffective.

Sometimes in-class time-out isn't possible or effective, and it's necessary to send a child out of the room. Barbara has worked out a system with another teacher so that she can send a child to his classroom if necessary. She simply writes the amount of time (e.g., "10 minutes") on a slip of paper that the child takes to the other teacher. In the other room, the child must sit quietly and do schoolwork, ignored by both teacher and students.

Time-out can be particularly effective with children who suffer from ADHD (Rief, 1993). These children have trouble dealing with the distraction and stimulation of the typical classroom environment; time-out can provide a much-needed opportunity to calm down and regain self-control. Try to direct the student to time-out in a calm, positive manner and to be specific about the behavior that is causing the problem (e.g., "Sean, I need you to keep your hands to yourself. Please go to the "think-about-it" chair until you are ready to sit without poking others" (Rief, 1993).

A few cautions are in order (Walker & Shea, 1995). First, you need to consider the characteristics of the child receiving time-out. Time-out may work well for a disruptive, aggressive child who is socially oriented, but it may actually be rewarding for a withdrawn child who tends to daydream. Second, children need to understand the reason they are being sent to time-out and what the rules are (e.g., sit quietly until a timer goes off; no participation in activities until time-out is over). Third, it's important to refrain from lecturing and chastising, since these can reinforce the inappropriate behavior. Fourth, the time-out area should be away from distraction and the possibility of interaction with others; however, it also needs to be a safe place that can be supervised. (For all these reasons, the hallway is *not* a good time-out area!) Lastly, time-out should be limited to approximately 2 to 5 minutes and never over 10 minutes.

WRITTEN REFLECTIONS ON THE PROBLEM. In Garnetta's classroom, students who consistently misbehave may have to write an essay about what they did, their thoughts about why it happened, and why it was inappropriate. In Ken's class, students who hurt other children write letters of apology to the individuals. Barbara sometimes has her students take out their journals and write about the problem that has occurred.

VISITS TO THE PRINCIPAL'S OFFICE. All four teachers believe that "kicking kids out" is a strategy that should be reserved for major disruption. Only rarely do any of them send a child to the principal. Nonetheless, they realize that in extreme cases (like physical aggression), exclusion from the classroom and a meeting with the principal or disciplinarian may be necessary. Even so, Garnetta tells us, "I send along a note telling the principal to send the child back right away. I want my kids in here. They're not going to learn any of my curriculum in the principal's office."

DETENTION. Sometimes Garnetta, Ken, and Barbara require students to meet with them after school for a few minutes. This gives them an opportunity to speak privately with students about the inappropriate behavior and to explore possible causes. Usually it's even possible for a "bus student" to meet for a brief period of time. If it's necessary for students to stay longer, parents are notified ahead of time. Ken also keeps students in the room at lunch time (although, as the student teacher we quoted at the beginning of this section observed, this requires him to eat his lunch in the room also). During this time, students make up missing work, and Ken can talk with students in a more private, less rushed manner.

CONTACTING PARENTS. All the teachers contact parents promptly if a student shows a pattern of repeated misbehavior. For example, in Barbara's classroom, the first time children don't do homework, she reminds them about her expectations. If shortly afterwards they "forget" again, she tells them, "It's my responsibility to let your parents know that you're not getting your work done and to ask them for help in seeing that you do it." She tries to say this, not in anger, but with an expression of serious concern. She wants to convey the idea that "between the two of us, maybe we can help you get it together."

These penalties illustrate the ways Viviana, Garnetta, Barbara, and Ken choose to deal with problems when they have a degree of flexibility. In addition, there are times when they are required to follow school policies mandating particular responses to specific misbehaviors. In Viviana's school, for example, the vice-principal (who serves as the school disciplinarian) requires that teachers send students to his office in cases of continual defiance, use of profanity, and fighting. Be sure to find out what your school policies are with respect to serious problem behaviors.

It's also important to note that almost all schools now have *"zero tolerance" policies* with predetermined consequences for the possession of firearms or other weapons, and about 80 percent have such policies for alcohol, drugs, violence, and tobacco (Johnston, 1999). Such policies usually result in automatic suspension or expulsion, although there may still be wide variation in severity.

If you have students with disabilities in your classes, it's essential that you consult with a special educator or a member of the child study team about appropriate intervention strategies. Serious behavior problems require a team effort, and parents, special education teachers, psychologists, social workers, and administrators can all provide valuable insights and suggestions. Also be aware that the 1997 reauthorization of the Individuals with Disabilities Education Act (IDEA 97) includes several stipulations about the rights of students with disabilities with respect to disciplinary procedures. For example, if the problematic behavior is a manifestation of a student's disability, suspension and expulsion may not be allowed (Janney & Snell, 2000). A recent case provides a good example of this policy. In June 2000, a federal magistrate ruled that a district near Madison, Wisconsin, was wrong to expel a student with disabilities who was involved in a vandalism spree that resulted in $40,000 damage to two elementary schools. A psychiatrist argued that the offense was a manifestation of the student's ADHD. The magistrate agreed (Sack, 2000).

Selecting Penalties That Are Logical Consequences

Whenever possible, penalties should be *logically related to the misbehavior* (e.g., Curwin & Mendler, 1988; Dreikurs, Grunwald, & Pepper, 1982). For example, if students make a mess at the science center, a logical penalty would be to make them clean it up. If a child forgets his book and can't do the assignment, he must borrow someone's book and do the assignment during free time or recess. A student who cannot work cooperatively in a group must leave the group until she decides she can cooperate. A student who hands in a carelessly done paper has to rewrite it.

Dreikurs, Grunwald, and Pepper (1982) distinguish logical consequences like these from traditional punishments, which bear no relationship to the misbehavior involved. An example of punishment would be to have students write "I will not mess up the science center" 50 times. Here are some other examples of punishments that are unrelated to the offense:

A child continually whispers to her neighbor. Instead of isolating the child (a logical consequence), the teacher makes her do an additional homework assignment in math.

A child forgets to get his spelling test signed by his parents. Instead of having the child write a letter home to parents about the need to sign the spelling test (a logical consequence), the teacher makes him stay in at recess.

A child continually calls out during a whole-class discussion. Instead of having the child make a cue-card to post on his desk ("I won't call out") or not allowing the child to participate in the discussion, the teacher makes him stay after school and clean the hamster cage.

According to Dreikurs and his colleagues, punishment is likely to be seen as an arbitrary exercise of power by a dictatorial teacher. Sometimes, children do not even associate the punishment with the misbehavior, but rather with the punisher. Instead of teaching students about the unpleasant results of their inappropriate behavior, unrelated punishments teach students only to make certain they don't get caught the next time around!

Imposing Penalties

It's frustrating when students misbehave, and sometimes we let our frustration color the way we impose penalties. We've seen teachers scream at students from across the room, lecture students on their history of misbehavior, insinuate that they come from terrible homes, and attack their personalities. Clearly, behavior like this destroys children's dignity and ruins the possibility of a good relationship with them. How can you avoid creating a situation like this?

First, if you're feeling really angry at a student, it's a good idea to *delay the discussion.* You can simply say to a child, "Sit there and think about what happened. I'll talk to you in a few minutes." Barbara sometimes tells her students, "I'm really angry about what just happened. Everybody take out journals; we're all going to write about this situation." After a few minutes of writing, she's better able to discuss the misbehavior with students in a calm, dispassionate manner. Similarly, Ken may tell an individual student, "I do not like what I just saw. See me for a few minutes during free time so we can discuss this." By delaying discussion, everyone has a chance to cool off, and you'll be better able to separate the child's character from the child's behavior. Your message must be: "*You're* okay, but your *behavior* is unacceptable."

Second, it's a good idea to *impose penalties privately, calmly, and quietly.* Despite the temptation to yell and scream, the softer your voice and the closer you stand, the more effective you tend to be (Curwin & Mendler, 1988). Remember, students are very concerned about saving face in front of their peers. Public sanction may have the advantage of "making an example" out of one student's misbehavior, but it has the disadvantage of creating resentment and embarrassment. In fact, a study by Turco and Elliott (1986) found that fifth-, seventh-, and ninth-graders viewed public reprimand as *the least acceptable method* of dealing with problems. Our four teachers agree. When Garnetta reprimands a child, she moves over to the individual and speaks so softly that no one else can hear what is going on. Even when speaking to the whole class about misbehavior, her voice is amazingly soft and low—a striking contrast to her "instructional voice," which is loud and strong.

In the following example, Barbara tells how she dealt with Robert:

> *Robert was used to being the focus of the teacher's attention because of his annoying habits. I think he really enjoyed being yelled at, being the center of attention. His records indicated that he often seemed angry and unwilling to do what the rest of the class was doing. I knew I had to get him early on or he'd mess up my class. I vowed not to allow him to pull me off task. I decided to work with him individually, privately. In the beginning of the year he was chronically late to school and late to get started on everything. He'd have to sharpen his pencil, or rearrange his desk, or get a dictionary—he always procrastinated. So the first thing I did was take him aside and tell him what my expectations were. If he didn't get work done because he was late to school or late starting, then he had to miss free time. For three days after that he missed free time and was really angry with me. I refused to talk with him about his anger; I ignored it. Then he tried tears, and I ignored the tears. After the third day I reminded him about getting his work done. He got it done that day and had free time. Robert needed to know that I meant what I said. In addition, of course, I made positive comments to him about other things, so he wouldn't think I was just picking on him.*

Finally, after imposing a penalty, it's a good idea to get back to the student and *reestablish a positive relationship.* At the beginning of this chapter, we saw how Garnetta sent Tanya on an errand after meeting with her in the hall. Similarly, complimenting a student's work or patting a back communicates that there are no hard feelings.

The Issue of Consistency

As Evertson, Emmer, and Worsham (2000) note, "The dictum 'be consistent' has been repeated more frequently than the pledge of allegiance" (p. 133). Beginning teachers are taught that if they do not consistently enforce the rules, students will become confused, will begin to test the limits, and misbehavior will escalate.

On the other hand, teachers often feel trapped by the need for consistency. (See the discussion in Chapter 5 about being fair.) When a normally conscientious student forgets a homework assignment, it seems unreasonable to send the same note home to parents that you would send if a child repeatedly missed assignments. Furthermore, what is an effective consequence for one child may not be effective for another (Dreikurs, Grunwald, & Pepper, 1982). Staying after school might be a negative experience for a child who is eager to go home to play; for a child who has nothing special waiting at home, staying after school could actually be a positive, rewarding experience.

In order to get out of this bind, it's desirable to develop a *hierarchy of generic consequences* that can be applied to all misbehaviors and that have enough flexibility that consequences can be tailored to the needs of particular individuals. Consider the following example:

First violation: Verbal warning
Second time: Name is written down
Third time: Conference with teacher to formulate individual action plan
Fourth time: Call parents
Fifth time: Send to principal.

Another approach is to develop a graduated list of consequences for specific classroom rules. Curwin and Mendler (1988) suggest the following consequences for not bringing in homework:

1. Reminder.
2. Warning.
3. Hand homework in before close of school that day.
4. Stay after school to finish homework.
5. A conference between teacher, student, and parent to develop an action plan for completing homework on time.

Similarly, consequences for fighting on the playground might be (1) sitting on the bench; (2) having to go inside early; or (3) not going out at all.

Curwin and Mendler (1988) recommend explaining in advance to students that "fair is not always equal." They contend that students should be taught it is impossible to have a single solution appropriate for everyone. Just as teachers design instruction to meet students' varying *academic* needs, they select consequences to meet students' varying *social* needs. A range of alternative consequences allows you to be *consistent* with respect to the behavior you expect from students, but *flexible* with respect to the selection of a consequence.

Penalizing the Group for Individual Misbehavior

Sometimes teachers impose a consequence on the whole class even if only one or two children have been misbehaving. The hope is that other students will be angry at receiving a penalty when they weren't misbehaving and will exert pressure on their peers to behave.

We decided to ask our four teachers what they think about this practice. Their responses were extremely consistent. All of them felt the practice was basically unfair and would undermine their efforts to create a caring community. They also believed the practice could backfire by teaching students that "it doesn't pay to be good since you'll be punished anyway." And Garnetta expressed concern about the animosity and physical fighting that might result from penalizing the group. She described instances of children vowing to "get back" at misbehaving students—"We'll take care of you after school."

When we asked our teachers if there were any situations that would prompt them to impose group penalties for individual wrongdoing, there was also remarkable consistency. All of the teachers cited the problem of stealing and described times when they had kept children after school or denied them free time in order to address the problem. Listen to Viviana:

> There was a time when one of my children stole some money from another child. I kept the whole class after school to discuss the problem. I told them, "I'm going to turn my back and I want the money returned. I don't need to know who did it. Let me know when I can turn back to you." Within a few minutes the money was returned, and I dismissed the class.

Garnetta described a similar way of dealing with stealing:

> I said the whole class had to stay after school and explained that the girl's money was "missing." I told them we were going to help find it by spending a few minutes looking around the room. I said that if someone found the money they should put it on my desk. I helped to look too, and a few minutes later I went back to my desk. The money was there.

Dealing with Chronic Misbehavior

Some students with persistent behavior problems fail to respond to the routine strategies we have described so far: nonverbal cues, verbal reminders, and penalties. What additional strategies are available? In this section, we consider three basic approaches. First, we examine a *problem-solving strategy*, which views inappropriate behavior as a conflict that can be solved through discussion and negotiation. Next, we take a look at *four self-management approaches based on principles of behavior modification—namely, self-monitoring, self-evaluation, self-instruction, and contingency contracting.* Finally, we discuss an unconventional strategy called *"reframing,"* in which teachers formulate a positive interpretation of problem behavior and then act in ways that are consistent with that interpretation (Molnar & Lindquist, 1989).

Resolving Conflicts through Problem Solving

Most teachers think in terms of winning or losing when they think about classroom conflicts. According to Thomas Gordon, author of *T.E.T.—Teacher Effectiveness Training* (1974),

> This win-lose orientation seems to be at the core of the knotty issue of discipline in schools. Teachers feel that they have only two approaches to choose from: They can be strict or lenient, tough or soft, authoritarian or permissive. They see the teacher-student relationship as a power struggle, a contest, a fight. . . . When conflicts arise, as they always do, most teachers try to resolve them so that they win, or at least don't lose. This obviously means that students end up losing, or at least not winning. (p. 183)

A third alternative is a "no-lose" problem-solving method of conflict resolution (Gordon, 1974) consisting of six steps. In Step 1, the teacher and the student (or students) *define the problem.* In Step 2, everyone *brainstorms possible solutions.* As in all brainstorming activities, suggestions are not evaluated at this stage. In Step 3, the *solutions are evaluated:* "Now let's take a look at all the solutions that have been proposed and decide which we like and which we don't like. Do you have some preferences?" It is important that you state your own opinions and preferences. Do not permit a solution to stand if it is not really acceptable to you. In Step 4, you and the students involved *decide on the solution that you will try.* If more than one student is involved, it is tempting to vote on the solution, but that's probably not a good idea. Voting always produces winners and losers unless the vote is unanimous, so some people leave the discussion feeling dissatisfied. Instead, try to work for consensus.

Once you have decided which solution to try, you move to Step 5 and *determine how to implement the decision:* Who will do what by when? Finally, in Step 6, *the solution is evaluated.* Sometimes the teacher may want to call everybody together again and ask, "Are you still satisfied with our solution?" It is important for everyone to realize that decisions are not chiseled in granite and that they can be discarded in search of a better solution to the problem.

Approaches Based on Principles of Behavior Modification

Behavior modification programs involve the systematic use of reinforcement to strengthen desired behavior. Probably more research has focused on the effectiveness of behavior modification than any other classroom management approach, and dozens of books on behavior modification techniques are available for teachers (e.g., Alberto & Troutman, 1999).

In recent years, educators have stressed behavioral approaches that involve the student in *self-management:* self-monitoring, self-evaluation, self-instruction, and contingency contracting. The goal of these self-management strategies is to help students learn to regulate their own behavior. The perception of control is crucial in this process: When we feel in control, we are much more likely to accept responsibility for our actions.

Self-Monitoring

Some students may not realize how often they're out of their seats, how frequently they sit daydreaming, or how often they call out during class discussions. Youngsters like this may benefit from a self-monitoring program, in which students learn to observe and record their own behavior during a designated period of time. Interestingly, self-monitoring can have positive effects even when youngsters are inaccurate (Graziano and Mooney, 1984).

Before beginning a self-monitoring program, you need to make sure that students can identify the behaviors targeted for change. For example, some children may not know what "working independently" looks like. You may have to demonstrate, explicitly noting all the component parts: "When I work independently, I am sitting down (without tilting back in my chair). I am looking at the paper on my desk. I am holding my pencil in my hand."

Students then learn how to observe and record their own behavior. This can be done in two ways. The first approach has individuals tally each time they engage in

FIGURE 12-1. An example of a "countoon." (Vernon F. Jones and Louise S. Jones, *Comprehensive Classroom Management: Creating communities of support and solving problems,* 6th ed. Copyright 2001 by Allyn and Bacon. Reprinted with permission.)

the targeted behavior. For example, students can learn to chart the number of math problems they complete during an in-class assignment, the number of times they blurt out irrelevant comments during a discussion, or the number of times they raise their hand to speak. For young children, the tally sheet might contain pictures of the appropriate and inappropriate behaviors. (See the "countoon" suggested by Jones and Jones, 2001, in Figure 12-1.) In the second approach, some sort of a timer is used to cue individuals to observe and record the targeted behavior at regular intervals. At the designated time, students mark a recording sheet with a + or a −, depending on whether they are engaged in the appropriate or inappropriate behavior.

Both Barbara and Ken have used self-monitoring approaches with students who did not respond to the simpler, routine strategies we have discussed. In Ken's class, we watched as this masterful teacher was driven to distraction by Jason, a boy who continually talked to his neighbors, to Ken, and to himself. Nonverbal signals, verbal directives, even penalties worked only momentarily. Eventually teacher and student agreed that Jason would sit at a separate desk in an isolated corner of the room, so he would not disrupt other students. But even there he constantly muttered while working on assignments, blurted out comments during class discussions, and chattered with anyone passing by. When Ken spoke with him about this excessive talking, Jason denied that he was doing it. He seemed like an obvious candidate for a self-monitoring program.

One evening, Ken described the system that he and Jason developed:

I decided to begin by focusing on only one of Jason's irritating behaviors— calling out during class discussions. I used the countoon form [see Figure 12-1] so Jason could record the times he raised his hand and the times he blurted out. In some ways, it wasn't entirely successful: I'd see Jason raise his hand even when he had nothing to say, just to collect marks on the positive side of the countoon. On the other hand, I frequently saw him start to blurt out a comment and then catch himself, so he wouldn't have to record a "call-out." And when he did call out, I could give him a look and he'd reluctantly realize that he had to make a check on that side of the countoon. That did make him more aware of his own behavior, and I did see some improvement.

In Barbara's case, self-monitoring proved useful with a child who continually left the room to go to the bathroom. As in Ken's situation, when Barbara spoke with Louis about how frequently he left, he adamantly rejected her claim. Finally, they decided that Louis would keep count. Barbara placed a tin of bingo markers next to the bathroom pass, which was kept on the chalkboard ledge near the door. Whenever Louis took the bathroom pass, he had to take a bingo marker and put it on his desk. Each day, Barbara and Louis counted the number of bingo markers on his desk. The chips served as indisputable, concrete evidence of his trips. Within days, the number of markers began to decrease.

Self-Evaluation

This self-management approach goes beyond simple self-monitoring by requiring children to judge the quality or acceptability of their behavior. Sometimes self-evaluation is linked with reinforcement, so that an improvement in behavior brings points or rewards.

There is evidence that even young children can learn to do this. In a study by Sainato, Strain, Lefebvre, and Rapp (1990), four preschool children who displayed high rates of inappropriate behaviors (hitting, tantrums, continual talking, lack of social responsiveness) were taught to assess whether they had exhibited appropriate independent seatwork behaviors (i.e., listening to the teacher's directions, sitting appropriately, working quietly). First, each child was photographed modeling the appropriate behaviors. These pictures were then mounted on construction paper, with a caption describing each behavior being modeled. Next to each picture were two faces: a happy face for "yes" and a frowning face for "no." The sheets of paper were covered with clear plastic and then placed in three-ring binders. Each of the four children received their own personalized binder. At the end of each independent seatwork period (20 minutes), the children assessed whether they had exhibited the behaviors, marking the yes or no with an erasable grease pencil. The results demonstrated that even these very young children could learn to accurately evaluate their behaviors. Furthermore, the self-evaluations produced immediate, substantial improvements in the children's behavior.

Self-Instruction

The third self-management approach is self-instruction, in which children learn to give themselves silent directions about how to behave. Most self-instruction strategies are based on Meichenbaum's (1977) five-step process of cognitive behavior modification: (1) an adult performs a task, while talking aloud about it, carefully describing each part; (2) the child performs the task while the adult talks aloud (overt, external guidance); (3) the child performs the task while talking aloud to self (overt self-guidance); (4) the child performs the task while whispering (faded, overt self-guidance); (5) the child performs the task while thinking the directions (covert, self-instruction). This approach has been used to teach impulsive students to approach tasks more deliberately, to help social isolates initiate peer activity, to teach aggressive students to control their anger, and to teach defeated students to try problem solving instead of giving up (Brophy, 1983).

Self-instruction has usually been used in special education classes or in one-to-one settings (e.g., between therapist and client), but a study by Brenda Manning (1988) suggests that it can be successful in general education classrooms as well. Manning worked with first- and third-grade students who had been identified by their teachers as exhibiting inappropriate behavior in class—shouting out, constantly being out of their seats, daydreaming, playing around with things in their desk, and disturbing others. Two times a week, for four consecutive weeks, Manning met with the children in a 50-minute session. First, she modeled appropriate behaviors (e.g., raising hands, staying seated, concentrating, keeping hands and feet to self). Then she had the students perform the behaviors while verbalizing aloud what to do: "If I scream out the answer, others will be disturbed. I will raise my hand and wait my turn. Good for me—see, I can wait!" Finally, students performed the behavior without speaking aloud, but they used "cue cards" as prompts ("I will raise my hand and wait my turn.") Observations of the students after the self-instruction training indicated significant increases in on-task behavior.

Although none of our four teachers have tried self-instruction with students, they have frequently used cue cards to prompt appropriate behavior. They tell us that Post-it notes are a useful "low-tech" tool for this purpose. Post-its can be stuck on desk tops to remind children not to call out, not to tattle, or not to whine. They can be stuck on lockers to help students remember to wear their glasses or to bring their books to class. And one student teacher with a tendency to dominate class discussions applied Post-its to her lesson plans in order to remind herself to "KEEP QUIET AND LET THE KIDS TALK."

Before we leave the discussion of self-monitoring, self-evaluation, and self-instruction, it is important to note that self-management strategies hold particular promise for students with disabilities in general education settings. Only a handful of studies have been conducted in inclusive classrooms, but they indicate that students with disabilities can be taught to use self-management to improve both their social and academic performance (McDougall, 1998). If you decide to try one of these self-management strategies, it would be a good idea to consult with your school's psychologist, a counselor, or a special education teacher.

Contingency Contracting

A contingency or behavior contract is an agreement between a teacher and an individual student that specifies what the student must do to earn a particular reward. Contingency contracts are negotiated with students; both parties must agree on the behaviors students must exhibit, the period of time involved, and the rewards that will result. To be most effective, contracts should be written and signed. And, of course, there should be an opportunity for review and renegotiation if the contract is not working.

Garnetta developed a contingency contract with Ronald, a child who was constantly out of his seat, did very little work, disrupted discussions, and frequently fought with other children. Garnetta told Ronald which behaviors she found most disruptive and irritating, and together they identified alternative, appropriate behaviors. Each week, they drew up a contract, listing the appropriate behaviors that Ronald agreed to work on (e.g., complete my work; raise my hand during discussion; don't get into fights). Then they discussed how many points each behavior was "worth" (e.g., don't get into fights = 4 points) so that daily point values would total 10. At the end of each day, Garnetta and Ronald met to determine how many points he had earned that day and what his reward would be. In addition, Ronald was able to select a GISMOS item from the school store when he reached 25 points. (See Chapter 8 for a description of GISMOS—Grand Incentive System for McKinley's Outstanding Students.) The contract system proved to be effective in reducing Ronald's disruptive behaviors and promoting more appropriate social and academic behaviors.

An example of a contract appears in Figure 12-2.

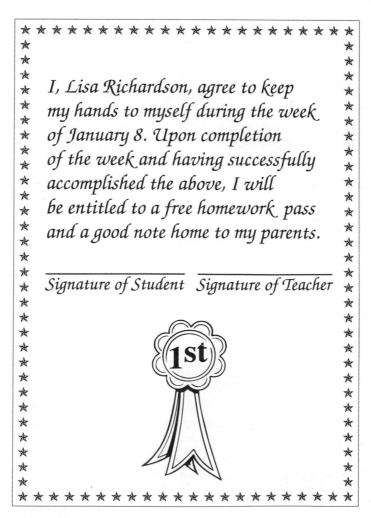

I, Lisa Richardson, agree to keep my hands to myself during the week of January 8. Upon completion of the week and having successfully accomplished the above, I will be entitled to a free homework pass and a good note home to my parents.

Signature of Student   Signature of Teacher

FIGURE 12-2. An example of a contract

Using an Ecosystemic Approach: Changing Problem Behavior by Reframing

We often explain problem behavior by focusing on the characteristics of individual students (e.g., "He's insolent and sarcastic because he comes from a broken home"; "She never participates in class because she's so shy"). These explanations may have some validity, but they are unlikely to help us bring about positive change. Since we cannot alter a student's home environment or basic personality, we may conclude there is nothing we can do and fail to consider ways in which the social context of the classroom is contributing to the problem.

On the other hand, if we take an *ecosystemic perspective,* we recognize that problem behaviors are part of a stable pattern of interpersonal interactions. In other words, the classroom constitutes an *ecosystem* in which every individual's behavior influences and is influenced by everyone else's behavior. According to Alex Molnar and Barbara Lindquist (1989), this is a more optimistic way of approaching problems because it means that we can influence problem behaviors by making changes to the ecosystem. As they put it, "when you want something to change, you must change something" (p. 10).

Given the fact that behaviors can have multiple interpretations, Molnar and Lindquist suggest that a powerful way to change the ecosystem is to formulate an *alternative, positive interpretation of the problem behavior and to act in ways that are consistent with the new interpretation.* This technique is called *reframing.* Let's look at a few examples adapted from Molnar and Linquist's book, *Changing Problem Behavior in Schools* (1989).

Problem behavior:	Brian continually blurts out answers during discussions.
Standard interpretation:	Brian is trying to get attention.
Standard response:	Teacher ignores Brian as long as possible, but eventually chastises him.
Alternative interpretation:	Brian is so intensely engaged in the discussion he forgets to raise his hand.
Problem behavior:	Shandra never participates in class discussions. She also takes a long time to get started on written classroom assignments, so she makes little progress by the end of class.
Standard interpretation:	Since Shandra is capable of doing the work, she is simply being resistant and lazy.
Standard response:	Teacher talks with Shandra about the importance of participating and doing classwork. When that doesn't work, teacher has conference with parents. Teacher also tries giving Shandra special attention for participation.
Alternative interpretation:	Shandra needs to think carefully before participating in discussions or doing written work. She wants to get all her thoughts together before speaking or writing. (Shandra is not resistant or lazy; she is careful and deliberate.)

Not all teachers will find these alternative interpretations plausible, but that doesn't matter. What *does* matter is that you generate an interpretation that is plausible to *you.* Then the *alternative frame can suggest alternative responses.* Reframing helps you to get "unstuck" from routine, unproductive ways of dealing with problem behavior and to consider fresh approaches that change the social context or ecosystem of the classroom.

The following example (adapted from Molnar & Lindquist, 1989, pp. 66–67) illustrates how reframing can transform the situation and influence the problem behavior:

Mike is a fifth-grader who often refused to take part in classroom discussions or to complete written classroom assignments. His teachers attributed his behavior to unwillingness, since he was academically capable of participating and completing his work. In accordance with this attribution, they tried various techniques to get him to work more consistently: they explained the importance of doing assigned work and participating in group discussions; they gave him smaller assignments to complete; they held conferences with his parents; they gave him special attention when he completed his work and showed an interest in discussions. None of these approaches had much effect.

After consultation with the school counselor, Mike's teachers agreed to try reframing. When Mike refused to participate in group discussions, they attributed his behavior to a desire to think before contributing: "We know it is important for you to consider all the facts and do a lot of good thinking before you raise your hand and enter into the group discussion. Take all the time you feel is necessary. . . ." For classroom work, the positive connotation was: "It is OK that you do a lot of good thinking before you start your written assignments. You need that time to get your thoughts together." Consistent with this positive connotation, Mike's teachers stopped nagging him to get his work done and be an active member in a discussion group.

For the first two days after these statements were made to him, Mike continued to refuse to do his work. Then he began to act as though he was thinking, but still did not complete his work or say much in discussions. Four days after the statements had been made to him, Mike began to finish his written work and enter into group discussions more consistently. Now Mike's teachers report that he seldom refuses to do his work and seems much happier.

Mike's teachers recognize that their interpretation of his problem behavior—*that he is simply unwilling to participate in class activities*—has led to unproductive responses. They and Mike are in a rut, and a different approach is obviously needed. With the counselor's help, they reframe the situation. They formulate an alternative, positive interpretation of the behavior that they find plausible: *Mike needs time to think.* They then act in ways that are consistent with the new interpretation: *They did not nag him about getting his work done or about being an active participant in the discussion.* This leads to an increase in Mike's participation and in finishing assignments. In short, by changing their own behavior to reflect the new interpretation, these teachers have changed the ecosystem of the classroom, bringing about a positive change in Mike's behavior.

Dealing with Thorny Problems

Every semester, student teachers from extremely different placements return to campus with similar tales of behavior that they find especially vexing or troublesome. It's impossible to generate recipes for dealing with these problems, since every instance is unique in terms of key players, circumstances, and history. Nonetheless, it is helpful to reflect on ways to deal with them *before* they occur and to hear some of the thinking that guides the actions of our four experienced teachers. In this section of the chapter, we will consider seven behaviors that keep teachers awake at night wondering what to do.

Tattling

Fortunately, tattling is generally confined to the lower grades; unfortunately, it can become an epidemic if allowed to go unchecked, creating a negative atmosphere and wasting instructional time. Furthermore, if tattling is encouraged or condoned, children receive the message that only "a higher authority" can settle disputes and resolve problems.

All four teachers stress the fact that children need to understand the difference between alerting the teacher to a dangerous or hurtful situation and reporting minor infractions or perceived injustices. This may require explicit lessons, during which the class discusses what tattling is, how it affects the atmosphere in the classroom, and the importance of learning to settle one's own problems (Charles & Senter, 1995). Sometimes students need practice in distinguishing among situations that call for different responses: instances when a particular situation demands an immediate report to the teacher (e.g., you see a classmate about to jab someone with a pair of scissors); situations that they should try to resolve by themselves (e.g., your neighbor is mumbling to herself and it's annoying you); and situations that can be ignored (e.g., you see a classmate use the pencil sharpener when he shouldn't be). Of course, if you encourage students to try resolving their own problems, then you need to equip them with some strategies (e.g., using an I-message to the student who is being a bother).

Viviana, Garnetta, Barbara, and Ken try to convey the message that they are available for students when serious problems arise, but that they are uninterested in minor, petty complaints. When tattling does occur, they try to discourage it. Ken sometimes asks, "Why are you telling me this?" When the student explains ("Well, he took my paper . . ."), Ken follows up with questions such as:

What else could you do, besides telling me?

Is this serious?

Can you talk to him?

Do you want to write about it?

Garnetta also suggests that children write about the problem and promises to read what they have written later, when she has the time. This usually discourages any further discussion, unless the situation is really upsetting to the child.

Very often, tattling occurs after lunch or recess, when students return to class with stories about problems that have occurred in the cafeteria or on the playground. Barbara deals with situations like these by telling students, "Unless you were hurt, I don't need to hear about it." If lunchtime or recess incidents begin to disrupt classroom life, however, it may be necessary to deal with the problem directly, either with the individual children involved or with the whole class. (See Barbara's problem-solving session described in Chapter 5.)

Cheating

As teachers increasingly emphasize collaboration, cooperative learning, and peer tutoring, both they and students are finding it harder to distinguish cheating from sharing. Furthermore, in classrooms where helping one another is the normal way of working, it can be difficult for students to shut off this mode of operation and move into individual, independent activities such as test taking. Desks arranged in clusters can also contribute to the difficulty. As we discussed in Chapter 3, clusters foster discussion and sharing— even during a test, when students are supposed to work independently.

It's obviously better to deal with cheating before it occurs, rather than afterwards. This means finding ways to *diminish the temptation to cheat.* You can discuss cheating in a class meeting, during which you can explain the difference between helping and cheating, demonstrate the expected behavior for various activities, and have students distinguish between situations when it's appropriate or inappropriate to share ideas. You can also explain the difference between *learning* and *performance* and make it clear that your job is to help students *learn.* Anderman, Griesinger, and Westerfield (1998) found that students are more likely to report that they have cheated when teachers are perceived as emphasizing performance over mastery (i.e., when it's more important to get an A on a test than to master the material). Similarly, students more often report that they have cheated when teachers rely on extrinsic incentives to stimulate motivation (e.g., giving homework passes to students who get As on a test) rather than trying to foster genuine interest in academic tasks.

In addition to reducing temptation, you can also take a number of simple precautions to *minimize opportunity.* When giving tests, for example, it's helpful to separate desks, circulate throughout the room, use new tests each year, and create different forms of the same test. In the case of standardized testing, it's a good idea to rearrange the desks several days in advance, so students can adjust to the new layout.

Obviously, despite all your precautions, incidents of cheating will occur. It then becomes necessary to confront the students involved. Here are some suggestions for handling those encounters:

Talk privately. Once again, avoid creating a situation where the student may be publicly humiliated. This is likely to lead to a series of accusations and denials that get more and more heated.

Present your reasons for suspecting cheating. Lay out your evidence calmly and firmly, even sorrowfully.

Express concern. Make it clear that you do not expect this kind of behavior from this student. Try to find out why students cheated (e.g., Were they simply unprepared? Are they under a lot of pressure to excel?)

Explain consequences. A common response to cheating is to give the student a low grade or a zero on the assignment or test. This seems like a sensible solution at first glance, but it confounds the act of cheating with the student's mastery of the content (Cangelosi, 1993). In other words, a person looking at the teacher's grade book would be unable to tell if the low grade meant the student had violated the test-taking procedures or if it indicated a failure to learn the material. We prefer using a logical consequence; namely, having the student redo the assignment or test under more carefully controlled conditions. Some schools have predetermined consequences for cheating, such as detention and parental notification. If so, you need to follow your school's policy.

Discuss the consequences for subsequent cheating. Alert the student to the consequences for additional cheating incidents. If the student continues to cheat, investigate the reasons for this behavior. Students may cheat on a test because they watched television instead of studying, but they may also cheat because their parents are putting excessive pressure on them to achieve, they have unrealistic goals for themselves, or they do not have the skills or background necessary to succeed on the test (Grossman, 1995). Clearly, these different causes of the cheating call for different responses.

Finally, you need to think about your response to the child who *gives* help on a task. Often, the desire to follow the teacher's directions and to stay out of trouble clashes with a child's desire to assist friends who are having difficulty (Bloome & Theodorou, 1988). This may be a particular dilemma for children who come from cultures that teach children to be generous; Hawaiian American and Hispanic students, for example, may feel that helping friends is a necessity even though the teacher views it as cheating (Grossman, 1995).

Stealing

Like tattling, most stealing incidents occur in the early grades when students have less control over their impulses and when they are still learning the difference between sharing and taking what doesn't belong to them. Again, it's important to help young children distinguish between these two situations. Usually, a simple reminder about rules relating to personal property should help, but remember that a rule like "respect other people's property" has to be clearly operationalized for children.

In addition to age, cultural differences may also play a role in the confusion between sharing and taking. Some cultures emphasize sharing and generosity, while others stress private ownership. For example, Grossman (1984) observes that when teachers try to explain that "what's mine is mine and what's yours is yours," Hispanic students may feel "bewildered, confused or even rejected and insulted" (p. 89).

If an incident of stealing does occur, and you know who the culprit is, you can have a quiet, private conversation about what has happened. If you are not sure that the child understands the difference between sharing and taking, it is best to avoid direct accusations: "I'm sure you forgot that his markers were in your backpack when you went home, but you need to bring them back tomorrow." When the child returns the markers, you can take a more instructional approach: "I'm glad you brought the markers back. You know, you shouldn't be putting other people's property in your backpack. Even though it was an accident, some people might call it stealing, and I know you wouldn't want to be accused of that."

Depending on the value of the property, the frequency of incidence, and the grade level you are teaching, it may be necessary to intervene more forcefully. As we mentioned earlier, all of our teachers have used whole-class pressure to have the stolen materials returned. Sometimes, you may even need to contact families or refer the problem to the principal. It's a good idea to confer with the principal before conducting a search of backpacks or lockers.

Profanity

The use of profanity in school has risen as children are increasingly exposed to inappropriate language at home and through the media. In deciding on a suitable response, it's useful to think about the reasons that students use profanity. Once again, age plays a role. Younger children may simply be echoing language they have heard used by friends, by family, or on television, with little or no understanding of the meaning. In this case, the appropriate response is instructional, not disciplinary. You need to explain that "we don't use words like that in school." You might ask the children if they know what the words mean and suggest they talk with their parents; it might also be helpful to contact parents and ask them to speak with their children.

Children may also use profanity because they hear it used frequently at home, and it has become a regular part of their speaking vocabulary. In this case, you can make it clear that language like that is inappropriate and unacceptable in school. Barbara reminds students that *she* doesn't use that language at school, and she doesn't expect *them* to use it either.

Finally, there are times when students angrily direct profanity toward another student or the teacher. When this happens, you need to stress that using language to hurt other people will not be tolerated and that there are more acceptable ways of expressing anger. Sometimes children are so angry that they blurt out profanities without thinking about the context. In this case, it's wise to allow them time to calm down before trying to discuss what happened. It's also helpful to address the reasons for their anger before addressing the inappropriateness of their language.

Defiance

When we asked Barbara, Garnetta, Ken, and Viviana to tell us about the ways they deal with defiance, our question was met with unusual silence. Finally, Ken ventured to explain that his students rarely acted in defiant ways, so it was hard for him to say what he'd do. The three other teachers murmured their agreement. We were initially skeptical, but as we talked, it became clear that the answer lay in the teachers' ability to prevent minor problems from escalating into major ones. Consider Garnetta's way of dealing with Ebony, a child who had "spent the entire second grade in the office":

> *Ebony was constantly picking fights, calling names, and talking back to the teacher. . . . Obviously, I couldn't wait to have her in my class. But when she came to me, one of the first things she said was "No one ever listens to me." I took that as my cue. I made sure to listen to her. And I'd always try to anticipate a problem. I'd see her beginning to act up—maybe going to poke someone—and I'd immediately go over and quietly tell her to come into the hall with me. I never got into an argument with her in front of everyone. I'd be real calm, and we'd go out, and I'd ask her what was happening. She'd tell me why she was mad, and I'd listen, and we'd talk about what she could do when she got that way. She hardly ever had to go to the office. But if I had let things go, the other child would have poked back. Then a fight would have erupted, and she'd have ended up in the principal's office again.*

Defiant situations can usually be avoided if teachers follow Garnetta's model. Having said that, we still need to consider what to do if a student *does* become defiant. Here are some suggestions:

Stay in control of yourself. Even though your first inclination may be to shout back, don't. (It may help to take a few deep breaths and to use self-talk: "I can handle this calmly. I'm going to speak quietly.")

Direct the rest of the class to work on something. (e.g., "Everyone do the next three problems" or "Start reading the next section").

Move the student away from peers. Talk to the student in an area where you can have more privacy. This eliminates the need for the student to worry about saving face.

Stand a few feet away from the student (i.e., don't get "in his face"). A student who is feeling angry and defiant may interpret closing in on him as an aggressive act (Wolfgang, 1999).

Acknowledge the student's feelings. "I can see that you're really angry. . ."

Avoid a power struggle. "I'm the boss in here and I'm telling you to . . ."

Offer a choice. "I can see that you're really upset, and we'll have to talk later. But meanwhile, here are the choices. You can go to the office, or I'll have to send for someone to come and get you."

Sexually Related Behavior

Our often-repeated reminder to consider children's developmental levels is particularly relevant here. In an early childhood classroom, it's not unusual to see children occasionally rubbing their genitals. Usually they will stop as soon as you divert their attention or get them more actively involved in the lesson. Viviana simply tells her first-graders that she wants to see everyone's hands on their desks. If the masturbation continues, however, she has a private conversation with the individual student:

I don't want to embarrass the child, but if I don't stop it, the other children will see and start to make fun. Maybe the child doesn't even know this is not proper to do in school. I'll say something like, "I don't want you to put your hands inside your pants. It's not bad, but it's not something people do at school."

Depending on the situation, you might also contact parents, ask them to speak with their child, and suggest some simple ways of curbing the behavior—for example, having children wear pants that require a belt instead of pants with an elastic waist.

By the time students reach fourth grade, they generally know that masturbation is inappropriate in school. If you do see a youngster engaging in this behavior, however, you need to deal with the situation very discreetly—and before the other children notice and begin to taunt. Barbara uses this approach: "I've seen what you've been doing at your seat during quiet times, and it's not something you should be doing in school. Is everything OK?"

It's also necessary to consider developmental level when you see a child touching another child in a sexual way. Again, it's not unusual for kindergarten children to explore each other's bodies; a simple directive to stop and a reminder to "keep your hands to yourself" will usually take care of the matter. At intermediate grade levels (four through six), students need to be aware of what constitutes sexual harassment and to know that it will not be tolerated in the school environment. They also need to know that they can report incidents of sexual harassment and that the adults in the school will take action.

At *any* elementary grade level, habitual masturbation and behaviors that are sexually precocious or explicit warrant investigation. Children who continue to masturbate even after you have spoken to them may have severe problems, and children who imitate adult sexual behavior may have witnessed such activity firsthand or experienced it themselves. In cases like these, you need to contact the appropriate child welfare agency. (See Chapter 13 for signs of abuse and reporting procedures.)

Failure to Do Homework

When students consistently fail to do homework assignments, it's important to consider just how valuable those assignments are and if you have communicated that value to students. It's also important to reflect on how much homework you're assigning, if it's too difficult for students to complete independently, and whether the time allotted is sufficient.

Here are some additional strategies that can help increase the likelihood of students completing homework:

Provide homework planners. Not only do homework planners help students to remember their assignments, they also allow parents to see what homework their children have and send messages to the child's teacher using the planner. Homework planners have a particularly positive effect on students with learning disabilities and average-achieving students who have homework problems (Bryan & Sullivan-Burstein, 1998).

Review, collect, or grade assignments. If you assign homework and then fail to check that students have done it, you're conveying the message that the homework just wasn't that important. Not all homework has to be graded, or even collected, but it's wise to check that students have done it and to record that fact in your grade book.

Have children graph their homework completion. Students can create their own graphs showing the homework assignments not turned in (red), complete and on time (green), or complete but late (yellow) (Bryan & Sullivan-Burstein, 1998).

Give "homework quizzes." Some teachers give a daily quiz with one or two questions that are just like those assigned the night before for homework. In addition, they give a "homework quiz" every week or two. They select a few problems that were previously given for homework and allow students to refer to their homework papers, but not their books.

Require a "product" in addition to reading. Students are far more likely to do reading if you also have them do something *with* it (e.g., use Post-it notes to mark your three favorite passages; list 10 words or phrases the author uses to give clues about the protagonist's character; generate three questions about the reading to ask your classmates).

Provide in-school support. Sometimes, students' home circumstances may interfere with doing homework. They may be in the midst of a family crisis. They may be living in an abusive situation. They may have after-school responsibilities (like caring for younger siblings) that leave little time for schoolwork. In situations like this, you might work with the student to develop a plan for getting homework done in school.

Despite your best efforts, some students will still not turn in homework. In this case, you need to meet individually to discuss the problem, generate possible solutions, and decide on an action plan. This might include contacting parents and asking for their co-operation and assistance, writing a contingency contract, or assigning a "homework buddy" to help the student remember and complete homework.

Concluding Comments

One afternoon after school, we talked with Garnetta about the problems her students bring with them to school. She displayed considerable empathy and insight into their home situations. Nonetheless, she emphasized that she had high expectations for their behavior and achievement:

It's up to us to teach students to be responsible, to have standards, and to demand that work gets done. We can't simply say, "They can't help it," or "They didn't do it, so it's a zero." You've got to discuss expectations and keep plugging away. I see so many kids kicked out of class, and I think to myself, "Did you talk with them? What did you try before you gave up and sent them out?" Some days I feel like I've had it too. But then I remind myself that I'm in charge of this classroom. I'm responsible for what goes on here.

Garnetta's comments recall findings from a study on the ways teachers cope with problem students (Brophy and Rohrkemper, 1981). One basic factor that distinguished more effective teachers from less effective teachers was their *willingness to take responsibility*. They used a variety of strategies: Some used behavioral approaches—negotiating contracts, providing rewards, praising desirable behavior—while others tried to build positive relationships, provide encouragement, and foster self-esteem. Regardless, effective teachers were willing to assume the responsibility for managing children's behavior. In sharp contrast, *less effective teachers tended to disclaim responsibility and to refer problems to other school personnel* (e.g., the principal, guidance counselor, etc.).

Clearly, our four teachers are willing to take responsibility for the behavior of their students. Like Garnetta, they recognize that they are "in charge" and that they are accountable for what happens in their classrooms. Furthermore, they are willing to admit when they themselves have contributed to misbehavior that occurs. Listen to Barbara:

Sometimes, everyone will be getting "into" a heated discussion, and I sort of suspend the rule about raising hands. All of a sudden I realize it's getting chaotic. That's not the kids' fault. I let it happen. It would be unfair to lash out at them for calling out. I just say, "Whoa . . .this is getting out of hand. Let's calm down and remember to raise hands."

We agree with Barbara, Garnetta, Viviana, and Ken that teachers need to assume responsibility for children's behavior problems, and we hope that this chapter will help you to feel more competent in this area. Nonetheless, there are times when you have to recognize that a child's problem is so deeply rooted that you need special assistance. In this case, it's your responsibility to see that the child receives the help you're unable to provide. As Barbara observes:

When you've gone the whole route, you've tried all the strategies you know, you've brainstormed solutions, and nothing works for more than one-and-a-half weeks, then you have to go for help. Sometimes you have to understand that the problem is bigger than what's going on in the classroom. The child has a greater need than you can fill. Sometimes I have someone from special services or a colleague come in and observe and then conference with me. The school psychologist has also been helpful.

For example, a few years ago I had a girl I just couldn't reach. She was a victim of sexual abuse. I liked her and she liked me, but I couldn't get her to change her behavior. She would sing in class. I'd say, "You can't do that. It disturbs other people." So she'd stop, but then she'd begin tapping her pencil. I'd take the pencil away, and then she'd take her beads off and rub the beads along the edge of the desk. I'd take her beads, and then she'd bang her head on the desk. She was finally classified as emotionally disturbed and is getting the kind of help she needs.

With experience, you learn to tell the difference between a student who's just being a pain in the neck and a student who's really in need. And then it's your responsibility to get help for that child.

We turn to this topic in Chapter 13, where we discuss helping children with special needs.

⊞ Summary

Inappropriate behavior threatens order by interrupting the flow of classroom activity. This chapter discussed ways of responding to a variety of problems—from minor, nondisruptive infractions to chronic, more serious misbehaviors.

Guidelines for dealing with misbehavior

- Use disciplinary strategies that preserve the dignity of the student.

    Separate the student's character from the specific misbehavior.
    Encourage students to take responsibility for regulating their own behavior.

- Try to keep the instructional program going with a minimum of disruption.
- Consider the context of students' actions. Behavior that is acceptable in one context may be unacceptable in another.
- Match your disciplinary strategy to the misbehavior.

Strategies for dealing with minor misbehavior

- Nonverbal interventions.
- Verbal interventions:

    Direct student to the task at hand.
    State student's name.
    Remind student of rule.

Call on student.
Use gentle humor.
Use an I-message.
- Ignore misbehavior that is fleeting.

Strategies for dealing with more serious misbehavior
- Plan penalties ahead of time.
- Choose penalties that are logically related to misbehavior.
- Impose penalties calmly and quietly.
- Reestablish a positive relationship with the student as quickly as possible.
- Develop a range of alternative consequences.

Strategies for dealing with chronic misbehavior
- Problem-solving process:
  Step 1: Define the problem.
  Step 2: Brainstorm possible solutions.
  Step 3: Evaluate solutions.
  Step 4: Decide on a solution to try.
  Step 5: Determine how to implement the decision.
  Step 6: Evaluate the solution.

- Behavior modification approaches:
  Self-monitoring.
  Self-evaluation.
  Self-instruction.
  Contingency contracting.

- An ecosystemic approach:
  Recognize your current interpretation of the problem.
  Formulate an alternative, positive interpretation (reframe the situation).
  Act in ways that are consistent with the new interpretation.

Dealing with thorny problems
- Tattling.
- Cheating.
- Stealing.
- Profanity.
- Defiance.
- Sexually related behavior.
- Failure to do homework.

Effective teachers are willing to take responsibility for managing students' behavior. Sometimes, however, you may have a student whose problems are just too severe for you to handle alone. If so, it is your responsibility to get this child outside help.

Activities

1. Beginning teachers sometimes overreact to misbehavior or take no action at all because they simply don't know what to do or say. Read each of the following situations and devise a nonverbal intervention, a verbal cue, and an "I message."

Example	Nonverbal	Verbal	I-Message
A student writes on the desk.	Hand the student an eraser.	"We use paper to write on."	"When you write on the desk, the custodian complains to me, and I get embarrassed."
A student makes a big show of looking through her book bag for her homework, distracting other students and delaying the start of the lesson.	Give the "look."	"We're ready to begin."	"When you take so long to get your things out, I can't begin the lesson, and I get very frustrated by the lost time."

   a. A student is copying from another student's paper.

   b. A student takes another student's notebook.

   c. A student sharpens his pencil during your presentation.

   d. A student calls out instead of raising her hand.

2. When a misbehavior occurs, there usually isn't much time for careful consideration of logical consequences. We've listed a few typical misbehaviors for your practice. What are two logical consequences for each example?

   a. Your class monitor keeps forgetting to clean the gerbil cage, and it is beginning to smell.

   b. Tom always takes longer than the other children to get settled in after snack time, and most times he is still eating when it is time to get back to work.

   c. Rachel spends her computer time playing with the contents of her purse.

   d. As part of a laboratory group, Lou mishandles supplies, causing spills and complaints from his group members.

e. Meagan draws all over Shelissa's face with a purple magic marker.

f. Ross rubs glue all over his hands so that he can peel it off when it dries.

g. Ariana returns her novel with ripped pages and the cover missing.

3. Develop a behavior modification plan (such as self-monitoring or a contingency contract) to deal with the following problems:

a. Arthur is larger than the other children in your second-grade class. A day has not gone by that a child hasn't come to you complaining of Arthur's hitting, pushing, or teasing. You've talked to his parents, but they are at a loss about what to do.

b. Cynthia, a fifth-grader, rarely completes her work. She daydreams, socializes with others, misunderstands directions, and gets upset when you speak to her about her incomplete work. The problem seems to be getting worse.

4. Try reframing a problem behavior according to an ecosystemic approach. First, think of a problem you are currently having. What is your current interpretation of the behavior? How do you typically respond to the behavior? Next, consider some positive alternative interpretations of the behavior. Based on one of the explanations, how might you respond differently?

5. What would you do in the following situation? You are reviewing homework from the night before. You call on James to do number 5. He slumps in his seat and fidgets with the chain around his neck. You tell him the class is waiting for his answer to number 5. Finally he mutters, "I didn't do the f____ homework."

For Further Reading

Curwin, R. L., & Mendler, A. N. (1988). *Discipline with dignity.* Alexandria, VA: Association for Supervision and Curriculum Development.

Dreikurs, R., Grunwald, B. B., & Pepper, F. C. (1982). *Maintaining sanity in the classroom: Classroom management techniques* (2nd ed.). New York: Harper & Row.

Gordon, T. (1974). *T.E.T.—Teacher Effectiveness Training.* New York: Peter H. Wyden.

Jones, F. H. (2001). *Fredric Jones's Tools for Teaching.* Santa Cruz, CA: Fredric H. Jones & Associates.

Walker, H. M., Colvin, G., & Ramsey, E. (1995). *Antisocial behavior in school: Strategies and best practices.* Pacific Grove, CA: Brooks/Cole.

References

Alberto, P. A., & Troutman, A. C. (1999). *Applied behavior analysis for teachers.* (5th ed.). Columbus, OH: Merrill.

Anderman, E. M., Griesinger, T., & Westerfield, G. (1998). Motivation and cheating during early adolescence. *Journal of Educational Psychology, 90*(1), 84–93.

Bloome, D., & Theodorou, E. (1988). Analyzing teacher–student and student–student discourse. In J. E. Green & J. O. Harker (Eds.), *Multiple perspective analyses of classroom discourse.* (pp. 217–248). Norwood, NJ: Ablex.

Brophy, J. E. (1983). Classroom organization and management. *The Elementary School Journal, 83*(4), 265–285.

Brophy, J., and Rohrkemper, M. (1981). The influence of problem ownership on teachers' perceptions of and strategies for coping with problem students. *Journal of Educational Psychology, 73,* 295–311.

Bryan, T., & Sullivan-Burstein, K. (1998). Teacher-selected strategies for improving homework completion. *Remedial and Special Education, 19*(5), 263–275.

Cairns, L. G. (1987). Behaviour problems. In M. J. Dunkin (Ed.), *The International Encyclopedia of Teaching and Teacher Education* (pp. 446–452). New York: Pergamon Press.

Cangelosi, J. S. (1993). *Classroom management strategies: Gaining and maintaining students' cooperation* (2nd ed.). New York: Longman.

Charles, C. M., and Senter, G. W. (1995). *Elementary classroom management* (2nd ed.). New York: Longman.

Créton, H. A., Wubbels, T., & Hooymayers, H. P. (1989). Escalated disorderly situations in the classroom and the improvement of these situations. *Teaching & Teacher Education, 5*(3), 205–215.

Curwin, R. L., & Mendler, A. N. (1988). *Discipline with dignity.* Alexandria, VA: Association for Supervision and Curriculum Development.

Delpit, L. (1995). *Other people's children.* New York: The New Press.

Doyle, W. (1986). Classroom organization and management. In M. C. Wittrock (Ed.), *Handbook of research on teaching* (pp. 392–431). New York: Macmillan.

Dreikurs, R., Grunwald, B. B., & Pepper, F. C. (1982). *Maintaining sanity in the classroom: Classroom management techniques* (2nd ed.). New York: Harper & Row.

Emmer, E. T., & Aussiker, A. (1990). School and classroom discipline programs: How well do they work? In O. C. Moles (Ed.), *Student discipline strategies* (pp. 129–165). New York: SUNY Press.

Emmer, E. T., Evertson, C. M., & Anderson, L. M. (1980). Effective classroom management at the beginning of the school year. *Elementary School Journal, 80*(5), 219–231.

Evans, W. H., Evans, S. S., & Schmid, R. E. (1989). *Behavior and instructional management: An ecological approach.* Boston: Allyn and Bacon.

Evertson, C. M. (1989). Classroom organization and management. In M. C. Reynolds (Ed.), *Knowledge base for the beginning teacher* (pp. 59–70). New York: Pergamon Press.

Evertson, C. M., Emmer, E. T., & Worsham, M. E. (2000). *Classroom management for elementary teachers* (5th ed.). Boston: Allyn & Bacon.

Good, T. L., and Brophy, J. E. (2000). *Looking in classrooms* (8th ed.). New York: HarperCollins.

Gordon, T. (1974). *T.E.T.—Teacher Effectiveness Training.* New York: Peter H. Wyden.

Graziano, A. M., and Mooney, K. C. (1984). *Children and behavior therapy.* New York: Aldine.

Grossman, H. (1984). *Educating Hispanic students: Cultural implications for instruction, classroom management, counseling, and assessment.* Springfield, IL: Thomas.

Grossman, H. (1995). *Classroom behavior management in a diverse society.* Mountain View, CA: Mayfield.

Janney, R., & Snell, M. E., with contributions from Elliott, J., Pitonyak, C. R., Burton, C. C., & Colley, K. M. (2000). *Behavioral Support.* Baltimore: Paul Brookes Publishing.

Johnston, R. C. (November 24, 1999). Decatur furor sparks wider policy debate. *Education Week, 19*(3), 1, 12.

Jones, F. H. (2001). *Fredric Jones's Tools for Teaching.* Santa Cruz, CA: Fredric H. Jones & Associates.

Jones, V. F., & Jones, L. S. (2001). *Comprehensive classroom management: Creating communities of support and solving problems* (6th ed.). Boston: Allyn and Bacon.

Kneedler, R. D., and Hallahan, D. P. (1981). Self-monitoring of on-task behavior with learning disabled children: Current studies and directions. *Exceptional Education Quarterly, 2,* 73–81.

Kounin, J. S. (1970). *Discipline and group management in classrooms.* New York: Holt, Rinehart and Winston.

Lasley, T. J., Lasley, J. O., & Ward, S. H. (1989). Activities and desists used by more and less effective classroom managers. Paper presented at the annual meeting of the American Educational Research Association, San Francisco.

Manning, B. H. (1988). Application of cognitive behavior modification: First and third graders' self-management of classroom behaviors. *American Educational Research Journal, 25*(2), 193–212.

McDougall, D. (1998). Research on self-management techniques used by students with disabilities in general education settings: A descriptive review. *Remedial and Special Education, 19*(5), 310–320.

Meichenbaum, D. (1977). *Cognitive behavior modification.* New York: Plenum.

Molnar, A., & Lindquist, B. (1989). *Changing problem behavior in schools.* San Francisco: Jossey-Bass.

Pittman, S. I. (1985). Cognitive ethnography and quantification of a first-grade teacher's selection routines for classroom management. *The Elementary School Journal, 85*(4), 541–558.

Rief, S. F. (1993). *How to reach and teach ADD/ADHD children.* West Nyack, NY: The Center for Applied Research in Education.

Sack, J. L. (June 7, 2000). ADHD student's expulsion voided. *Education Week, 19*(39), 4.

Sainato, D. M., Strain, P. S. Lefebvre, D., & Rapp, N. (1990). Effects of self-evaluation on the independent work skills of preschool children with disabilities. *Exceptional Children, 56*(6), 540–549.

Turco, T. L., and Elliott, S. N. (1986). Assessment of students' acceptability ratings of teacher-initiated interventions for classroom misbehavior. *Journal of School Psychology, 24,* 277–283.

Valentine, G. Fall, (1998). Lessons from home (an interview with Lisa Delpit). *Teaching Tolerance, 7*(2), 15–19.

Walker, J. E., & Shea, T. M. (1995). *Behavior management: A practical approach for educators.* Englewood Cliffs, NJ: Merrill/Prentice Hall.

Wolfgang, C. H. (1999). *Solving discipline problems: Methods and models for today's teachers.* Boston: Allyn and Bacon.

Chapter Thirteen

Helping Students with Special Needs

Today's elementary classrooms are far more diverse than ever before. Recent increases in immigration have led to classes in which children come from a wide range of cultural and linguistic backgrounds. Efforts to achieve inclusive classrooms have meant that children with disabilities, who would have previously been taught in separate classrooms or even special schools, are now educated in general education classrooms.

In addition to being more diverse, classrooms contain a greater number of children who suffer from conditions associated with poverty. Consider these statistics from the Annie E. Casey Foundation (1999) and the Children's Defense Fund (1999):

Despite the economic boom of the 1990s, the proportion of children living in poverty—14.7 million or nearly 21 percent—has changed little over the past decade. During the 1990s, there was a significant increase in the number of children living in "working-poor" families, from 4.3 million in 1989 to 5.6 million in 1997.

The U.S. child poverty rate is among the highest (if not *the* highest) in the developed world.

More than 10.7 million children, or 15 percent, do not have health insurance. These children are more likely to suffer from health problems because they have fewer physician visits each year and are less likely to receive adequate preventive services and immunizations.

Nineteen percent of American children, or nearly 13.3 million, are growing up in homes where the head of the household is not a high school graduate. Children born to a mother without a high school diploma are twice as likely to drop out of school as the children of a mother who is a high school graduate.

The United States ranks first among industrialized nations in rates of teenage pregnancy. The teen birth rate is twice as high as the next highest country (United Kingdom). Children born to teenage mothers are more likely to drop out of school, give birth out of wedlock, divorce or separate, and be dependent on welfare.

The number of abused and neglected children doubled between 1986 and 1993. Child abuse, neglect, and family violence are all closely linked with alcohol and other drug use. Three-quarters of the 12 million Americans who say they regularly use illegal drugs have children under the age of 12 at home. Illicit drugs are involved in half the reported incidents of family violence, while alcohol is involved in three-quarters of the cases.

Nationally, 9.2 million children, or 13 percent, are growing up with four or more risk factors (e.g., poverty, absence of health insurance, low parental educational level). Nearly 30 percent of all Black children and nearly 25 percent of all Hispanic children are in this high-risk category, compared to only 6 percent of all White children.

The message in these alarming statistics is clear: Large numbers of America's youth are growing up in circumstances that delay their development; create physical, emotional, and psychological problems; and jeopardize their futures. (For a chilling picture of the plight of America's children, see Figure 13-1.) Furthermore, *when these youngsters come to school, their problems come with them.* Children who are frightened, hungry, or abused can't leave their problems at the door and participate wholeheartedly in classroom activities.

How can you help the children with special needs who may be in your classroom? One answer is to be informed about the various special services that are available and to know how to obtain access to those services. Maynard Reynolds, a leading special educator, writes:

> *It is too much to ask that a beginning teacher know about all of the problems he or she will encounter in teaching; but it is not too much to ask that the beginning teacher recognize needs for support and assistance when challenging problems arise, and to understand that it is a sign of*

Every 1 second	a public high school student is suspended.*
Every 9 seconds	a high school student drops out.*
Every 10 seconds	a public school student is corporally punished.*
Every 20 seconds	a child is arrested.
Every 24 seconds	a baby is born to an unmarried mother.
Every 37 seconds	a baby is born to a mother who is not a high school graduate.
Every 44 seconds	a baby is born into poverty.
Every 1 minute	a baby is born to a teen mother.
Every 2 minutes	a baby is born at low birthweight (less than 5 lbs., 8 oz.).
Every 4 minutes	a baby is born to a mother who had late or no prenatal care.
Every 4 minutes	a child is arrested for drug abuse.
Every 8 minutes	a child is arrested for a violent crime.
Every 9 minutes	a baby is born at very low birthweight (less than 3lbs., 4 oz.)
Every 19 minutes	a baby dies.
Every 42 minutes	a child or youth under 20 dies from an accident.
Every 2 hours 20 minutes	a child or youth under 20 is killed by a firearm.
Every 3 hours	a child or youth under 20 is a homicide victim.
Every 4 hours	a child or youth under 20 commits suicide.
Every day	a young person under 25 dies from HIV infection.

*Based on calculations per school day (180 days of seven hours each)

FIGURE 13-1. Moments in America for All Children. Reprinted with permission. Children's Defense Fund, The State of America's Children Yearbook 2001. Washington, D.C.: Children's Defense Fund, 2001.

professionalism to seek help when needed rather than a sign of weakness. (Reynolds, 1989, p. 138)

Seeking help does *not* mean that you are "off the hook." We strongly believe that *teachers are responsible for all the children in their classes, including those with special needs.* This may mean communicating and collaborating with special services personnel in order to provide children with appropriate educational experiences. It *also* means working with special-needs children when they are in your room—not putting them in the back and ignoring them—like the teacher in this journal entry written by one of our students:

There's a boy in my classroom who goes to a resource room every day for reading and math. When he's in the classroom, he sits in a back corner, basically doing nothing. My cooperating teacher gives him some worksheets to do, but doesn't even really monitor to see if he does them. He never includes him in any of the class's activities. Sometimes the boy wanders around the room, looking at what the other kids are doing, and I get the feeling he'd like to do the lesson too, but my teacher doesn't make any attempt to involve him. When I asked about the boy, my teacher told me he can't do anything for the child, that his learning disabilities are just too great. He said he doesn't have the necessary expertise to help him—that he's not a special educator. So he just lets him sit. It makes me want to cry.

It is not unusual for regular classroom teachers to feel that they lack the professional preparation necessary to help children with special needs (Semmel, Abernathy, Butera, & Lesar, 1991), and we can empathize with this feeling. Nonetheless, *those who are hard to teach or to manage are just as much your responsibility as those who are easy.* The question is not *whether* to help, but *how.*

This chapter begins by examining ways of helping children with disabilities and attention-deficit/hyperactivity disorder, the most commonly diagnosed behavior disorder among children in the United States (Coles, 2000). Then we consider strategies for supporting children who are second-language learners. Finally, we discuss the needs of children who are troubled—namely, those who suffer from the problems associated with substance abuse, child abuse and neglect, and depression.

Helping Children with Disabilities and ADHD

Stuart is an autistic child in Barbara's classroom. His vocal speech is very limited and difficult to understand, but he is able to type independently to communicate. For brief exchanges, Stuart uses an electronic organizer; for more elaborate interactions, academic writing, and note taking, he uses a laptop. In mathematics, he uses a calculator. Stuart's individualized education program (IEP) specifies that he is to have a full-time, male aide (a "teacher associate" or TA) to assist him during the day. The TA helps to refocus Stuart when his attention wanders and to calm him when he becomes frustrated, distressed, or agitated. Stuart appears to be flourishing in the general education classroom. In February, when asked how things were going, Stuart typed this message: "SCHOOL IS REALLY THE GREATEST."

Malika is in Garnetta's third-grade classroom. Her skills in reading and math are far below those of her classmates. In addition, Malika is extremely immature: She cries a lot, gets frustrated easily, and frequently falls out of her chair. Sometimes Garnetta finds Malika sitting under her desk. She's often defensive and denies her involvement in any misbehavior ("I didn't do it!"). Classified as "learning disabled," Malika has an individualized education program that specifies the goals and objectives for the academic year and how instruction is to be modified to meet her needs. In addition, it specifies that Malika is to go to a resource room every day, where a special education teacher provides instruction in reading and math.

Stuart and Malika's presence in general education classrooms, the supplemental services they receive, and their individualized education programs are a direct result of the Individuals with Disabilities Education Act (IDEA), federal legislation mandating a "free appropriate public education" for all children with disabilities. According to the IDEA, disability is defined as mental retardation, a hearing impairment including deafness, a speech or language impairment, a visual impairment including blindness, serious emotional disturbance, an orthopedic impairment, autism, traumatic brain injury, other health impairment (e.g., limited strength or vitality due to chronic or acute health problems such as asthma or diabetes), a specific learning disability, deaf-blindness, or multiple disabilities.

Sometimes called the "mainstreaming law," the IDEA requires *students with disabilities to be educated with their nondisabled peers to the maximum extent appropriate, with the supplementary aids and services needed to help them achieve.* However, the law also requires schools to have available a *continuum of alternative placements* (e.g., a special classroom or school, hospital, residential institution) if the nature or severity of a child's disability precludes the possibility of a satisfactory education in a general education setting.

In recent years, increasing numbers of educators have rejected the notion of a continuum of *placements;* they argue that it is far preferable to provide a continuum of *services* in the general education setting. Advocates of this position, often referred to as *inclusion,* contend that the general classroom benefits children with disabilities academically because they are held to higher expectations and are exposed to more stimulating content. Furthermore, they benefit socially, since they can make friends with children from their own neighborhoods and can observe peers behaving in a socially appropriate manner. (Table 13-1 lists the assumptions that underlie arguments about inclusion.) Mara Sapon-Shevin is a proponent of full inclusion:

The idea is that these [inclusive] schools would be restructured so that they are supportive, nurturing communities that really meet the needs of all the children within them: rich in resources and support for both students and teachers. . . . As far as a rationale, we should not have to defend inclusion— we should make others defend exclusion. There's very little evidence that some children need segregated settings in which to be educated. . . [W]e know that the world is an inclusive community. There are lots of people in it who vary not only in terms of disabilities, but in race, class, gender, and religious background. It's very important for children to have the opportunity to learn and grow within communities that represent the kind of world they'll live in when they finish school. (O'Neil, 1994/95, p. 7)

On the other side of the debate are educators who argue that it is essential to maintain a continuum of placements (e.g., Zigmond, Jenkins, Fuchs, Deno, & Fuchs, 1995; Zigmond, et al., 1995). Jim Kauffman reflects this point of view:

TABLE 13-1. The Inclusion Argument

Proponents of Full Inclusion	Opponents of Full Inclusion
1. Labeling and segregation are inherently bad.	1. Labeling is not bad if the labels indicate real differences; it's the only way to ensure that funds go to the neediest children.
2. Students with disabilities aren't different from nondisabled students in any meaningful way; everyone is unique.	2. Students with disabilities are different from nondisabled children, precisely because of their disabilities.
3. Students with disabilities can best be served in regular classrooms because	3. Some children with disabilities may be best served in regular classrooms, but some may be better served in separate special educational programs because
teachers have lower expectations when all students in a class have disabilities	special education teachers have appropriate expectations for their students
they benefit academically because they are held to higher expectations and are exposed to more stimulating curriculum	they benefit academically because teachers are specially trained, can implement an appropriate curriculum, and can give more individualized attention
virtually all regular teachers can teach disabled students and are willing to do so	regular education teachers don't want children with disabilities in their classes and don't consider themselves prepared to serve them
students with disabilities can make friends with children in their neighborhoods and model appropriate behavior of nondisabled peers	students with disabilities are often isolated and rejected by their nondisabled peers; they need the social acceptance and camaraderie of peers with similar disabilities
4. Special education is too costly, fragmented, and inefficient.	4. Opponents of special education just want to save money at the expense of needy students.
5. Many students in special education are not actually disabled, but are placed there because of faulty evaluations.	5. Most children in special education belong there; evaluations are generally reliable.
6. Nondisabled students benefit from having children with disabilities in their classes because they learn to accept and respect differences.	6. Nondisabled students suffer from having children with disabilities in their classes because the teacher has to spend too much time working with the disabled students.

Source: Adapted from Webb, 1994, p. 4.

I'm convinced that we must *maintain the alternative of moving kids to other places when that appears necessary in the judgment of teachers and parents. . . . Sure, we ought to meet special needs in a regular class when that's possible. But there isn't anything wrong with meeting special needs outside the regular class if that is required. In fact, the law and best practice say we must consider both possibilities. (O'Neil, 1994/95, p. 7)*

Critics of inclusion also worry that financially desperate school districts will use inclusion to reduce special education costs and "dump" children with disabilities in regular classrooms without support. Not surprisingly, many regular classroom teachers share this view. Indeed, they often resist inclusion, afraid that they lack the expertise to meet children's special needs and worried about the time and effort that children with disabilities take away from other students (Semmel, et al., 1991). On the other hand, inclusion advocates point out that including children with disabilities in the regular classroom does not mean placing unreasonable demands on teachers. A good program provides the supports necessary to make it work: aides, interpreters, planning time, administrative assistance, special materials, and equipment.

Attention-Deficit/Hyperactivity Disorder

Although teachers often find it particularly challenging to work with children who have attention-deficit/hyperactivity disorder (ADHD), this condition is *not* included in the IDEA's definition of children with disabilities. For this reason, students with ADHD are not eligible for services under IDEA unless they fall into other disability categories (e.g., learning disabilities, serious emotional disturbance, other health impairment). They may, however, be able to receive special services under Section 504 of the Rehabilitation Act of 1973. Section 504 prohibits discrimination on the basis of disability by recipients of federal funds and requires that public schools receiving federal funding address the needs of children with disabilities. As defined in Section 504, a person with a disability is any person who has a physical or mental impairment substantially limiting a major life activity such as learning. Thus, children with ADHD may fit within that definition.

No diagnostic test for ADHD is currently available, but Table 13-2 lists the criteria for identifying a child as having ADHD. As the table notes, four conditions must be met for a positive diagnosis: (1) Six or more symptoms must be present; (2) the symptoms have to have persisted for at least six months; (3) the symptoms had to have appeared before seven years of age; and (4) the symptoms must result in impaired functioning in at least two settings. Keep in mind that any one of the behaviors can be normal, especially in young children. It is when a child frequently displays a large number of these behaviors at a developmentally inappropriate age that the possibility of ADHD should be considered.

It is estimated that 3 percent to 5 percent of school-age children in the United States have ADHD, with far more boys than girls affected (Wodrich, 2000). The reason for the disparity is not clear. Some researchers believe the explanation lies in brain biochemistry or structure; others point to the way boys are socialized, which may make it harder to sit quietly and attend. Still others suggest subtle discrimination on the part of elementary teachers, who are predominantly women (Wodrich, 2000).

Children with ADHD often have difficulties in school. They may be underproductive or disorganized, failing to complete their work, or even losing it. They may also have problems with memory, language, visual perception, and fine motor control, which interfere with academic achievement. Indeed, as many as 35 percent of children with ADHD may have learning disabilities, compared with 3 percent of all children (Wodrich, 2000). Finally—and not surprisingly—children with ADHD may have problems meeting behavioral expectations and getting along with other children.

TABLE 13-2. DSM-IV Definition of Attention-Deficit/Hyperactivity Disorder

A. Either (1) or (2):

  (1) Six (or more) of the following symptoms of inattention have persisted for at least 6 months to a degree that is maladaptive and inconsistent with developmental level:

    Inattention

    (a) Often fails to give close attention to details or makes careless mistakes in schoolwork, work, or other activities

    (b) Often has difficulty sustaining attention in tasks or play activities

    (c) Often does not seem to listen when spoken to directly

    (d) Often does not follow through on instructions and fails to finish schoolwork, chores, or duties in the workplace (not due to oppositional behavior or failure to understand instructions)

    (e) Often has difficulty organizing tasks and activities

    (f) Often avoids, dislikes, or is reluctant to engage in tasks that require sustained mental effort (such as schoolwork or homework)

    (g) Often loses things necessary for tasks or activities (e.g., toys, school assignments, pencils, books, tools)

    (h) Is often easily distracted by extraneous stimuli

    (i) Is often forgetful in daily activities

  (2) Six (or more) of the following symptoms of hyperactivity-impulsivity have persisted for at least 6 months to a degree that is maladaptive and inconsistent with developmental level:

    Hyperactivity

    (a) Often fidgets with hands or feet or squirms in seat

    (b) Often leaves seat in classroom or in other situations in which remaining seated is expected

    (c) Often runs about or climbs excessively in situations in which it is inappropriate (in adolescents or adults, may be limited to subjective feelings of restlessness)

    (d) Often has difficulty playing or engaging in leisure activities quietly

    (e) Is often "on the go" or often acts as if "driven by a motor"

    (f) Often talks excessively

    Impulsivity

    (g) Often blurts out answers before questions have been completed

    (h) Often has difficulty awaiting turn

    (i) Often interrupts or intrudes on others (e.g., butts into conversations or games)

B. Some hyperactive-impulsive symptoms that caused impairment were present before age 7 years.

C. Some impairment from the symptoms is present in two or more settings (e.g., at school [or work] and at home).

D. There must be clear evidence of clinically significant impairment in social, academic, or occupational functioning.

E. The symptoms do not occur exclusively during the course of a Pervasive Developmental Disorder, Schizophrenia, or other Psychotic Disorder and are not better accounted for by another mental disorder (e.g., Mood Disorder, Anxiety Disorder, Dissociative Disorder, or a Personality Disorder).

(continued)

TABLE 13-2. DSM-IV Definition of Attention-Deficit/Hyperactivity Disorder *(continued)*

Code based on type:
Attention-deficit/hyperactivity disorder, combined type: If both Criteria A1 and A2 are met for the past 6 months.
Attention-deficit/hyperactivity disorder, predominantly inattentive type: If Criterion A1 is met but Criterion A2 is not met for the past 6 months.
Attention-deficit/hyperactivity disorder, predominantly hyperactive-impulsive type: If Criterion A2 is met but Criterion A1 is not met for the past 6 months.

Source: American Psychiatric Association (APA). (1994). *Diagnostic and statistical manual of mental disorders* (4th ed., pp. 83–85). Washington, DC: Author. Reprinted with permission from the Diagnostic and Statistical Manual of Mental Disorders, 4th ed.

Strategies for Helping Children with Disabilities and ADHD

Examine Your Classroom Environment for Possible Mismatch

It's important to remember that problems do not always reside exclusively within a child. Sometimes problems are the result of a discrepancy between a child's needs and the classroom environment. Barbara shares this example of an obvious mismatch:

> *I have a boy in my class who's 5'6" and weighs about 200 pounds. He's constantly picking up his desk with his knees and dropping it on the floor. It's disturbing and disruptive, but I can't blame him. I've had a request in for months for a bigger desk, but so far nothing has happened. Meanwhile, he's always fumbling and bumping into things and knocking things over. It's easy to get frustrated with him—he's got lots of other problems too—but it's clear that one contributing factor is that the physical setting is just too small for him!*

As Barbara's story points out, we sometimes think of a child as disabled, when actually the problem is the result of a *disabling situation* (Gearheart, Weishahn, & Gearheart, 1992). For example, since children with ADHD are easily distracted, you need to arrange the classroom environment so that distractions are minimized. Furthermore, children with ADHD have a special need for classrooms that are predictable, secure, and structured, where behavioral expectations are clear, and where there are clear, fair consequences. Table 13-3 offers some more specific suggestions.

In sum, before concluding that "the entire problem is the kid," examine your classroom situation and reflect on ways the environment may be contributing to the child's difficulties. Here are some questions that our teachers ask themselves when they reflect on ways their classroom settings might be exacerbating students' problems:

> Where is the child sitting? Is the seat near a source of distraction? Is it too far from the teacher?

TABLE 13-3. Helping Children with ADD/ADHD

Provide structure, routine, predictability, and consistency.

Make sure that behavioral expectations are clear.

Tape a copy of the schedule on their desks.

Seat them close to you, among attentive, well-focused students (the second row is better than the first).

Make frequent eye contact.

Make sure their desks are free of distractions (e.g., provide cardboard dividers to block out distractions).

Provide a quiet work area or a "private office" to which children can move for better concentration.

Provide headphones to block out noise during seatwork or other times that require concentration.

Provide opportunities to move around in legitimate ways (e.g., exercise breaks, doing errands).

Use physical contact to focus attention (e.g., a hand on a shoulder).

Develop private signals to help focus attention.

Ease transitions by providing cues and warnings.

Use positive reinforcement and behavior modification techniques.

Modify assignments (e.g., cut the written workload, break the assignment into manageable parts).

Limit the amount of homework.

Allow more time on assignments or tests.

Assist with organization (e.g., assignment pads; checklists; color coded notebooks for different subjects; accordion folders for loose papers).

Try to give students at least one task each day that they can do successfully.

Try to call on students when they are paying attention; use their first names before calling on them.

Provide extra sets of books to keep at home so that children are not overwhelmed after an absence and to prevent problems caused by forgetting books.

Provide access to a computer, along with keyboard and word processing instruction; do not remove access to the computer as a penalty.

DO NOT PUNISH; DO NOT ASSUME CHILDREN ARE LAZY; DO NOT GIVE UP.

Source: Adapted from Rief, 1993, and CH.A.D.D. Facts, 1993.

Is sitting in clusters too difficult for the child to handle? Should I move the child to a pair or to individual seating?

What type of academic work am I providing? Are assignments too mechanical? too dry? too long? Do they require too much independence? Do I ever allow choice?

How do I speak with the child? How do I praise the child? *Do* I praise the child?

What rules and routines have I set up and are they contrary to the student's ability to comply? Am I expecting quiet behavior too long? Am I setting the child up for failure?

Am I allowing an appropriate amount of time for completing assignments? For transitions?

Reflect on the Appropriateness of Your Expectations

Sometimes, in our efforts to be understanding and sympathetic, we lower our expectations so much that we teach students to "be less than they are." We water down curriculum; we set "ceilings" rather than floors (Good & Brophy, 2000); we forgive inappropriate behavior since "they can't help it"; we place children in safe environments where they will never be asked to do things we "know they cannot do" (Gartner & Lipsky, 1987). And when, in fact, they cannot do them, when they behave inappropriately, and when they do not learn, our beliefs seem justified.

On the other hand, it's important not to set unreasonably high expectations that children cannot meet. Your expectations have to be achievable, appropriate, and flexible. Viviana shares this incident:

> *Last year I had a child who had just moved here as a first-grader. This boy would learn something one day and forget it the next. I couldn't understand what was going on. I began to get so frustrated; I'd say, "But you knew this yesterday!" The child was frustrated too, of course. Finally, I talked with the parents about the problem. The mother told me that she had been taking him to a clinic for lead poisoning. When he was a baby, he had eaten the paint chips in his apartment. I said, "Why didn't you tell me? I wouldn't have gotten so frustrated with him!" Once I understood the problem, my entire attitude changed. That didn't mean I left him in the corner not doing anything, but I understood what was causing his memory problems.*

Use Groupwork and Cooperative Learning to Foster Real Inclusion

Teachers sometimes think that all support and assistance must come from them. But students can serve as *tutors* on academic tasks, *buddies* who assist with difficult activities, or *advocates* who "watch out" for the welfare of children who have special needs (Gearheart, Weishahn, & Gearheart, 1992). Ken tells us about a two-person team he created that has been beneficial to both students:

> *I have one kid, Jeannie, who goes to a resource room, and another kid, Suzanne, who's considered "gifted and talented." When the class works on* Voyage of the Mimi *activities on the computer, they function as a team. Let's say their task is to find a whale that's caught in a trap. You're someplace in the ocean, you've got different nautical instruments and you're supposed to get to the whale. I know that Jeannie isn't going to be able to follow the complicated instructions on her own, and she doesn't have the patience to go through the necessary six or seven steps to come close to the whale. She's just not accurate enough. Also, you never get it on the first shot, so you have to deal with that frustration, and she's easily frustrated. But she can be a valuable part of the team. She can work the rulers to plot the points on the map, for example. And Suzanne can do the planning and the strategizing. She's not held back at all. Together, they do fine.*

As we stressed in Chapter 10, research has demonstrated that cooperative learning can promote positive social relationships between children with disabilities and their peers. The use of cooperative learning can help to minimize the problem of children with special needs being isolated and rejected *socially*, even though they are included *physically* in the regular classroom. This year, for example, Barbara has teamed up for science with a special education teacher who teaches a self-contained class. Each day during science, the special education teacher and her class come to Barbara's room where children work in cooperative learning groups:

All the children are integrated into cooperative learning teams. Each member of the group always has a special job, like materials gatherer, timekeeper, reader, recorder. Since the special ed kids have a communication disability, they have problems with reading and writing, but they don't get out of the reading and writing responsibilities. Instead, they all have a "buddy" from my class who helps them do their jobs. There's been no embarrassment or nervousness about this at all. They know they have trouble with reading and writing, and my kids know they have trouble, and everyone approaches the matter very matter-of-factly. It's been really wonderful. The special ed teacher and I have a great time working together, and the kids really enjoy it.

Unfortunately, research indicates that cooperative learning is not always this successful. As we mentioned in Chapter 10, O'Connor and Jenkins (1996) observed 22 children with mild disabilities and 12 average-performing children in grades three through six. They classified only 40 percent of the disabled students as successfully participating in cooperative groups. Successful participation depended on the selection of suitable partners, careful monitoring, the teaching of cooperative behaviors, and the establishment of a cooperative ethic.

Use a Variety of Instructional Strategies

Diverse classrooms demand diverse teaching approaches. It is unlikely that a steady diet of traditional instruction—whole-group teacher presentation, recitation, independent seatwork—will be successful when classrooms contain children who vary in academic ability and have a range of disabilities. The use of cooperative learning is one instructional alternative. There are others: group problem solving, role playing, debates, writing and reading workshop, computer-assisted instruction, peer tutoring, cross-age tutoring.

In recent years, teachers have become increasingly aware of the need to vary instructional approaches so that children who learn differently have equal access to instruction. Numerous schools have developed programs based on Howard Gardner's (1993, 1995) theory of "multiple intelligences" (MI). According to Gardner, people have at least eight types of intellectual capacities: linguistic (capacity to use language); logical-mathematical (capacity to reason and recognize patterns); spatial (capacity to perceive the visual world accurately); musical (sensitivity to pitch, melody, rhythm, and tone); bodily-kinesthetic (capacity to use the body and to handle objects skillfully); interpersonal (capacity to understand others); intrapersonal (capacity to understand oneself); and naturalist (capacity to understand nature). Schools have traditionally emphasized the development of linguistic and logical-mathematical intelligences (and have favored those who are relatively strong in these), while they have neglected and undervalued the other intelligences. Although Gardner does not advocate one "right way" to implement a multiple intelligences education, he does recommend that teachers approach topics in a variety of ways, so that more children will be reached and more children can experience "what it is like to be an expert" (1995, p. 208). With this in mind, Barbara plans curriculum units that allow for a wide range of activities, from report writing, to puppet shows, to murals, to hands-on demonstrations and experiments. As Barbara puts it,

> *I want all students to have the chance to work in ways that are comfortable for them, but I also want to "stretch" them and have them work in ways that are less comfortable. Children who are artistic should have the chance to do murals, but they also have to do writing!*

Remember the Principles of Effective Management

Although you may feel you lack the skills needed to teach children who are especially low-achieving or those who have mild academic disabilities, research indicates that the teaching behaviors associated with outstanding achievement gains for these students are similar to the behaviors that are effective with *all* students (Slavin, 1989). In fact, effective teaching behaviors include many of the strategies we've discussed in earlier chapters:

- Providing feedback to students.
- Providing specific, informative praise.
- Providing learning tasks that students can accomplish with a high rate of success.
- Using classroom time efficiently, minimizing transitional or noninstructional time.
- Limiting the use of punishment.
- Maintaining high engagement rates.
- Focusing on preventive management strategies, rather than disciplinary interventions.
- Creating a supportive, nonthreatening learning environment.

This list reinforces Ken's viewpoint that working with children who have special needs often doesn't require different skills. As he puts it, "It's not such special stuff."

Obtain Access to Support and Services

In order to obtain appropriate assistance, you need to become familiar with the procedures and resources in your own school. The best way to do this is to speak with people who can provide guidance and direction—experienced teachers, the principal, the school nurse, special educators, school psychologists, guidance counselors. Ken emphasizes that

> *what's important is that you talk with people. The more you talk with people, the less the problem is just yours, and that makes it easier to deal with. You also need to keep in mind that if you go to one special services*

person and you're in the wrong place, they'll bounce you to the right place. And be sure to build rapport with people involved in special services. If you build rapport, you're going to get help.

Exactly what kind of help will you receive when you make contact with your school's special services personnel? Generally, the first step is to provide you with additional suggestions for addressing the child's needs. These suggestions may include adjusting the curriculum, tutoring by a peer or an aide, implementing a behavior modification plan—even something as simple as changing the child's seat. If these interventions are not successful, and special services personnel believe the child should be considered for placement in special education, the classroom teacher initiates a formal request for evaluation.

Specific referral procedures vary from district to district, but the teacher usually completes a form describing the child's academic performance and classroom behavior and the interventions that have already been tried. The form used in New Brunswick, the district in which Garnetta and Viviana teach, asks for the following information:

• Family information (parents' birthplace, education, occupation, residence, marital status; siblings).
• Contact with parents with regard to problem.
• Steps that the teacher has taken to deal with the problem.
• Description of the child's social and emotional adjustment (e.g., relationship with other children; attitude toward authority; effort; special interests and aptitudes).
• Previous schools attended.
• Attendance record for last two years.
• Standardized test data.
• Achievement level in reading and mathematics.
• Remedial services received.
• Health record (to be completed by the school nurse).

The IDEA requires that parental consent be obtained before a child can be evaluated. When parents give their permission, the referral process can proceed: The child is given a variety of tests, a conference is held with parents, and the results of the evaluation are discussed. If it is determined that the student's problems result from a disability, a classification is agreed upon, and an individualized education program is developed. A flow chart outlining this generic referral process appears in Figure 13-2.

It's important to approach special services armed with specific information about the child and about the interventions you've already tried. Complaints like "He's driving me crazy," "She constantly demands attention," or "He just can't hack it in fourth grade" are not helpful. The more detailed your information can be, the more likely you are to receive assistance. Here are some of our teachers' suggestions about the kinds of information to bring:

• An overall description of the child (both strengths and weaknesses).
• A detailed description of the child's inappropriate behavior:
    When does the child exhibit the behavior?
    How frequently does the child exhibit the behavior?

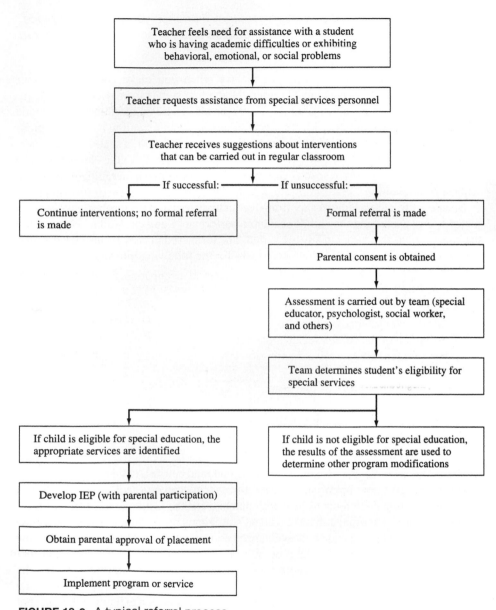

FIGURE 13-2. A typical referral process

What antecedent events set off the behavior?

What is the duration of the behavior?

What is the reaction of other students in the class?

- A detailed description of the child's academic difficulties (with work samples to support your description).
- Information about the family (if possible).
- Efforts on your part to correct or deal with the problem.
- How you'd like to be helped or what type of help you believe the child needs.

Once you've reported a problem, it's human nature to expect everybody to drop whatever they're doing and provide you with immediate help. But special services tend to be overworked and understaffed, and help is not always prompt. Barbara reminds us:

You're dealing with the problem every day, and you're frustrated. You want an immediate resolution, but you have to be realistic. Special services is a slow process. I'm not the only person they deal with. They work with all the teachers in the building and with the kids who are already classified. It can take a long time for a child to be evaluated. But special services people will come in and consult with me. They'll give me ideas for working with a child, strategies I've forgotten to use. Or they'll fill me in on family histories. You've got to remember that they're not miracle workers. They're not wonders. But they will validate my problem, provide me with advice and support, and give time and understanding to a student.

Helping Children Who Are Second-Language Learners

The past two decades have seen a tremendous increase in the number of students who come from homes where a language other than English is spoken. In 1994, the number of "language minority" students or "second-language learners" was estimated to be 9.9 million (Nieto, 2000). Although they live throughout the United States, about 62 percent of second-language learners are clustered in Arizona, Colorado, California, New Mexico, and Texas. The vast majority are of Spanish language background, but there are also sizable numbers of children with other European language backgrounds, Southeast Asian backgrounds (e.g., Vietnamese, Cambodian, Hmong), Asian backgrounds (Chinese, Korean), and Native American backgrounds. It is not uncommon in large school districts to have children representing as many as 25 different languages; in 1991, California's public schools served children speaking any one of about 100 languages (Lessow-Hurley, 1991).

Some second-language learners may be fluent in English. Others, like Viviana's students, may enter school with limited English proficiency (LEP)—that is, their lack of facility in English may have negative consequences for their academic achievement in monolingual English classrooms (Nieto, 2000). It is currently estimated that about 7.3

percent of all public school students have limited proficiency in English, and the great majority spend most or part of their time in English-only classrooms (Nieto, 2000).

Federal legislation provides funding and encouragement for programs to assist these children; however, there are no federally mandated programs like those provided for children who have disabilities. In fact, a landmark statement supporting the rights of LEP students comes not from the legislature, but from a Supreme Court case, *Lau v. Nichols* (1974), in which a group of Chinese students sued the San Francisco Unified School District for providing them with an education they could not understand. The Court found for the plaintiffs, stating:

> *[T]here is no equality of treatment merely by providing students with the same facilities, textbooks, teachers, and curriculum: for students who do not understand English are effectively foreclosed from any meaningful education. Basic English skills are at the very core of what these public schools teach. Imposition of a requirement that, before a child can effectively participate in the education program he must already have acquired those basic skills is to make a mockery of public education. We know that those who do not understand English are certain to find their classroom experiences wholly incomprehensible and in no way meaningful. (p. 27)*

As a result of *Lau,* a number of states enacted legislation requiring services for LEP students, but laws change constantly and vary substantially from state to state. The state in which you teach may mandate such services or merely permit them; it may even prohibit them! Despite the variability, state laws generally call for the identification and assessment of second-language learners and describe options for special services. One option is a *bilingual education program,* which teaches children in their native language as well as in English, thus allowing them to learn academic subjects while they're learning English. In some states, if there are a given number of second-language learners in a district, speaking a common native language at approximately the same grade level, the district is required to provide bilingual programs.

When second-language learners come from many different language backgrounds, bilingual education programs are not practical. In this case, schools typically place children in regular English-only classrooms and pull them out for instruction from a specially trained teacher in *English as a Second Language.* Since the focus is on learning English, children with different native languages can be in the same room. A few years ago, for example, Ken had six students—from Mexico, Korea, India, Sri Lanka, and Turkey—who regularly left his room for ESL instruction; there they joined students who spoke Russian, Hebrew, and Chinese.

In a general education, English-only classroom, second-language learners may have problems if you tend to talk quickly, use idioms like "It's raining cats and dogs," and speak in complex sentences. They may be able to function admirably, however, if you implement specific environmental supports. For example, you can ask questions that require different degrees of English proficiency in responding (e.g., nonverbal signals to communicate

TABLE 13-4. Strategies for Helping Second-Language Learners

Provide a safe environment for language risk taking.

Increase time and opportunities for meaningful talk.

Encourage English speaking while honoring students' first language and culture.

Offer periodic summaries and paraphrases.

Emphasize collaborative over individual work.

Emphasize process over product, wholes over pieces.

Apply Specially Designed Academic Instruction in English (SDAIE) strategies across the curriculum. Often known as "sheltered instruction," SDAIE focuses on core curriculum content and uses a rich variety of techniques and materials such as artifacts, visuals, video, storyboarding, movement, role plays, and collaborative learning.

Think aloud and model a variety of reading comprehension strategies (e.g., making connections, predicting, inferring).

Use a variety of reading supports such as text tours and picture walks (to preview material), graphic organizers (story maps, character analyses), and text signposts (chapter headings, bold print).

Encourage students to write about topics of their choice and for real-world purposes.

Use a variety of writing supports, such as group composing, graphic organizers, and drawing-based texts.

Source: Cary, 2000.

agreement or disagreement, yes–no, single-word or short answers). Table 13-4 lists additional suggestions provided by Stephen Cary (2000).

Having a number of second-language learners in your class will add to the cultural richness and global understanding of your students. It may also be a source of stress, especially for new teachers. Although questions will undoubtedly arise about how to meet the needs of your second-language learners while not shortchanging the rest of the class, implementing the suggestions from Table 13-4 should benefit *everyone.*

Helping Students Who Are Troubled

During one meeting, our four teachers spoke sadly about the increasing problems their students face. They talked about six children sleeping in one bed; about absent fathers and drug-addicted mothers; about parents who are in and out of jail; about a youngster finding the body of his older brother who had committed suicide; about a child sleeping, eating, and doing homework in the car while his mother delivered newspapers; about a first-grader who had to bring her mother home from a bar every afternoon after school. As they talked, their anger and compassion were obvious. Also obvious was their recognition that in today's society, teachers have to deal with issues that were unimaginable in an earlier era—issues that require knowledge and skills far beyond those needed to be an effective instructor.

In order to help the troubled children in your class, *you need to be alert to the indicators of potential problems.* As an adult immersed in the culture of youth, you will probably develop a good idea of what the behavior of a typical elementary student is like. This allows you to detect deviations or changes in a student's behavior that might signal the presence of a problem. In *Teacher as Counselor: Developing the Helping Skills You Need* (1993), Jeffrey and Ellen Kottler suggest that you learn to ask yourself a series of questions when you notice atypical behavior:

What is unusual about this student's behavior?

Is there a pattern to what I have observed?

What additional information do I need to make an informed judgment?

Whom might I contact to collect this background information?

What are the risks of waiting longer to figure out what is going on?

Does this student seem to be in any imminent danger?

Whom can I consult about this case?

Viviana tells us how she tries to be alert to problems her students might be experiencing:

Even when I'm giving a lesson, I'm always scanning the room from one end to the other. You have to have your eyes all over. When the children are supposed to be paying attention, it's easy to notice behavior that might mean there's a problem—sleeping, putting a head down on the desk, masturbating, fidgeting. I also watch for bruises. The other day, for example, Carlita came in with a bruise under her eye. I said, "How did you get that bruise?" She said that she had fallen. I was not too concerned because I have known the family for a long time—I had two of Carlita's siblings—and there's never been any indication of abuse. But I decided to consult with the school nurse anyway. She examined the bruise, got the same story from Carlita, and talked with her grandmother, who happens to work in the cafeteria. She said, "You know, Carlita has a bruise under her eye." The grandmother said that she knew, that Carlita had fallen. Since the story checked out, we decided to leave it at that. But I still watch. If a child seems to be "falling" too much, then I report it. DYFS [Division of Youth and Family Services] would have to be notified.

Substance Abuse

Substance abuse affects elementary classrooms in two ways: when children from chemically dependent families enter school and when children themselves are substance abusers. Let's turn first to the problems of children from chemically dependent families.

Amanda's father is an alcoholic who becomes aggressive and abusive when he drinks. At age 13, Amanda is her mother's primary source of support and works hard to make her family appear normal. She has assumed many adult responsibilities that would normally be carried out by the father of a household. At school, she is a very successful student; her teachers describe her as superdependable and motivated. They don't realize that she is filled with feelings of inadequacy and confusion, that her behavior is prompted by a compulsive need to be perfect. Nor do they notice that in between classes and at lunch time Amanda spends most of her time alone. Amanda avoids forming friendships because she is afraid of revealing the family secret. (Powell, Zehm, & Kottler, 1995)

Ricky, Amanda's 10-year-old brother, is a fourth-grader whose teacher describes him as sullen, disrespectful, and obstructive. He frequently fights with other children and is often in the principal's office being reprimanded for some antisocial behavior. His mother claims not to understand his behavior; she reports that Ricky never acts this way at home and implies that the teacher is the cause of his perpetual negative attitude. Yet he often runs around the house, screaming and tearing things apart. At the core of Ricky's behavior is anger: He is enraged by the rejection he feels from his alcoholic father and resentful that his mother spends so much time wallowing in self-pity. He soothes his pain by planning ways to run away. He is on the verge of jumping into his own life of addiction. (Powell, Zehm, & Kottler, 1995)

It is estimated that *one in every four children* sitting in a classroom comes from a family in which one or both parents are addicted to drugs or alcohol (Powell, Zehm, & Kottler, 1995). When these children of alcoholics/addicts (COAs) are angry and disruptive like Ricky, it is relatively easy to recognize that a problem exists; it is far more difficult when children are compliant perfectionists like Amanda. Leslie Lillian, the student assistance counselor (SAC) at Ken's school, stresses that COAs can exhibit a wide variety of behaviors (see Table 13-5):

Some children become perfectionists. It's as if they think to themselves, "I'm not going to disturb anything, I'm not going to do anything wrong, so no one can be angry with me." Some children become class clowns; maybe they've found that making people laugh breaks the tension, or maybe they're seeking attention. Others become very angry; they may begin to lie, or steal, or cheat. Some become sad and melancholy; everything about them says, "Nurture me." We see a whole spectrum of reactions—and it's the same spectrum of behaviors that we see in kids from violent homes.

It's important to understand that for COAs, family life revolves around the addiction. Rules are arbitrary and irrational; boundaries between parents and children are blurred; and life is marked by unpredictability and inconsistency. Leslie comments:

These kids never know what they're going home to. One day, they may bring a paper home from school that's gotten a low grade, and the parent might say, "That's OK, just do it over." Another day, they might get beaten up for bringing home a paper like that.

TABLE 13-5. Characteristics of Children of Alcoholics/Addicts

Difficulty in creating and maintaining trusting relationships, often leading to isolation.

Low self-esteem.

Self-doubt.

Difficulty in being spontaneous and open, caused by a need to be in control and to minimize the risk of being surprised.

Denial and repression because of the need to collaborate with other family members in keeping "the secret."

General feelings of guilt about areas for which the child had no responsibility.

Uncertainty about his/her own feelings and desires caused by shifting parental roles.

Seeing things in an "all or nothing" context, which sometimes manifests itself in a perfectionist fear of failure.

Poor impulse control, which may result in acting-out behavior, probably caused by lack of parental guidance, love, and discipline.

Potential for depression, phobias, panic reactions, and hyperactivity.

Preoccupation with the family.

Abuse of alcohol and/or drugs.

Source: Adapted from Towers, 1989.

Sadly, it's often difficult for COAs to reach out for help. In a chemically dependent family, everyone works to maintain the family secret. Tonia Moore, Highland Park's student assistance counselor, finds that COAs move back and forth between "wanting to report the lies and wanting to believe the lies":

> *A while back I worked with a sister and brother; the girl was in elementary school and the boy was in high school. Their mother was an alcoholic, and she would tell them if they did well on their report cards, she would stop drinking. They'd go to church and pray for that; they'd even dream about it. I would tell them, "Don't count on it. It's not that easy for your mom to stop drinking, even though she wants to." But they wanted to believe it would happen. They really tried to improve their grades, and they did, and she still didn't stop. They were heartbroken.*
>
> *Sometimes, she'd come to back-to-school night, and you could tell she'd been drinking. The boy would put his arm around her and try to keep her from making a scene. And then the next day, he'd come in to see me, all embarrassed, and apologize for her behavior. He'd say she wasn't feeling well, that she had the flu, even though he knew that I knew she was an alcoholic. He'd participate in the secret, he'd try to cover up, even as he confided in me. Children of substance abusers have such a tremendous need to have things be normal.*

One of the most frustrating aspects of working with COAs is the realization that you do not have the power to change the child's home life. Instead, you must concentrate on

TABLE 13-6. Ways of Helping Children of Alcoholics/Addicts

---

1. **Be observant.** Watch your students not just for academic or behavior problems, but also for the more subtle signs of addiction and emotional distress. Remember that COAs can be over-achieving, cooperative, and quiet, as well as disruptive and angry.

2. **Set boundaries that are enforced consistently.** When chaos exists at home, some sense of order is crucial at school.

3. **Be flexible.** Although it is necessary to set boundaries, classroom rules that are too rigid and unyielding may invite students to act out.

4. **Make addiction a focus of discussion.** Find a way to deal with this subject. Incorporate addiction into literacy instruction (e.g., through children's literature, writing), science, and social studies.

5. **Make it clear you are available.** Communicate that you are eager and open to talk to children. Reach out to the troubled child in a gentle, caring way. "I notice you are having some difficulty. I just want you to know that I care about you. Call me any time you are ready to talk. And if you would rather speak to someone else, let me find you someone you can trust."

6. **Develop a referral network.** Find out what services are available to help and refer the child for appropriate professional care.

7. **Accept what you can do little about.** You can't make people stop drinking or taking drugs.

Source: Adapted from Powell, Zehm, & Kottler, 1995.

what you *are* able to do during the six hours each day that the child is in school. Many of the strategies are not different from those we have espoused for all children. (See Table 13-6.) For example, it is essential that you establish clear, consistent rules and work to create a climate of trust and caring. It is also useful to focus attention directly and indirectly on topics related to addiction. In *Classrooms Under the Influence* (Powell, Zehm, & Kottler, 1995), Dennis Thompson, a seventh- and eighth-grade language arts teacher, describes the ways he teaches about addiction:

> *When we first began to read and talk about the effects of addiction, I discovered that I could begin to help students from addicted families develop some of the important coping skills they needed to deal with the anger and shame they brought from home. I also found that students from addicted families could begin to find the words they needed to describe and vent their anger and shame. They did this privately within the pages of their confidential journals. Later, they even began to do it publicly in the safety of role-playing and creative drama activities. . . . I'll never forget the day that Julie, one of my eighth-graders, brought me her journal and said, "Mr. Thompson, please read page 31 of my journal, and only page 31." It was the beginning of her story about her alcoholic father. She trusted me enough to want me to know this about her.*
>
> *[Another] strategy I use to reduce the negative effects students from addicted families bring into my classroom is to select and read adolescent literature to my students that focuses on the topic of healthy and unhealthy*

family living. . . . I am pleased to find lately that there are many new books of fiction for adolescents that focus on the topic of family addiction. My students enjoyed Elisa Carbone's My Dad's Definitely Not a Drunk, *a short novel about the revelation of a family's secret and the eventual recovery of an alcoholic father. . . . I [also] use selections from children's literature like Judith Viorst's* Terrible, Horrible, No-Good, Very Bad Day, *and Bernard Waber's* Ira Sleeps Over *as examples of how kids learn to solve problems in healthy families. I then ask each of my students to use these stories as models for writing their own children's books about how their characters can solve problems at home in healthy ways. (Powell, Zehm, & Kottler, 1995, pp. 112–113)*

In addition to using these strategies, you should find out if your school has student assistance counselors or other special services personnel who can provide help. Find out if support groups for COAs are available. For example, Tonia Moore runs groups at Barbara's school, sometimes alone and sometimes with the school's guidance counselor. Tonia speaks about the benefits that joining such a group can bring:

There's such a sense of relief. The comments are always the same: "I thought I was the only one." "I didn't know anyone else was going through this stuff." The shame is so great, even at a very young age, and the need to keep it all a secret is so hard. There's instant camaraderie.

We'll often start off by asking, "On a scale from 1 to 10, how are you feeling today?" That allows us to get a sense of the group and to learn quickly who's in the middle of a crisis. Then we'll ask them to share something positive that happened this week and something negative that happened. We'll ask who needs group time. We do activities that help to build self-esteem. We do role playing to get at feelings—being disappointed, being unsafe, being embarrassed, being angry that you can never make plans, that you can never say, "My mother will be there," or even "I'll be there."

If there are no groups for COAs in your school, find out if your community has any support groups like *Alateen*, for children from 8 to 19, and *Alatot*, for children under 8. These groups are part of the Al-Anon Family Groups and abide by the same 12 steps as Alcoholics Anonymous.

A second way that substance abuse can affect elementary classrooms is when *children themselves abuse drugs and alcohol.* At the elementary level, the problems of COAs are far more prevalent, but it would be naive to think that there is no substance abuse among youngsters at the intermediate grade levels. The New Jersey Alcohol/Drug Resource Center and Clearinghouse (1994) reports that nearly 100,000 children aged 10 or 11 report getting drunk once a week. Significant alcohol, inhalant, and cigarette use is reported as early as fourth grade, and alcohol experimentation increases from 6 to

17 percent between fourth and sixth grades. Viviana even tells of a first-grader whose mother not only taught him to use drugs, she also had him selling on street corners.

To a large extent, SACs rely on teachers to refer students who might be having problems with alcohol and other drugs or who might be at risk for such problems. But teachers may be particularly reluctant to make referrals about suspected drug use because they are unsure about the indicators. Tonia Moore is very sensitive to this problem:

> *Teachers tell me, "I have no idea what substance abuse looks like. It wasn't a part of my training. I wouldn't know when to refer a student." I tell them, that's OK. You can't tell substance abuse just by looking. There has to be a chemical screening. But you can see changes in behavior. You know enough about kids to know when somebody's behavior has changed, or if their behavior is different from all the other kids. You don't need to know the student is using; you just need to suspect that there may be drug use or a problem related to drug use.*

What are the behaviors that might lead you to suspect drug use and to make a referral? Figure 13-3 shows the behavior checklist used in South Brunswick. Many schools use forms that are very similar to this one. Keeping your school's behavior checklist handy can help you stay alert to the possibility that students are using drugs or living with addiction in their families.

It's important to distinguish between situations in which a pattern of behavior problems suggests possible drug use *outside of school* and situations in which a student appears to be *under the influence of drugs during school, at school functions, or on school property*. When you see students who might be "under the influence," you cannot wait to fill out a behavior checklist; you need to alert the appropriate personnel as soon as you possibly can. In New Jersey, teachers are legally required to report "as soon as possible" a student who appears to be under the influence of drugs. Tonia explains one of the reasons for mandating an immediate response:

> *It used to be that teachers would come to me at the end of the day and say, "I was really worried about X today. I think he was really on something." That's no good.* I need to know at the time. *After all, that student could fall down the stairs, or the student could leave the building . . . and get killed crossing the street.* We have to deal with the problem immediately. *It can really be a matter of life and death.*

Since you cannot be sure that a student is using drugs just by looking, it's important not to be accusatory when you talk with the student. Ken would ask, "Are you feeling OK? You don't look like yourself. Would you like to go to the nurse?" He would then alert the nurse that he was sending her a student whose behavior suggested possible drug or alcohol use. Making a referral like this is not easy, but you need to remember that turning away and remaining silent can send the message that you condone the behavior—or that you don't care enough to do anything.

STUDENT ASSISTANCE PROGRAM
BEHAVIOR CHECKLIST

The goal of the Student Assistance Program is to help students who may be experiencing problems in their lives. These problems can be manifested in school through any combination of behaviors. The following is a list of typical behaviors students having problems may exhibit. While most students engage in many of the behaviors at one time or another, the student who may be having trouble will show a combination or pattern of these behaviors.

Student: _____ Grade: _____

Staff
Member: _____ Date: _____

Academic Performance
_____Drop in grades
_____Decrease in participation
_____Inconsistent work
_____Works below potential
_____Compulsive overachievement
(preoccupied w/school success)

School Attendance
_____Change in attendance
_____Absenteeism
_____Tardiness
_____Class cutting
_____Frequent visits to nurse
_____Frequent visits to counselor
_____Frequent restroom visits
_____Frequent request for hall passes

Social Problems
_____Family problems
_____Run away
_____Job problems
_____Peer problems
_____Constantly borrowing money
_____Relationship problems

Physical Symptoms
_____Staggering/stumbling
_____Incoherent
_____Smelling of alcohol/marijuana
_____Vomiting/nausea

_____Glassy, bloodshot eyes/dark
_____Poor coordination
_____Slurred speech
_____Deteriorating physical appearance
_____Sleeping in class
_____Physical injuries
_____Frequent physical complaints
_____Dramatic change in musculature

Extracurricular Activities
_____Lack of participation
_____Possession of drugs/alcohol
_____Involvement in thefts and assaults
_____Vandalism
_____Talking about involvement in illegal activities
_____Possession of paraphernalia
_____Increasing noninvolvement
_____Decrease in motivation
_____Dropping out missing practice(s)
_____Not fulfilling responsibilities
_____Performance changes

Disruptive Behavior
_____Defiance of rules
_____Irresponsibility, blaming, lying, fighting
_____Cheating

FIGURE 13-3. The referral form used in South Brunswick

_____Sudden outburst, verbal abuse	_____Defensive
_____Obscene language, gesture	_____Withdrawn/difficulty relating
_____Attention-getting behavior	_____Unrealistic goals
_____Frequently in wrong area	_____Sexual behavior in public
_____Extreme negativism	_____Seeking adult advice without a
_____Hyperactivity, nervousness	specific problem
_____Lack of motivation, apathy	_____Rigid obedience
_____Problem with authority figures	_____Constantly seeks approval

Atypical Behavior

_____Difficulty in accepting mistakes

_____Boasts about alcohol or drug use, "partying bravado"

_____Erratic behavior

_____Change of friends

_____Overly sensitive

_____Disoriented

_____Inappropriate responses

_____Depression

Other

_____Students talking about alcohol or other drugs

_____Having beeper

_____Bragging about sexual exploits

_____Mentions concerns about significant other's alcohol or other drug use, gambling

_____Staff knowledge of addiction in family

Additional Comments:

_____

FIGURE 13-3. The referral form used in South Brunswick (*continued*)

One final note: If you suspect that a student is in possession of drugs or alcohol in school (e.g., in a purse or backpack), it's best to bring that person to the appropriate school official rather than undertake a search by yourself. In a landmark case (*New Jersey v. T.L.O.,* 1985), the United States Supreme Court ruled that a school official may properly conduct a search of a student "when there are reasonable grounds for suspecting that the search will turn up evidence that the student has violated or is violating either the law or the rules of the school" (Fischer, Schimmel, & Kelly, 1999). In other words, students in school have fewer protections than are normally afforded to citizens under the stricter "probable cause" standard (Stefkovich & Miller, 1998). Nonetheless, searching a student's belongings is best left to an administrator who is aware of the subtleties of the law.

Abuse and Neglect

During one meeting with our teachers, they related sad, frightening stories that illustrate the important role teachers serve in identifying victims of abuse. Listen to Garnetta:

> *Libby had moved from another country with her mother and sisters, and they were living in her grandmother's house. Her father stayed back home, but within three or four years, he rejoined his family. Shortly after, I noticed physical bruises on Libby's arms and legs. I also noticed that her older*

brother had bruises, too. We reported the case to DYFS (Division of Youth and Family Services), and they sent a caseworker to the home to investigate. DYFS reported back to us that the father admitted he had hit the children because they hadn't gone to bed when he told them to. Apparently this wasn't the first time. According to the mother, when the children were very young, the father had been jailed for "hurting" the children. This time he agreed to counseling.

Libby and her brother are not alone. It has been estimated that almost 2 million children are victims of child abuse or neglect each year (Parkay & Stanford, 1992). In order to protect these young people, most states have laws requiring educators to report suspected abuse to the state's "child protective service" or "child welfare agency." Garnetta, for example, contacted New Jersey's Division of Youth and Family Services, the agency charged with receiving and investigating all reports of suspected child abuse and neglect.

Amazingly, only 10 percent of abuse and neglect reports originate in schools, even though at least half of the nation's abused and neglected children are in school on any given day (McIntyre, 1990). One simple reason is teachers' lack of familiarity with the signs of abuse. Thomas McIntyre (1990) found that only 4 percent of the teachers he surveyed were "very aware" of the signs of sexual abuse; 17 percent could recognize obvious signs; and 75 percent could not recognize signs of sexual abuse at any point. These findings clearly underscore the need for teachers to become familiar with the physical and behavioral indicators of these problems. (See Table 13-7.)

Unfortunately, the signs of abuse can be difficult to detect. As Table 13-7 indicates, teachers not only need to watch for physical evidence, they must also be alert to behavioral indicators such as apprehension when other children are upset, reluctance to go home at the end of the school day, and wariness of adult contact. Children who give improbable explanations for their injuries, refuse to talk about them, or pretend they don't hurt may also be victims of physical abuse.

According to Leslie Lillian, the SAC at Ken's school, the teachers at Brunswick Acres see more neglect than abuse:

We'll see parents who don't make sure that their kids get to school; parents who know that their first-grader is lying and stealing but "don't want to hear"; parents who send their kid to school smelling of stale smoke—and won't do anything even when we tell them that the other kids tease him unmercifully. People tend to think that neglect occurs in poor families, but cases like this cross SES lines. I remember one girl in particular who would cry when she got sick and beg us not to send her home. She knew that her high-powered parents would be angry if their day was disrupted.

Teachers are often reluctant to file a report unless they have absolute proof of abuse or neglect. They worry about invading the family's privacy and causing unnecessary embarrassment to everyone involved. Nonetheless, it's important to keep in mind that *no state requires the reporter to have absolute proof before reporting.* What most states do

TABLE 13-7. Physical and Behavioral Indicators of Child Abuse and Neglect

Type of child abuse or neglect	Physical Indicators	Behavioral Indicators
Physical abuse	Unexplained bruises and welts: —on face, lips, mouth —on torso, back, buttocks, thighs —in various stages of healing —clustered, forming regular patterns —reflecting shape of article used to inflict (electric cord, belt buckle) —on several different surface areas —regularly appear after absence, weekend or vacation Unexplained burns: —cigar, cigarette burns, especially on soles, palms, back or buttocks —immersion burns (sock-like, glove-like doughnut shaped on buttocks or genitalia) —patterned like electric burner, iron, etc. —rope burns on arms, legs, neck or torso Unexplained fractures: —to skull, nose, facial structure —in various stages of healing —multiple or spiral fractures Unexplained lacerations or abrasions: —to mouth, lips, gums, eyes —to external genitalia	Wary of adult contacts Apprehensive when other children cry Behavioral extremes: —aggressiveness —withdrawal Frightened of parents Afraid to go home Reports injury by parents
Physical neglect	Consistent hunger, poor hygiene, inappropriate dress Consistent lack of supervision, especially in dangerous activities or long periods	Begging, stealing food Extended stays at school (early arrival and late departure) Constantly falling alseep in class

(continued)

TABLE 13-7. Physical and Behavioral Indicators of Child Abuse and Neglect *(continued)*

Type of child abuse or neglect	Physical Indicators	Behavioral Indicators
physical neglect (continued)	Constant fatigue or listlessness Unattended physical problems or medical needs Abandonment	Alcohol or drug abuse Delinquency (e.g., thefts) States there is no caretaker
Sexual abuse	Difficulty in walking or sitting Torn, stained or bloody underclothing Pain or itching in genital area Bruises or bleeding in external genitalia, vaginal or anal areas Venereal disease, especially in preteens Pregnancy	Unwilling to change for gym or participate in PE Withdrawal, fantasy or infantile behavior Bizarre, sophisticated, or unusual sexual behavior or knowledge Poor peer relationships Delinquent or runaway Reports sexual assault by caretaker
Emotional maltreatment	Habit disorders (sucking, biting, rocking, etc.) Conduct disorders (antisocial, destructive, etc.) Neurotic traits (sleep disorders, speech disorders, inhibition of play) Psychoneurotic reactions (hysteria, obsession, compulsion, phobias, hypochondria)	Behavior extremes: —compliant, passive —aggressive, demanding Overly adaptive behavior: —inappropriately adult —inappropriately infantile Developmental lags (physical, mental, emotional) Attempted sulcide

require is reasonable "cause to suspect" or "believe" that abuse has occurred (Michaelis, 1993). If you are uncertain whether abuse is occurring, but have reasonable cause, you should err in favor of the youngster and file a report. Waiting for proof can be dangerous; it may also be illegal. If a child is later harmed, and it becomes clear that you failed to report suspected abuse, both you and your school district may be subject to civil and criminal liability (Michaelis, 1993).

It's essential that you learn about the reporting procedures in your state *before* you are faced with a situation of suspected child abuse. Some states explicitly name the school personnel who are required to file the report. (In New Jersey, for example, teachers are required to file a report directly to the state's child protective service in order to avoid unnecessary delays.) Other states have more general provisions that require reporting by "any person" who works with children; this would clearly include teachers, nurses, therapists, and counselors (Fischer, Schimmel, & Kelly, 1999). Often, a teacher who suspects child abuse notifies the principal, who then reports to the appropriate state agency. If, however, the administrator fails to make the report, the teacher should do so. Studies suggest that two-thirds of reports from teachers stop at the principal's desk (Bancroft, 1997). Also keep in mind that every state provides immunity from any civil suit or criminal prosecution that might result from the reporting of suspected child abuse or neglect—as long as you have acted "in good faith" (Fischer, Schimmel, & Kelly, 1999).

States also vary with respect to the form and content of reports required. Most states require an oral report, followed by a more detailed written report, and some states also have a 24-hour, toll-free "hot line." Generally, you should be prepared to provide the student's name and address; the nature and extent of injury or condition observed; and your own name and address (Fischer, Schimmel, & Kelly, 1999).

The variation among states underscores the importance of becoming familiar with the procedures and resources in your own school. The best way to do this is to speak with people who can provide guidance and direction: experienced teachers, the principal, the school nurse, members of the CORE team, and the student assistance counselor.

Depression

Not too long ago, a student teacher we know wrote the following journal entry:

I'm really worried about one of my kids. She's unbelievably shy and withdrawn. It took me a long time to even notice her. She never participates in class discussions, never raises her hand, and never volunteers for anything. When I call on her, she looks down and doesn't answer, or her answer is so soft that I can't hear her. I've watched her during lunch time in the cafeteria, and she doesn't seem to have any friends. The other kids aren't mean to her—they act like she doesn't even exist—and that's sort of the way I feel too!

When teachers are asked to talk about "problem children," they tend to speak about those who are disruptive, aggressive, and defiant. But quiet children like the one described by this student teacher may also have serious problems. Indeed, students who act sad, reserved, withdrawn, or irritable may actually be suffering from childhood depression. Table 13-8 lists the signs that suggest depression in children.

In "Too Sad to Learn," Steven Schlozman (2001), a clinical instructor in psychiatry at Harvard, suggests that teachers consult with a guidance counselor or school psychologist if they are concerned that a child is depressed. Certainly, classroom behavior that is dangerous or journals, drawings, or essays that suggest suicidal or homicidal thoughts warrant a formal referral. In addition, teachers need to understand that depressed students frequently feel as though they have little to contribute. To counter these feelings, you need to communicate respect and confidence in the student's abilities, minimize the possibility of embarrassment (e.g., by calling on depressed students to answer questions that have no clearly correct answer), and encourage them to assist younger or less able students. Most importantly, you need to forge a connection with the depressed student. As

TABLE 13-8. Indicators of Early-Onset Depression

Indecision, lack of concentration, or forgetfulness
Change in personality, such as increased anger, irritability, moodiness, agitation, or whining
Change in sleep patterns and appetite
Loss of energy
Lack of enthusiasm or motivation
Loss of interest in personal appearance and hygiene
Hopelessness, helplessness, and sadness
Frequent physical complaints such as headaches and stomachaches
Thoughts of suicide or death
Low self-esteem, frequently expressed through self-blame and self-criticism
Withdrawal from friends and activities once enjoyed
Poor school performance

Schlozman writes, "Studies have shown that adults who suffered from depression when they were younger often recall a specific teacher as central to their recovery" (p. 81).

Concluding Comments

The problems that students bring to school can seem overwhelming, especially for beginning teachers who are still learning the basics. And in fact, there may be students whose problems are so great, you really cannot help very much. That *doesn't* mean giving up. When students have serious problems, it's more important than ever to create a classroom that is safe, orderly, and humane. You may not be able to eliminate a child's disability, but you can make sure that your classroom is not disabling. You may not be able to change youngsters' relationships with their families, but you can work to establish positive teacher–student relationships. You may not be able to provide students with control over unstable, chaotic home lives, but you can allow them opportunities to make decisions and to have some control over their time in school. You may not be able to change students' lives, but you can try to make their time in school as productive and meaningful as possible.

Summary

Today's heterogeneous classrooms are more diverse than ever before. Recent increases in immigration have led to classes in which children come from a wide range of cultural and linguistic backgrounds. Efforts to achieve inclusive classrooms have meant that children with disabilities are now educated alongside their nondisabled peers. In addition, classrooms contain a greater number of children who suffer from conditions associated with poverty.

This chapter reflects our belief that teachers are responsible for all the children in the class—not just the ones who are easy to teach. We began by examining ways of helping children with disabilities and ADHD. Then we considered strategies for supporting children who are second-language learners. Finally, we discussed the needs of children who are troubled—those who suffer from the problems associated with substance abuse, child abuse and neglect, and depression.

Helping children with disabilities and ADHD

- Examine your classroom environment for possible mismatch.
- Reflect on the appropriateness of your expectations.
- Use groupwork and cooperative learning to foster real inclusion.
- Use a variety of instructional strategies.
- Remember the principles of effective management.
- Obtain access to support and services.

Helping children who are second-language learners

- Paraphrase questions and statements to allow for different levels of proficiency.
- Use synonyms to clarify the meaning of unknown words.
- Make the language of the text comprehensible by interpreting it in simple, everyday language.
- Enunciate clearly, with your mouth in direct view of the students.
- Encourage classroom discussion of new information.
- Establish a classroom environment in which children are not afraid to take risks and to use English.
- Ask questions that require different degrees of English proficiency in responding.
- When students respond to your questions, focus on the content, rather than on the form of the response.
- Encourage children to tell about their culture.

Helping children who are troubled

- Substance abuse:
  Students may be children of alcoholics/addicts (COAs) and/or may be abusing drugs and alcohol themselves.
  COAs can benefit from support groups.
  Teachers must be watchful for students who may be abusing drugs and alcohol and refer students to the SAC or other appropriate persons.

Distinguish between situations in which drugs are being used outside of school and situations in which students are under the influence during school.

- Abuse and neglect:

    Educators are required to report suspected abuse and neglect to the state's child protective service.
    No state requires the reporter to have absolute proof before reporting.
    Most states require "reason to believe" or "reasonable cause to believe or suspect."

- Depression:

    Be aware of the signs that suggest depression.
    Behavior that is dangerous or journals, drawings, or essays that suggest suicidal or homicidal thoughts warrant a referral.
    Consult with a guidance counselor or school psychologist.

Sometimes the problems that students bring to school can be overwhelming, especially for beginning teachers who are still learning the basics. And in fact, there may be students whose problems are so great, you just cannot help. Nonetheless, you can still try to create a classroom environment that is safe, orderly, and humane. You can show students you care by working to make their time in school as meaningful and productive as possible.

Activities

1. In the school where you are observing or teaching, interview the principal or the director of special services to learn about the district's policies and procedures for supporting children with disabilities. Are any children with severe disabilities being educated in the general education classroom? If so, what kind of special supports are being provided for those children? Interview a teacher about his/her attitudes toward including a child with special needs who would have previously been educated in a special education classroom or sent to a special school.

2. In the school where you are observing or teaching, interview the principal or an ESL teacher about the district's policies and programs for supporting children who are second-language learners. How many languages are represented in the school? Interview a teacher in an English-only classroom who has second-language learners in his/her classroom. How does the teacher provide supports for second-language learners?

3. In the school where you are observing or teaching, interview the student assistance counselor, a guidance counselor, or the director of special services to determine what services are available for children who come from substance-abusing families.

4. Reporting suspected abuse and neglect varies from state to state. Find out the policies used in your state. Also find out if your school has particular policies and procedures you are to follow. In particular, get answers to the following questions:

Who is required to report abuse and neglect?
When should you report child abuse? (When you have reasonable cause to suspect? Reasonable cause to believe?)
To what state agency do you report?
What information must be included in the report?
Do you have to give your name when reporting?

5. At XYZ School, a meeting of the special services team was called to discuss two children having academic and emotional difficulties. The teacher of each child was invited to describe the situation. Mr. Ryan, a fifth-grade teacher, made the following presentation:

Mr. Ryan began by saying that he thought Olivia was having some difficulties at home that were affecting her ability to do her work in school. "Olivia's academic problems have been evident since the beginning of the school year. She's reading at a third-grade level, and she's doing fourth-grade math." He distributed reading and math worksheets for the committee to see. "However, recently her work and her work habits have gotten worse. I've talked to Olivia and her mom. Since her mother started working nights, Olivia has shown little interest in school. In a typical week, she'll have her homework done only one or two days, and she rarely finishes assignments in class. She has difficulty following oral directions and is slow at getting her ideas down on paper. Here are two typical writing papers; in each case, she only managed to get down two sentences in 25 minutes, and you can see that her handwriting is somewhat immature." He showed the committee two papers. "I have tried to limit the number of directions I give her and when oral directions are given, I also write them on the board. I've offered after-school help, but she needs to get home to watch her little sister. She's also having problems socially; in the last two weeks, she's gotten into five fights with the children in the class." He referred to a note pad he had brought. "On November fifth, for example, she accused another child of stealing a pencil and an eraser from her desk. It resulted in a lot of name calling and loud insults. We finally found the pencil and eraser in the back of her desk, behind all her papers and books. I was worried about her before the problems at home surfaced, and now I'm really at a loss for how to help her. Do you have any ideas for me?" He took out a pen and opened the note pad to a clean sheet.

After Mr. Ryan's presentation, the team discussed ways of helping Olivia. Mr. Ryan left the meeting feeling that his concerns had been taken seriously and that he had received useful advice. Next, Mrs. Teller, a third-grade teacher, presented her concerns about Daniel:

> *Mrs. Teller began by stating that it was about time that someone did something for Daniel. "He has been disturbing my class since September. Look at his work." She handed out papers with many red circles and negative comments. "His work is sloppy, and he never finishes anything. I keep him after school and call his mother and still he doesn't try to get any better. He's one year below level in reading and still can't figure out long vowel sounds. I've had it with him. He doesn't seem to listen to me anymore. In all my years of teaching third grade, this boy is the worst one yet! He always interrupts the lesson by fooling around. I always end up yelling at him or sending him to the principal. What can you do to help me? I think he belongs in a special class."*

The team members told Mrs. Teller that they needed more information before they could provide meaningful assistance and asked her to attend the next meeting when Daniel's case would again be discussed. Based on the guidelines presented in this chapter and the model provided by Mr. Ryan, rewrite Mrs. Teller's presentation to make it more effective.

✲For Further Reading

Cary, S. (2000). *Working with second language learners: Answers to teachers' top ten questions.* Portsmouth, NH: Heinemann.

Nieto, S. (2000). *Affirming diversity: The sociopolitical context of multicultural education* (3rd ed.). New York: Longman.

Powell, R. R., Zehm, S. J., & Kottler, J. A. (1995). *Classrooms under the influence: Addicted families/addicted students.* Newbury Park, CA: Corwin Press, Inc.

Tannock, R., & Martinussen, R. (2001). Reconceptualizing ADHD. *Educational Leadership, 59*(3), 20–25.

Wodrich, D. L. (2000). *Attention-Deficit/Hyperactivity Disorder: What every parent wants to know* (2nd ed.). Baltimore, MD: Paul Brookes Publishing Co.

✲References

Annie E. Casey Foundation (1999). *Kids count data book: State profiles of child well-being (1999).* Baltimore, MD: Annie E. Casey Foundation.

Bancroft, S. (1997). Becoming heroes: Teachers can help abused children. *Educational Leadership, 55*(2), 69–71.

Cary, S. (2000). *Working with second language learners: Answers to teachers' top ten questions.* Portsmouth, NH: Heinemann.

CH.A.D.D. (1993). *Attention deficit disorders: an educator's guide (CH.A.D.D. Facts #5).* Plantation, FL: Childen and Adults with Attention Deficit Disorders.

Children's Defense Fund (1999). *The state of America's children yearbook 1999.* Washington, DC: Children's Defense Fund.

Coles, A. D. (May 10, 2000). Educators welcome guidelines for diagnosing ADHD. *Education Week, 19*(35), 6.

Fischer, L., Schimmel, D., & Kelly, C. (1999). *Teachers and the law.* New York: Longman.

Gardner, H. (1993). *Multiple intelligences: The theory in practice.* New York: Basic Books.

Gardner, H. (1995). Reflections on multiple intelligences: Myths and messages. *Phi Delta Kappan, 77*(3), 200–209.

Gartner, A., & Lipsky, D. K. (1987). Beyond special education: Toward a quality system for all students. *Harvard Educational Review, 57*(4), 367–395.

Gearheart, B. R., Weishahn, M. W., & Gearheart, C. J. (1992). *The exceptional student in the regular classroom* (5th ed.). New York: Macmillan.

Gonet, M. M. (1994). *Counseling the adolescent substance abuser: School-based intervention and prevention.* Thousand Oaks, CA: Sage Publications.

Good, T. L., & Brophy, J. E. (2000). *Looking in classrooms* (8th ed.). New York: Addison Wesley Longman.

Gordon, T. (1974). *T.E.T.—Teacher Effectiveness Training.* New York: Peter H. Wyden.

Grossman, H. (1995). *Classroom behavior management in a diverse society* (2nd edition). Mountain View, CA: Mayfield Publishing Company.

Johnson, D. W., & Johnson, R. T. (1995). *Reducing school violence through conflict resolution.* Alexandria: VA: ASCD.

Johnson, D. W., Johnson, R., Dudley, B., Ward, M., & Magnuson, D. (1995). The impact of peer mediation training on the management of school and home conflicts. *AERJ, 32*(4), 829–844.

Kottler, J. A., & Kottler, E. (1993). *Teacher as counselor: Developing the helping skills you need.* Newbury Park, CA: Corwin Press, Inc.

Lessow-Hurley, J. (1991). *A commonsense guide to bilingual education.* Alexandria, VA: Association for Supervision and Curriculum Development.

McIntyre, T. (1990). The teacher's role in cases of suspected child abuse. *Education and Urban Society, 22*(3), 300–306.

Michaelis, K. L. (1993). *Reporting child abuse: A guide to mandatory requirements for school personnel.* Newbury Park, CA: Corwin Press, Inc.

Miller, E. (1994). Peer mediation catches on, but some adults don't. *Harvard Education Letter, 10*(3), 8.

New Jersey Alcohol/Drug Resource Center & Clearinghouse, Center of Alcohol Studies, Rutgers University (1994). *Facts on Adolescent substance abuse.* Clearinghouse Fact Sheet.

Newsam, B. S. (1992). *Complete Student Assistance Program Handbook.* West Nyack, NY: The Center for Applied Research in Education.

O'Neil, J. (1994/95). Can inclusion work? A conversation with Jim Kauffman and Mara Sapon-Shevin. *Educational Leadership, 52*(4), 7–11.

Parkay, F. W., & Stanford, B. H. (1992). *Becoming a teacher* (2nd ed.). Boston: Allyn and Bacon.

Powell, R. R., Zehm, S. J., & Kottler, J. A. (1995). *Classrooms under the influence: Addicted families/addicted students.* Newbury Park, CA: Corwin Press, Inc.

Reynolds, M. C. (1989). Students with special needs. In M. C. Reynolds (Ed.), *Knowledge base for the beginning teacher.* Oxford, England: Pergamon Press.

Rief, S. F. (1993). *How to reach and teach ADD/ADHD children.* West Nyack, NY: The Center for Applied Research in Education.

Rist, M. C. (1990). The shadow children. *American School Board Journal, 177*(1), 19–24.

Schlozman, S. C. (2001). Too sad to learn? *Educational Leadership, 59*(1), 80–81.

Semmel, M. I., Abernathy, T. V., Butera, G., & Lesar, S. (1991). Teacher perceptions of the regular education initiative. *Exceptional Children, 58,* 9–24.

Slavin, R. E. (1989). Students at risk of school failure: The problems and its dimensions. In R. E. Slavin, N. L. Karweit, & N. A. Madden (Eds.), *Effective programs for students at risk.* Boston: Allyn and Bacon, 3–19.

Stefkovich, J. A., & Miller, J. A. (April 13, 1998). Law enforcement officers in public schools: Student citizens in safe havens? Paper presented at the annual meeting of the American Educational Research Association.

Tower, C. C. (1987). *How schools can help combat child abuse and neglect* (2nd ed.). Washington, DC: National Education Association.

Towers, R. L. (1989). *Children of alcoholics/addicts.* Washington, DC: National Education Association.

Wodrich, D. L. (2000). *Attention-Deficit/Hyperactivity Disorder: What every parent wants to know* (2nd ed.). Baltimore, MD: Paul Brookes Publishing Co.

Zigmond, N., Jenkins, J., Fuchs, D., Deno, S., & Fuchs, L. S. (1995). When students fail to achieve satisfactorily: A reply to McLeskey and Waldron. *Phi Delta Kappan, 77*(4), 303–306.

Zigmond, N., Jenkins, J., Fuchs, L., Deno, S., Fuchs, D., Baker, J., Jenkins, L., & Couthino, M. (1995). Special education in restructured schools: Findings from three multi-year studies. *Phi Delta Kappan, 76*(7), 533–540.

Chapter Fourteen

Preventing and Responding to Violence

By the year 2000 all schools in America will be free of drugs and violence and the unauthorized presence of firearms and alcohol, and offer a disciplined environment that is conducive to learning. (HR 1804: Goals 2000: Educate America Act, 1994)

In the late 1990s, a series of school shootings in Mississippi, Kentucky, Arkansas, Pennsylvania, Tennessee, and Oregon made it clear that this laudable national goal, adopted by Congress and signed by President Clinton, was certainly out of reach. But nothing prepared the country for the events of April 20, 1999. On that day, two seniors at Columbine High School in Littleton, Colorado, shot and killed 12 students and a teacher before turning their guns on themselves. Overnight, the topic of school violence catapulted to the front page. Copycat shootings, bomb scares, and threats of violence created unprecedented terror and upheaval during the final weeks of the school year. Parents agonized about sending their children to school. Politicians, policy makers, and pundits talked about youth violence as a "national epidemic" and speculated on the causes (Drummond & Portner, 1999). Perceptions of an epidemic were heightened in March 2000, when a six-year-old in Michigan took a gun to school and killed his first-grade classmate (Naughton & Thomas, 2000).

But just how widespread is school violence? Was Columbine symptomatic of a growing epidemic, or a horrible, but isolated incident? Let's look at some facts and figures.

How Much Violence Is There?

Data on the frequency and severity of school violence come from a study conducted by researchers at the Centers for Disease Control (Brener, Simon, Krug, & Lowry, 1999). *Surprisingly, the study found that violence in schools had actually decreased in the 1990s.* From 1993 to 1997, for example, the number of high school students who said they had carried a weapon "such as a gun, knife, or club" on school property decreased 28 percent, from 11.8 percent to 8.5 percent. The number of students who carried a gun decreased 25 percent, from 7.9 percent to 5.9 percent. And the percentage of students in a physical fight on school property decreased 9 percent, from 16.2 percent to 14.8 percent.

Other research supports these findings. The Justice Department has reported that the number of violent crimes committed by children and teenagers has declined substantially since 1993 and is at the lowest rate since 1986 (Glassner, 1999). The Washington-based Justice Policy Institute found that the number of school-associated violent deaths has decreased 40 percent, from 43 in 1998 to 26 in 1999 (Portner, 2000). The U. S. Departments of Education and Justice have confirmed that schools remain among the safest places for children and youth. During the 1999–2000 school year, for example, 90 percent of the nation's schools reported no serious crime, while 43 percent said they experienced no crime at all (U.S. Department of Education, 2001).

It is hard to believe numbers like these when we read headlines about murderous rampages and see television news clips of students fleeing from schools under siege. Indeed, surveys indicate that students do not *feel* safer, even though they report fewer fights and weapons. On the contrary, the number of public school students who said they always feel safe in school fell from 44 percent in 1998 to 37 percent in 1999 (Glassner, 1999). And in a telephone poll conducted by *The Wall Street Journal* and NBC News in 1998, 71 percent of the respondents said they thought it was likely a school shooting could happen in their community (Portner, 2000). Clearly, teachers and administrators must work to decrease students' fears and anxiety, as well as actual incidents of school violence. But what can actually be done?

Strategies for Preventing Violence

Building Supportive School Communities

Although we focused on creating safer, more caring classrooms in Chapter 5, it's important to revisit this topic in relationship to violence prevention. Numerous educators argue that violence prevention has to focus on the creation of more humane environments in which students are known and feel supported (Astor, Meyer, & Behre, 1999; Noguera, 1995). Indeed, Richard Riley, President Clinton's Secretary of Education, has suggested that schools look beyond traditional security issues to find better solutions for students who need help: "We need to make sure that in every community, in school, every child is connected to at least one responsible, caring adult" (Richard, 1999). Marylu Simon, the superintendent of Barbara's district, echoes this sentiment:

> *A safe school is one that is responsive to students, where the staff knows the kids, where you can get help for troubled kids right away. . . .We don't talk much about metal detectors or security measures here. Our approach to violence prevention emphasizes connecting to kids and addressing their social–emotional needs. We try hard to make sure that one group isn't elevated over another. . .and to respect differences among kids.*

Creating a supportive school community is not easy, especially in large schools. Following the suggestions in Chapter 5 should help to build a sense of community in the classes you teach. In addition, a number of useful suggestions come from *Responding to Hate at School* (1999) published by Teaching Tolerance, a project of the Southern Poverty Law Center.

Be Alert to Signs of Hate

Take note if book reports, essays, drawings, or journal entries convey messages of hate or violence, and report your concerns to the principal, a school counselor, or the district's affirmative action officer. Help students recognize hate symbols, such as swastikas, and derogatory labels for race, ethnicity, and sexual orientation. At Halloween time, discourage costumes that involve negative stereotyping (e.g., "Gypsy" costumes or "homeless person" outfits), organizations that promote hate (e.g., Ku Klux Klan robes), or the display of weapons.

Curb Peer Harassment

We already touched on peer harassment in Chapter 5 but this problem clearly warrants further discussion. Every day, students suffer teasing, name calling, ridicule, humiliation, ostracism, and even physical injury at the hands of their peers. The problem is substantial: In a large-scale, national study of 15,686 students in grades 6 through 10

(Nansel, Overpeck, Pilla, Ruan, Simons-Morton, & Scheidt, 2001), about 30 percent of the sample reported moderate or frequent involvement in bullying—as a bully (13 percent), one who was bullied (10.6 percent), or both (6.3 percent). Also frightening is the fact that peer harassment is quasi-acceptable (Hoover & Oliver, 1996). Bullies can be popular, and their behavior is often dismissed as normal. When the bullies are males, for example, it is not uncommon to hear adults dismiss their behavior by reminding us that "boys will be boys."

Teasing is the most frequent bullying behavior at all ages, but it can be difficult for students to draw the line between playful exchanges and hurtful harassment. Hoover and Oliver (1996) suggest that whether an exchange represents teasing or friendly banter may have to do with the social level or popularity of the individuals involved. If a higher-status student mocks a lower-status student, the exchange is likely to be seen as an attack. Teasing someone of the same status is more likely to be interpreted as playful. Figure 14-1 contains some "Teasing Dos and Don'ts" that may help your students understand when teasing is acceptable and when it is not.

In an effort to curb peer harassment, you need to be alert to hurtful comments about race and ethnicity, body size, disabilities, sexual orientation, unfashionable or eccentric dress, use of languages other than English, and socioeconomic status. Barone (1997) reports that counselors, teachers, and administrators tend to underestimate the amount of bullying that exists in their schools. In a survey administered to eighth-graders and school staff, Barone found that almost 60 percent of students reported having "been bothered by a bully or bullies" in middle school. In contrast, staff members believed that only 16 percent of the students had been victims of bullies.

Teachers also need to make it clear that disrespectful speech and slurs—even when used in a joking manner—are absolutely unacceptable. This means intervening if you hear a student use a hateful epithet (e.g., "That word hurts people, so you may not use it in this classroom" or "Disrespectful words are never acceptable in this school" or even "Watch your language, please!"). According to Stephen Wessler (2000/2001), a former prosecutor of school hate crimes, intervention "breaks the pattern of escalation from language to more focused harassment to threats and, finally to violence" (p. 31). If you stay silent, students are likely to think you condone the degrading language. You're also serving as a poor role model for students—modeling passivity instead of the courage, skills, and empathy to speak up.

Teaching Conflict Resolution

Concerns about safety and order have led to a raft of violence prevention programs such as conflict resolution training, peer mediation, and social problem solving. These programs emphasize anger management and impulse control, effective communication skills, social perspective taking (i.e., understanding that others can have a different and equally valid perspective on the same situation), resisting peer pressure, and fighting prejudice, sexism, and racism (Dusenbury, Falco, Lake, Brannigan, & Bosworth, 1997). All programs also teach students a series of steps for dealing constructively with conflicts. These generally consist of strategies for cooling down, expressing feelings (in the form of I-messages), generating solutions, evaluating consequences, selecting the best action, and implementing the plan.

TEASING DOs AND DON'Ts

DO:

1. Be careful of others' feelings.
2. Use humor gently and carefully.
3. Ask whether teasing about a certain topic hurts someone's feelings.
4. Accept teasing from others if you tease.
5. Tell others if teasing about a certain topic hurts your feelings.
6. Know the difference between friendly gentle teasing and hurtful ridicule or harassment.
7. Try to read others' "body language" to see if their feelings are hurt—even when they don't tell you.
8. Help a weaker student when he or she is being ridiculed.

DON'T:

1. Tease someone you don't know well.
2. [If you are a boy] tease girls about sex.
3. Tease about a person's body.
4. Tease about a person's family members.
5. Tease about a topic when a student has asked you not to.
6. Tease someone who seems agitated or who you know is having a bad day.
7. Be thin-skinned about teasing that is meant in a friendly way.
8. Swallow your feelings about teasing—tell someone in a direct and clear way what is bothering you.

FIGURE 14-1. Teasing dos and don'ts
Reprinted, with permission, from *The Bullying Prevention Handbook: A Guide for Principals, Teachers, and Counselors* by John H. Hoover and Ronald Oliver. Copyright 1996 by the National Educational Service, 304 W. Kirkwood Ave., Suite 2, Bloomington, IN 47404, 800–733–6786, www.nesonline.com

There is great diversity in approaches, but generally the programs fall into two categories: those that train the entire student body in social problem-solving and conflict resolution strategies and those that train a particular cadre of students to mediate disputes among their peers (Johnson & Johnson, 1996). An example of a program that targets the entire student body is Johnson and Johnson's *Teaching Students to be Peacemakers* (1995). The program spans grades 1 through 12; each year all students learn increasingly sophisticated negotiation and mediation procedures. Research conducted by Johnson and Johnson indicates that students trained in the peacemaker program are able to apply the negotiation and mediation procedures to a variety of conflicts—both in and out of the classroom. In addition, training results in fewer discipline problems that have to be managed by the teacher and the principal (Bodine & Crawford, 1998).

Ken's school has tried to implement a broad-based program like this, although Leslie Lillian, the student assistance counselor at Ken's school, admits that an ever-increasing number of crises has begun to limit the time she has for preventive programs. Beginning with the kindergartners, Leslie teaches children to use "I messages," much like those described in Chapter 12 ("When you. . .I feel. . ."). In fourth grade, she trains children in conflict resolution and peer mediation techniques. Once children are trained, they may sign up to be peer mediators.

Children in Barbara's school also participate in a broad-based program. Designed by psychologists Maurice Elias and John Clabby, the program focuses on social decision making and social problem solving (SDM/SPS; Elias & Clabby, 1988, 1989). It is based on two premises: first, that a hierarchy of skills underlies competent interpersonal behavior, in particular, social–cognitive problem-solving skills; and second, that children can be taught these skills so that they can analyze, understand, and prepare to respond to everyday problems, decisions, and conflict. Whereas traditional approaches to social decision making have often been organized around a particular issue (drug and alcohol use, violence, nutrition), SDM/SPS believes that children need to learn social–cognitive skills that can be applied to a variety of decision-making situations. Figure 14-2 lists the sequence of skills that children are taught to use.

Vicky Poedubicky, the health teacher at Bartle, has incorporated SDM/SPS into the health curriculum for all third- and fourth-graders. There, children are taught to deal with conflicts by being their **BEST**: monitoring **B**ody posture, making **E**ye contact, **S**aying nice words, and using a respectful **T**one of voice. In the classroom, teachers reinforce the SDM/SPS curriculum by having children complete "Hassle Logs" when they are

---

1. Look for signs of different feelings.

   Recognize your feelings of stress, anxiety, or uncertainty as a signal to begin problem solving, rather than a feeling to be eliminated or ignored; also recognize signs of others' feelings.

2. Tell yourself what the problem is.

   "I feel nervous because I have a test tomorrow."

   "I'm worried because those kids look really tough."

3. Decide on your goal.

   "I want to do well on that test."

   "I want to keep away from those tough kids."

4. Stop and think of as many solutions to the problem as you can.

   "I'll study in the library tonight instead of staying home. That way I won't be able to talk on the phone."

5. For each solution, think of all the things that might happen next.

   "Of course, if I meet friends in the library, I might waste time talking to them."

6. Choose your best solution.

7. Plan it and make a final check.

8. Try it and rethink it.

FIGURE 14-2. Skills children are taught to use in SDM/SPS
Source: Elias & Clabby, 1988.

having a problem. (Figure 14-3 shows a Hassle Log completed by a third-grade girl when her classmate started to "bug" her. Figure 14-4 shows a Hassle Log that uses a different format.) If, after three Hassle Logs, a problem still persists, a teacher can refer a child to the Social Problem Solving Lab—not as a punishment, but as an opportunity to get special help. There, children can have a one-on-one conference with Vicky, role play solutions to their problems, or use a software program, also developed by Elias and Clabby, to go through the problem-solving steps.

In contrast to these broad-based programs, peer mediation programs select a few students to guide disputants through the problem-solving process. The advantage of using peers as mediators rather than adults is that students can frame disputes in a way that is age-appropriate. Generally working in pairs, mediators explain the ground rules for mediation, provide an opportunity for disputants to identify the problem from their differing perspectives, explain how they feel, brainstorm solutions, evaluate the advantages and disadvantages of each proposed solution, and select a course of action. These steps can be seen in the example of a peer mediation that appears in Figure 14-5.

Peer mediation programs are becoming increasingly popular in schools across the country, and thus far, anecdotal evidence suggests that they can substantially reduce violent incidents. Some researchers contend that peer mediation actually has more impact on the *mediators* than on the disputants, since they acquire valuable conflict resolution skills and earn the respect of their peers (Bodine & Crawford, 1998; Miller, 1994). If this is so, it means that high-risk students—not just the "good kids"—must be trained and used as mediators.

In schools with ethnic and racial diversity, it's extremely important to sensitize peer mediators to cultural differences (Hyman, 1997). For example, African-American, Italian, and Eastern European cultures encourage emotional expressiveness, and this frequently involves the dramatic use of hands and body language. On the other hand, English and Scandinavian cultures value the control of overt emotionality. Thus, an innocuous interaction can turn into an angry exchange if students from these different backgrounds misread cues. Consider an argument between Salim, who comes from Lebanon, and Jim, whose family heritage is British and German:

> SALIM: Jim, why did you laugh in class when I was reading that part from *Romeo and Juliet* out loud?
>
> JIM: I don't know. Something was funny.
>
> SALIM: What was funny? (Salim wonders if Jim was laughing at him. His voice becomes louder as he uses his hands to help express himself.)
>
> JIM: Listen, I have to get to my next class. I'll talk to you later. (Jim begins to get uncomfortable about Salim's raised voice and hand waving.)
>
> SALIM: Just tell me what was funny. (Salim now feels he is being ignored. He steps in front of Jim, who has turned to walk away.)
>
> JIM: Why are you waving your fist at me? I told you I don't have time now. Now get out of my way. You better not try anything! (Salim's hand waving and attempt to get Jim's attention was misinterpreted.)

Hassle Log

Name: Madeleine

Date: Nov. 28

Time: 12:00

(1) I am feeling:

MAD!

My feeling looks like this: ▶

(2) Tell the problem.

What did you say and do?

Lena just startid buging me

Draw it.

(3) Now what do you want to happen?

I want her to stop it!

Draw it.

(4) What could you do to have that happen?

I could have hit her but I rilised that shel wine about it, so I got a hassle log.

Draw it.

FIGURE 14-3. Hassle log completed by third-grade girl

Hassle Log

Name _____ Homeroom Teacher _____

Date _____ Grade _____

Time of day: (Circle one)   morning   afternoon   evening

Where were you? _____

Who was involved? _____

What is the **problem?**_____

_____

What did you do? _____

_____

How did you **feel** before you did this? _____

_____

What was your **goal** (what were you trying to do)? _____

_____

How satisifed are you with the way(s) you have tried to solve the problem?
(Circle one)   not at all   only a little   okay   pretty satisfied   very satisifed
How easy or hard was it for you to keep calm and stay in control of yourself?
(Circle one)   very easy   pretty easy   okay   pretty hard   very hard

****************What else could you have done to be your **BEST?******************
Think of as many possible **solutions** as you can.

Solutions (what I could do)   **Consequences** (what could happen)

FIGURE 14-4. Another type of hassle log

SALIM: I am not waving my fist. I just want to know why you laughed.
   JIM: I wasn't laughing at you. I was laughing about what those words
         meant. This is ridiculous. I'm not going to stand here and argue
         about such a silly thing.
SALIM: What words were so funny? (Salim will forget the matter if he be-
         lieves he wasn't insulted.)
   JIM: I don't have time for this. (Jim turns to walk way. This action is a
         direct insult to Salim. It means he is being treated with contempt,
         when all he asked for were the words that were funny. He would ac-
         tually like to know what he missed.) (Hyman, 1997, p. 255)

Trouble in the Classroom

Situation: Jimmy has been sitting in front of Eduardo all year in math class. Eduardo has this habit of tapping his foot on Jimmy's chair. It's been driving Jimmy crazy.

Jimmy: You jerk! Why don't you stop bothering me?

Eduardo: Who are you calling a jerk? I don't know what you are talking about.

Jimmy: If you touch my chair one more time, I'm going to let you have it.

Eduardo: I'll touch your chair all I want. See if I care.

The boys start pushing and the teacher asks them if they would like to go to mediation.

The boys agree.

▶ **Step 1**   **Introductions and Ground Rules**
Mediator 1:
Our names are _____ and _____ and we are student mediators. We are not here to punish you or tell you what to do. We are here to help you solve your conflict. What are your names? (Write them on the form.) Thank you for coming. Everything you say here is CONFIDENTIAL, except if it involves drugs, weapons, or abuse. Then, we'll have to report it to our advisor or stop the mediation.

Mediator 2:
There are five rules you must agree to before we begin. They are:
1. **Be willing to solve the problem.**   2. **Tell the truth.**
3. **Listen without interrupting.**   4. **Be respectful: no name calling or fighting.**
        5. **Take responsibility for carrying out your agreement.**
Do you agree to the rules? (Be sure the students agree.)

▶ **Step 2**   **Telling the Story**
(Each person tells his/her side of the story. Mediator chooses the person who begins.)

Mediator 1:   Jimmy, tell us what happened.

Jimmy: I was minding my own business when this creep starts hitting my chair.

Mediator 1:   No name calling, please.

Jimmy: Okay. Like I said, I was sitting in my chair when he started hitting it, like he always does, just to bother me. I'm not going to take it anymore.

Mediator 1:   You said that you were sitting in your chair when Eduardo started hitting it. How do you feel about this situation?

FIGURE 14-5. Peer mediation script
(from Grace Contrino Abrams Peace Education Foundation Inc., 1992)

Jimmy:	I feel angry because he's doing this all the time. He does it just to get me mad.
Mediator 1:	You feel angry because he does it all the time just to get you mad.
Mediator 2:	Eduardo, tell us what happened.
Eduardo:	I always tap my foot. I do it to keep myself awake. It's just a nervous habit. You can ask anybody, I always tap my foot.
Mediator 2:	You said that you always tap your foot to keep yourself awake and it's a habit. How do you feel about what happened?
Eduardo:	I feel upset because I really didn't mean to start a fight. He's too picky.
Mediator 2:	You feel upset because you didn't mean to start a fight and you also think that Jimmy is too picky. Is there any other information that we need to know? (If yes, ask each one to speak following the same rules. If no, continue to Step 3.)

▶ **Step 3** **Searching For Solutions**

One mediator asks questions, the other writes the suggested solutions on paper. This is not the time for choosing—only thinking.

Mediator 1:	You both listened to each other's side of the story. How do you think this conflict can be solved? What could you do to solve this conflict? We're going to write down all your ideas. Later, you'll pick the idea or ideas you like best.
Jimmy:	I could apologize for calling Eduardo a creep.
Eduardo:	I could tap my foot on my bookbag, instead of his chair so it won't make a noise.
Jimmy:	I could ask the teacher to move my seat to the front of the room.
Eduardo:	We could exchange seats with each other.
Mediator 1:	Any more ideas? (If none, go to Step 4.)

▶ **Step 4** **Choosing the Solution**

Mediator 2:	Let's go over the suggestions you both made. Which ones do you think will solve this conflict?
Jimmy:	I'll apologize for calling you a creep. I got mad and the words just came out.
Eduardo:	I'll apologize for tapping on your chair. I didn't know that it was bothering you. I will tap on my bookbag from now on.
Jimmy:	It sounds good to me.
Mediator 2:	Is this conflict solved? (If they both say "yes" have them fill out their section of the Mediation Report Form. If not, go back to Step 3.)

FIGURE 14-5. Peer mediation script   *(continued)*

❯ **Step 5**	**In The Future**
Mediator 1:	What do you think you could do differently to prevent this from happening again?
Jimmy:	I'm going to try to tell people what is bothering me before I explode.
Eduardo:	I'm going to try to be more aware of bothering other people.
❯ **Step 6**	**Choosing**
Mediator 2:	Jimmy and Eduardo, congratulations for solving your conflict. To keep rumors from spreading, please tell your friends that the conflict has been resolved: Thank you for coming to mediation.

FIGURE 14-5. Peer mediation script

Hyman suggests that Jim's immediate response might have been adequate for someone he knew well or who was not part of a culture in which any possible insult is not treated lightly:

Salim, who does not believe in violence, had no intention of becoming aggressive, but he was worried that he did not understand if there was something funny in the text he was reading. However, Jim's initial response made him wonder if Jim were laughing at him. Salim's hand waving and animated body language are typical in his culture, but to Jim, they suggest real danger. (p. 255)

Obviously, peer mediation is not an option when the conflict involves drugs, alcohol, theft, or violence, since these are criminal actions. But mediation *can* help to resolve disputes involving behavior such as gossiping, name calling, racial putdowns, and bullying, as well as conflicts over property (e.g., borrowing a book and losing it). Even then, mediation must be voluntary and confidential. In cases where school rules have been violated, mediation should not substitute for disciplinary action; rather, it can be offered as an opportunity to solve problems and "clear the air."

Knowing the Early Warning Signs of Potential for Violence

In 1998, at the request of President Clinton, the U. S. Department of Education and the Department of Justice published a guide to assist schools in developing comprehensive violence prevention plans (Dwyer, Osher, & Warger, 1998). The guide contains a list of "early warning signs" that can alert teachers and other school staff to students' potential for violence, as well as signs that violence is imminent. These appear in Tables 14-1 and 14-2.

It's important to remember that the early warning signs are not an infallible predictor that a child or youth will commit a violent act toward self or others (Dwyer, Osher, & Warger, 1998). Also keep in mind that potentially violent students typically exhibit mul-

TABLE 14-1. Early Warning Signs of Potential for Violence

Social withdrawal.
Excessive feelings of isolation and being alone.
Excessive feelings of rejection.
Being a victim of violence.
Feelings of being picked on and persecuted.
Low school interest and poor academic performance.
Expression of violence in writings and drawings.
Uncontrolled anger.
Patterns of impulsive and chronic hitting, intimidating, and bullying behaviors.
History of discipline problems.
Past history of violent and aggressive behavior.
Intolerance for differences and prejudicial attitudes.
Drug use and alcohol use.
Affiliation with gangs.
Inappropriate access to, possession of, and use of firearms.
Serious threats of violence.

TABLE 14-2. Imminent Signs of Violence

Serious physical fighting with peers or family members.
Severe destruction of property.
Severe rage for seemingly minor reasons.
Detailed threats of lethal violence.
Possession and/or use of firearms and other weapons.
Self-injurious behaviors or threats of suicide.

tiple warning signs. Thus, be careful about overreacting to single signs, words, or actions, and don't be biased by a student's race, socioeconomic status, academic ability, or physical appearance.

The difficulty of distinguishing between a real threat to safety and harmless student expression is underscored by a 2000 federal court ruling in Washington state (Walsh, 2000). In this case, a high school junior submitted a poem to his English teacher about a lonely student who roamed his high school with a pounding heart. The poem contained this passage:

> *As I approached the classroom door, I drew my gun and threw open the door. Bang, Bang, Bang-Bang. When it was all over, 28 were dead, and all I remember was not felling [sic] any remorce [sic], for I felt, I was, cleansing my soul. . .*

The student's teacher alerted administrators, and the poem was reviewed by a psychologist, who determined that the student was unlikely to cause harm to himself or others. Nonetheless, the district decided to expel him on an emergency basis. After the student was examined by a psychiatrist, the district rescinded the expulsion, and the student completed his junior year. The boy's parents then sued the district, claiming that the school had violated his First Amendment right to free speech and asking that the expulsion be removed from their son's record. On February 24, 2000, a federal district judge ruled for the family, maintaining that the district had overreacted in expelling the student. She suggested that there were less restrictive ways the district could have ensured the safety of students and school personnel, such as imposing a temporary suspension pending psychiatric examination.

Stories like this can discourage teachers from reporting essays or artwork that contain threatening messages or behavior that suggests a potential for violence. But it's better to alert school officials about what you have learned than to ignore indicators and be sorry later. Find out what the reporting procedures are in your school: Do you report your concerns to the principal? the school nurse? a counselor? Do you notify parents? Remember that parental involvement and consent are required before personally identifiable information is shared with agencies outside the school (except in case of emergencies or suspicion of abuse). The Family Educational Rights and Privacy Act (FERPA), a federal law that addresses the privacy of educational records, must be observed in all referrals to community agencies (Dwyer, Osher, & Warger, 1998).

In addition to knowing the early warning signs, teachers can help prevent violence by being observant in hallways, cafeterias, stairwells, and locker rooms—"unowned" spaces where violence is most likely to erupt. Astor, Meyer, and Pitner (2001) interviewed elementary and middle school students about the places in their schools that seemed unsafe and violence-prone. Areas that students perceived to be unsafe tended to lack adult supervision and monitoring and were overcrowded. As one elementary student put it,

> *[Fights are likely to occur] in the hallway. . .'cause it's like the biggest space in the school. And like most teachers don't look in the hallway if they're going to get coffee.*

Being Attentive to Whispers and Rumors

The high-profile school shootings that we have witnessed in the last decade are what the Secret Service calls *targeted violence*—incidents in which the attacker selects a particular target prior to the violent attack. As part of the Safe School Initiative (October 2000) of the U.S. Secret Service and the U.S. Department of Education, researchers studied 37 school shootings involving 41 attackers who were current or recent students at the school. Here are some of the preliminary findings:

> Incidents of targeted violence at school are rarely impulsive. In well over three-quarters of the incidents, the attacker *planned* the attack. A few attackers developed the plan the same day as the attack, but more than half developed the plan at least two days before.

In more than three-quarters of the cases, the attacker told someone about his idea or plan. Some peers knew details of the attack, while others just knew that something "spectacular" was going to happen in school on a particular day.

In over two-thirds of the cases, the attackers felt persecuted, bullied, harassed, and injured.

More than three-quarters of the attackers were known to hold a grievance at the time of the attack. Half had revenge as a motive.

These findings contradict the common perception that students who commit targeted acts of violence have simply "snapped." Nor are they loners who keep their plans to themselves. This means that school staff must be attentive to whispers that something is afoot and impress upon students the need to report rumors of potential violence. As Tonia Moore, the SAC in Barbara's district, puts it, "You have to have your radar out all the time."

De-Escalating Potentially Explosive Situations

Explosive situations often begin benignly. You make a reasonable request ("Would you join the group over there?") or give an ordinary directive ("Get started on the questions at the end of this section"). But the student is feeling angry—maybe he has just been taunted and humiliated in the hallway; maybe her mother has just grounded her for a month; maybe the teacher in the previous class has ridiculed an answer. The anger may have nothing to do with you at all, but it finds its outlet in your class. In a hostile mood, the student fails to comply immediately and may even respond defiantly. Unfortunately, at this point, teachers often contribute to the escalation of a conflict by becoming angry and impatient. They issue an ultimatum: "Do what I say or else." And now teacher and student are combatants in a potentially explosive situation neither of them wanted.

Let's consider an example (adapted from Walker, Colvin, and Ramsey, 1995) of a teacher–student interaction that begins innocuously enough, but quickly escalates into an explosive situation:

Students are working on a set of math problems the teacher has assigned. Michael sits slouched in his seat staring at the floor, an angry expression on his face. The teacher sees that Michael is not doing his math and calls over to him from the back of the room where she is working with other students.

TEACHER: Michael, why aren't you working on the assignment?
MICHAEL: I finished it.
TEACHER: Well, let me see it then. [She walks over to Michael's desk and sees that he has four problems completed.] Good. You've done 4 but you need to do 10.
MICHAEL: Nobody told me that!
TEACHER: Michael, I went over the assignment very clearly and asked if there were any questions about what to do!
MICHAEL: I don't remember that.

TEACHER: Look at the board. I wrote it there. See, page 163, numbers 11–20.

MICHAEL: I didn't see it. Anyway, I hate this boring stuff.

TEACHER: OK, that's enough. No more arguments. Page 163, 11 through 20. Now.

MICHAEL: It's dumb. I'm not going to do it.

TEACHER: Yes you are, mister.

MICHAEL: Yeah? Make me.

TEACHER: If you don't do it now, you're going to the office.

MICHAEL: F———you!

TEACHER: That's enough!

MICHAEL: You want math? Here it is! [He throws the math book across the room.]

At first glance, it appears that the teacher is being remarkably patient and reasonable in the face of Michael's stubbornness, defiance, and abuse. On closer examination, however, we can detect a chain of successive escalating interactions, in which Michael's behavior moves from questioning and challenging the teacher to defiance and abuse, and for which the teacher is also responsible (Walker, Colvin, & Ramsey, 1995). Could the teacher have broken this chain earlier? The probable answer is yes.

First, the teacher should have been sensitive to Michael's angry facial expression and the fact that he was slouching down in his seat. Facial expression, flushing, squinty eyes, clenched fists, rigid body posture, pacing and stomping—these all suggest an impending eruption (Hyman, 1997). Second, teachers can usually avoid defiant situations if they do not corner a student, do not argue, do not engage in a power struggle ("I'm the boss in this classroom, and I'm telling you to. . .") and do not embarrass the student in front of peers. Table 14-3 summarizes specific recommendations.

With this background, let's go back to Michael and see how the teacher might have dealt with the situation to prevent it from escalating.

Students are working on a set of math problems the teacher has assigned. Michael sits slouched in his seat staring at the floor, an angry expression on his face. The teacher notices Michael's posture and realizes that he is feeling upset about something. She goes over, bends down so that she is on eye-level with Michael, and speaks very quietly.

TEACHER: Are you doing OK, Michael? You look upset. [Teacher demonstrates empathy.]

MICHAEL: I'm okay.

TEACHER: Well, good, but if you'd like to talk later, let me know. [Teacher invites further communication.] Meanwhile, you need to get going on this assignment.

MICHAEL: I already did it.

TEACHER: Oh, good. Let me see how you did. [She checks the paper.] OK, you've done the first four, and they're fine. Now do the next four problems and let me see them when you're done. [She walks away, giving the student space.]

TABLE 14-3. Managing potentially explosive situations

- Move slowly and deliberately toward the problem situation.
- Speak privately, quietly, and calmly. Do not threaten. Be as matter-of-fact as possible.
- Be as still as possible. Avoid pointing or gesturing.
- Keep a reasonable distance. Do not crowd the student. Do not get "in the student's face."
- Speak respectfully. Use the student's name.
- Establish eye-level position.
- Be brief. Avoid long-winded statements or nagging.
- Stay with the agenda. Stay focused on the problem at hand. Do not get sidetracked. Deal with less severe problems later.
- Avoid power struggles. Do not get drawn into "I won't, you will" arguments.
- Inform the student of the expected behavior and the negative consequence as a choice or decision for the student to make. Then withdraw from the student and allow some time for the student to decide. ("Michael, you need to return to your desk, or I will have to send for the principal. You have a few seconds to decide." The teacher then moves away, perhaps attending to other students. If Michael does not choose the appropriate behavior, deliver the negative consequence. "You are choosing to have me call the principal.") Follow through with the consequence.

Source: Adapted from Walker, Colvin, & Ramsey, 1995.

Responding to Violence

Coping with Aggressive Behavior

Despite your best efforts at prevention, there are times when students erupt in hostile, aggressive behavior. A girl screams profanities and knocks a pile of dictionaries to the floor. A boy explodes in anger and throws a chair across the room. Someone yells, "I'll kill you," and hurls a notebook at another student. In situations like this—every teacher's nightmare—it's easy to lose self-control and lash out. That's the *normal* reaction. But teachers can't afford to react normally. That will only make things worse, and your responsibility is to make things better.

Let's consider an episode that occurred in Garnetta's classroom:

> *My class was working in small groups of three or four students on their "five senses" projects. Each group was collecting information on a different sense. I was circulating, helping groups that were having difficulty, directing others to additional resources. All of a sudden, I heard a commotion on the other side of the room. Larry had turned over the desk he was working at, and he was yelling to Jeffrey, "I'm going to get you after school." Jeffrey was on his feet, and he looked as though he was about to tackle Larry.*

My first instinct was to shout, "Now stop that at once!," but I kept my cool and immediately started walking over to the two boys. The first thing I said was "Jeffrey, keep your hands down. Go over to the library corner. Larry, you come over to me." I kept repeating that. Finally, Larry looked at me and started coming towards me, mumbling under his breath about how Jeffrey's little brother had hit his [Larry's] younger sister for the last time. As we got closer, I put my arm around him (something that was natural since I had done that many times before) and quietly said, "Let's move over to the door so we can talk." I wanted to talk with him privately, but I also wanted to be able to keep an eye on the class. I told the rest of the students that I needed to speak with Larry, but that I wanted them to continue working on their projects. I told them that if they acted responsibly, we would have lunch together in the classroom on Friday.

When we got to the doorway, a security guard was passing by. I asked him to go get the vice-principal, Mr. Williams. Meanwhile, I tried to get Larry to calm down. It was clear he was still ready to burst. I said, "Obviously you're really angry about something. Tell me about it." He told me how Jeffrey's younger brother kept beating up his [Larry's] younger sister.

When Mr. Williams came, I explained what had happened. He took Larry to the office, along with Jeffrey (collecting the two younger siblings on the way), so that everyone could tell their version of the situation. I went back into the room, where my students all wanted to know what had happened, of course. I told them that the two boys were having a feud, but that they were going to talk about it with Mr. Williams and get everything settled. I complimented them on their behavior and got us back on track.

About 20 minutes later, Larry came back with a note from the vice-principal saying that he needed to get his jacket and bookbag because he was going home for the day. I gave him a hug and told him that I was glad to see he had calmed down. I told him that I could understand why he had been angry, but that we all needed to learn better ways to express our anger. I made sure he had the necessary materials so that he could work on his project at home. Once Larry left, Jeffrey came with the same note. I gave him a hug too and helped him pack up his things. I told him how glad I was that he had listened to me and not fought back.

After the boys left, Mr. Williams called on the intercom and asked me to stop by to see him at the end of the school day. I found out that it was the boys' mothers who were having the dispute and they had dragged the kids in. Mr. Williams had met with them both, and they had agreed to see the *school guidance counselor—with and without their children—to work out their problems. Given their agreement, he agreed not to suspend Larry.*

My class handled itself really well during the whole thing—I was really proud of them. On Friday, I kept my promise: We had a pizza lunch together in the classroom.

Analysis of Garnetta's response to Larry's outburst reveals some important guidelines for dealing with aggression in the classroom. Let's examine her behavior more closely and consider the lessons to be learned.

1. Although Garnetta's first instinct was to shout, she remained outwardly calm and in control. By doing so, she was able to lower the level of emotion in the class and *prevent the situation from escalating.* She then directed Jeffrey to keep his hands down and to move to the library corner. This prevented Larry's aggressive actions from escalating into a full-scale physical fight. Next, she issued quiet, firm, repetitive instructions for Larry to move away from Jeffrey and come over to her.

2. Garnetta's next action was to *summon help* by asking the passing security guard to get the vice-principal. Never send angry, aggressive students to the office alone: You cannot be certain they will actually get there, nor do you know what they will do on the way. If you do not have a telephone or intercom (and no security guard shows up at the right moment), quietly instruct a responsible student to go for assistance.

3. While Garnetta waited for the vice-principal, she spoke privately and quietly with Larry in an attempt to *defuse the aggression.* She did not rebuke or threaten punishment. Instead, she acknowledged his anger and showed her willingness to listen.

   Again, it's critical that you resist the temptation to "react normally" and lash out at the student. You need to speak slowly and softly and to minimize threat by not invading the student's space and keeping your hands by your side. Allow the student to relate facts and feelings, even if it involves profanity, and use active listening ("So you were really furious when you found out what was happening. . ."). Do not disagree or argue.

   If, despite your efforts to restore calm, the student's aggression escalates, it is best to move away unless you are trained in physical restraint techniques. Even then, don't use restraint unless you are strong enough and there are no other options. As Hyman (1997) emphasizes, "The last thing you ever want to do is to physically engage an enraged student who may be out of control" (p. 251).

4. Once Larry and Jeffrey were on their way to the office, Garnetta turned her attention to her class in order to *determine how the other students were feeling* and what to do next. She decided to briefly explain what was going on and to continue the lesson.

Sometimes, your students may be so upset and frightened that it's impossible to continue working. Tonia Moore, the Highland Park SAC, suggests that it's important to allow them to express their feelings:

If the students are upset, you have to give them the opportunity to talk about what happened and to acknowledge their fear. You don't want to pretend nothing happened and then send them on to the next class all churned up inside.

5. When Larry came back to the room to get his belongings, he gave Garnetta the chance to *reestablish a positive relationship.* She gave him a hug, helped him to get his materials together, and acknowledged his anger. Her actions reassured him that he was still a member of the class, and that he could learn from this.

Responding Effectively to Physical Fights

What do you do if you're on the scene when a fight erupts? I asked the teachers that question one evening, as we talked about the problem of violence in schools. They were unanimous in their response:

1. **Get help.** All four teachers stressed the importance of immediately calling for other teachers and for the principal or vice-principal. Once other people are there to help, it's easier—and safer—to get the situation under control.
2. **Tell students to stop.** Often, students don't want to continue the fight, and they'll respond to a short, clear, firm command. If you know the combatants' names, use them.
3. **Disperse other students.** There's no need for an audience, and you don't want on-lookers to become part of the fray. If you're in the hallway, direct students to be on their way. If you're in the classroom, send your students to the library or to some other safe place.
4. **Do not intervene physically**—unless the age, size, and number of combatants indicates that it's safe to do so, there are three or four people to help, or you have learned physical restraint.

As we discussed the issue of fighting in school, the teachers repeatedly stressed the fact that *fights are fast.* They can erupt quickly—so you don't have a lot of time to think through a response—and they're usually over in less than 30 seconds (although that can seem like a lifetime).

Finally, it's important to remember that you must report violent acts. Every school system needs to have a violent incident reporting system that requires you to report what happened, when and where it happened, who was involved and what action was taken (Blauvelt, 1990). Remember that assault and battery, possession of a weapon on school property, and vandalism are *crimes*—not just violations of school rules—and that they must be reported to the police (Blauvelt, 1990).

Concluding Comments

In the wake of Columbine, school officials all across the country reexamined their safety and security measures. Schools installed metal detectors and surveillance cameras, stationed police officers in high schools, introduced photo identification cards, practiced "lock-downs" and safety drills, and required clear plastic backpacks or banned them completely. Although these measures are a logical reaction to the threat of violent crime, enhanced security *alone* will not solve the problem of school violence, nor will it allay students' fears and anxieties. In fact, studies suggest that measures like these may actually make students feel *less* safe and may not reduce incidents of violent crime (Barton, Coley, & Wenglinsky, 1998; Portner, 2000). Furthermore, some educators worry that security measures create a negative environment, turning schools into prisonlike, oppressive institutions (Astor, Meyer, & Behre, 1999; Berreth & Berman, 1997; Noguera, 1995).

Creating safer schools—and schools that *feel* safer—requires a collaborative effort to reach out to students (especially those on the margins), build connections, and promote a climate of tolerance. In the final analysis, it is the presence of caring administrators and teachers that holds the greatest promise for preventing violence.

Summary

In the late 1990s, a series of horrific school shootings catapulted the topic of school violence to the front page. Politicians, policy makers, and pundits talked about youth violence as a national epidemic. Although data on the frequency and severity of school violence indicate a decrease, students, teachers, and parents are fearful, and the perception that violence is increasing is widespread.

School officials have tried to counter the problem of school violence by installing metal detectors and sophisticated security systems, but it is clear that these will not solve all the problems. This chapter presented a variety of strategies for preventing and responding to violence.

Prevention Strategies

Build supportive school communities:
  Be alert to signs of hate.
  Curb peer harassment.
Teach conflict resolution.
Know the early warning signs of potential for violence.
Be attentive to whispers and rumors.
De-escalate potentially explosive situations.

Responding to Violence

Cope with aggressive behavior:
    Prevent escalation.
    Summon help.
    Defuse the aggression.
    Reestablish a positive relationship with the aggressor.
    Determine how the other students are feeling.
Respond effectively to physical fights:
    Get help.
    Tell the students to stop.
    Disperse onlookers.
    Do not intervene physically unless it is safe.
Metal detectors and security systems can only go so far. It's essential to build connections with students. In the final analysis, it is the presence of caring administrators and teachers that holds the greatest promise for preventing violence.

Activities

1. Interview an experienced teacher, the student assistance counselor, the school nurse, or a guidance counselor about the school's efforts to prevent violence.

   If you think a student exhibits some of the early warning signs of potential for violence, to whom do you report?
   Is there an official form to file?
   Do you contact parents?

2. Consider the following situations. What would you do in each case?

   a. As students enter your classroom, you overhear a girl teasing Annamarie about being overweight. They go to their seats, but the taunts continue. Suddenly, Annamarie stands up, turns to the girl, and shouts, "You shut up! Just shut up, or I'll get you!"

   b. Your students are taking a brief quiz on the homework. Those who have finished already are reading. As you circulate throughout the room, collecting the finished papers, you notice that James is drawing gruesome pictures of people fighting with knives and guns. He's labeled one of the victims with the name of a classmate.

   c. You catch Joe passing a note to Pete. It says, "Michael is a fag. Let's go after him at lunchtime."

   d. You ask Taysha where her homework is. She mutters something under her breath. When you tell her you didn't hear what she said, she shouts, "I didn't do it, you bitch!"

3. Find out if the school where you are observing or teaching has a peer mediation program.

How are students selected to be peer mediators?
Who schedules peer mediation sessions?
What is the procedure for requesting peer mediation?
Can a teacher insist/suggest that two students go to peer mediation?

For Further Reading

Beane, A. L. (1999). *The bully free classroom: Over 100 tips and strategies for teachers K–8.* Minneapolis, MN: Free Spirit.

Bodine, R. J., & Crawford, D. K. (1998). *The handbook of conflict resolution education: A guide to building quality programs in schools.* San Francisco: Jossey-Bass.

Byrnes, D. A. (1995). *"Teacher, they called me a———!"* New York: Anti-Defamation League and Utah State Office of Education.

Canter, L., with Garrison, R. (1994). *Scared or prepared: Preventing conflict and violence in your classroom.* Santa Monica, CA: Lee Canter & Associates.

Schrumpf, F., Crawford, D. K., & Bodine, R. J. (1997). *Peer mediation: Conflict resolution in schools* (revised ed.). Champaign, IL: Research Press.

Teaching Tolerance (1999). *Responding to hate at school: A guide for teachers, counselors and administrators.* Montgomery, AL: The Southern Poverty Law Center.

Walker, H. M., Colvin, G., Ramsey, E. (1995). *Antisocial behavior in school: Strategies and best practices.* Pacific Grove, CA: Brooks/Cole.

Organizational Resources

The Anti-Defamation League (ADL), 823 United Nations Plaza, New York, NY 10017 (www.adl.org; 212-885-7800). Dedicated to combating hate crime and promoting intergroup cooperation and understanding.

Drug Strategies, 1575 Eye Street, NW, Suite 210, Washington, DC 20005 (www.drugstrategies. org; 202-289-9070). Publishes a guide on conflict resolution and violence prevention curricula.

National Educational Service, 1252 Loessch Rd., Bloomington, IN 47401 (www.nesonline.com; 1-800-733-6786). Provides a variety of resources and materials for understanding, preventing, and reducing violence in schools.

National School Safety Center, 141 Duesenberg Dr., Suite 11, Westlake Village, CA 91362 (www.nssc1.org; 805-373-9977). Resource for school safety information, training, and violence prevention.

The Safe and Drug Free Schools website for the U.S. Department of Education (www.ed.gov/offices/OESE/SDFS/news.html). Provides reports and articles on school safety and school violence.

The Southern Poverty Law Center, 400 Washington Avenue, Montgomery, AL 36104 (www.teachingtolerance.org). The Teaching Tolerance project provides teachers at all levels with ideas and free resources for building community, fighting bias, and celebrating diversity.

✦References

Astor, R. A., Meyer, H. A., & Behre, W. J. (1999). Unowned places and times: Maps and interviews about violence in high schools. *American Educational Research Journal, 36,* 3–42.

Astor, R. A., Meyer, H. A., & Pitner, R. O. (2001). Elementary and middle school students' perceptions of violence-prone school subcontexts. *The Elementary School Journal, 101*(5), 511–528.

Barone, F. J. (1997). Bullying in school: It doesn't have to happen. *Phi Delta Kappan, 79,* 80–82.

Barton, P. E., Coley, R. J., & Wenglinsky, H. (1998). *Order in the classroom: Violence, discipline, and student achievement.* Princeton, NJ: Educational Testing Service.

Berreth, D., & Berman, S. (1997) The moral dimensions of schools. *Educational Leadership, 54*(8), 24–26.

Blauvelt, P. D. (1990). School security: "Who you gonna call?" *School Safety Newsjournal,* Fall, 4–8.

Bodine, R. J., & Crawford, D. K. (1998). *The handbook of conflict resolution education: A guide to building quality programs in schools.* San Francisco: Jossey-Bass.

Brener, N. D., Simon, T. R., Krug, E. G., Lowry, R. (1999). Recent trends in violence-related behaviors among high school students in the United States. *Journal of the American Medical Association, 282,* 440–446.

Drummond, S., & Portner, J. (May 26, 1999). Arrests top 350 in threats, bomb scares. *Education Week,* 1, 12–13.

Dusenbury, L., Falco, M., Lake, A., Brannigan, R., & Bosworth, K. (1997). Nine critical elements of promising violence prevention programs. *Journal of School Health, 67*(10), 409–414.

Dwyer, K., Osher, D., & Warger, C. (1998). *Early warning, timely response: A guide to safe schools.* Washington, DC: U.S. Department of Education.

Elias, M. J., & Clabby, J. F. (1989). *SDM skills: A curriculum guide for the elementary grades.* Gaithersburg, MD: Aspen Publishers.

Elias, M. J., & Clabby, J. F. (1988). Teaching social decision making. *Educational Leadership, 45*(6), 52–55.

Glassner, B. (August 13, 1999). School violence: The fears, the facts. *New York Times,* A21.

Hoover, J., & Oliver, R. (1996). *The bullying prevention handbook: A guide for teachers, principals and counselors.* Bloomington, IN: National Educational Service.

HR 1804: *Goals 2000: Educate America Act,* 103rd Cong., 2nd session. 1994.

Hyman, I. A. (1997). *School discipline and school violence: The teacher variance approach.* Boston: Allyn and Bacon.

Johnson, D. W., & Johnson, R. T. (1995). *Teaching students to be peacemakers* (3rd ed.). Edina, MN: Interaction Book Co.

Johnson, D. W., & Johnson, R. T. (1996). Reducing school violence through conflict resolution training. *NASSP Bulletin, 80* (579), 11–18.

Miller, E. (1994). Peer mediation catches on, but some adults don't. *Harvard Education Letter, 10*(3), 8.

Nansel, T. R., Overpeck, M., Pilla, R. S., Ruan, W. J., Simons-Morton, B., & Scheidt, P. (2001). Bullying behaviors among US youth: Prevalence and association with psychosocial adjustment. *Journal of the American Medical Association, 285*(16), 2094–2100.

Naughton, K., & Thomas, E. (March 13, 2000). Did Kayla have to die? *Newsweek,* 24–29.

Noguera, P. A. (1995). Preventing and producing violence: A critical analysis of responses to school violence. *Harvard Educational Review, 65*(2), 189–212.

Portner, J. (April 12, 2000). School violence down, report says, but worry high. *Education Week,* 3.

Richard, A. (September 8, 1999). As students return, focus is on security. *Education Week,* 1, 14–15.

Teaching Tolerance (1999). *Responding to hate at school: A guide for teachers, counselors and administrators.* Montgomery, AL: The Southern Poverty Law Center.

U.S. Department of Education (February/March 2001). Studies report declining rate of school violence. *Community Update, 85,* 1–2.

U.S. Secret Service Safe School Initiative (October 2000). *An interim report on the prevention of targeted violence in schools.* Washington, DC: U.S. Secret Service National Threat Assessment Center in collaboration with the U.S. Department of Education.

Walker, H. M., Colvin, G., Ramsey, E. (1995). *Antisocial behavior in school: Strategies and best practices.* Pacific Grove, CA: Brooks/Cole Publishing Company.

Walsh, M. (March 8, 2000). Law update: A fine line between dangerous and harmless student expression. *Education Week,* 14.

Wessler, S. L. (2000/2001). Sticks and stones. *Educational Leadership, 58*(4), 28–33.

Name Index

Subject Index